T0304827

Moederland

Moederland

Nine Daughters of South Africa

CATO PEDDER

JOHN MURRAY

First published in Great Britain in 2024 by John Murray (Publishers)

I

Copyright © Cato Pedder 2024

The right of Cato Pedder to be identified as the Author of the Work has been
asserted by her in accordance with the Copyright, Designs and Patents Act 1988.

Family tree and map drawn by Nicky Barneby (barneby.co.uk)

A CIP catalogue record for this title is available from the British Library

Hardback ISBN 9781399810791
Trade Paperback ISBN 9781399810807
ebook ISBN 9781399810821

Typeset in Bembo MT by Hewer Text UK Ltd, Edinburgh
Printed and bound in Great Britain by Clays Ltd, Elcograf S.p.A.

John Murray policy is to use papers that are natural, renewable and recyclable products and
made from wood grown in sustainable forests. The logging and manufacturing processes
are expected to conform to the environmental regulations of the country of origin.

Carmelite House
50 Victoria Embankment
London EC4Y 0DZ

www.johnmurraypress.co.uk

John Murray Press, part of Hodder & Stoughton Limited
An Hachette UK company

For my mother,
my aunts
and
all the other women
who walked ahead

Contents

Author's Note

I have tried to be as historically accurate as possible, using primary texts, academic articles, published books, family archives, interviews and so on. Where I have been unable to find information about individual women's lives, I have used contemporary memoir and history to flesh out scenes. All these sources are listed in a bibliography at the end.

Moederland:
The Family Tree

Sophia van der Merwe 1670–1735
m. ————————————————————
Roelof Pasman 1660–1695

Elsje Cloete 1655–1702
m. ————
Willem Schalk van der Merwe
1648–1668

Johann Siek 1670–1715
m. ————————————————————
Hans Helm 1644–1690
m. ————————————————— Geertruida Helm 1678–1707
Gertruida Willems –1642–1699

Krotoa, 1643–1674
m. ————————————————— Pieternella van Meerhoff 1663–1713
Pieter van Meerhoff 1637–1668   *m.* ————————————————————
Daniel Zaaiman 1660–1714

Angela van Bengale c.1646–1720
m. ————————————————— Michael Basson 1679–1772
Arnoldus Willemsz Basson 1647–1698   *m.* ————————————
Maria Daensdons 1682–1706

Sibella Pasman 1693–1778

m. —————————————————— Rudolf Laubser

Jan Laubser 1685–1719   1715–1752

m. ——————————————————▶

Hester van den Heyden

1729–1753

Madgalena van der Merwe 1690–1765

m. ——————————————————▶

Pieter van Heerden 1677–1763

Anna Margaretha Siek 1695–1773

m. ——————————————————▶

Michiel Otto 1688–1743

Magdalena Zaaiman

682–1704

1. ——————————————— Petronella Bockelenberg

ohannes Bockelenberg   1698–1720

668–1709   m. ——————————— Anna Catharina Feyt 1714–1758

Coenraad Feyt   m. ——————————————————▶

1683–1727   Nicolaas Loubser 1710–1782

Johannes Basson 1706–1778

m. ——————————————————▶

Johanna Catharina van Jaarsveld 1716–1778

Debora Joubert 1749–1814
m. ————————————————————————
Jacobus Retief 1754–1821

Sibella Margaretha Laubser 1745–1828
m. ————————————————————————
Johannes Louw 1732–1812

Maria van Heerden
1733–1816
m. ———————————— Maria du Plessis 1744–?
Daniel du Plessis   m. ————————————————————
1732–1795   Philippus Hartog 1756–?

Sophia Otto 1734–1803
m. ———————————————————————— Sophia Pas 1767–1839
Jurgen Pas 1739–1773   m. ————————————————
                                              Rudolfus Davel 1767–181

Aletta Loubser 1743–1802
m. ———————————— Anna Catharina Mostert
Johannes Mostert   1766–1810
1727–1774   m. ————————————————
                    ⌐ Pieter van der Bijl
                    │ 1762–1800
Maria Magdelena Basson 1735–1789
m. ————————————————————————————⌡
Pieter van der Bijl 1714–1789

— Francois Retief 1773–1838
m. ————————————————————— **Anna Elisabeth Retief 1797–1891**
Martha Joubert 1776–1809

— **Piet Retief 1780–1838**

— **Margaretha Louisa Retief 1787–1884**
m. ————————————————————— Margaretha Wilhelmina Joubert
Gideon Joubert 1782–1851   1822–1866
                                    m. ————————————————————▸--
                                    Jacob Daniel Krige 1819–1894

— Jacob Winand Louw 1778–1847
m. ————————————————————— Sibella Margaretha Louw
Johanna Catharina Furstenberg 1794–1854   1818–1892
                                    m. ————————————————————▸--
                                    Petrus Johannes Schabort
                                    1804–1880

— Maria Hartog 1799–?1866
m. ————————————————————— Maria Niehaus 1819–1873
Christoffel Niehaus 1793–?1862   m. ————————————————————▸···
                                    — Jan Christian de Vries 1815–1879

— Maria Davel 1793–1857
m. ——————————————————
Boudewyn de Vries 1789–1841

— Maria Magdalena van der Bijl 1794–1850
m. ————————————————————— Michiel Nicolaas Smuts
Michiel Nicolaas Smuts 1788–1848   1813–1868
                                    m. ————————————————————▸-
                                    Adrianna Martha van Aarde
                                    1819–1853

Jacob Daniel Krige 1845–1919
m. ———————————————
Susanna Johanna Schabort
1848–1933

Sibella Margaretha Krige 1870–1954
m. ———————————————
Jan Christiaan Smuts 1870–1950

Catharina Petronella de Vries
1847–1901
m. ———————————————
Jacobus Abraham Smuts 1845–1914

Catharina Petronella
nuts 1904–1968

illiam Bancroft Clark
02–1993

Petronella Clark
1940–
m.
Lionel Sylvester 1943–

Roger Sylvester 1974–

Sarah Sylvester 1977–

Sibella Margaretha Clark
1943–
m.
Roger Anthony Pedder
1941–2015

**Catharina
Petronella Pedder
1973–**

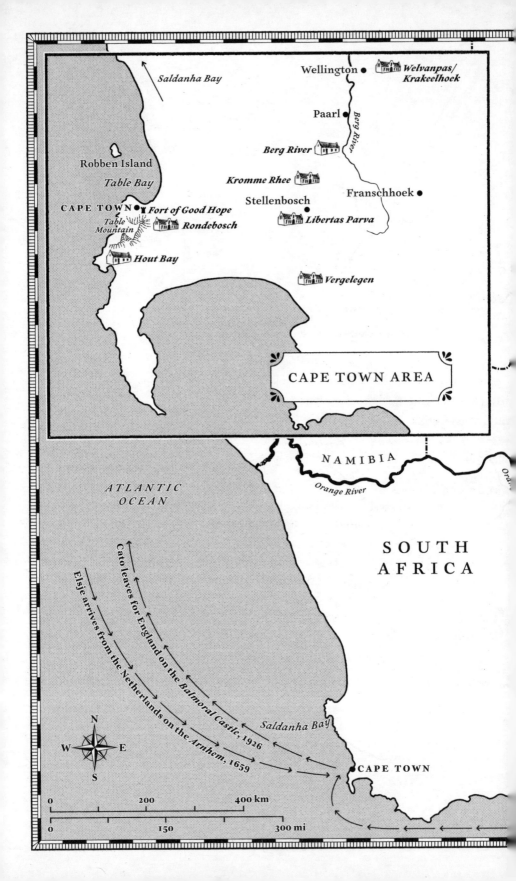

CAPE TOWN AREA

Saldanha Bay

Wellington ●
Welvanpas/
Krakeelhoek

Paarl ●

Berg River

Robben Island

Table Bay

Berg River

Kromme Rhee

Stellenbosch

Franschhoek ●

CAPE TOWN ● ▼ Fort of Good Hope

Table
Mountain

Rondebosch

Libertas Parva

Hout Bay

Vergelegen

NAMIBIA

ATLANTIC
OCEAN

Orange River

Orange

SOUTH
AFRICA

Cato leaves for England on the Balmoral Castle, 1926

Elsje arrives from the Netherlands on the Arnhem, 1659

Saldanha Bay

N
W ✦ E
S

CAPE TOWN

0   200   400 km

0   150   300 mi

Petronella flies in from London, 1966

ZIMBABWE

MOZAMBIQUIE

BOTSWANA

Modjadjiskloof, home of the Rain Queen

PRETORIA ● 🏠 *Sunnyside*
Irene ● 🏠 *Doornkloof*
JOHANNESBURG ●

ESWATINI
(SWAZILAND)

Vaal River

Blood River

Bethlehem 🏠
Blood River ●

Tugela River
● uMgungundlovu,
Dingaan's kraal

BLOEMFONTEIN ●

Weenen

Maseru
Thaba Nchu ●
🏠 *Roma*
Morija 🏠 LESOTHO

Albert Falls ●
● Pietermaritzburg
● DURBAN/
PORT NATAL

Drakensberg Mountains

Orange River

Anna Retief's trek route

INDIAN OCEAN

🏠
raaff-Reinet

SOUTH AFRICA

...la arrives from Batavia on the *Amersfoort*, 1657

The conditions under which the obscure mass of women live and fulfil their duties as human beings have a vital influence upon the destinies of the human race.

Alice Clark, *Working Life of Women in the Seventeenth Century*, 1920

Prologue

All my life I have been mistaken for someone else, a misfortune for which I blame my parents, who choose to name me after a long-lost mother, a strange, humorous name that affords me no anonymity at all. Cato, I am called, a name mispronounced by well-meaning strangers in line with the Roman senator or Inspector Clouseau's sidekick, so I must say the same thing, over and over, 'No, not Kate-o, Cuh-too. It's Afrikaans, short for Catharina. No, I'm not Afrikaans, just named for my grandmother.' Sometimes, when this label gets too heavy, I exaggerate to lighten the load, 'No, half South African, through my mum.' And, sometimes, there's the suggestion of an erasing. 'Why don't you just change it to something more English?' asks the creepy old poet, trousers tucked into his socks and sandals.

In calling me Cato, my parents are not trying to burden me, but to follow an Afrikaans tradition where names are passed down through generations, and where, as second daughter, I am named for my maternal grandmother, the only Afrikaner among them. It is an owning and a commitment that ensures I am forever connected to a country 6,000 miles from home, to a culture freighted with shame. In 1973, perhaps, claiming descent from a world statesman, warrior, philosopher, from Prime Minister Jan Smuts, is a source of pride, not shame. But surely even then, I think, the stain of apartheid must have been apparent. Still, here I am. My name is Cato – pleased to meet you.

As children, we are fresh film on which no light has fallen, pristine. Until the reel starts to turn, and the light falls, and we too fall, into knowledge. It is all new to us, all strange, unsullied. Backlit with an unholy light. Our South African grandmother might die before we are born, but we make the long journey south nevertheless, take trips cross-country to trees, monuments, landscapes. South Africa is stitched into the fabric of our selves from the beginning, from before the beginning, in all the actions and reactions of other lives that coalesce in our bodies.

For so long, that first film seems to be the only one. That the world has always been the same and will always stay the same. The stories we are told are huge, enormous. Creation myths. And if there are things we don't know about the creation, we can ask. But time turns. People die. It all gets a bit lonelier. Until there is no one left to ask; there is only the ephemera they leave behind.

I take down a volume of Hancock and Van der Poel's *Selections from the Smuts Papers*. 'Renée Chiffers' it says on the fly leaf, and below that: 'from Cato Smuts Clark, Christmas 1966' and then further down: 'Catharina Petronella Pedder, from Renée Chiffers, January 1994'. These books have sat on my shelves for decades, unread. I think of my grandfather's secretary, Renée, with her neat white hair and bright pink lipstick, who passed them on to me because of the name I share with my grandmother. Of my mother who carefully transported them to university for me when I turned twenty-one: ten volumes in a cardboard box with grapes stencilled on the side. Of how, full of the preoccupations of Finals and irritated by the endless repetition of old stories, I pushed the box under the armchair in my college room and forgot about it.

By the time I turn to them, those old stories prove hard to unravel. Even my own memories are occluded. Here is an example: Lesotho, 1982. Under blue gum trees, we are stopped at a roadblock. The dusty leaves flicker in the sunlight. The soldiers are dressed in khaki and carry guns. With a jerk of those guns, they urge us out of the minivan. I struggle again with time, against memory; the looped film is patchy, incomplete. All this friable footage. The frames that show whether this is Lesotho or South Africa are missing. I think it might be Lesotho because the soldiers are black. I can remember that, and their faces: business-like. My father tries to use his fountain pen to sign the papers, but it has dried out.

'It must have been the aeroplane,' he says, making a nervous noise in his throat. My father is not a nervous man.

I phone my mother, whose film does not have the same gaps. Lesotho, not South Africa. And the aftermath of a murderous cross-border raid by South African commandos. Travelling with my cousin Hugh, they were worried he might be taken for a South African mercenary, with his hairy white legs, his shorts. A gentle soul, Hugh is not likely to have taken up a machine gun, grenade or bazooka and killed any of the forty-two people slaughtered on 10 December. Which was just a fortnight before this moment we are remembering together, my mother reliving her relief as we drove on. She sends me a photograph. There are no gum trees on the stretch of tarmac occupied by army trucks. Only rocks and a couple of scrubby bushes. And the blue mountain range in the distance.

My Great-Aunt Daphne dies in Cape Town in 2009. 'Bury me in a bin bag,' she said. Years since she arrived in the retirement complex with its little white houses, when children were already learning about her era from textbooks. 'What beautiful skin you have,' she tells me, a dishevelled teenager in a shapeless skirt. That fine grace standing her in good stead when she is cast adrift in a land suddenly foreign. The society beauty who entertained the king of a diminishing empire on a farm on the veld. In the photograph from the archive, she leans fetchingly on a cane, slim in her pussy-bow floral blouse and waisted jumpsuit, dark hair beautifully shingled. Behind stretches the dry veld, with its wire fences and rocky margins.

History has begun. Daphne's reel of memory burnt out. But even when people are still here, documents can reveal more than their memory, or lips. I keep rediscovering that a question must be asked in exactly the right way, as if it were a key to a secret door to the doll's house of memory where each room is exactly as it was left. I don't have that key, only a chisel, which breaks the doll's house as it enters, so I must try to reconstruct it.

It is important, suddenly, to reconstruct this lost past, where we came from. Because time does turn and twenty-five years after the racist paraphernalia of apartheid has been dismantled, after black people are legally entitled to vote, to have sex with and marry white people, to live wherever they like instead of in so-called 'tribal homelands' or slums on the outskirts of white cities, twenty-five years after this has all become history, race has been mobilised in post-Rainbow Nation South Africa by an embattled African National Congress (ANC) and a proletariat fed up with the slow pace of change and the entrenchment of white power. #RhodesMustFall, proclaim students as they occupy universities, topple statues of old white men: South Africa begins to appear less a miracle of reconciliation and more a weeping sore. Globally, identity politics catch fire, #BlackLivesMatter activists protest against the continuing violence visited upon black people, #MeToo activists against the continuing violence visited upon women and girls.

I struggle with my place in all this, what ties me to it, to the white male power that continues to saturate South Africa and further afield: Jan Smuts, a South African statesman so revered by the British that in the 1950s a statue is raised to him in Parliament Square. My great-grandfather was the only man to sign the peace treaties after both world wars. He was father of the Royal Air Force, central to the creation of the League of Nations and drafter of the Preamble to the United Nations Charter. He was prime minister of South Africa, twice, and Albert Einstein held him to be one of only ten people who truly understood the theory of relativity. But Jan Smuts was also a white supremacist who supported racial segregation in South Africa. Moral narratives shift and Smuts falls out of the history books, at least until the summer of 2020, when anti-racist campaigners, having thrown a statue of Edward Colston in Bristol Harbour, turn to the statue of Jan Christiaan Smuts in Parliament Square.

Struggling to understand on which page to find myself in this contested history, I construct family trees, pin them to the back of my study door. The same names, my names, hang like fruit on this tree. I run my finger down lists of the dead where women's names are misplaced as they marry, the lost girl sliding into the depths as the grown woman takes her husband's identity. I try on the masks of the past, consider how South Africa has a powerful narrative attached to it, of tragedy, oppression, blood. How it is a narrative populated by men. Those old half-truths frustrate me, those battles and political wrangles, with their exclusive masculine patina, the women consigned to silence, swelling a crowd, swaddling a baby. How do people like me fit in? Where are we while the camera is on the men?

The family tree remains silent, a palimpsest written over by successive generations. It does not say a word about a woman's greed for honey, or whether she showed her teeth when she smiled. It does not say a word about how a white woman in Africa might fit into the jigsaw of her country, how she might relate to men in that country, or people of a different colour, how she might shape the past, and so the present and the future. Not a word about this secret history. Identity is fluid and contingent, and those names are no more than gravestones, all present together in death. But, once asked, a question cannot be unasked.

Complicit, (adj.) meaning: involved with others in an activity that is unlawful or morally wrong. Also, culpable, Middle English, (adj.) meaning: deserving blame.

The family tree remains silent about all of this. About what it means when the people whose DNA threads through yours, from whose wealth you benefit, put together the cage that entrapped and maimed millions of human beings. About what it means to live in the heart of whiteness, with the *sjambok* of the slave owner in your ancestral hand, the sweat of an African feeding your body. What it means to live six thousand miles distant, so the result of those beatings, those separations, is hidden by mountains and deserts. The bloodline that ties me to South Africa leads directly down into this abyss. Inside its most celebrated son, my great-grandfather Prime Minister Jan Smuts, pools a dark slick of pride and shame.

Working through the past, the Germans call it as they struggle to come to terms with the Third Reich: *Vergangenheitsbewältigung*. Which you will also find listed under South Africa's Truth and Reconciliation Commission, designed to lay the horrors of apartheid to rest. But apartheid's legacy persists, the *Vergangenheitsbewältigung* unfinished, these ancient tangles too complex to unravel, too divisive to lay bare. I think about belonging and exclusion; about those leaky frontiers between guilt and innocence; about whether that burden can be unpacked, its parts used to construct something more worthwhile.

It is an ongoing process, delivering us from evil. I wonder about looking the basilisk in the eye, if I am brave enough to hurt people I love by bringing our shame into the light, by unpicking the tapestry of our identity. I think about collective guilt and individual responsibility, how impunity allows sin to continue to walk among us. How Archbishop Desmond Tutu says that because human beings live in communities, groups must acknowledge their part in the past in a symbolic confession of wrong-doing. I think about the collective looking away from violence done to black bodies, the theft, dispossession and denial of black people as human beings. All the centuries that edifice took to build, the weight of the ship of history, how long she takes to turn. And how empty she is of women's stories, not only of our triumphs, but of our crimes, our complicity.

How would it be, I think, if I could excavate the life stories of these women, all the way back to the beginning? If I could find their stories and try to understand how we got here? How I got here? I picture the women of my prehistory lined up, daughter to mother to mother, back and further back in a chain, an insane game of Chinese whispers where what the first mother said is changed in almost all its essentials: language, form, content. How all those lost words shape South Africa into her monstrous, distorted present. And I think it would help us all bear it, this history: to understand where it, where we, come from.

After a while, I pick up my pen, turn on my laptop, begin to reconstruct.

I

Krotoa • Angela van Bengale • Elsje Cloete

1652–1720

A host country is neither a tabula rasa, nor a fait accompli, but a page in the process of being written.

Amin Maalouf, *In the Name of Identity*, 2012

'A savage set, living without conscience'

Seeking a path, I jump straight in. This story of the knotted lives of women weaving the framework of apartheid could begin with the wife of an Afrikaner statesman in 1920. Or with the *Voortrekker* who hauls her wagons over mountains in 1837. But I am going to start at the furthest point I can find, the furthest point from us in time where I have information about women in my ancestry on South African soil: 1652.

After all, all Afrikaners descend from the small group of white settlers who arrived at the Cape of Good Hope, the southern tip of Africa, in the 1600s. And all Afrikaners have an estimated seven per cent non-white ancestors, the result of early unions between these settlers, slaves and local Khoikhoi people. So our first ancestor will not be white at all. But she will interact with white people, and with brown people from further afield. In the racialised bodies of three women, unrelated to each other, but all related to me, I will find the start of a centuries-long and ongoing race war on South African soil.

7 April 1652

Three tall ships are at anchor in Table Bay. Each vessel is a spider's web of rigging and masts. They fly the blue, white and red tricolour of the Dutch emblazoned with the black entwined VOC of the Dutch East India Company (the *Vereenigde Oostindische Compagnie*). The reed huts of the Goringhaikona people are visible on the slopes of the mountain above, and by evening Autshumao, their leader, boards one of the ships: the English he learnt from sailors on his travels to Java and back proving useful once again. The following morning the

9

Dutch row ashore, dressed in their coarse woollen trousers and linen shirts. Autshumao wears only a small leather apron.

The white men put up their canvas tents near the Camissa River, which has sweet-tasting water, and soon they are hacking away at the ground, building long thick walls. Autshumao and his people carry their reed huts down the slopes of the mountain and set them up by the canvas tents, planting the green poles into the ground, bending and tying them together, covering them with reed mats. They are offered white man's food – rice, mutton – at every meal, although sometimes they forage still for mussels and wild roots along the seashore. The arrival of the Europeans is a boon, and they do not expect them to stay long: the previous group only stayed a year before being picked up by another ship.

What do these people think of each other? Autshumao is well used to Europeans, having travelled to the Far East on their ships, observed their practices and facilitated local trade for twenty years. Pragmatic and flexible, he sees them as a useful source of income, but not to be depended upon. And we know what the leader of the white men thinks because he tells us: 'They are by no means to be trusted, but are a savage set, living without conscience.' But without Autshumao and his smattering of English, Van Riebeeck's trade for cattle and sheep would be impossible.

We can tell something of Commander Jan van Riebeeck from the thousands of documents the Dutch leave behind: at thirty-two, he is a small, fiery-tempered, resolute man who has sailed the world's oceans from the Caribbean to Northern China. His wife, Maria de la Quellerie, and his infant son accompany him on this fast journey from the Netherlands: 104 days, with only two deaths. But why, after fifty years of using Table Bay as a stopover on their voyages east, are the Dutch coming ashore with tents and building mud walls twenty feet thick and twelve feet high?

The Dutch East India Company, a consortium of Dutch trading companies that monopolises trade in the southern oceans for almost two hundred years, is at the height of its powers in the 1650s. No company has ever approached the VOC for influence and size: it is worth an adjusted £6.3 trillion at its peak and acts in all ways like a state, with no control from any political authority. Trading in spices, silk, tea, coffee and precious metals, the VOC's power is concentrated in Batavia, modern-day Jakarta: it needs a way station to re-provision its ships on the long voyage to and from Amsterdam.

For their part, the 'half-naked band of savages' are the Khoikhoi people, pastoralists who compete with subsistence hunter-gatherers, known as the San people. They live in clans, each clan united into a larger group. No one owns the land, but clans can use the water, vegetation and animals of the ground they range over. The San share everything but the Khoikhoi own goats, sheep and cattle. Some are rich, some poor. Cattle symbolise wealth, only slaughtered for weddings and funerals.

Isolated for millennia by mountains, deserts and oceans, and far removed from the Bantu-speaking people to the east, for the past hundred and fifty years the Khoikhoi have had contact with Europeans, starting with the Portuguese. By the late 1590s, the Portuguese are eclipsed by the Dutch and English, who visit Table Bay for provisions before sailing across the Indian Ocean. In 1647, Dutch sailors are ship-wrecked at the Cape for a year. Safely back in the Netherlands, they tell tales of the cabbages, pumpkins, turnips and onions that thrive in the Cape climate; the game that fell under their guns in abundance. Cows can be bred, and cheese and butter made, enough hogs can be reared and fattened to supply all the Company's ships, they promise. So Commander van Riebeeck sails into Table Bay.

It is here that Krotoa enters recorded history, a girl aged nine or ten living with her uncle Autshumao across the lower slopes of Table Mountain – *Hoerikwaggo*, they call it, 'mountain of the sea' – and the dunes of the hinterland. Autshumao's Goringhaikona are outcasts, refugees, orphans, the poor, people who scavenge for stranded whales, shellfish, fish and herbs along where tourists now buy curios at the Victoria and Alfred Waterfront, beneath the mirrored windows of anonymous apartments.

Krotoa, small, spirited and golden-skinned, with curls tight as peppercorns, lives in and around what will become the most prime real estate in Africa. But the tower blocks clinging to cliffs, the tour-ists walking the narrow pavement next to the drop-off into the Atlantic, none of that exists yet. The mountain is as it has always been, with Lion's Head and Signal Hill watching over Table Bay, but where Church Square now sits, at the top of Adderley Street, hippopotami wallow in a great swamp. The wild animals give the strongest sense of how different the Cape of 1652 is: to the Europeans, starved of fresh meat after a hundred days at sea, the flesh of hippopotamus is a great delicacy, said to taste of veal.

Krotoa is the ward of Autshumao, or so this name suggests. But all these relationships are opaque to the Dutch and to us, thanks to the discrepancy between European and Khoikhoi designations of kinfolk. We don't even know her real name – Krotoa is probably just the Dutch transcription of '!Oroloas', a Khoikhoi designation meaning 'ward-girl'. When Maria de la Quellerie takes a fancy to the little girl and installs her in the Van Riebeeck tent she can't be bothered with the child's name and calls her Eva instead.

So much of this history is ironic: 'Khoikhoi', as the Cape pastoralists call themselves, means just 'real people', but these 'real people' are precisely those regarded as less than real, less than human, by the Europeans. Early on, they are given the name 'Hottentot' by the Dutch, a derivation of the German 'hotteren-totteren', meaning 'stutter', which is how, to the European ear, the implosive clicks and staccato pronunciation of the Khoikhoi language sounds. Or is it the sound they make when they dance? Later 'Hottentot' evolves to mean 'person of inferior intellect or culture' and, by the early eighteenth century, English novelist Daniel Defoe is referring to the 'Hottentots' as the 'worst and most savage of all savages'. Today the word is a racial slur.

But this first winter, vulnerable and exposed, the Dutch are still dependent on these despised 'Hottentots'. Living in tents, they are battered by the Cape's wind and rain and stricken with dysentery, the dreaded 'red flux'. Nearly every day there is a death. The fort is semi-habitable four months after the Dutch arrive, and Krotoa moves inside. She learns to speak Dutch and wears an Indonesian sarong and blouse. She is not a slave but a servant, 'being trained to civilised habits' Victorian historian George McCall Theal later remarks, without irony.

In October, the rich Goringhaiqua arrive with ten thousand cattle and, with Autshumao's help, Van Riebeeck trades copper plates, brass wire and tobacco for cattle, sheep, ivory and ostriches. The Khoikhoi

won't hunt elephant or ostriches to trade; they just bring along whatever they can pick up. The Dutch sneer – such sloth! – but by January
1653 Van Riebeeck has hundreds of sheep and cattle. There are
enough vegetables and livestock to provision the VOC fleet returning
from Japan, Ceylon, Malacca and other points east of the Netherlands,
even if the Dutch are terrorised by lions so bold they invade the cattle
kraal at night and leopards that carry sheep away in broad daylight.

But wild animals are not the only threat and the Dutch are weak
and exposed here, at the tip of the African continent, thousands of
miles from home.

19 October 1653

Table Valley is quiet, a fine mizzling rain blowing in off the Atlantic.
Commander van Riebeeck's wife, Maria, has given birth to a son the
previous day. Sentries patrol the thick mud walls, long muskets over
their shoulders. The fort is deserted, all the soldiers inside listening to
the pastor, *Dominie* Wylant, and his droning sermon. The VOC cattle
graze on the slopes of the Lion Mountain.

As the soldiers listen to the *dominie*, little Krotoa takes off her
sarong, puts on her leather apron and slinks out of the fort. Only
when the sermon ends does Commander van Riebeeck hear that
'Herry' (as the Dutch call Autshumao) has gone and 'Eva' too. As he
sits down to his midday meal, more news arrives: all the cattle have
disappeared. Soldiers set out for the fine green pasture at the tail end
of the Lion Mountain, where Hendrik Wilders, the cattle herd, left
the herd boy while he went to fetch lunch from the cook.

They find no sign of the cattle, nor David Janssen, the Company's
herd boy. Calling his name, they mill about, scanning the grass for the
tracks of the cattle, which seem to be heading away from the settlement. Suddenly a shout goes up. A soldier has found the boy's body,
crumpled next to a stream. He has been stabbed to death. The soldiers
set off in pursuit of the Goringhaikona, but the Khoikhoi drive the
cattle around the peninsula so fast they cannot catch them. Cornered
in the dunes on the other side of the mountain, the Khoikhoi escape
again, fleet-footed over the heavy sand. Late on the second day, they
take refuge among the herds of the Goringhaiqua, and the soldiers
reluctantly abandon their pursuit.

This is the first fracture in the Dutch relationship with the Khoikhoi, but Commander van Riebeeck is not allowed to retaliate. Unable to trade for cattle, the Dutch eat penguins and salted seal and carry palisades for the fort on their shoulders instead of using an ox wagon. They mutter about bloody retribution and carry muskets for protection while different groups of Khoikhoi wash in and out of Table Bay, stealing food and metal, preventing the Dutch from collecting wood or grass. The Khoikhoi's perceived dishonesty, their 'savagery', are a *leitmotif* in the Commander's journal, but they are too important to be punished, even for murder.

All that second summer, little Krotoa sleeps on grass scented with sprigs of woody, herby *buchu* instead of a straw mattress and drinks sour sheep's milk from a skin bag. But, after months of coaxing, Autshumao's people are back at the fort when the weather starts to turn, even if, privately, the Dutch continue to sneer: 'We embraced each other, like the greatest friends in the world, so that we had again a suit of clothes destroyed, from the greasiness of the oil and filth with which they [. . .] had so besmeared themselves.'

It is clear now that the Dutch mean to stay. They have replaced frail wooden houses with substantial brick, turned twelve *morgen* (ten hectares) of land into market gardens. What can the Khoikhoi do? In February 1655, Commander van Riebeeck records that fifty 'Hottentoos' have erected huts near the fort, telling him boldly that the land belongs to them, and that they will build their huts wherever they like. If the Dutch try to stop them, they will kill them with the help of the inland clans. But even this mild rebellion falters when Van Riebeeck continues, reluctantly, to turn the other cheek.

Meanwhile, astute Krotoa, more flexible than her uncle, learns to speak Dutch 'almost as well as a Dutch girl', making herself central as interpreter and trade broker. No European masters the Khoikhoi languages, spiked as they are with implosive clicks, and Krotoa runs through the fabric of Commander van Riebeeck's journal like a thread now, scurrying here and there, saying what she thinks they want to hear. At fifteen, on the cusp of maturity (she has not yet 'seen the moon', as the Khoikhoi call menstruation, but soon will, Khoikhoi girls starting later than European), she shines with beauty.

Standing in the council chamber, hair neatly covered by a cotton head-wrap over slanted cheekbones, she tells Commander van Riebeeck that her uncle secretly plans to build huts near the fort, but later alleges that another clan is massing to plunder Dutch cattle. They mean only to barter, not attack, claims the other interpreter Doman.

'Look, Mr van Riebeeck,' Krotoa says quickly, brown eyes snapping, 'Doman jokes and curries favour. He only flatters you, but I speak sincerely.'

Van Riebeeck records: 'It appears that the every-where-travelling Eva does the Company the greatest service by conciliating these tribes' and Krotoa's position appears secure. But five years after the Dutch arrive at the Cape, the feeding station is evolving, pushing against its boundaries as more and more humans alight from ships, stepping onto the shore and altering its fragile balance.

Mooi *Ansela*

21 February 1657

'Land hoi!' comes the cry from high above the deck: faint on the horizon lies a low grey mass, the Cape of Good Hope. After 5,900 nautical miles and two and a half months, the *Amersfoort* is nearing the end of the first leg of her voyage home. Aboard is an eleven-year-old girl, slave to Rear-Admiral Pieter Kemp, a VOC official on his way back to Amsterdam. Snatched from her parents by pirates in Bengal and taken to a VOC station on the Ganges Delta where the Dutch purchase clothing, opium and saltpetre for export, Angela was transported by ship to Batavia, just a small child in the dark below deck for a month with little to eat or drink. Slavery is firmly established in Bengal, with new slaves branded on their forehead and breast. Does Angela spend a lifetime bearing the physical mark of her slave past?

The big Dutch East Indiaman lumbers on, its hold full of cloves, nutmeg and pepper, part of the VOC return fleet from Batavia. Batavia (modern-day Jakarta) is a new town: in need of a secure location to store goods and run the spice trade, in 1619 the VOC found an Eastern headquarters on the coast of Java. Angela was a housemaid in Master Kemp's Batavia home, built in the Dutch style and completely different from the wood and thatch hut in which she last lived, next to the estuary in Bengal. Batavian streets are in an efficient grid, crisscrossed with canals and arched bridges. Angela would accompany Master Kemp to church, trotting amenably behind with a parasol to keep him cool, pretty slave girls being a status symbol here. Walking through the main square, Master Kemp and his slave would run the gamut of merchants, bankers, engineers, soldiers and tax collectors; packed warehouses share space with busy trading houses, VOC administrative offices and alehouses.

Angela van Bengale – one of the many names her captors give her. The Dutch don't bother with accurate records of brown-skinned people, partly because they don't care and partly because to rename someone is to claim their identity. Angela lines up alongside Krotoa/ Eva, her given name not recorded anywhere, her names in the literature varying so widely that we cannot know what name an acquaintance passing her in the street would have called out.

Ancilla she is called, Latin for slave girl. Or – in another classical tradition – Angela, Greek for messenger and angel. The gulf between these two meanings illuminates the voyage she will take. Later she is *mooi* Ansela ('pretty' in Dutch), or is it (in the Cape muster roll of 1692) *maaij* Ansela, *maaij* the creolised Dutch or Portuguese for 'mother'. *Maaij* Ansela is an elderly matriarch, a woman widely respected in her community: what price now the Ancilla of 1657? Slave girl, pretty angel, mother.

Then there is the surname: Van Bengale. A name laden with meaning and yet essentially meaningless. Slaves are given the tag *'van'* ('from' in Dutch), followed by the region from which they are acquired. The VOC does not care where its slaves originate, only the law under which they live before capture: the slave transforms into a new being, with no roots to tempt them to rebellion. Angela van Bengale might be from Bangladesh, of 'pariah' or untouchable status, or from a small mountain community. She might be from Burma or Assam or somewhere else entirely.

These names are more tenacious than any slave irons: once freed, slaves are still known by the country where they were captured. Once a slave, always a slave, in the eyes of society, at least. For many humans, this parallel loss of identity and imposition of a slave persona represents an insurmountable hurdle, but not for Angela.

The Cape Angela arrives at in the late summer of 1657 is a tiny settlement, quite different from bustling Batavia, with only fourteen other non-native women. A small hospital lies along the shoreline, and there is a jetty out into the bay. Around the fort, streets lie in three neat grids. Krotoa is living with the Van Riebeecks and is something of a favourite. Slavery is not legal in the Netherlands; slaves must be freed on arrival or sold en route, and so Rear-Admiral Kemp sells Angela to Commander Jan van Riebeeck. Soon she sleeps alongside Krotoa in the cramped and dirty Van Riebeeck quarters, cooking, cleaning and washing alongside the other young slaves. Water is collected from the stream; candles are scarce, so they go to bed with the sun and get up with the sun: there is not much here, except for clean air and wild animals.

Slavery and the slave trade are integral to the VOC from its inception in the early seventeenth century, and at the Cape, as we shall see. As a house slave, Angela is sheltered from the floggings and shackles of collective slave labour: in 1658, the first official slave consignment docks, carrying people captured off the coast of Angola, bound for Brazil. There are sourcing trips to Madagascar and Mozambique; slaves are brought from Batavia (Jakarta) and Ceylon (Sri Lanka) on the VOC's return fleets. But the Khoikhoi are never enslaved: it is too risky to capture these people who can easily abscond and retaliate. So, while Angela washes clothes and sweeps out the grate, Krotoa is free to come and go. She is in ascendance, for now.

October 1658

Spring and the fynbos, that distinctive shrubland of the Cape peninsula, is vibrant with life: red disa flowers in the streams, sugarbirds swoop between the proteas, searching for nectar. Honeybees drone over the sweet thorn and bushwillow, and the sky is a great arc of blue. Krotoa walks through the clear air, laden under the weight of brass, iron, beads, bread and brandy. Hearing of another clan, the Cochoqua, and their Chief Oedasoa's store of assegais (short spears), bows and arrows; that he is 'so greased over, that the fat ran in drops down his body, which was the highest mark of distinction'; and that his cattle are so numerous that there is 'no end of them to be seen', Commander van Riebeeck longs to trade with him.

When Krotoa first suggests she undertake this visit, Van Riebeeck resists; she is too young, too vulnerable, too unschooled in trade. But Krotoa persists, wheedling, reminding him of the elephant tusks, civet, amber, seed pearls and buckskins that she could bring back. Commander van Riebeeck capitulates, and, setting aside her soft eastern garments, Krotoa departs, confident and at ease. First stop will be the Goringhaiqua encampment where her mother, or the woman identified by the Dutch as her mother, lives. Then a few hours fast walk further on to the Cochoqua and, with them, Chief Oedasoa and his wife: Krotoa's sister.

As she enters Gogosa's kraal, Krotoa looks around for her mother. All the women are dressed as she is: skin cloak and apron of sheep hide, little pointed skin cap, leather shoulder bag and leather sandals. Some of these women have necks and ears, fingers and arms, draped with beads of copper and coloured glass. But Krotoa trumps them all with her brass bracelets, which replaced the copper, which in turn replaced the traditional ivory. And her face is clean of the detailed swirls and points of red ochre, mixed with fat, which adorns the faces of the other women; her body is free of the fat and *buchu* that smears theirs.

When Krotoa finally spies her mother and walks toward her, the older woman barely acknowledges her. And when Krotoa wakes in the morning to find the iron beads, the bread and the brandy, all her trade goods, have disappeared, her mother will not meet her eyes, stalking off into the fynbos, the sugar bushes swinging shut behind her. Nonplussed, Krotoa leaves the kraal while the dew still glints on the fynbos. In the late afternoon, she reaches the vast herds of Oedasoa's cattle, and Khoikhoi erupt all around her, chattering excitedly. Contented, Krotoa allows herself to be led to Oedasoa's kraal. Oedasoa, a small, lean, but kingly man, welcomes her, and the two sisters, who have not seen each other since Krotoa was an infant, fall into each other's arms, gossiping away in their quick, plosive tongue.

That night, the Khoikhoi dance around the fire, skipping on the spot, leg rings rattling, while Krotoa spins tales of the hairy Dutchmen.

She accepts ostrich eggs and the softest part of the buck, sleeps with her sister on straw mats in the chief's big hut and the following morning she is seated on an ox as if she were a chief's daughter. Not only does Oedasoa want to trade with the Dutch, but Krotoa's sister promises to find her a rich husband.

Krotoa returns to the fort with some of Oedasoa's men, regaling Commander van Riebeeck with tales of Oedasoa's wealth and friendliness. Her rival, Doman, spreads rumours that the Cochoqua plan to burn down the Fort and kill the Dutch, but Krotoa brushes it off: he is a liar who speaks with a double tongue, she retorts. A party sets off from the fort: Europeans, Krotoa and Oedasoa's men, followed by an ox swaying under the weight of gifts – brass, beads, tobacco, brandy, a hundred pounds of bread. When the Europeans reach the Cochoqua, they cannot help smiling: the herds are 'in number like the grass in the field', stripping the pasture bare in minutes.

Trading brass wire and beads for hundreds of cows and sheep, they return to the fort a few days later. But Krotoa is not with them. 'Eva', they report, has set off into the interior with her sister, telling them 'that she had a Dutch heart in her body and would never forget this, but do everything for our benefit wherever this was possible'. Krotoa's future as a Khoikhoi princess is mapped out.

Yet six weeks later she is back at the fort. I think about Khoikhoi puberty rituals, held at the start of menstruation, of Krotoa, like other Khoikhoi girls, isolated in a hut and taught how to be a mother, a wife, a Khoikhoi woman. Of Khoikhoi society, where men hunt and guard the herds while women forage, choose when to butcher livestock. But Krotoa cannot resist what ties her to the Dutch: childish loyalty to Maria de la Quellerie; the thrill through her bones when she talks in the council chamber; the comfort of soft cloth on her skin, soft rice in her mouth. Departure, return: this pattern endures for the rest of her life. Each time she leaves, she removes her cloth garments, putting on her skins. Each time she returns, she swaps her skins for her sarong. The Dutch are appalled: she is not civilised at all!

Krotoa experiences the flux in Cape society, the collision of African pastoralist and European capitalist, on her skin. And all we can do is watch as new arrivals continue to disembark, in their white skins, ready to take everything away from her. Land, freedom, belonging. As Krotoa sets out on her first trading visit, a little girl, standing on the docks in the Netherlands, catches my eye. Waiting to board a ship to take her down the long sea road to the Cape, this child, the final character in our opening trio, has skin that is not golden like Krotoa, or coppery like Angela's, but a pallid ivory, and hair the colour of straw.

The open ocean

Vlie, Netherlands, October 1658
It is cold on the dock, a clear day. The young Cloete family shiver. The air smells salty, autumnal. Three-year-old Elsje mirrors her mother in miniature: linen shift under blouse and petticoats, apron and a white linen cap, woollen shawls for warmth if they are lucky. Elsje has travelled with her mother, brother and uncle from the small village of Oedt near the bishopric of Cologne.

In the 1650s, much of north-central Europe comprises a hotch-potch of kingdoms, baronies and bishoprics. I find a map drawn by Dutch cartographer Willem Blaeu in the 1600s. Tiny trees scatter this plan, red castles, heraldic lions and crossed swords. Rivers and their confluences, borders in green, pink and yellow. And at the top, under a river, sits Oedt. I flick through web pages to the present day: here is Oedt, encircled by a small commuter town on the Niers River. The photographs show deep woods, campervans and elderly people litter-picking. The Pearl of the Niers, they call it.

Oedt is a hundred and eighty miles from Vlie, a long way for Elsje's little legs. People walk everywhere, transporting goods in wheelbar-rows and handcarts, although the network of canals, rivers and streams makes travelling by boat possible and, in the winter, by skate. Elsje's mother, Fytje (a diminutive of Sophia), is following her husband Jacob Cloete, who signed on as a sailor bound for the Cape the previ-ous year. Most European immigrants are illiterate peasants or labour-ers employed by the VOC. VOC soldiers earn less than peat-cutters, and fifteen to twenty per cent of those who set sail on Company voyages die every year. Penniless and ragged, some migrants are helped by agents while waiting for a VOC job and then take five years to repay the debt: people trafficking, seventeenth–century style.

It is a long and dangerous journey, overland from Oedt. Fytje and her brother shelter Elsje and her older brother Gerrit as they run the gauntlet of criminals in the back streets, although since the late 1500s the roads have been lit by lanterns to prevent people falling in the canals. Fytje and Elsje walk past people living on the streets during the day, markets selling fish, cheese, butter, wood, cattle. Girls stay near the house, playing tag, hopscotch, blind-man's bluff. There are porters who deliver letters or act as a childminder, *kargadoors* whose job it is to pull handcarts over the steep canal bridges, night watch-men, lamplighters. There are fire and water shops where you can buy a bucket of hot water or a bucket of hot coal.

In the Netherlands, poor people do not get old: women marry at twenty-two and live for another twenty-five years; death rates are so high that remarriage is very common. A widow, especially with chil-dren, must be rich or beautiful, or she faces a life grubbing around for charity. Plague is rife, medical care basic. Surrounded by death, uncertainty and despair, people celebrate hard when they get the chance. Feast days are loud and vulgar: fires on corners and in squares, magicians and jugglers in the inns and streets, women wearing men's clothes and men women's, and everyone wearing a mask. Secret drinking, and sex.

Fytje's children might be educated in poor schools run by the church and city councils. Elsje might be hired very young as a servant to make the fire and breakfast, to ventilate the house, make beds, clean clothes, polish the tin and copper. She would be lucky: the Dutch do not beat their servants. Or she might become a prostitute. But Elsje's life is going to look nothing like this.

The changes of the seventeenth century are dramatic. Ships carry European sailors (Spanish, Portuguese, Dutch, English) around the globe; they explore and colonise new continents. European states grow, merge and strengthen; they extend their long trading arms across the world's oceans. The fate of Africa's southern tip is directly involved with these changes.

Seven provinces that now make up the Netherlands rebel against Spain in 1568 and slowly win independence. With cheap energy from windmills and peat burning, the Dutch Republic, formed in 1648, becomes a powerhouse of trade, industry, the arts and the sciences. This is the era of Rembrandt, Vermeer, Van Ruisdael. Christiaan Huygens invents the pendulum clock and explains Saturn's planetary rings. Always keen sailors and mapmakers, in the 1600s, the Dutch begin to trade with the Far East. In 1602, the Dutch East India Company appears. The Dutch dominate trade with Japan and within Europe. Eighty years later, Louis XIV, the Sun King, repeals the Edict of Nantes – which allowed the Protestant Huguenots religious and political freedom in France – forcing two hundred thousand Huguenots to flee as far as the Americas and even South Africa.

Dutch society revolves around trade and wealth, and people climb up and down the social ladder. The nobility has no special privilege, and this Calvinist country reveres humility. Dutch women are strong stuff, their penchant for kissing in public, frank conversations and walks without chaperones shocking the French. Unmarried mothers can force the child's father into marriage and women can initiate legal proceedings, even against husbands. This is the culture that influences the character of the Cape most: Roman-Dutch law applies, the Calvinist Reformed Church is the only church for more than a century and Dutch is the official language, giving rise to the creolised dialect, Afrikaans.

The small party wait on the docks in the shadow of the *Arnhem* and its ornate stern, a ship that can carry two hundred and fifty to three hundred people to the Cape and beyond. On average, four thousand people leave Europe for East Asia every year in the seventeenth century on ships that travel at what now seems like a snail's pace: seven knots or eight miles per hour. Given the scale of the VOC enterprise and the profits involved, it is not surprising that it is well managed, with relatively few shipwrecks. Ships follow prescribed routes and are issued with maps and coastal descriptions with dangers detailed from rocks to shallows. But sailing the world's oceans remains a risky business. Four years later, the *Arnhem* sinks in a violent storm off the coast of Mauritius. Struggling ashore on an islet, some of her crew are the last to see a living dodo.

Fytje holds tightly to Elsje's hand as they walk up the swaying gangplank, clutching a bundle of clothes and a small Bible. She is trusting their lives to this floating wooden vessel with barnacles and seaweed on its hull. They will travel across open oceans where seas reach as high as the townhouses lining the quay. The passengers are herded below deck, stumbling over ropes and barrels in the dimness. The stench is so overpowering they breathe through their mouths. The bunks are narrow and stacked high, a thin mattress on each, a chamber pot beneath the lowest. Meagre possessions are stowed in bunks, coins strapped securely round the waist or sewn into clothes. Fytje keeps to herself: a woman among so many men does not wish to draw attention. The deck starts to move, masts creak, ropes snap and a fresh wind comes down through the hatch. The great ship is making its way towards the open sea.

The *Arnhem* leaves the Netherlands in the autumn, setting sail across the North Sea for the English Channel. The captain has waited for favourable winds as the heavy ship takes half an hour to turn and cannot sail close to the wind. This leaves her vulnerable to running aground on the shores of France or England. (Visit Bexhill-on-Sea in East Sussex 350 years later, and the price of such a mistake can still be seen. At low tide, the *Amsterdam*'s wooden ribs protrude through the sand where they have rested since she was lost on her maiden voyage in 1749.)

During storms, the hatch is latched down and the stink of urine, faeces and vomit becomes unbearable. Seasickness is a constant problem. High-ranking officials and passengers have cabins behind the main mast with more space and better food. But Fytje and her family sleep, eat and live crammed in with hundreds of sailors before the mast. There are provisions of salt beef or pork, fish, cheese, ale. The longer the ship sails, the worse the food becomes until only ship's biscuit is left: hard as a rock and full of weevils and maggots. Everything is dirty and covered with flies. Sailors suffer with the bloody flux, with bleeding gums and loose teeth.

Once out into the Atlantic, the *Arnhem* sails across the stormy Bay of Biscay, round Cape Finisterre and makes for her first stop: Cape Verde for fresh water and supplies. From there, she catches the northeast trade wind toward Fernando Po off the Brazilian coast. Here she risks getting caught in the Doldrums, converging winds along the equator where ships can lie becalmed for days. Then it is a run on the west winds of the southern hemisphere to the islands of Tristan da Cunha and from there to Cape Town.

As the *Arnhem* sails into Table Bay on 16 March 1659, Fytje and the children make out the mountain's flat shape. The *Arnhem* drops anchor, and goods and passengers are rowed ashore in small boats. Clutching Elsje, Fytje struggles down the steep ladder into the boat as the water seethes below, although there is only a light breeze from the north-west. On the quayside are faces darker than Fytje recognises, in a settlement where there are nearly two hundred slaves to the fifty-one freemen, and ninety-five VOC soldiers and officials. Fytje and her children are vastly outnumbered. And, unbeknownst to her, they are walking into a guttering conflict.

Eighteen months earlier, in 1657, Commander van Riebeeck, in need of more supplies, releases VOC men to live as farmers outside the fort ('burghers' they call them, including Jacob Cloete, Fytje's husband). From her vantage point in the Dutch inner circle, Krotoa watches as these men occupy Khoikhoi land and stop them sending their cattle to the river to drink, listens while Khoikhoi mutter about violent attacks from these new farmers. She watches as runaway slaves are fitted with heavy chains that rub their skin raw, sees her fellow Goringhaikona loiter in the fort and cut the brass buttons from the coats of passers-by.

Van Riebeeck talks of barricading off the Cape Peninsula with a canal or border wall, enslaving the Goringhaikona, and preventing them from influencing trade, but his Amsterdam overlords dismiss the scheme as too expensive. Increasingly barred from their traditional way of life, the Khoikhoi are reduced to stock raids. In 1659, just as Fytje and her family disembark at the Cape, the first of two Khoikhoi–Dutch wars breaks out.

Liesbeeck River, Cape settlement, May 1659
Skirts tucked up, bare feet placed carefully between reeds on the soft riverbed, Fytje scrubs at the petticoat draped over a rock. An observer might note her tight back, her frequent glances around. Lions, snakes, hippopotamuses are all still common – even the Khoikhoi, so naked and so brown, and she can't get used to how they appear, silent with their spears. Elsje plays on the bank, close to a pair of breeches and a

dress drying over the wild almond bushes. In the distance Jacob and Gerrit are turning the earth. The fields around the thatched cottage with its earthen floor and mud walls already show green with rye and wheat.

The sudden burr of insect, whistle of bird in the humming silence of the wilderness – how different does this feel to five months aboard ship, surrounded by stinking bodies? The fort lies six miles away, and a fold in the land hides the nearest cottage: Harman Remajenne is a bachelor from Cologne and shares their dialect. It is a harsh life; even Commander van Riebeeck admits they can hardly survive on what he paid Jacob for last year's wheat. Other farmers have already given up, finding work as carpenters, bricklayers and innkeepers.

Fytje wipes at the perspiration trickling into her eyes. It is heavy work, and she sweats despite the cool weather. Behind the cottage rises the mountain, with its strange flowers and flitting birds. Harman complains that the climate is too changeable, with too little rain too often, and the vicious south-west wind destroys his harvests; that he can't grow the sugar or tobacco the sailors describe from their voyages. She takes Harman's complaints on advisement, given that she has seen with her own eyes the cattle he has traded from the Khoikhoi for bits of iron. Which the Company forbids them from doing, keeping all the trade for themselves. Which leaves them reliant on low pay for meagre harvests, so poor that they share their cottage with two sheep and a cow, sleeping on straw and the naked earth.

What I know, and Fytje doesn't, being so far from the settlement, is that the Khoikhoi have attacked the *Arnhem*'s skipper and mate, and that a European has been stabbed seven times and killed, his gun stolen by Doman – Krotoa's rival, who turns out to be just as loyal to his own people as she claimed. A bounty has been put on any Khoikhoi, caught dead or alive. Livestock, crops, ploughshares and tobacco have been stolen from other farmers. Yesterday, under dark grey skies, the Company animals were hustled into the fort.

The first she knows of it all is a messenger from the fort running through the fields, shouting, trampling on all the new wheat, Jacob and Gerrit standing suddenly straight. She lifts the petticoat from its rock, pulls the other clothes carefully under her arm (how could she replace such things?) and hurries up the narrow path to the cottage.

Within two hours, she, Elsje and Gerrit are stuck in a fortified redoubt with their animals and iron tools. Jacob is left to defend the farm from the Khoikhoi who, under Doman, are fighting to use the land as they have for the past few hundred years, to reach the river with their cattle, so the animals can graze on the rich grass of the river plain. From the very next day, Commander van Riebeeck forces all the free burghers to take part in commando drills every Sunday after church, a martial unit that will dominate Afrikaner culture for centuries.

Krotoa and Angela remain in the fort as throughout May and June, under cover of rain, which prevents the Dutch from keeping their matches alight to fire their guns, the Goringhaiqua attack the settlers. Krotoa is the only Khoikhoi to stay. When Commander van Riebeeck sends for her, she walks confidently into the council chamber, a slight brown-skinned girl among the bearded Dutchmen. Her brother-in-law, Oedasoa, has promised to help the Europeans. Will she discuss terms with him, Commander van Riebeeck asks?

Krotoa travels north to Saldanha Bay where Oedasoa is camped, but when she arrives her brother-in-law avoids her, or so she tells Van Riebeeck. For months, she travels to and fro by small boat or on foot, but to no avail. In the council chamber Van Riebeeck grows tired of his protégé: 'She has been found to fib a little, and is a little given to flattery, and to saying whatever she thinks one would be pleased to hear,' he records. Later historians speculate that Krotoa is working for Oedasoa, who has no intention of siding with the Dutch and is instead trying to contain them and control trade for himself. As for other Khoikhoi, well, they despise Krotoa as a traitor. But they sue for peace in the end, seeing no road to victory, and are forced off the Liesbeeck lands forever.

The Cloetes return to their mud farmstead and Fytje gives birth to another daughter (Catryn, for Jacob's mother, back in Oedt). Angela, thirteen now, is a washerwoman. Krotoa can still pull a little magic out of her apron. In 1660, she persuades Oedasoa to visit the fort, and the grateful Dutch give her tobacco pipes, knives, sticks of brass wire, pounds and pounds of tobacco, strings of beads, axes. This is the only time that her putative true name is recorded in the journal – 'Eva, named by them Krotoa' – and even this is inaccurate. But the honeymoon period is over: at home in neither European nor Khoikhoi society, she floats between the two, shipping more and more water. As Van Riebeeck notes: 'She seems so much habituated to Dutch customs and Dutch food that she will never be able entirely to relinquish them.'

'This is a kind of death'

Elsje is still only five, but both Krotoa and Angela are growing into womanhood early, because they must: to survive, to thrive. Angela lives in the Van Riebeecks' rooms, breathes in and out alongside Krotoa. I wonder at their relationship, if there is one.

August 1660

It is murky in the castle even by day, and now, at gone ten at night, the light comes only from the pitch torch Commander van Riebeeck carries as he leads three soldiers past the gunpowder magazine further down a passageway to a door, where they all stop. Turning the iron ring set into wooden planks to lift the latch, Van Riebeeck pushes the door open. In the flaring light, Gunner Willem Cornelisz can be seen, undressed on the rough sheets. Alongside him lies the woman they are searching for, the Commander's slave Maria.

As the pair struggle to find their clothes, the Commander tells Maria to return to his quarters. Cornelisz is locked in a cell for the night, protesting. The next day the soldiers testify that they found Cornelisz in bed with Maria when he was supposed to be on duty. Cornelisz accuses Commander van Riebeeck of victimising him: other soldiers regularly keep slaves as concubines and escape scot-free! It is not his fault they are not allowed to marry! Yet here he is dismissed from his post and fined fifty reals!

Fellow soldier and stonemason, Francois de Coninck, keeps his eyes on the floor. Later, he watches covertly as another slave crosses the courtyard, sleek black hair caught up at the nape of her neck. Pretty, charming, and able to flirt in both Portuguese and Dutch. Angela keeps her eyes downcast, her smooth brown cheeks flushing as she feels his eyes on her. She is fourteen and slight. Better the free stonemason than the enslaved Africans who also stare, she might think. In this isolated community, male slaves, their masters and other Europeans all assault female slaves and Khoikhoi women. Commander van Riebeeck does not disapprove of his men having relationships with slaves or indeed, as he calls it, 'fructifying' them and creating new slaves; Cornelisz is only in trouble because he neglected his work. For a slave woman, too much resistance is risky, and it is far more sensible to pair off with the least unpalatable man.

A year later, in August 1661, we find Angela, aged fifteen, in labour. There is no midwife at the Cape yet, but the other slave women light a fire, walk her up and down through contractions, hold her upright as she strains. The baby, Anna de Coninck, is destined to be a great society beauty, but her father does not stick around for long, disappearing from the Cape records in 1662. Angela has already moved on; her first child with the Belgian cooper Jan van As is baptised this year. She is still only seventeen. Together they have Jacobus in 1662 and his brother Jan in 1665. (Born bastard slaves, one of these sons will break Angela's heart, but not for a couple of decades yet.) Although unbaptised herself, Angela attends church regularly, as does Krotoa. It is all part of taking on the rites and customs of white society. Krotoa cannot tolerate this framework in the long term, but Angela can: easier to assimilate when you have no access to, and little memory of, your own people. What is more, when the Van Riebeecks leave the Cape in 1662, they sell Angela to a kind man named Abraham Gabbema, but leave Krotoa out in the cold.

3 May 1662
Dutchmen crowd the hall at the fort of Good Hope: soldiers with long lank hair, thin moustaches and beards, tall boots; Company servants in grey curled wigs under wide-brimmed black hats, wearing white collars, knee breeches, fitted jackets. The stench of unwashed bodies is pungent as the minister gives the sermon. It is cold, the rain pattering on the thatch overhead.

At nineteen, Krotoa has fallen out of favour, perhaps because, like Angela, she has recently given birth to a baby that is half white. The new Commander, Zacharias Wagenaar, old and ill, despises her, speaks to her as if she were a slave or a prostitute. The Van Riebeecks haven't even bothered to turn up for Krotoa's baptism. The sermon rumbles on. Krotoa knows her catechism and can read the big old Bible with its Dutch lettering. '*Gelooft u in de enige ware God?*' asks the minister, a stranger who arrived on the ship due to take the Commander and Maria away. Dost thou believe in the only true God?

'*Ja,*' Krotoa says – yes – but she might be thinking of Tsui-//goab, creator of rain, clouds, thunder and lightning. At full moon, the Khoikhoi still dance in his honour. How can we know what she thinks as the water washes over her head?

Within the last year, Krotoa has lost her mother, her sister, her uncle Autshumao, and given birth to a child she could not purify in the Khoikhoi way, where she would have been confined to a hut for seven days, untouched by water, learning how to feed him. No, she gave birth in the fort, like the Dutch. Perhaps another Khoikhoi woman helped her, rubbing the new baby with fresh cow dung, leaving him green and sweet-smelling. But I think not.

And now this: appointed head of the Company in Malacca, Jan van Riebeeck and his wife are leaving. Van Riebeeck mentions Eva two hundred times in sixty-five diary entries, but in his official letter of transfer he can only bring himself to say that, while Eva can speak Dutch well, her reports should be taken with a pinch of salt. As the rain continues pattering on the thatch and Krotoa takes her place back on the rough bench, her body loosens. Baptism will surely prove to Commander Wagenaar that she is nearly Dutch. And it will allow her to marry the sober young Dane who smiles at her as she sits down and murmurs something in Dutch. She touches the cross at her throat, smooths her cotton sarong and reaches out for baby Jacobus.

When, years earlier, Commander van Riebeeck shows Krotoa the map from Amsterdam, of a north-flowing river and the kingdom of Monomotapa, the kingdom he says is rich in gold, ivory and pearls, she thinks of the Namaqua people, who live to the north. Could he mean them? No reason for her not to tell the commander that the Namaqua are rich, which pleases him no end; he stays fired up for days. The other Khoikhoi mutter in displeasure.

And when the young man who watches her in the council chamber volunteers for all six expeditions to the north, it opens a path to the future. A story goes around that the men come across Bosjesmans women and children in a camp and Corporal Cruythof orders them put to death, but that Pieter van Meerhof refuses, and all the other men stand by him. That Pieter finds the Namaqua, gaining their trust and starting a craze for red nightcaps when he gives his to the chief, Krotoa understands as proof of his promise. Although as it turns out, the Namaqua are not rich at all.

Pieter can read, like Krotoa, and he can write, and has been promoted to under-surgeon since arriving three years previously. Born Peter Havgard, Krotoa knows him by the name the VOC give him: Pieter van Meerhof. Most of the VOC men visit the female slaves in the Company slave lodge, but those women can offer nothing but sex and companionship, while Krotoa provides a leg-up into the world of Commander van Riebeeck. She is the only Khoikhoi woman with a European partner; the others are kept in the kraals and, besides, the Dutchmen are revolted when the Khoikhoi women smear themselves in sheep fat.

By June 1664, the couple are in the hall again, exchanging vows beneath the leopard and lion skins that line the walls. Sunlight falls on the planks of the floor thanks to glass windows that have replaced the old calico screens. Later, the Cape's Council provides a feast, having agreed to the marriage because Krotoa has 'long since' been baptised. Pieter is promoted to surgeon. Two months later, Krotoa and Pieter set out to visit Oedasoa, but the moment has passed, and her brother-in-law will only trade five skinny bullocks and fourteen sheep. He promises Krotoa cattle and sheep as a wedding present, but they never materialise. With his wife, Krotoa's lovely sister, dead, the chief leaves her life.

When Krotoa is a teenager, time and change are vague theories. Only as the days and years accrue does she realise that the treasured role of translator and go-between will be irrelevant within five years once the Dutch find there are no rich clans, no mythical kingdoms inland; once they complete their plundering of Khoikhoi land; once more and more Khoikhoi speak Dutch. Krotoa has become an irrelevance, and the old hidden disdain seeps out. When her husband travels abroad, she is ordered to stay within the fort. But Krotoa is not Dutch, nor a slave, so when her niece gives birth in November 1663, she takes her small half-European children to visit. How this looks to Wagenaar: 'the thoughtless wench has often played us the same trick before, throwing aside her clean and neat clothing, and resuming old stinking skins of animals, like all the other filthy female Hottentoos'.

19 May 1665

Krotoa is aboard *De Bruydegom*, the children turning green as the little ship wallows all seven miles to Robben Island. The island is already a penal colony, and Pieter is not being promoted. As superintendent, he will watch for ships entering the bay, monitor the convicts who collect shells for lime and quarry stone for the castle. The small town dwindles in the lee of the mountain. How long the family will be isolated on the island Krotoa does not know. It will be quiet after the fort, where the Khoikhoi rest on their haunches, chewing tobacco, as the dark African slaves play their instruments and dance in the dusk.

In theory, the boat crosses from Cape Town every day to collect the lime, but wind and storms often conspire to leave the residents marooned. Pieter can slaughter sheep for his family, but must feed the prisoners through fishing while ridding the island of snakes and spiders. Under Krotoa's hands, her belly is rounded: there are no other women on Robben Island, no one to deliver the child. Was it inevitable, this posting? The two superintendents before Pieter were also married to women with skin darker than their own pale, burning pelts. Van Riebeeck, who appropriated the child Krotoa, his wife who moulded her into this curious hybrid, are long gone, and the new order finds her so embarrassing, this 'filthy native' with her Dutch language, that they banish the entire family. The devious vines of colonisation are creeping over Krotoa now, up her legs, towards her throat.

April 1667

Krotoa lies on the beaten earth, an overturned bench next to her, blood tracking from the cut above her left eyebrow, across her nose and dripping onto the ground. Little Pieternella runs to where her father is supervising the boat's unloading at the slipway with their new slave, Jan Vos of the Cape Verde Islands. April winds whip across the dry grass and rocks. Pieter comes at a run and stoops over his wife before carrying her inside. Jan Vos heats water, and cleans the wound, but it won't stop bleeding. Pieter tears a sheet and binds it round Krotoa's unconscious head. He finds paper and an old quill and scribbles a note to the mainland, asking for surgical assistance. Handing the captain of *De Bruydegom* the note, he urges him on his way.

With no women on the island, Pieter and Jan Vos nurse Krotoa until the boat returns with the surgeon onboard. Krotoa comes round, confused and vomiting, and keeps 'fainting away'. The surgeon can do no more than suggest she has a skull fracture and hope for the best. He is accompanied back to the mainland by thirty fat sheep and sacks of lime.

There are coincidences in the commander's journal, unexplained lacunae and little interest in Krotoa, so I cannot tell when she succumbs to alcohol. Beer and wine are drunk by everyone, and harder spirits, including Eastern rice brandy, or *arrack*, are supplied as part of the convicts' rations. The Khoikhoi are fond of alcohol, but it is not as initially catastrophic as it is to Native American populations, as the Khoikhoi already brew traditional drinks from fruits and grains. Yet several Khoikhoi integrated into the white community fall prey to drunkenness, their in-between state too much to carry.

May 1667

After the boat carrying Pieter has left the shore, Krotoa walks up the *Vuurberg*, where they light the great bonfires to warn passing ships of rocks. From here Table Mountain, *Hoerikwaggo* to her still, seems close. You could almost lay a hand on its flat top. Robben Island is so small, just two miles long, the walk so short, that the boat is still struggling on its way to the mainland. How it worked was that, first, the Company stopped building at the castle, so Pieter had no work. And then, a few days later, they asked him to go on a trading expedition somewhere over the ocean.

For a man who jumps on the back of wild animals and volunteers to travel deep into the African interior six times, there would be no question of refusing even if he hadn't been stuck on the island for two years. The VOC allows Krotoa to stay in *d'baas zijn woning*, the boss's house, until he returns. What she might do, alone on an island full of criminals with three children under six, is never explained.

A few days later, Pieter van Meerhof sets sail for Mauritius and Madagascar. Krotoa never sees him again. In February the following year, word arrives at the Cape: Van Meerhof and eight of his men have been murdered after going ashore at the Bay of Antongil, Madagascar. 'While unsuspicious of danger the little party was attacked by local people and all were murdered,' the journal records. This dreadful news is written down on a paper and passed to the captain of *De Bruydegom*. He, in turn, carries it in his pocket when *De Bruydegom* makes her daily crossing to Robben Island, along with a cargo of rice and prisoners. The captain passes the paper to Krotoa when the boat docks at the island.

I don't know what happens to the paper after that, but I think Krotoa has had enough. There is no invitation back to the mainland. She and the children stay on Robben Island for seven long months more before they return to Cape Town in September 1668, under constant heavy rain, accompanied by a load of slate. A home has been fitted out for them in the old pottery, between the castle (being built on the grounds of the old fort) and the Company's Garden, an act that reflects not kindness but the fact that Krotoa's children are half European and, as such, the responsibility of the Company.

The town is radically different from the tiny settlement of Krotoa's teens. There are more than three hundred inhabitants, half of them European; free farmers have settled around the town, and slaves work the land. But Krotoa, still only twenty-six, is no longer accepted by the whites, especially now that she has lost her white husband, and with the remnants of her clan in tatters, her ties with other clans frayed, she has nowhere to go. It's the double-bind of assimilation: in reaching for European identity Krotoa has sacrificed her indigenous soul, only to fall between two worlds.

'Uijt puijre genegentheijt'

July 1668
Six years after we last saw her being sold to Abraham Gabbema, Angela lifts the heavy dough, turns it, drops it back down, pushing the heels of her hands into it, the rhythm helping her not think of her

son Pieter's tiny body, now under the soil. Turn, fold, knead. It becomes glossy and elastic under her patient hands. On an early morning in mid-winter, the short walk from home to the bakery is cold, the wind shoving its icy fingers under her shawl. Angela leaves her three children at home with her slave, Scipio, and Zara, her Khoikhoi servant, in the little thatched house on Heerestraat, awarded to her last year.

Jan van As is long gone, but Angela makes a good living from her vegetable garden and the bakery job. She is saving to set up her own business, trading in essential supplies. Baptised three months previously, she is taking on the structure of a European; it settles on her bones like dust on church beams. How far she has come from just two years ago when she was still a slave to Abraham Gabbema! *Mijnheer* Gabbema had grown gloomy after the death of his five-month-old son, a baby Angela breastfed herself, and eventually the couple left for Batavia. They could have taken her with them or sold her, but, instead, they set her free. '*Uijt puijre genegentheijt*': out of pure affection, Abraham wrote in the manumission document of 13 April 1666.

How generous *Mijnheer* Gabbema had been, helping her into her new life, persuading the baker to take her on as an apprentice. Angela divides the dough into sections and rounds them into fat sausage shapes, placing them next to the warm oven to rise. Wiping the flour from her hands, Angela thinks of the mess slave women get into over men: with three men to every woman, things get out of hand very fast. And beyond the castle everyone lives so far apart, speaks such different languages, that there is no solidarity, nothing shared. Female slaves fade into their masters' families, become carriers of the emerging Cape culture, which is European, although whispers of the East can still be heard three hundred years later in the Afrikaans language, and Cape cuisine.

Some whites already equate the non-white with the dishonourable, 'the blood of Ham', but it is being a slave, or a convict, or a non-Christian, that really marks people out as inferior. Pragmatic and warm, Angela knows she stands alongside, but not quite equal to, the other free people of the colony and their wives, all fourteen of them. But she has her own house and a slave, she is baptised and she is the only single woman in the colony to own property: Angela is, in fact, ripe for marriage, and marriage to a free white man. In December 1669, she marries burgher Arnoldus Basson. Between them, they own eighty sheep and a flintlock.

Back at the Cloetes' mud farmhouse on the banks of the Liesbeeck River, the very squalor of which Commander Wagenaar accuses the 'Hottentoos' is a daily reality and little Elsje Cloete's life is rough and ready: in 1663 a lion kills a calf and two sheep and her father and his neighbours set off in pursuit, only to return empty-handed that night, wet and dirty, thanks to the 'boisterous weather'. Jacob is caught bartering with the Khoikhoi again: first, he blasts the leg of a young rhino with his musket, then he bargains for five sheep. We're not in Oedt any more.

In the Cape winter, it can rain for days, the damp seeping under clothes to leave skin clammy and goose-bumped. Jacob and Gerrit will be out all day, sowing wheat and barley in the wet fields. Left alone with her mother and two little siblings, if Fytje becomes ill, Elsje had better look after her. She is nine years old. Catryn is five and Coenradus three. Elsje stops the little ones falling in the fire, or eating animal droppings, offers her mother a thin broth from the mutton stewing in the pot hung on chains over the kitchen hearth. She sweeps the dung floor, heats water to rinse the dirty bedlinen, plays a game with Catryn and her old rag dolly. Illness is hard to control in squalid surroundings with no running water, no doctors, no hospitals or roads. Women die during childbirth or in the days afterwards. Childbed fever gives the mother chills and a headache; there is a stench around the bed. Tiny infants are buried in small family grave-yards near farm cottages.

On 28 May 1665, Commander Wagenaar writes in his journal: 'In the afternoon we heard from our chief surgeon that shortly before, the wife of the agriculturist Jacob Cloeten had died in the Lord. In her the poor man and his four little children have lost much.' Elsje's father might take his gun and walk the two hours into town to visit his friends, but there are no spare European women at the Cape. He cannot remarry, let alone find someone to look after the children. Elsje must do it. The family struggle on, clothes threadbare and the pot too often empty, and as soon as there is a chance of divesting himself of a child Jacob jumps at it.

Cape Town, 9 September 1668

Spring and a wedding day. The thirteen-year-old bride stands awkward in her gown, which is just a cotton overskirt covering her child's body, green eyes round in her plain open face. The bride and groom have walked into the town together, along with her family. Coenradus and Catryn, who are six and eight, stare at the sea, the tall ship anchored in the bay, the bustle of sailors, slaves and merchants peddling their wares on the waterfront. Elsje knows her bridegroom as her father's friend, a regular visitor at the cottage. Willem Schalk van der Merwe is twenty-eight. She is barely more than a child and only just menstruating, letting the slight flow of blood trickle down under her petticoats as they all do.

Her eyes shift to Coenradus and Catryn, dwarfed by the castle. Who will look after them? At least she will be close by, in Willem's hut. Elsje wonders if the story Barbara Geems told her can be true. Whispering in Elsje's ear, Barbara had told her about the African woman in the Company's slave quarters. How Willem had been so in love that he had kept her secretly in the soldiers' kitchen while she was having their child, waiting on her hand and foot. Koddo van Guinea. She wonders if Willem still thinks about Koddo, or the child, Maria, who must be four now. She thinks too of what Barbara told her about men and women, how that might feel.

Yet she is excited about her marriage, about her husband. They will have their own farm; she will have her own kitchen, even if it is a smoky fire inside a mud-walled hut. Willem farms well, his crops growing flexible and tall. She sneaks a glance at him, his straight nose, the bristle on his cheeks. His talk is different to her father's – of Holland, of his parents – and he tells Bible stories, although he cannot read or write. Watching her as Krotoa sails back from Robben Island, wife to a murdered husband, I consider how the married unit offers shelter in this lonely, arbitrary landscape. Elsje holds Catryn's hand on the way home, her father and husband up ahead, the monotony of the two-hour walk dulling the anxiety in her stomach. The evening is chilly as the two parties separate, and for the first time she follows Willem into his hut.

Two years later we find Elsje kneeling in clean straw before the fire which Willem has made up before leaving to smoke his pipe with Jacob Cloete. Perhaps her aunt, fetched by a servant, coaxes her through this, her first labour. Has Willem refrained from having sex with his child bride for eighteen months? Aged fifteen, Elsje is strong and feisty, but still not fully developed. She is four times more likely to die than a mother in her twenties, her baby significantly more likely to die in its first month. The aunt offers a spoonful of broth, or a swig of brandy, rubs Elsje's lower back with linseed oil. This labour is slow but steady and baby Sophia, named for Elsje's mother, is born onto the straw, the afterbirth slithering out later. Elsje has borrowed string and scissors, laying them out on the rough table, ready for the umbilical cord. Later, the straw is swept into the fire, the afterbirth buried.

Against the odds, mother and daughter both survive and Elsje starts to build her own family just as her father Jacob places his two young-est children with other settlers and returns to Europe. Out here on the frontier, children are labour force, bank account and nursing home. The younger the bride, the more children she can have, and Elsje is very young. She will spend a decade of her life homing two lives in one body, twenty-eight years looking after thirteen children, eight more than her European contemporaries. Cape settlers choose to have so many children, to one degree or another; women have practised basic contraception for millennia, and Elsje spreads her children out at two-year intervals.

While Elsje begins the long journey of fostering thirteen infants towards adulthood, Krotoa is struggling to keep custody of just three as the VOC grasps the European half of them, unprotected as she is by the fortress of settler family life, or the reed huts of the Khoikhoi.

8 February 1669

The assembly hall seethes with soldiers and Company servants in for the evening service when three children enter. Stark naked, they trail past the long benches, up to the front row, to Commander Borghorst, who takes in their golden skin, their orange peppercorn curls. '*Wat?*' he barks. Their mother has stripped the potting shed bare; they have no clothes, no food, no bedding, Jacobus, the oldest, tells the

Commander. What of the nine rix-dollars she is given every month, of the pots and furniture she received when the family returned from Robben Island? She has sold everything, Jacobus replies, to buy *arrack*. Commander Borghorst's florid face burns even redder.

Hours previously, Krotoa is admitted to the hall as Eva ('almost as good as a Dutch girl') before spewing *arrack*-soaked insults at the Company, her spirit undaunted. Censorious officials warn her to behave better, describing with horrified relish how she 'plays the beast at night with one or another' and does nothing but 'lead a life of debauchery'. The Church Council decrees that Krotoa's children must be taken away from her. Jacobus, Pieternella and Salomon are housed with Jan Reyniersz, a cattle rustler and sheep thief. Three weeks later, they are placed with Barbara Geems in her brothel.

And Krotoa? I try to get a feeling for where she is now, place her in her situation and regard it from all angles. But it is akin to looking at a diorama in a museum, the plaster showing through the paint on her forehead, the fur on her *kaross* worn thin. She is trapped inside a scene: this hut kitted out with European pots and furniture, no European husband to anchor the family. No way of stepping over the rope into the real world. To begin with, Krotoa felt slick as a frog, at home with Dutch or Khoikhoi, but by now her carapace is rubbed raw and she cannot belong in either place, each change of clothes chafing until she must put them off again.

Krotoa sells her mattress for tobacco and drink, rattles around town before being arrested in 'front of the dunes with the Hottentoos', drunk and with a pipe in her mouth. She is thrown into the black hole of the castle's prison in semi-darkness, stinking, starving. A month later, the south-west wind is blowing hard when she is forced aboard the *De Bruydegom* once more, bound for Robben Island along with criminals so aggressive the island's new superintendent must fend them off with a cane. This time she is a prisoner.

December 1671

Dutch contempt for the Khoikhoi bursts open like a boil once the need for trade has passed and in 1671, three years after Krotoa is banished to Robben Island, Angela too becomes mired in it. High summer and her Table Valley garden seethes with growth. There are weeds to be pulled, vines to be trained. In the early morning, Angela and Francois Champelier, workmate of her husband, go out to the sheep-pen to feed and water the animals. Pushing open the gate, Angela stops suddenly. Hanging from the rafters is Zara, the Khoikhoi woman who has been living with Angela for three years. Her face glowers, swollen and purple.

Pushing the hungry milling sheep out of the way, Angela stumbles towards her. She thinks she sees movement in the veins of the slowly twisting neck and urges Francois to cut the body down. Patting Zara's face, pulling her dress straight, Angela begs her friend to wake up. It is futile. After that, the Company gets involved, ordering Zara's body to be dragged under the threshold of Angela's house so it does not sully the household with her suicide, and then hung by the head from a forked pole in the street. There Zara stays rotting, where the birds can peck out her eyes, where the stench can wash over passers-by, warning them not to consider a similar course. For weeks Angela takes a long way round, avoiding her friend's bloated, dishonoured corpse.

Why did Zara die of suicide? If we believe Willem ten Rhyne, a Dutch doctor and author who never met her, her death results from the old story: seduced by a white man on the promise of marriage and then abandoned. Ten Rhyne suggests that Zara had a double-nippled breast, and that a stone of diamond-like brilliance was cut from a Khoikhoi man's testicle, so I don't entirely believe him.

Did Zara, like Krotoa, get lost somewhere between the Dutch and the Khoikhoi? Creeping westernisation ('civilisation', as the Europeans would have it) does not sit well with the Khoikhoi. They often return to Khoikhoi life, even after twenty years with the Europeans, but Zara has lived among Europeans since she was five. By the time she kills herself, aged twenty-four, she speaks Dutch and Portuguese, dresses in European clothes, and attends church. There is violent, vengeful hypocrisy afoot. The VOC regards suicide as a sin and a crime against the state, and Company officials claim Zara has become sufficiently European to be judged as one. Yet when Europeans die of suicide at the Cape, officials treat each case as an act of temporary insanity. Not Zara: they violate her body, refer to her as a 'beast', whose 'brutal soul' 'Satan had already taken possession of'.

Angela is not Khoikhoi, but she has a tenuous hold on society, still Angela *van Bengale*, despite her marriage. The sight of Zara's rotting body against the backdrop of Table Mountain is a sobering reminder. On top of this, the social situation at the Cape is unravelling. Visiting Khoikhoi become aggressive and two years later, in July 1673, Arnoldus's sloop returns from the north, carrying horrible news alongside the fish, lime, salt and seal meat. Khoikhoi have attacked the Company's post and Francois, who discovered Zara's body with Angela, has been massacred alongside seven other burghers and a slave.

This second Khoikhoi war – primarily Dutch raids on the Cochoqua – drags on for four years until the Dutch emerge victorious with thousands of pilfered cattle and sheep. The Khoikhoi are increasingly fragmented: the native is being eliminated, which means greater prosperity for settlers who take over their land. For Angela and Arnoldus it means slaves, animals, wheat, rye and barley, not to mention four flintlocks and three rapiers.

Pretty, pragmatic Angela builds a wall of capital: status is everything in a new colony where social rules act as a bulwark against chaos. Anna de Coninck helps to cement Angela's position. Legitimised by her mother's marriage and renowned as a great beauty, in 1678, she marries Olof Bergh, a maverick Swede two years older than her mother. By 1679 he has made Angela a grandmother at the age of thirty-four. But none of Angela's children or grandchildren bears her name (or her parents' names, if she even remembers them): who wants to draw attention to slave heritage?

'You have not experienced me'

On 29 July 1674, the west wind, which has spent the last two days battering the coast, blows itself out, leaving Table Bay as smooth and bright as a mirror. And on a day such as this, when the Cape basks in its beauty, Krotoa dies. Her dying happens suddenly in the historical record, which has not mentioned her in years. Swiftly she is there, and just as swiftly gone: 'This day departed this life, a certain female Hottentoo, named Eva'.

In these records, nobody mourns. The Dutch are busy with the second Khoikhoi war, erasing Krotoa's people as they erase Krotoa herself. Krotoa has spent the final years of her life to-ing and fro-ing between the island and the mainland. No longer protected by her marriage to Van Meerhof, she staggers on among these violent men and has at least two more children. Unlike her three older children, these are not sanctioned by Dutch society, not part of Khoikhoi society either. Others die in infancy, and the journal rants about her 'drinking herself drunk' and her 'vile unchastity'.

To read what the Dutch write about Krotoa after her death is a desecration. What they have to say is this:

> She, like the dogs, always returned to her own vomit, so that finally she quenched the fire of her sensuality by death affording a manifest example that nature, however closely and firmly muzzled by imprinted principles, nevertheless at its one time triumphing over all precepts, again rushes back to its inborn qualities.

To settle the Cape, they must dream the land empty, a *terra nullis*, theirs to claim, and so the existing population must be made less than human: Krotoa's essential nature is that of a dog, which European habits could not vanquish.

I prefer to listen to Danish author J. P. Cortemunde, visiting Robben Island in 1672, who speaks highly of Krotoa's beauty, her fluency in Dutch, her wide-ranging knowledge of the Bible. And to Willem ten Rhyne who praises her civility, her wisdom. She is still in there, the sparkling girl who learnt Dutch and parleyed with commanders and chieftains.

On 30 July 1674, the journal notes: 'The body of the deceased Hottentoo, Eva, was not withstanding her unchristian life, buried today according to Christian usage in the church of the new Castle.' The scribe then records three men sentenced to keelhauling and banishment, public scourge and conviction in irons for theft and wounding.

Krotoa exists at the confluence of eras and oceans – pre-colonial and colonial, Atlantic and Indian, with her fluid, tricky tongue. Her children live on. How many times in the unwritten history do they think of this mother? One – Pieternella – leaves descendants in their thousands. It is *de rigueur* to start this kind of history – personal, white, insecure – with Krotoa, *de rigueur* to claim her. After all, I share a middle name with her daughter, Pieternella/Petronella, connected through this to the lost Danish husband. But this pursuit of Krotoa as the Mother of the Rainbow Nation is another domestication like the Dutch one, and motherhood is precisely the role most denied her. 'Mother': origin or source. The origin of white South Africa, and all the grim fruit that bears.

Caught in a moment of history, the decade before mutual reliance dissolves into coercion and violence, the experiences that enrich Krotoa's life – the new language on her tongue, the clothes on her skin, the manners, the religion – are an acid burning into her, destroying her inside and out.

The Khoikhoi and the San stand alongside the Australian Aboriginals and the Native Americans as First Peoples, all but annihilated by European settlers. History has tended to elide these crimes, but they should stand alongside the national anthems, the patriotism. If South African, Australian, American history is a history of roads built, cities raised, democracy achieved, it is also a history of domination and killing. Once Dutch settlers spill out of the original feeding station and begin to farm land around the Cape of Good Hope, they need that land to be empty, just as Australia does for white settlers two hundred years later. But – just like Australia – the land isn't empty. It blossoms with people. The 'real people' as they know themselves. And then – so fast – it doesn't.

The original people don't stand a chance against what Jared Diamond calls the triple threat of guns, germs and steel. Land is taken. Cultures are derided and destroyed. People die of disease, or they are hunted like animals. They are exiled from their land, from their culture and traditions, from their way of being. Only remnants remain, people filled with shame and self-hatred on the margins of modern society, seeking solace in alcohol and violence. Ancient nomadic cultures contradict modern nation states' existence and must be assimilated, by force or otherwise. So Krotoa blazes down through the years, exemplar and ruin.

In the years following her death, the Khoikhoi suffer more and more loss through war, disease and societal decline. A smallpox epidemic in 1713 kills ninety per cent of their population. Infighting and weak social structures render them incapable of withstanding the pressure from Europeans on the one side and amaXhosa on the other.

In a museum in the Cape, I pick up a CD of lost Khoisan languages. Across the top of the case runs the title, edged in black: 'Extinct,' it says. The voices crackle across the years from 1936. Some are aggressive, some soft. They click and slur from the back of their throats; speak of leopards and spoor, of jackals and hyenas. One voice speaks of a young girl becoming a woman. The young girl must stay in the hut and become lovely and flower there. She is made beautiful with *buchu*, ointment and ochre. She is so comely the men cannot take their eyes off her, 'as the fire lights her up'. Just for a moment, I see Krotoa.

The CD draws to a close, the speaker lamenting: 'You have not experienced me that you may know me, that you may realise that the people in this country speak a beautiful language.' This is Mukulap, an !Ora speaker, recorded in 1938. The clicks and whirrs go on. I imagine those small brown men and women disappearing from the land, flickering out like lights around the mountain, the dunes.

Running the gauntlet of lions

With Krotoa gone, we are left with Elsje and Angela, both married mothers, building their fortress families on the uncertain sands of the Cape. And both, despite their differing antecedents, part of the travelling wave of colonisation that washes the tatters of Krotoa's people further and further inland.

For seventeen years after Jan van Riebeeck's departure, the settlement remains within the cordon of sandy plains surrounding the Cape Peninsula, swelled by the crews of the thirty to forty ships that visit each year. Known as the Tavern of the Two Seas, its population scratches a livelihood from trading with ships, putting up sailors, providing alcohol and prostitutes. But Cape Town does not produce enough food for these ships and by the time Commander Simon van der Stel arrives in 1679, the second Khoikhoi war has ended in their defeat: in need of land, the expansion of the white man across southern Africa commences.

Cape Colony, 1689

Elsje and her family travel twenty-five miles along uneven dirt tracks from Cape Town before turning north. She keeps a close eye on the children: three are still under five and might fall under the wagon wheels. The wagon she drives is loaded with pots, kettles, bedsteads, ploughs, hoes. Willem guides more than sixty cattle ahead, and the older children herd the sheep. Chickens cluck indignantly as a wagon lurches over a rock. The family have been travelling for two days and will sleep in the canvas-covered wagons again tonight. Sometimes they hear lions roaring. How different this is to Hout Bay, with its curve of white sand between the steep walls of the mountain, great ribbons of kelp washed up on the shore.

Elsje and Willem van der Merwe have already moved once – in 1677, after nearly twenty years on the Liesbeeck River, they travel over the neck of Table Mountain and into the bay named for its dense woods – 'wood bay': *Houtbaai*. Hout Bay is still wild enough that the last two elephants are only shot in 1689, and the family and their slaves huddle in the small mud-walled house at night, out of reach of leopards. The Khoikhoi have used the land around Hout Bay for millennia, fishing and grazing their cattle, and when in 1678 officials scold Elsje for giving food and tobacco to fugitive Khoikhoi I wonder at how flexible the boundaries between peoples still are. But I recognise too how the generous Elsje will prove to be a vector of rigidity, so that 'white' will equal master, and 'brown' will equal servant.

Farming here suits the Van der Merwes because in 1678, when Elsje has her fourth child, they are the wealthiest they will ever be with slaves, cattle and two horses and six and a half tonnes of grain. Riches, but something keeps these people moving on, the possibility of perhaps more land, more cattle, and now, after another decade and five more children, they are on the move again, thanks to Commander van der Stel.

The next day, the family arrive at the Berg River. They have been allocated two hundred yards of water frontage, shrubs and thickets stretching more than a mile back, near Drakenstein (now the bustling town of Paarl). The Van der Merwes live in their wagons as the farmhouse rises, a rudimentary cottage of several rooms in a row with a steep thatched roof. They make the floors of clay mixed with cowdung, cover the window openings with linen. The men clear and flatten a threshing floor, build a cattle-fold out of thorn bushes. They have wheat and rye to sow, rice to eat. Game is still plentiful: eland, bontebok, hippopotamus.

Every square inch of land must be painstakingly, backbreakingly, cleared. Later, when the fields are planted with grain, it is harvested with a sickle and winnowed with a sieve. Livestock is sent out to pasture, helped through calving or lambing, slaughtered and butchered. Elsje, aged thirty-four now and stout after all those children, is aided by Jacoba, who is ten and Maria, thirteen, as she cooks over an open fire, and washes clothes in the Berg River, beating the multiple petticoats women wear as dresses, the men's breeches, on a plank or stone.

Later Elsje, coarse blonde hair pulled back in a bun, face tanned a deep brown, wrinkles fanning out from bright green eyes, gossips with her daughters and slave women as she repairs precious clothes in the murky gloom of the cottage. After dark, the only light comes from smoky tallow candles, but despite her work coarsened fingers Elsje sews nimbly, with the neat tiny stitches she learnt from Fytje in the cottage on the Liesbeeck River. After all, this is just another of the frontier homesteads over which she has spent a lifetime toiling.

But the change for the Cape itself is fundamental. When he arrives in 1679, Van der Stel – a vigorous, innovative man with a prominent nose – explores the surrounding areas, looking for suitable land for farming. He picks out the Eerste River Valley, thirty miles inland, and Stellenbosch is – perhaps unwisely – constructed on the river, which proves to flood regularly. A church is built, and houses for officials. It's civilisation, of a sort, although travellers from Cape Town run the gauntlet of lions, which continue to roam the area for another hundred and twenty years. By the 1720s, the whole area has been colonised, and in Stellenbosch there are well-established farms and wealthy farmers. The feeding station has become a colony, after all.

★

Life is uncertain out here. It is a society on the edge: of the known world, of social cohesion, of danger. And matters are even more fraught for a freed slave. The year after Elsje moves inland, Angela follows, settling nearby. Her move is motivated not only by the pull of opportunity, but by the push of scandal when in 1687 her son Jan van As commits an unspeakable crime. Jan is always a frightening combination of violence and stupidity and never more so than when he steals fifty sheep, drives them down the Cape peninsula before hacking off their ears and slitting their throats. That he then murders his accomplice, a slave called Anthonij van Malabar, who looks remarkably similar to him in skin and hair, is the final nail in his coffin. Because it doesn't matter if one is still a slave and the other freed by his mother's marriage to a free burgher, or that free burghers are never executed for killing a slave. Despite both those facts, Jan van As is still executed on 23 January 1688.

Later Jan's family retrieve his bullet-riddled corpse and I think about Angela and whether she watches her son die – she has nine other surviving children, but parental love does not rely upon scarcity or good behaviour. Jan's sister Anna and his brother Jacobus, also born bastard slaves, live successful lives, maintaining stable marriages and several children. Destiny is contingent not only on circumstance, but also on character. But it seems to me that over this whole long life Angela can never stop being vigilant, never forget her origins.

Slavery is embedded in South Africa's history from almost the moment the Dutch set foot at the Cape until abolition in 1834. By the 1700s, most free men own slaves – they work in fields, hospitals, warehouses and shops as craftsmen, fishermen and labourers. Working with their hands, or for someone else, brings a person closer to slave status and a society based on the avoidance of hard physical labour evolves. People like Elsje are more likely to have been a servant than to have owned a slave, but they take to the custom with alacrity: later historians find that European immigrants across the world refuse to work the land if they can find someone else to do it. Van Riebeeck notes that Dutch women, once outside their motherland, consider themselves 'too good and too precious' for laundry work.

Captured slaves, like Angela, have no experience of being slaves, either: nobody knows how to behave. This is not the large-scale plantation slavery of the Americas. Elsje and Willem share their isolated farmhouse with their slaves and it can feel like a joint enterprise: fighting off lions, clearing land, making candles to light the dark. But this is not a joint enterprise. The Van der Merwe's slaves call Willem '*baas*', boss or master, and he calls them '*jongen*' and '*meid*', boy and girl, regardless of age. (These forms of address remain in place until the end of the apartheid era.) Slave women – including Angela – breastfeed their owner's children or carry within their wombs babies conceived through rape by their owner.

Cape slaves are scourged, branded, riveted in chains, flogged, pilloried, have their ears cut off, or their nose, or the middle finger of each hand, or are hanged. They can be roasted alive or impaled on a sharp stick running under their skin next to the backbone and left sitting upright until they die. Their owners live in constant fear of retaliation and the line between normality and depravity becomes blurred in this silent seething war staged against the beauty of the Cape, giving rise to virulent racism. Once white people have treated other humans in this inhumane way, they must despise them or risk recognising their own sin. This necessary hatred passes down through centuries and spreads across the landscape.

The roots of white fear in twenty-first-century South Africa run deep into this appalling past, but Elsje's husband Willem van der Merwe fell in love with a slave, Koddo van Guinea, when he was young and fresh. What might have happened if they had all chosen another path across this alien landscape? But here comes Koddo, just down the wagon track from Elsje, in Stellenbosch. Free, and farming. What can Elsje do but keep a close eye on the one her husband loved? And here too is Maria Schalks, bearing part of Willem's name and his nose, that four-year-old child, free now, married to a German, with six children. And so Elsje builds the barriers of whiteness higher, always protecting herself and her children against Koddo.

After all, there was that mass escape in 1690, and now Elsje must report any escaped humans who hurry through the darkness, bare feet cut by stones on the rough ground, within twenty-four hours so that a blue warning flag can be hoisted at the castle, and on the road to Stellenbosch. And those forested slopes her mother loved, the slopes of Table Mountain, are home to runaway slaves. Life is dangerous and short, so Elsje keeps it tight and controlled. No one else will: look at her father, returning to Oedt, having more children and then abandoning them too, returning here in 1680, a humble corporal at the age of fifty. Jacob Cloete never did commit, and she holds how it ended for him in her mind, as a reminder.

Cape Town, May 1693

The evening is chilly; winter is near. Blood spreads around the head of the man lying in the dirty street. His sword is still in its scabbard by his side. Close by, the soldiers on the ramparts of the new brick-built fortress change their watch. Half an hour ago, perhaps the man was playing draughts in the tavern, making ribald remarks to the barmaid as she bent to refill his empty tankard. Pockets empty, he had stepped out, pulling his blue coat with its red lining closer around his shoulders, placing his black tricorn hat on his head.

Picking his way over the chicken bones and potato peelings, he had turned towards the sea as the shortest way back to the barracks. It is still a small town, the Cape, with one hundred houses and two thousand souls. Did he turn when he heard footsteps behind him, put up an arm to protect himself? Or did he know his attacker? The iron bar had come down hard on his skull, pitching him forward, hitting him twice more for good measure. Then the knife, stabbing twice deep into his chest, and then on and on, twenty-five more times.

Jacob Cloete, the oldest member of the Cape garrison at sixty-three, lies in the street, empty eyes staring up at the sky. Who is the killer? Why the frenzied attack? No one ever knows. Simon van der Stel records in his journal: 'the attack must have been treacherous as he was still very agile and as fit as a twenty-five-year-old young man'. Elsje's father represents the joker in the pack, the anti-settler. His life does not fit the neat pattern of a proto-Afrikaner, and any legacy he leaves is an accident, despite his eager adoption as a founding father by later descendants. I find it fits the scene, that Jacob Cloete and his wife Fytje Radergoertens are among the first Europeans to leave descendants at the Cape.

The founder effect

While Elsje and her slaves pick stones from the soil by the Berg River, west around the mountains, Sophia, her first-born, is settling into her own marital home, history having repeated itself when, aged just fourteen, she married Roelof Pasman. Pasman, a German immigrant, is granted the farm Rustenberg in 1682. Later in life, Sophia is renowned for being tough as old boots, and in 1705 diarist Adam Tas records that the 'rude wife of the old northern *Landdrost* Robberts', which is Sophia, hurled swear words at his sister and threatened to hit her. During the smallpox epidemic of 1713, during which she loses her husband and two daughters, Sophia is reportedly so determined to collect on debts that she tackles people on their deathbeds.

Not just a rude wife: Sophia suffers from Huntington's chorea, a neuro-psychiatric disorder which leads to irritability, loss of mental abilities, lack of coordination and worsened gait, and finally dementia and death. In nine per cent of cases, the sufferer commits suicide. There is no cure, although medication can alleviate some symptoms. Children of a sufferer have a fifty per cent chance of inheriting the disease. Nearly half of Huntington's sufferers in South Africa – 210 – are descended from Sophia van der Merwe.

Because Afrikaners all descend from a small group of immigrants, they share hereditary diseases carried by those ancestors. Called 'the founder effect', this propensity flourishes in settler colonies with a small number of original immigrants, including the French Canadians, the Amish and the British population of the remote South Atlantic islands of Tristan da Cunha. Willem and Elsje have so many grandchildren that they are a common ancestor for most Afrikaners and have been held responsible for introducing four diseases into the Afrikaner bloodline: Huntington's chorea, pseudoxanthoma elasticum, lipoid proteinosis and, in a more complex genetic fashion, schizophrenia.

The law of unintended consequences. Stoical Elsje, who lost both her parents so young, plants an orchard of family trees, tending them with the care of a master arborist, but there is rot in the wood: not only the founder effect but its corollary, racial exclusivity. The Van der Merwes have thirteen children, and those thirteen children have

118 children of their own. It is a European population explosion, and Elsje ensures her offspring come out on top. She does this through gossip. Invisible, protean conversations with her daughters, her sisters-in-law, multiple threads of talk across their needlework, side by side at the stove, after church on Sundays, the way two women together might hatch a plan to encourage romance. Two of Elsje's children marry their first cousins, her older brother Gerrit's children.

It is the Dutch law of partible inheritance that enables white dominance: half a parent's estate goes to the surviving spouse, and the rest is divided between the children. Elsje's daughters and nieces can inherit from their husbands and parents. Suppose siblings from Elsje's family marry siblings from her brother's family. In that case, they can exchange interest in farms, or an almost equal inheritance from a spouse's family can allow a sibling to be bought out. Farms do not have to be divided into tiny useless parcels; they can pool energy and capital. Willem and Elsje's grandchildren have seventy-three marriages, and, despite the Calvinist church prohibiting first-cousin marriage, twenty-five of these marriages are to first cousins.

But in 1688 the game is complicated by the arrival of another group of people, a people as pale as Elsje under her dress, but speaking another language, and only to each other. They are French Huguenots, Protestant refugees from Catholic France. Afrikaners are thought of as Dutch, so far as anyone thinks about them at all, but a current of French blood runs through their veins. The colour-coded family trees pinned to my study door show more red (for French) than orange (for Dutch), forty-six per cent to thirty-three per cent. Around two hundred Huguenots arrive at the Cape, skilled bourgeoisie, unlike the impoverished Dutch and German settlers. They arrive as traders, doctors, hat-makers, but soon they are all farmers. Commander van der Stel scatters them, bans a French congregation and ensures schools and official correspondence are held in Dutch. Within a couple of generations, no one speaks French any more.

Still, the Huguenots don't intermarry, at least not on the branches of my trees, not for two hundred years: a Huguenot marries a Huguenot, and their children marry other Huguenots. It is a remarkable exclusionary practice: only one of Elsje's thirteen children marries a Huguenot. If they do not marry out, the Huguenots bring a great gift to make up for it: the Cape, it turns out, has ideal conditions for growing vines. Cape wines are soon celebrated in Europe, thanks to Huguenot wine-making prowess, and land closer to Cape Town is rapidly taken up with these vines, in addition to wheat and vegetables.

But the Cape is evolving, and in 1703 the ban on grazing stock more than a day's journey from farms is reversed. The further white farmers reach into the vast interior, the more they take up cattle farming: cattle can be left to graze while they are relieved of the tedious business of clearing land, planting, weeding, harvesting. Of working, in fact. The burghers are – unwittingly – imitating the despised Khoikhoi. Roads and other services are supposed to be supplied by the *heemraad* (magistrate), using local taxes and burgher labour, but the burghers don't pay their taxes and send their – poorly motivated – slaves to do the work instead. Distances remain great, roads poor or non-existent.

The Puritans who emigrated to North America fifty years previously put to sea with dreams of building their own society with roads and houses, schools and courtrooms. Elsje and her contemporaries have no such dreams. Peasants who make the voyage – Jacob and Fytje Cloete, Willem van der Merwe – do not expect to build their own society, which is just as well as they are allowed no freedom to do anything of the sort. This lack of independence makes the settlers reliant on the VOC, physically and mentally. They have no interest in building roads in a society where they have no influence: the roads go unmade, and the farmers become ever more isolated.

Europeans drift further inland, an unruly destructive swarm pushing the frontier of the colonial state outward. I picture Elsje in this wave: arriving from Germany in 1659, rolling from the Liesbeeck River to Hout Bay to Drakenstein, washing away Khoikhoi as she goes, even as she offers them food. Her marriage, and that of her children, consolidates white power. It is not Koddo, who Willem loves, who gets the prize, but the European girl. Elsje is not only domesticated herself, but domesticates the southern African terrain, setting the scene for the European expansion of the next century. To her, it is just day-to-day life, survival.

Elsje is dead by January 1702, aged forty-six, leaving five children still at home, and her husband, dying fourteen years later, leaves only ploughs, cattle and kettles. But their Van der Merwe descendants are among the richest in the colony. This is Elsje's legacy, making her family safe, which she spends a lifetime constructing.

Now only a widowed Angela is left. Her mixed-race children and grandchildren assimilate into white society; they are prosperous land-owners, aldermen, and Anna de Coninck and her husband are even part of the VOC inner circle. But undercurrents of exclusive racism swirl, soon to settle into a hardened mass, and they must negotiate this territory carefully. Angela knows how to court authority, and her children have learnt their lessons well, but in 1706 they end up on the losing side of a constitutional crisis.

This is how it comes about. Company officials are not supposed to own land, but Simon van der Stel's son Willem Adriaan, appointed governor in 1699, carves out a considerable chunk at the foot of the Hottentots Holland mountains. Within six years, his Vergelegen farm produces enough wheat, livestock and wine to supply all the ships, and the colony. This drives the farmers crazy: how are they supposed to earn a living if Company servants monopolise trade? In Stellenbosch, rowdy burghers jostle *Landdrost* Johannes Starrenburg in the street, taunting him. He hides at home, complaining: 'The women are as dangerous as the men and do not keep quiet.'

The farmers compose a petition highlighting Company corruption and the difficulty of making a living. They complain:

> Kaffirs, Mulattoes, Mestiços and Castiços and all that black brood living among us, who have been bred from marriages and other forms of mingling with Europeans and African Christians. To our amazement they have so grown in power, numbers and arrogance and have been allowed to handle arms and participate with Christians.

(The word *k****r*, originally an offensive word for a non-Muslim or infidel, is adopted as an ethnic slur by white South Africans. It is unacceptable now, much like the 'n' word.)

Perhaps this is why Angela's sons take Willem Adriaan's side, but they have backed the wrong horse: the Lords Seventeen recall Willem Adriaan and other officials to Amsterdam and forbid Company employees from owning land or trading. It is a significant victory for the farmers, and for racial stratification. Angela's children successfully cross the colour line, but the door shuts behind them.

Angela might hope to sink into quiet old age, but in February 1713, a Dutch ship docks in Table Bay. Sailors on board are suffering from fever and vomiting, their skin covered in fluid-filled bumps. The ship's dirty linen travels ashore to be laundered in the Slave Lodge and by May so many people are dying of smallpox that bodies are buried without coffins in shallow graves, only to be dug up by hyenas and jackals. Corpses rot along wagon tracks and paths. Farming comes to a standstill. Emergency supplies are imported. The smallpox kills many colonists, but the indigenous population suffers the most: with no resistance, they die *en masse*; fleeing inland to escape the disease, they spread it further.

By 1714 only ten per cent of the Khoikhoi population remains. Guns, germs and steel. Over a quarter of white people also die, including three of Angela's children. (Krotoa's daughter Pieternella also dies this year, in Stellenbosch, where she lives with her husband Daniel Zaaiman.) Angela retreats to Table Bay to garden and make brandy. In 1718, confined to her four-poster bed, propped up by seven pillows, a gilded mirror on the dresser, she draws up her will. As I watch, I finger her jewellery, the four gold rings, the string of pearls with matching drop earrings, the English silver watch. I glance inside her kitchen, with its copper pots where she cooks the food she half remembers from her childhood in faraway Batavia, the spicy stews and sauces, the food that evolves into Cape Malay cuisine, into *bobotie*. For twenty years of loyal service, she leaves her youngest son Michiel Basson two slaves. But Michiel dies the following year, and then only Anna de Coninck remains. Firstborn of eleven children, last standing.

In 1720, aged seventy-five, Angela dies, decades after Krotoa and Elsje lost that last fight. Her grandchildren spread through the interior and her estate is worth more than double that which her husband left. Wealth cushions her, but it is more than that. Luck? It is all luck in the end, of course: that she is supple as a cat, landing on her feet time after time, that she is pragmatic, hardworking, beautiful. And that other people love her, 'out of pure affection,' as they say.

With Krotoa, Angela and Elsje dies an alternate future for South Africa, a parallel universe where fate is not determined by skin colour. All

Afrikaners have non-white ancestors, the result of unions such as theirs. But it is disingenuous to suggest that Afrikaner origins are anything other than primarily European: of the 185 of my ancestors identifiable as first arrivals at the Cape, only nine are non-European – five per cent. Twenty-three originate from Germany, sixty-two are Dutch, and eighty-three are French Huguenots. Because after this first wave of arrivals, as we will see, generations of white people work to ensure that slaves remain slaves, slave owners remain slave owners, and mixed-race babies are born headfirst into the nascent coloured community.

Khoikhoi legacies at the Cape have not been wiped out, but they are obscured. The South African coloured community (I use the word 'coloured' tentatively, in the South African sense, which, despite being an apartheid designation of mixed race, has stuck) has the highest levels of mixed ancestry in the world: more than sixty per cent of their maternal DNA comes from Khoikhoi women, virtually none from European women. They descend from children born to Khoikhoi and Indian and Asian women – women like Krotoa and Angela – and European, Indian and African men three hundred and fifty years ago. Visible and aural traces thread through the Coloured population, within Afrikaans and on people's faces. My cousin Sarah, whose father is coloured, lives in the UK. She has long, curling hair and a beautiful light brown face with eyes that slant like a cat's.

'I hate it when people comment on my great tan,' she says. 'How do they not realise this is the colour I am?'

Increasingly, the Khoikhoi are being rehabilitated into South African history, even if this sometimes smacks of appropriation. (The stigma of descending from enslaved people means that slave ancestors continue to be denied and obscured.) Sarah (Saartjie) Baartman – the Hottentot Venus – is one of several Khoikhoi people taken to Europe in the nineteenth century and exhibited as freak-show attractions. After her death, her body parts are put on display in the Musée de l'Homme in Paris for a hundred and fifty years – I am not French, not from the nineteenth century, but I burn with shame. Baartman's remains finally return to South Africa in 2002, and she is buried in the Eastern Cape, the ceremony attended by President Thabo Mbeki.

At the burial, Mbeki claims Baartman for all African people: 'The story of Sarah Baartman is the story of the African people,' he said.

'It is the story of the loss of our ancient freedom.' Yet the fate of Khoikhoi descendants, the coloured people, is not an easy one in post-apartheid South Africa. Five million people, almost nine per cent of the population, are the embodiment of the Rainbow Nation, their very skin a signal of racial blending. That skin leaves them caught between, not white enough under apartheid, not black enough afterwards. Even if Sarah Baartman operates as a useful focal point for nation-building, the people who sit between white and black, never sure which way to jump, are not so useful. Much like Krotoa, Baartman's body, her life, have been endlessly pawed in the search for meaning of one sort or another, from scientific racism to feminist criticism. I, too, navigate these waters, these endless ripples of vision and revision.

But for white South Africans it is Elsje Cloete who is most relevant, not Angela van Bengale, and certainly not the girl we know only as Krotoa. When Elsje's daughter, that 'rude wife' Sophia Pasman, gives birth to her first daughter in 1693, she calls her Sibella. In 1778 Sibella Pasman's son Hendrik Cloete buys the original Cape Dutch farm, iconic Groot Constantia, making a sweet Constantia wine so famous it graces the pages of Austen, Dickens and even Baudelaire. The Constantia vines are decimated by phylloxera in the late nineteenth century, but revived in the 1980s, and with them the sweet wine. Later my family makes a regular pilgrimage to visit the portrait of Sibella Pasman, which hangs within the entrance hall of Groot Constantia. We photograph her with two other Sibellas – my mother and my reluctant sister, her seventh and eighth great-granddaughters – before sitting down to lunch. Beneath us, the vines roll out towards the False Bay suburbs, and beyond them lies the sea.

A slow dawning

As the curtain falls on this first act, I find myself thinking again about what is passed on, what the connection might be between us, between Krotoa, Angela, Elsje and myself. They are so far away, so alien in their three-hundred-year-old world. But what they chose to do then affects us now, and their names are written in indelible ink all over my life.

Moederland, Dutch and Afrikaans: motherland. The first sound any of us hear is the slow drumming of our mother's heart. We are shaped not only by her DNA but by a forgotten swirl of touch, sound, smell. I think about Krotoa, how I can have inherited virtually nothing from her, given that she is one of 8,192 possible ancestors in that generation. How even in her daughter's generation her legacy is all but erased: six years old when she is taken from her mother, Krotoa's daughter Pieternella marries a European and has eight children. She names one daughter Catharina (there's the indelible ink again), after her husband's mother, and another Eva after her own: the public memory she saves of her mother is the Dutch, Krotoa's alter ego.

Pieternella's *moederland* becomes foreign to her, an impossible past. As she moves forward into her European future, the chasm between Khoikhoi mother and European daughter can never be crossed. (Angela too is exiled from her *moederland*, while Elsje carries hers with her in the person of Fytje, and the languages and customs of Europe.) But how durable childhood habits are, sneaking silently in round the back. Not acceptable Eva, but the sly hidden memories of Krotoa: a taste for sour milk, or the scent of *buchu*. What do mothers pass on? What do migrant mothers pass on? How many generations down can these quiet customs, these connections, stretch? I ask because some customs persist across implausibly long stretches of time and distance, leaching into my own life in those early days before I understand anything, the underpinnings of my existence.

My mother's mother, my namesake, dies just over four years before I am born. When I remind my mother of this, there is deep silence down the telephone line. 'Hello?' I ask. She is doing the mental maths, having separated the two eras of her life with a deep unfillable chasm. No wonder we children think of our maternal grandmother as part of pre-history; she does not belong to the continuity of which we are part. But she lives in my mother's mind all the time I am growing up, even if my mother keeps her to herself. Some reminders are kept, taken out and polished every now and again. Odd things, and mostly to do with food. Do all stories begin with families, and the foods eaten together?

Biltong, when we can get it, is treasured. Tough strips of beef, cured and dried by *trekboers*, following the ways of the Khoikhoi people, with the addition of Eastern spices – coriander, pepper. We like it with a thick layer of fat, still slightly red and damp inside. *Mebos* arrives every year from my aunt, shipped from Cape Town in a neat cardboard box: salty-sweet dried and pulped apricots, compressed into neat medallions. Rolled in granulated sugar, they are rough as a cat's tongue. '*Mebos*', from the Dutch, deriving from the Japanese '*umeboshi*', preserved plums. A word carried down ocean trade routes, alongside the plums to which it belongs.

At home in Hampshire, my mother follows a recipe for *bobotie* from a book with a yellow spine where chillies, spring onions, olives and a big juicy soup terrine jostle together against a salmon pink background. *Ouma's Cookery Book*, first published in 1940. Minced lamb and curry powder, fried onions, raisins, flaked almonds, bay leaf. All mixed together in a glass dish, covered with a thin milk and egg custard, and baked in the oven.

One or other of us always complains about the grey lump of spicy meat that materialises, but we don't forget it. In Johannesburg fifteen years later, my housemate makes another version, from *Cook with Ina Paarman*. Ina Paarman herself appears on the front cover, looking rather like Britain's own TV cook Delia Smith, although her helmet of hair is blonde, not brown. This book too contains South African delicacies: avocado soup, chicken curry. It is the same, but different, this *bobotie*. Better. More suited to modern mouths. My mother is an excellent cook, following a recipe forty years out of date. It is as if we all started trying to cook with Mrs Beeton. Expatriates are caught in aspic, remembering a culture that no longer exists and yet, somehow, does.

In 1981 when I visit Johannesburg, I am still in innocence, not yet fallen into knowledge of my own difference, my own distance from this *moederland*. This is still the first reel, for me. For South Africa, it is nearing the end, or the present, in any case a long way from Krotoa, from Angela and Elsje. I make lemonade with my cousin Richard from the lemons growing in his garden, round the back of the swimming pool. I am eight years old and here with my English grandfather, who I call Bancroft. Driving across the highveld, we stop and watch a lightning storm in the distance. The light is heavy, charged with waiting rain. The storm hits us in torrents. Five minutes later, the sun is drying patches of rain on the road. The cicadas are humming in the grass. The car, white, boxy, chugs down avenues of gum trees, still, dusty.

On the side of the road are stalls selling pineapples, lychees. We stop for pineapple, but do not have a knife, so stop again to buy one. This knife, orange-handled, serrated, cheap, is transported home in a suitcase and floats around the house for years after. The lychees are sold in bunches still attached to the twig, the orangey-pink rough fruit nestling among the dark green leaves like fat jewels. I nip the bitter skin, pull it off with my teeth, use delicate bites to eat the smooth flesh. It is almost slimy, but not. Underneath is a dark-brown shiny pip.

At the hotel in Pietermaritzburg, there is a swimming pool full of frogs. At the bushveld farm, I get to choose whether I want to sleep under the lion's head or the buffalo. I choose the lion. At another farm, there is a snake in the sitting room. I find my Aunt Sarah and they kill it with a poker. Later I overhear her talking to Bancroft: 'Don't tell Cato,' she says, 'but it was a puff adder.' If a puff adder bites you, you die.

My aunt lives in Durban, down a narrow cul-de-sac that runs out into a footpath. It is off Musgrave Road, on a hill above the city. When we walk down Musgrave Road, dogs bark from every driveway, or there are signs about the dogs, how dangerous they are. Across the road and to the left is Musgrave Centre, where we visit the Pick 'n Pay supermarket. All the African women wear pastel uniforms – pink, lilac, green, yellow, blue – with white collars and pockets. The men wear thick royal-blue boiler suits. Fountains of bougainvillaea hang over garden walls; the flowers are purple and papery. The weather always weighs heavy and hot, and it always smells the same. Fecund. Downtown Durban is pinky-brown and gusty with warm wind. You can get something called a bunny chow to eat. It is a hollowed-out loaf of white bread filled with curry. I never get one.

I write a journal for my teacher in Hampshire. We buy her a thick blanket from Lesotho. It is pale blue with a design of a Basotho hat in brown. We drive north to Umdloti to swim in the Indian Ocean. The waves are too rough for Bancroft, who walks with two sticks and in the water can only use his right arm, over and over. On my ninth birthday, I swim nine times in the pool with tiled dolphins on the bottom. I wear an oversized white rubber swim cap with a strap under the chin. My teeth are uneven from sucking my thumb. There is a ginger kitten and a black dog called Pedro, who we walk in the park across Musgrave Road, where the grass is not like English grass, being rough and full of ants.

I make this particular visit because when my grandfather and my parents discussed his trip to South Africa in the kitchen at Middle Leigh, I said, 'I'll go.' They looked at each other, and here I am. This is not a family to mollycoddle its offspring. Away from my mother, I am not scared nor homesick. I do know that when my aunt calls me 'chicky', she is trying to hide that she is annoyed with me. Bancroft is never annoyed with me and cuts me thick slices of *biltong* with his pocket knife.

In the 1970s and 80s, flying from London to Durban is not the easy process it is now. Getting across the six thousand miles between the two involves leapfrogging down the African continent for refuelling and – if you are flying South African Airlines – avoiding the airspace of countries hostile to the apartheid regime, adding two and a half hours to the twelve-hour flight. Each time we fly, we stop at airstrips from Brazzaville to the Ilha do Sal, four hundred miles off the coast of Senegal. Sometimes there are local wars, and we are herded across the tarmac and into the airport terminal by armed guards, and kept inside until the plane refuels. At other times, cattle roam across the runway.

There are still smoking sections on these aircraft, the cabin stale and fuggy. We sleep head to toe across the seats or – my favoured position – on the floor beneath. It is hard down there, covered in thin carpeting, the metal struts of the seat cold as they press into your back. The aircraft roars and shudders through the night. Sometimes there are TVs on the bulkheads, showing a fuzzy film, or a tiny aircraft inching down a map of the continent, which lies in darkness below. I love everything about flying: the cars receding into toys as we take off, the plastic meals, the dry roll in its cellophane, stepping out of the plane into the warm dark somewhere in Africa, the neat slide and wallop of suitcases onto the carousel.

In Durban, security is so slack my Aunt Sarah sometimes comes to find us at the baggage reclaim; she wears white cotton sundresses and sunglasses. Around us are white children tanned a deep brown, towheaded, slapping around on the lino in their flip-flops. Black people in overalls push wide mops around the floor and collect trolleys.

The supermarkets with their long strips of sweets at the till; the thick smell of meat in the butcher's where we buy *biltong*; the viscous heavy perfume of guava juice; evening meals on the veranda with its deep shiny terracotta tiles, the insect hum beneath the chatter of conversation; the swimming pool with its dancing dolphins; the bitter malaria pills in their spoonful of honey. Everything has an intense glamour from which I never recover.

One Christmas Day, the tree is a sparse angular fir with pale green needles. My mother glares at me when I try and pass on to my baby sister my newfound knowledge about the existence of Father Christmas. We visit the beach for a hotdog lunch, *braai* meat over hot coals in a wheelbarrow for supper, melt marshmallows over the embers.

'Listen to this,' says my uncle proudly, pulling a record from its sleeve, a clean cream with a red and black painting in the centre. Accordion, drums, a solo voice and then the thrumming Zulu harmonies. It is Paul Simon's *Graceland*. The live-in gardener is a Zulu himself, Reginald Dlamini. One evening a fight breaks out between two women behind the house. They are quarrelling over Reginald. One is very young and holds a baby. My mother takes the child while the fight rumbles on. The young woman is desperate to recover her baby, but my mother maintains hold of it. I am wrenched with embarrassment until my mother hands the infant back.

Later we visit my Aunt Petronella in Lesotho. She feeds us wholemeal spaghetti. It tastes of cardboard. I fall in love with the boy next door, through the haphazard wooden fence. He is a year older than me with dusty black skin and hair that my hand bounces off. My cousin Roger teaches us to say *Qhekella, Bancroft* in Sesotho. 'It means fuck off, Bancroft,' he claims.

We go swimming in a pool so green you cannot see your hands. There are so many children in the pool that it is a sea of bodies. Later, after we are not there any more, a child goes under, and nobody notices for too long, thanks to the fatal murkiness. Other times we swim in the pool at the Victoria Hotel in Maseru. Or in the cold of a mountain stream. A man on a horse, wrapped in a thick blanket, watches us. These men are everywhere. They wear the *mokorotlo*, the conical straw hat, which also appears on licence plates and on the flag. There are also dogs everywhere, just hanging around. Children chase the car as we leave, shouting. I wish I could be a child who chases cars, shouting.

We transit through an airport that bears a name which we learn is important and belongs to us: Jan Smuts. This is our great-grandfather and also the travellers' shorthand for Johannesburg's international airport. The name appears on road maps, on the South African Monopoly board. Much of what we learn about this name is legend, the mythology of fame combined with family in a curious amalgam. He learnt Greek in two weeks, was the only foreigner to be on the Imperial War Cabinet in the First World War. It all seems normal, part of the wallpaper. And distant, some old man, some part of the adult world we will never visit. Not like the beloved grandfather who gives us the cucumber off his plate and eats our potatoes when we don't want them. Who tells us about visiting South Africa as a young man and wooing our grandmother. 'We couldn't get a driving licence,' he says, 'so I asked her, shall we get a marriage licence instead?'

We are taught not to use the name Jan Smuts outside the family. Not because it is a guilty secret, but because to share would be bragging. He was a man of his time, the reassuring mantra goes, less racist than others, not nearly as bad as those National Party fascists. The Oubaas, as they call him – even this name is disturbing, 'old master' the English translation, obscuring the connotations of slavery embedded in that word, *baas* – was my mother's actual grandfather. Photographs of him holding her in the family garden in Somerset appear in books.

Swellendam, 1988

The slow waking into adulthood is a slow dawning of knowledge. In this town, the white Cape Dutch buildings glow in the evening light, the Dutch Reformed Church tiered like a wedding cake against the deepening Karoo sky. We admire the mill house, VOC Drostdy, stables, coach house, all tucked into the lee of the blue Overberg. The Groote Wagenweg, the Old Cape Wagon Road; the square lined with ancient oaks. But in the hotel restaurant the coloured waiting staff keep their heads bowed and duck backwards as they put down the plates.

Scraps of memory filed away. Incomplete. Another murky swimming pool, a dog with distended dugs and her pups in the hedge. My Uncle Lionel, who in apartheid South Africa is designated coloured, was denied a bed in this town two decades previously, spending the night in the car. We take a strange prurient pride in this story, bringing it out and holding it up against the light with a laugh of disbelief. The things we don't see: the coloured township across the railway tracks, Railton. Cheap wine in its foil bag, *papsak*. Mandrax (those dreamy Quaaludes of 1970s USA) aka 'white buttons', ground up, mixed with marijuana and smoked. Farm labourers who work twelve hours a day for wages that don't cover food, clothing or tiny school fees.

Northern Transvaal, 1991

We make the long trip cross country to visit Modjadji, queen of the Balobedu people, up near the border with Mozambique, in a white minivan, bumping along over the dirt roads. Modjadji is the Rain Queen, who the Balobedu believe controls the clouds and rain. My uncle Dan Krige, son of an eminent anthropologist who spent months living near Modjadji in the 1930s, is greeted warmly by Simeon, the Rain Queen's retainer. It is damp in the Royal Compound, rain dripping from the eaves of the thatched huts, a sheen on the concrete forecourt, and the red earth smells luxuriant, the pawpaw (papaya) tree's leaves glossy in the dim light. From the veranda of the reception hut, we can see across to the ridge beyond, a dark misty green.

Queen Modjadji V keeps us waiting for half an hour before she enters and sits on a mat on the floor, her shoulders wrapped in a beach towel over a shiny cream blouse, her head wrapped in a leopard-print scarf. She watches in silent disdain as Dan, a grown man, crawls on his belly over the lino tiles towards her. Gauche English teenagers, we do not understand why we feel awkward, but I tuck my hands inside the arms of my sweater for comfort. Before we leave, we visit the Modjadji forest. Here the miraculous rain that gives the Rain Queen her power results in the only cycad forest in southern Africa. This valley of strange fern-like trees, which first grew when dinosaurs foraged on these hills, only adds to her mystique. As we drive off, we glimpse the queen hanging out the washing behind the Royal Compound.

When I first go to South Africa, I think myself a member of humanity, not a white person. (I also think myself human, not female: when I read all those books with their male protagonists, I am right there, on that horse, brandishing my sword.) Later, I begin to read and interpret the world differently. I have an epiphany about the evils of apartheid, write an essay in biro and show it to my parents. They offer praise, but I know when they are patronising me, making that easy adult gesture towards complexity and impotence, which means divesting ourselves of responsibility.

I am indignant, Che Guevara at thirteen. Uncorrupted, I think myself not culpable. With the naivety and courage of youth, I rant at an uncle. 'Do you want us to go the way of Zimbabwe?' he asks angrily, rhetorically. 'Don't call me racist; I went into the township and helped build Elizabeth's house for her.' My great-grandfather can never be criticised for his policies on race. 'He was a man of his time,' they repeat. I am too young to know how to argue with any of this. As the years roll by, my own skin begins to feel shameful, to burn. Much later I read Antjie Krog who in *Begging to Be Black* suggests: 'It is not always easy to work out how to live a righteous life. That apartheid is wrong is relatively obvious, but how to live against apartheid is the harder question.'

This is not a question we have to answer directly: South Africa seeps into our consciousness, but there is an incongruity between the fieldmice and badgers of home in England and the empty grasslands of the highveld, the emerald greens of the Indian Ocean coast.

Between the whiteness of an English market town and the blackness even apartheid can't hide. And, mostly, we are not there anymore. Foreign: from the Middle English, meaning not in one's own land, not domestic or native. Is foreign a finite adjective? Is it possible to stop being foreign? Two hundred and thirty-two million people worldwide live in a country other than that of their birth. Who are we when we do this? Who do we think we are?

We are all many people, multiple, multiplying, as our lives move on. My ten-year-old self lists who she is by country: English, but – by an accident of birth – American too. And South African, by ancestry but also by affiliation and experience. When I leave the golden grasslands of California, I am only six months old – they barely singe the edges of my mind – and it is the beech woods of Hampshire, the wild garlic and bluebells, which shape who I become. But the small navy rectangle embossed with a bald eagle, its head surrounded by a glory of stars, the small rectangle my mother tucks in her handbag, the retention of this passport, adds another dimension to the mould of my person.

Consider all the children who leave their birthplace still unformed when they arrive at the shores of another country. The clay of the self, not yet fired by experience, age, consciousness, moulded by the journey, by the new landscape, and in turn moulding that landscape to their own image. Still malleable children, Angela and Elsje arrive at a location itself unformed, geography fixed but identity unknown. On the frontier, the grounds for belonging weave backwards and forwards. There are no passports to bind person to place, place to nation. People are immaculate: at the mercy of good fortune and timing, they must fall back on charm, beauty, guile.

When the first whites arrive at the Cape more than three centuries before my tentative entrance, they are ignorant too, but at the other end of the scale. These men, women and children, wrapped in their dirty clean white skins, are unable to understand white supremacy because it hasn't happened yet, because they are the labourers who are going to construct it, rule by exclusive rule, marriage by exclusive marriage.

II

Anna Siek

1695–1773

Dutch girls carry an aura of property with them. They are first of all themselves: they bring not only so many pounds of white flesh but also so many morgen of land and so many head of cattle and so many servants.

J. M. Coetzee, 'The Narrative of
Jacobus Coetzee', *Dusklands*, 1974

Some buttons, an empty coffin

As the Enlightenment sweeps Europe, southern Africa is in the formative stages of a modern nation state. As Bach writes his cantatas, the
trekboers pack their Bibles and head for the blue horizons of the Karoo.
During this century, the death knell rings for the Khoikhoi, and the
white man comes up against an adversary he cannot trick or beat into
submission. But this white man is no longer a European: cast in the
cauldron of the Cape, German, French, Italian, Belgian and Dutch
emerge speaking a new tongue, a blend of Dutch with the languages
of slaves, phrases from dispossessed Khoikhoi. No longer immigrants,
no longer foreign, they have become static, have become Afrikaners.

No longer immigrants, are they natives? Native, noun, meaning: a
person born in a specified place or associated with a place by birth.
From Latin *nativus*, from *nat-*, 'born'. Although of course this is
something we cannot call these Afrikaners because in a century or so
this word will gain a specifically toxic resonance. 'Native' will refer to
a non-white original inhabitant as seen by European colonists, and it
will carry a burden of cultural inferiority, of lewd, greedy, shameless
animal behaviour. Whereas being European will mean civilised,
normal, the centre of the world. And two centuries after that the
word will come full circle, representing a person who belongs without question. The battle over who is native and who is not will rage
on, three hundred years of history not enough to convince Africans,
fed up with being the underdog, that those with white skins are
anything other than immigrants.

Anna Siek, the next character on our roll call of ancestors, lives her
life right through the years when these seeds of the Afrikaner

character are planted in African soil, the long quietude of the eighteenth century. Not for her the shock of a new landscape; she is third-generation, born more than forty years after Van Riebeeck takes Krotoa into the fort. Anna Siek's truest relationship is a secret one; her rapport with the whitewashed Cape Dutch farmhouse at Vergelegen unrecorded. It is the men who shape its history who are acknowledged on celebratory websites. Anna remains a footnote, her only recognition through the men she marries, men who die or leave her, while the house remains.

As it is so often, women are a roaring absence at the heart of the historical record. But life is as much about the quotidian as it is affairs of state, and it is women who shape that everyday reality, from the sheets on which a body wakes up, through the day to the evening meal that feeds it. And through the relationships shared at that table, in that bed. Through the pattern of her life, Anna Siek shapes eighteenth-century Cape society.

Cape Town, 1707

Everywhere people bustle, shouting out their wares, bargaining over eggs. A sailor weaves in front, leers at twelve-year-old Anna. With a sudden memory of her mother Geertruij warning her again in her low German dialect not to fall into the tree-lined canal that runs down the Heerengracht, meeting the sea by the castle, she holds her basket closer and scurries along. Carpenters and blacksmiths labour away with hammer, saw and chisel, repairing boats. The stink of horse dung on the streets mixes with the yeasted scent of bakeries.

The air is tranquil: sometimes, in the summer, the south-east wind blows so hard that parasols are torn to shreds and closed boxes and cupboards filled with dust. People caught outside in the wind risk being hit in the head with small stones and cling from house to house to make headway along the street. Putting the eggs carefully into her basket, Anna retraces her steps to her home near the Company's Garden, with its avenues of oak, its beds of lettuce, parsley and 'exceptionally lovely' cauliflowers. Since her mother's death three years ago, she has shared the falling-down cottage with her father, two sisters, and her father's odds and ends including some buttons and an empty coffin.

She finds her father Johann weighing clay in the backyard, waiting for the new pots to dry. Anna has work to do: stewing beans and root vegetables over the fire, swatting the flies that infest the town thanks to sheep slaughtering, sweeping the earth floor. But as she measures beans into the pot her father steps into the kitchen, stooping under the lintel. She stops, looks up at him, noticing him worrying at a cleaning rag with his muddy hands. Something is going on, and she knows what, being neither blind nor stupid and having watched him catch eyes with the rich widow Margaretha van Neerkassel at church on Sundays. 'Marriage', he says, and 'new home', and she thinks: I will not have to sweep this dirt floor ever again. And then she thinks of her mother.

Within a couple of weeks, Anna's life has changed completely: the widow Van Neerkassel lives well in a three-room house of Cape brick with a reed roof, stuffed full of porcelain, mirrors, books, paintings. Anna sleeps on a feather mattress, her head nestled on feather pillows. For three years, she watches her shrewd, kind stepmother navigate Cape society. She and her sisters do not go to school, but the widow ensures they can read and write, which is more than her father does, although the sources are confused – either Johann Siek dies in 1707, or he doesn't, either Anna and her sisters are orphans, or they are not.

Every Sunday, the Van Neerkassel household attends the octagonal Dutch Reformed Church, completed in 1704, with its high glass windows, ebony pulpit and red-and-white marbled portals. Every Sunday, they see the wealthy Gildenhuyses, who live nearby in one of their three townhouses. In 1710, as the church shudders in the strong wind, Anna, demure in the neat oak pew, blue eyes under dark brows and hair the colour of ripe barley, catches the eye of Barend Gildenhuys, son of the widowed Margaretha Hoefnagels.

They marry a few months later. Barend is twenty-eight, Anna only fifteen, but she has set her foot on the path that will see her reach the heights of this new society.

'This lovely homestead'

Vergelegen, 1710

Anna's husband breathes beside her, but Cape Town, where she has lived all her life, where there is always noise, slaves stirring in the kitchen next door, a drunk outside in the street kicking a stone and singing, that Cape Town is six hours' fast gallop away. Here there are only owls hooting and perhaps the distant roar of a lion. Anna is far away from everything she knows. Does she wake suddenly during those first weeks, at the deep silence in the house?

Barend rises at first light and the slave Januarie even earlier, stoking the fire in the kitchen to boil the water, heat the bread oven. Anna must relieve herself in a chamber pot, wash her face and armpits from the pitcher and bowl on the nightstand. After a shared breakfast of coffee and rusks, Barend and Januarie work on the land, leaving the house to Anna. All day she walks barefoot over the smooth polished boards of her new home. Past the small panes of the windows, the smart green shutters, the flowers of the garden, surrounded by its thick, high octagonal wall, the blue mountains beyond.

In the kitchen are neat glass canisters, flour and sugar, the ever-simmering pot filling the house with the smell of coffee. In the heat of the afternoon, Anna sits out in the deep shade of the veranda, her slave girl Rosa for company. The rest of the time, they are busy: there is bread to be baked, beer to be brewed, meat to be salted. Pickles, jellies and preserves to be laid down; candles and soap to be made.

Recalling the scandal that engulfs corrupt Governor Willem Adriaan van der Stel in 1706, I did not expect to be returning to Vergelegen as we step down into the next generation. But the Cape population remains tiny in the early 1700s, just a thousand white souls, and Anna's good fortune glimmers down the centuries, ready for me to find. Vergelegen, 'faraway' in Dutch, is isolated fynbos until scores of slaves, under the lash of white overseers, build a mill, a granary and threshing floor, reservoirs, irrigation channels, a smithy, stables, sheep pens, and a large slave house. Willem Adriaan pours Company money into recreating Europe in Africa, a Dutch idyll.

But by 1708 Willem Adriaan is on his way to the Netherlands in disgrace and the once glorious Vergelegen estate is divided into four and sold. Left a substantial inheritance by his father in 1709, Barend Gildenhuys buys the best section, which includes the house. This is Anna's home, now and for the next forty years. From potter's daughter to mistress of one of the grandest estates in the colony in two moves. White Cape women are in such short supply that they nearly always marry up, but Anna has reason to be grateful to her stepmother.

Vergelegen, August 1712

Barend's friends are in the house again. They drink all the good red wine and eat all the tender asparagus, all the tastiest *steenbrassem* and other fish, gossiping all the while, and Anna feels nauseous from their stinking pipe smoke, especially now she is pregnant. Brother-in-law Jacobus van der Heijden is up from Cape Town, visiting his farm next door, so Anna listens as he retells the story of how he was thrown into the Black Hole at the castle by Willem Adriaan van der Stel. Later they play cards by candlelight, chatting and drinking.

At sixteen, like most Cape girls, she is not backward about coming forward, flirting over her pronounced bump. The baby will come soon, according to her mother-in-law, a midwife of long standing who has invited herself to stay for the duration. (Like many midwives, *Juffrou* Margaretha Hoefnagels is an outspoken widow who, in another century, another country, would run the risk of being burnt as a witch.) The bed must be freshly made up with the childbed linen, softer than the usual sheets, she directs; the house kept free of rats, mice and cockroaches. Vergelegen is far from the germ-ridden streets and water of Cape Town and having *Juffrou* Hoefnagels on hand is, at least in this, a good thing. An obstructed delivery can kill mother and child, and Caesarean sections are not successfully carried out at the Cape for another hundred years. Two in every hundred births result in the mother's death and women have so many children that the risk of dying in childbirth runs at perhaps one in eight.

When Anna goes into labour two days later, *Juffrou* Hoefnagels coaxes her along, joined by the house slave Rosa and female neighbours, while the husbands gather elsewhere to drink and smoke.

They offer wine and gossip, wiping Anna's face with a warm damp cloth. Later, Anna leans back on Rosa and *Juffrou* Hoefnagels catches a grandson, Albert, safely in her apron. The womenfolk stay for days, taking care of Anna, dressing the baby, changing the bed.

But the perils are not yet over: more than one in ten babies die before they reach the age of one, one in three before they reach fifteen. Later, when Albert falls ill or gets injured, Anna will nurse him at home: iron filings in beer for pale skin, dried dill in honey for a cough. He is too young to see a doctor who would give him a rectal purge, or cut his veins open, or prescribe emetics to force him to vomit. Then there are horses for trampling, fires for falling into, siblings for dropping, water troughs for drowning. Poor Albert. He survives all these hazards only to die aged eighteen. By March 1715, Anna is pregnant again, but baby Geertruij does not even survive childhood. Third time lucky and Hendrik survives all the way from 1717 to 1770.

Sometimes it seems as if these Cape women all live the same life, trapped on farms, having endless children. German traveller Peter Kolbe notes: 'They are excellent breeders. In most houses in the Colonies are seen from six to a dozen Children and upwards; brave Lads and Lasses with Limbs and Countenances strongly declarative of the ardour with which they were begotten.' Kolbe's delight in Cape women's sexual proclivities aside, the figures bear out his observations on family size: in 1735, women in the rural Western Cape have eight children on average. With all this land seemingly free for cattle, why not?

But a darkness hides behind this abundance of babies, seeping out between the copperplate of names inscribed in great ledgers of birth. Because rumour has it that these Cape women become 'excellent breeders' by proxy, using the bodies of slave women. When Albert is born, it is not his mother who breastfeeds him, but Rosa, who must sleep at the door to Anna and Barend's room in case Albert wakes hungry in the night while Anna's breasts ache with unused milk. Breastfeeding suppresses ovulation, making it harder to fall pregnant. By using a slave to breastfeed her babies, Anna can fall pregnant again, increase her bank of children, and prevent the slave from falling pregnant.

Slave wet nurses are treated generously, fed well, offered gifts and even later their freedom, but I can only touch this subject delicately, afraid of the terrible intimacy of it, the violation, the stripping away of bodily integrity. Who is involuntarily offering tender care? Who living amidst a confusion of love and resentment? I shudder and picture these white spores exploding across the landscape, seeding themselves by rivers, on grassy plains, in forests, their range increasing by nearly ten times from 1703 to 1780. By 1795 there are almost fifteen thousand settlers. Anna has eleven children and an incredible eighty grandchildren.

By the end of 1720, she is heavily pregnant with number five and has been married to Barend for over a decade. He serves as deacon of the Stellenbosch church and sergeant in the infantry, saddling up and leading his small commando to recover cattle and the 'Hottentots' who had taken them. If the Company will not look after them, they will have to do it themselves, he tells her. Life is good. But just three months later, once the slaves have reaped all the December wheat, barley and rye, Barend is dead.

No meek housewife

Vergelegen, 1722

A year later and Anna listens as the foremen squabble across the smooth surface of the stinkwood dining table, the dish of fried mullet. Perhaps Paul has been drinking too much wine again, or Jan has taken his boots. They chew over their argument with the mutton and potatoes. Anna soaks some bread in milk and hands it to the baby, Johanna, who grabs it in her chubby hands and gums it to a pulp. Her back aches from working in the cellar with Hendrik, the cooper, using her strong wrists to scrub the barrels ready for the grape harvest.

After little Albert arrived back in 1712, Anna had pestered Barend until he took her to the German, Peter Kolbe, to draw up a will, making each other their heir, as Roman-Dutch law allows. So when Barend dies suddenly aged thirty-eight, Anna takes on sole charge of the Vergelegen estate. *Godzijdank voor* brother-in-law Jacobus, she thinks, thank God, who lent her his barrel-maker, Hendrik van Heezel, and two foremen. Good barrels are so scarce they are often worth more than the wine they contain. Although the two *knechten* (servants) are not an unmitigated blessing, what with Paul and the slave girl in his room and Jan chasing his cat. She can't go on like this, all these children, this great house and the farm, and no man to stop these two stupid *knechten* from bickering, to keep the slaves under control.

She feels her frustration rise, that she can own this considerable house, raise the children to be God-fearing burghers, mount a horse and ride astride all the way into Cape Town, but she cannot be a burgher herself. She can't be a magistrate; she can't join the militia. She needs to marry again, and it must be a burgher to give her the status. Snapping at the idiot foremen and taking Johanna into the kitchen to wipe her face, Anna does at least have a good idea who she might marry. Somewhere inside, she knows the old story, where rushing into a second marriage to shelter from the brutal loss of the first can end up. But when she wakes up disorientated, or can't decide whether to plant oats or barley, Michiel Otto seems a good prospect.

The wedding takes place in Stellenbosch in March 1722, the floor strewn with fresh sea sand and the minister waiting in his banded toga and tricorn hat. Anna keeps her mouth closed over her teeth, which are as bad as everyone else's; she trips slightly, unaccustomed to her shoes and stockings and lifts her feet a bit higher. Nose still straight and true, Anna wears a gown of Amsterdam silk. She has pinned a silk square over her low neckline and carries a wreath of wild evergreen and *zevenjaartje* flowers, small and white as a tiny daisy, but stiff and long-lasting.

She remembers meeting Michiel when he came asking in his broken Dutch to borrow her wine press, or maybe it was to offer to share a carriage to church. She had not known him when he was a woodcutter behind the Steenberg, having no occasion to visit the woodcutters, and, besides, Barend was alive then. Anna frets that Michiel is a little too angry with the children, a little too short with the slaves. She notes the smell of wine on his breath after his quick visit to the taproom nearby. Too late to change her mind now. She covers her face with her fan as the minister rises to pray, the men standing with their hats before their faces.

Originally from the Baltic coast in Pomerania (now Poland), Michiel Otto arrives at the Cape in 1714. Marriage to Anna means a huge step up: Vergelegen is more luxurious than the homes of even the wealthiest farmers. He takes his marital prerogative, too, getting Anna pregnant within a few months and Michiel Otto junior is followed by five daughters in quick succession.

Otto Mentzel, a German who lives at the Cape a decade later, doubtless feels that Michiel has the better deal. 'In general, the farm women surpass the men in natural intelligence, good behaviour and ability to learn and understand anything,' he says. 'They are usually industrious, good housekeepers and excellent mothers.' But, he adds, 'their conversation does not go beyond household affairs'. It is hard to see how their conversation could be more sophisticated. There are no books, plays or newspapers. And no schooling. They are, Mentzel reports, delighted to have visitors to relieve their daily boredom.

By 1729, Michiel is away from home more and more, maintaining one of the few wagon roads into the hinterland, which peters out just a hundred miles from Cape Town. But the hills rise blue and alluring beyond Stellenbosch, especially for land-poor people suffocated by the bonds of society and the VOC.

A century before disaffected Afrikaners, fed up with British rule, outraged at the abolition of slavery, set out on their Great Trek across the South African interior, landless *trekboers* drive their stock over the first mountain range into the dry scrubland beyond. Women go too, with their one long dress of East Indian chintz for Sundays, their small dowry of cattle or sheep. They carry grain, but once they eat or plant it the *trekboers* must rely on dried meat and game, peas and beans. Houses are rough, four limestone walls with a shrub roof. A far cry from Vergelegen, these.

When a *trekboer* falls pregnant, she has no one to deliver her baby, no *Juffrou* Hoefnagels, no sister or mother. Some white men take Khoikhoi wives and lay the foundation of mixed-race groups. Some consort with Khoikhoi women even when they have 'quite tolerable' wives of their own, according to a contemporary observer. The

Khoikhoi bear children who look like the farmer who puts them to work under the nose of the farmer's wife.

From the Khoikhoi, the *trekboers* learn to store milk in skin bags, to make the rough skin shoes called *velskoene*. They wear leather clothes and use termite mounds as ovens, eat *biltong* and rusks. But they need coffee, salt, tobacco, sugar and ammunition, and when supplies run low they load the wagon with skins, horns, butter, wax and dried fruit to barter in distant towns. No schools, no churches, months on horseback, the only book the Bible. These people are wholly isolated: from Europe, from the Cape, from most other humans.

Ironically, their intense love for the land turns out to be ignorant and destructive. The Khoikhoi move on quickly, allowing the soil to recover. The Xhosa people across the horizon settle and improve the soil. The *trekboers*? They allow their cattle to graze at will, leaving the veld useless within eight years. By the late 1770s, the *trekboers* have reached the Fish River, five hundred miles east of Cape Town. Only in the 1830s will the momentum of this isolationist impulse sweep the white man across the Karoo and up onto the highveld and beyond.

Baltic Jekyll and Hyde

In 1722, Michiel Otto's true self cannot be visible to Anna, or she would not accept the match with this Baltic Jekyll and Hyde, hiding his fleshy evil under the cloak of courtesy. The marriage lasts for nearly two decades. How many of those years are intolerable? How long does she fear the drumming of his horse's hooves, the violent slam of the *voorkamer* door, the shouting? The unbuttoning of his breeches? How long does he drink wine at breakfast and belch, roar and threaten the children, sweating and spitting?

Michiel Otto is a savage, tyrannical to his slaves, punished again and again by the Company for his floggings, his brutality. He is a bogeyman. 'Behave, or I will sell you to Michel Otto,' the burghers growl. In the summer, he binds disobedient slaves to a tree or pole in the sun and has their naked bodies smeared with honey. Tempted by sweetness, wasps, flies, mosquitoes, bumblebees buzz and taste, their chitinous legs stuck fast in the stickiness.

Or so the stories go. Otto Mentzel admits some of his tales are plain gossip, but when he dedicates a whole page of his *Geographical and Topographical Description of the Cape of Good Hope* of 1787 to how Michiel Otto treats his slaves, something rattles around inside the nested boxes of time. I read the box labelled 'Michiel Otto' on my screen, click on a link, turn the key in the lock, and there it is: 'Michiel Otto, SV/PROG is your seventh great-grandfather' reads the banner at the top of the website, laying bare my proximity to a slave-owning torturer, his marriage to my seventh great-grandmother.

Anna is entangled in this violence, married to it, complicit in it, subject to it. Dutch women are more powerful than most and have the backing of the law if their husband steps too far out of line: if he commits adultery with a female slave, the wife can take him to court, demand a divorce. Anna can even refuse to have sex with Michiel (but only if there is a risk she will catch syphilis, or herpes, or some other unspeakable disease). In contrast, during more than a hundred and eighty years of slavery at the Cape, no man, slave or free, is convicted of raping a slave woman. (The Slave Lodge, which houses all the VOC slaves, is also the town's de facto brothel.) Slave women, being less than human, do not merit legal protection. (This toleration of violence leaches down the centuries: one in four women over eighteen in South Africa today has been assaulted by a partner; twelve in every hundred thousand women are victims of femicide, five times the global average.)

At forty-six, tempered by thirty years of marriage, child-rearing and loss, empowered by Roman-Dutch law, Anna Siek finds herself up to the challenge. And by January 1741 she becomes the 'separated house-wife of Michael Otto'. To ensure '*ruste, vreede en welstand, van hare persoonen en familie*', the State Generaal has been told: 'rest, peace and prosperity of her persons [*sic*] and family'. Divorces are rare and only granted for adultery or desertion. So Anna and Michiel separate: separation of table and bed, the legal term. These are not common either, but they are easier; the marriage commitment remains intact, and neither partner can remarry.

And so Anna frees her family and her status from Michel Otto's coarse brutality, gains control of her own business and becomes legally independent. She brought Vergelegen into the marriage; it remains hers. From now on, she wakes up alone in her stinkwood four-poster, is brought coffee by her slave, who removes the smelly pot from under her bed. Helped into her chemise, stays and petticoats, Anna ties her pockets round her waist, slips the ring of keys inside, puts on her embroidered gown. Treading the smooth yellowwood boards to the dining room, she takes breakfast at her table: bread, butter, bacon, early grapes.

Around the table, the family laugh and bicker. Hendrik and Barend, her grown sons, help run the farm. Michiel junior lives out on the loan farm with his father, thirty miles away. Her daughters dally over their morning tea, but the *knecht* Bernard Wit waits at the door, ready to teach them their catechism and arithmetic. He costs fifteen florins a month, not to mention the tobacco, tea and bread he consumes, nor his bed. Beyond the green shutters are Anna's vineyards, her wheat fields, her cattle, her sheep. Finally, she is mistress of the horizon.

A queen bee in her hive, Anna knows every chamber, every plant. The way the land lies. Her nineteen slaves must be kept under control, grievances and rebellions harnessed. These slaves cost Anna to feed and clothe: one rix-dollar a month for food, a length of tobacco a week, two new pairs of trousers and a coat every year. They live in the slave house, sleep on quilted Eastern *palempore*. Beds are so scarce that a male slave with a bed can rely on a female body to warm it at night – a bed feels like 'home', precious privacy.

A year later, Michiel abandons all pretence of farming and buries himself in his warehouse in Cape Town, drinking his way through barrels of wine, squatting in the front room of the warehouse, selling yarn, tea, saffron and silver spoons from the back. In late 1743 he dies, leaving 2,332 rix-dollars (£80,000 today) stuffed in a copper kettle. Anna is wealthy too, but, considering the estate she inherited in 1720, she might have expected to have accumulated more. Life is not just capital: it is being a woman in a man's world. Or having an alcoholic husband in charge of your farm.

The camphor trees grow and protect the house from the afternoon sun. The children marry and move away, and Anna makes more wine per vine than the average. In 1751, aged fifty-six, tired and lonely, her golden hair faded and coarse under her white cap, she transfers the northern section to her son-in-law Jurgen Radyn and six years later, after nearly half a century, she sells the farmhouse, winery and mill to a man called Arnoldus Maasdorp.

A name is just letters until it is attached to a life. And this life is that of a man whose grandmother was a slave – Angela van Bengale – but Arnoldus Maasdorp is forgetting her, forgetting the tag that follows her around her whole life, 'van Bengale'. It means nothing to him, born into white society, son of Maria Basson and Christian Maasdorp. Later Maria dies and Christian marries his sister-in-law, Helena van der Merwe, daughter of Elsje Cloete. And former wife of Jacobus van As, Maria Basson's brother. Feminine networking spreads like crop circles across the wheat of the Western Cape.

Arnoldus can forget the quarter of Indian blood his veins carry around his body, but it becomes harder and harder. From the outset it is true: white, European, Christian, free at the top; brown, slave, non-Christian at the bottom. Cape Town retains some racial fluidity for centuries, the busy port offering jobs for free blacks as barbers, innkeepers, craftsmen. But, in the Western Cape, Europeans own the land, and the slaves work it, with no space for un-landed free blacks.

Brazil and South Africa are often brought together, bookended across the Atlantic Ocean. Compare and contrast: why does South Africa not look like Brazil, with huge racial inequality, but no stark black–white divide? In 2010 there are 91 million white Brazilians, 82 million mixed-race Brazilians and 14 million black Brazilians. At the same time, there are 41 million black South Africans, 4.5 million white South Africans and just 4.6 million coloured (mixed-race) South Africans. In Brazil, the black population are imported as slaves from Africa. In South Africa, the black population is the native population. No matter how Europeans try to justify the theft, the land belongs to them. Demographically dominant, they cannot be assimilated and must be subdued.

But there is something else. Something that lies at the node of race and gender. In modern parlance, 'intersectionality', a word coined by Kimberlé Williams Crenshaw in 1989. This happens again and again, in both time scales. Historical time, of which I write, and temporal time, in which I write. That not only do black and white women have very different female experiences, but white women often create or compound the difficult experiences of black women. Specifically, that the white women resident in South Africa from whom my blood flows, women like Anna Siek, maintain their small portion of power by denying it to all the black, Indian, coloured and Khoikhoi women around them.

Anna can do this because she has more legal rights and because the burgher family is the building block of this society. In Brazil, because of its relation to Portugal, to Spain, and to the Catholic Church, white women have few rights. They cannot divorce the husbands who sleep with slave women – or drink the estate's profits away – and they cannot prevent the children of those unions clustering around the patriarch. At the Cape, white women can punish their husbands for adultery and bastard children do not have rights. White Cape women can keep the race pure to maintain their status.

Conduits for wealth

I find no record of how Anna dies or where she is buried after this long life, so much longer than her mother's, cushioned as she is by luck, which makes her white, and brings her Barend, and Vergelegen; which makes her intelligent, diligent and attractive. She last appears on the *opgaaf* in 1771, aged seventy-six, having survived the smallpox epidemics of 1755 and 1767. But I do have physical contact with this energetic soul: more than three hundred years after she and Barend sign their will while Peter Kolbe looks on, I order it up from the stacks at the Cape Archives in Cape Town. I don't know that I am going to have this contact. Mystified by the arcane codes of archival filing and how these Afrikaners seem to share just five names between them, I fill my request slip with numbers.

The assistant is reluctant. The lift is broken, and he sweats as he struggles up and down the stairs into the vaults of the past with the big old ledgers, these giant lozenges of oppression. Here I am, another white person turning over the tilth of whiteness. 'Only six requisitions allowed,' he mutters as he dumps the ledgers. The manager intervenes. 'Are you the lady who phoned earlier,' she asks, 'from the UK?' Given how far I have travelled in space and time, I am to be allowed special dispensation. I can have more than six volumes. Guiltily, I fill in another slip. Half an hour later, a leatherbound tome is placed on my desk.

I turn the frayed pages reverentially, and there it is. Pale blue, covered in ornate, old-fashioned Dutch in a beautiful high script. I touch the parchment. The writing is illegible. But there is Anna's signature. Small, cramped and all lowercase but distinct: anna margareta siek. I give thanks for the Dutch East India Company's incomparable filing.

In this world, it is not love that will remain of us, but pots. The detritus of colonists' lives are painstakingly inscribed onto thick rag-based paper by VOC officials and stored in the VOC records. Digging through probate inventories, I unearth more ancestors: Susanna de Villiers, dying in childbirth in 1730, leaving pewter plates and dishes, forty knives and spoons but just four forks (a reminder of the relative novelty of that implement). Two pewter chamber pots, three sailcloth sacks, two buckets and a copper funnel. Cornelia Nel, miles from Cape Town on Boesmansdrift, who in 1756 leaves two tea canisters and a pepper box, four paintings, a mirror and a Siamese jar.

These copper funnels and tea canisters are not frivolous. They are the thin threads of culture that tie isolated farmhouses across the empty miles of scrub, across the mountains and rivers, to Cape Town. Cape women are described as 'conduits for the accumulation and transmission of property' – just a passage for something else to travel through. Or, in a discussion of the importance of widows, a woman's name goes unspecified in favour of her dead husband. How hard it is to see through the mesh of the patriarchy. Patronymic naming conventions are blinding, reading historical records like gazing at the sun. But looked at sideways, these women can be glimpsed: holograms walking, working, riding, managing relationships across the Cape's mountain ranges and generations.

Anna lives a settled life, shaping Cape society, but others are on the move, as they always are: at her birth in 1695, settlers have barely reached Drakenstein; by the time of her death, they have reached as far north as the Orange River and as far east as the Fish River. Here they stop: beyond the Fish River are the amaXhosa, a people more populous and capable than any they have yet met. The battle between these two peoples will set the tone for South Africa's struggles for the next several centuries.

~

A tenuous hold

Two hundred and twenty years later, 1994, and I am arriving in a South Africa that seems as if it might have finally reached the end of this battle. Black and white, people stood in line together for hours earlier this year to vote in the newly dubbed Rainbow Nation's first multiracial elections. I am here to stay, learning the lie of the land, but fall foul of the airport immigration officials who want to know exactly what it is I think I am doing here. What I am doing here, post-university, adrift, is casting around for a path into the future, but I can't tell them that, which means, in the end, that my sojourn will prove all too temporary.

Here are some words: domestic/domesticate. Belonging to the home, but also: made compliant, tamed. Domestic: site of belonging and safety. Also: site where women are trapped, and men go out into the world. Here are some more words: alien, belonging to another person, place or family, *esp.* to a foreign nation or allegiance. Or this one: wild, of an animal, living in a state of nature, not tame, not domesticated. The domestic is always the same, or so it seems, keeping wildness at bay with its rules and routines. And most domesticated are those who most remain in the home, the women.

In a foreign country, human beings can become wild, undomesticated, or at least become someone else. Not entirely, but enough. It is not, as the cliché goes, 'discovering yourself', because to discover something, it must already be there, and humans are not static entities, so I consider it more invention, or building. And, I think, it is not only economic necessity, forced migration or political oppression that fuels movement, but change, difference, escape. What serendipity that I am made new in a country that has woken up and found itself made new. Newly minted. Sometimes I think this luck colours everything that comes afterwards in my life. I am shaped by hope, carry the seed of gladness around in my pocket.

Durban, 1994

I have been visiting this house my whole life: the avocado tree shading the drive; the vegetable patch with its red earth, its basil and chilli plants; the yesterday, today and tomorrow bush by the front door with its purple, lilac and white flowers. The frangipani tree with its fleshy, perfumed blooms. I pick, sniff and sniff again, and am lost in a childhood world of inchoate desire. Nowadays, tower blocks dwarf the elegant colonial bungalow, windows framed with beautifully scrolled burglar bars, but the house has not changed, not the threadbare olive carpets, nor the 1950s tilework in the kitchen.

It is I who have changed. The seam of time is ripped: before, I was a visitor, travelling from one place to another. Now I am static, at rest. In a place that is strange, foreign. My body is static, but my mind is ever travelling away from who I was, ever becoming other. Durban nights are velvety, the air warm, the sky dark and close. I am fingering photographs of friends, considering how far I am from home, when suddenly outside God is being praised under the palm prints of the pawpaw tree. In time I get used to it: every Friday night, without fail, Reginald holds a prayer meeting in his room out the back.

In all the years I visit and live in this house I never go into Reginald's room. Often in the evenings, I see him from the kitchen window, sitting on an upturned crate, the sweet smell of dope percolating the dusk. In the flowerbed under my window I find marijuana plants, self-seeded. *Dagga*, they call it. But on Friday nights, there is no *dagga*, only Reginald in clean white robes, preaching. His voice rises and falls while his congregation ululate in praise. They are mostly women, this congregation, dressed in their own flowing robes.

My uncle and aunt talk of Reginald with a mix of pride and fascination, about his role as a player, the multiple children with multiple mothers, his high standing in his community. Despite living in a small pokey room at the back of the house, Reginald is not diminished. He has a wife and children in rural KwaZulu-Natal, but he spends most of his life away from that family: gardening, cleaning the pool, doing odd jobs. It is a story common among black South Africans: the absent parent and the family, divided by apartheid's Group Areas Act. Later two of the children Reginald leaves behind die after being hit by lightning. How does he make sense of this split? I can never ask such a thing, step over the invisible line. I don't even know his Zulu name.

I never get used to having a stranger in the house. For that is what servants are, in the end: strangers. You might be walking to the bathroom in your towel, and suddenly there they are. You might be getting a snack, leaving a trail of crumbs behind you, and there they are, waiting to wipe up. Jeans come back from the wash beautifully ironed, with a crease down the front of each leg. They might know everything about you, your habits and human vulnerabilities, and you don't know anything about them. Meanwhile, here they are, scrubbing your lavatory.

I never get over my discomfort, but every white home I visit in South Africa contains a live-in servant, or at the very least someone who comes in every day to clean, cook, do the washing. And they are always African. One in five South African women is a domestic worker, and in South Africa's vastly unequal landscape domestic workers have higher incomes than many and beneficial social ties to rich white households, so there are some benefits. But for a twentieth-century European, this fundamental stratification bears the imprint of Angela's life, of the slavery abolished nearly two centuries earlier in the Cape; it contains the same seed of resentment. I think again about domestication, how white South Africa tried to domesticate the African population by penning them up on tiny patches of land, forcing them to work in its homes, its mines, its farms.

A complex network of obligation and tradition, isolation and domicile, persists on farms. Visiting old friends on their *mealie* farm two decades later, we *braai* and chat late into the night. Eyeing the piles of plates and pans, the salad bowl, the smeared glasses, I offer to do the washing up.

'No, don't worry,' says Danielle. 'Someone will do it in the morning.'

All these people are trapped in a universe not of their own making. The servants, with no opportunity for alternative employment, are tied to a locale where they have little influence after generations of servitude. Danielle and Chris, inclined to do their own washing up and childcare but honour-bound to share their privilege in this peculiar way. This country can't find its way out of the labyrinth.

I come down the following day to find two women doing our washing up, chatting in another language. I greet them, and they respond before going back to their conversation. My inability to understand allows them surprising privacy, something like a wall walling them off from my ears. As if they are in a separate space. We are separate.

Durban, 1995

'We love you Miss Cato because you do not care though we are black.' The blue biro is scrawled on a scrap torn from an exercise book. Hidden in my bag while I was teaching. Outside, the sun shines as usual in Kwazulu-Natal: Nelson Mandela is president, and after decades of a sporting boycott South Africa is winning the Rugby World Cup on its own turf. Everywhere I go is delight.

But the past festers on. I make some friends, meet their friends in turn: it is the first time I have met people like this, for whom black people are definitely lesser and definitely dangerous. 'He's not bad for one of those okes,' one says of a black colleague. 'Usually they drink all the time and lie around.' These people are white, but they are not the kind of whites my aunt and uncle know, the university lecturers, the Quakers, the Afrikaner elite. There is something else here, in the army service, the houses in the outer suburbs.

We spend our weekends playing pool and volunteering at the harbour, visit a white surfer hangout every Saturday night, where we hit pool balls around and listen to grunge, this being the 1990s. One night my friend and I have got so good at pool that we beat the boys. 'You girls don't need the table, do you? Can't we have it back?' they ask. Chauvinism, another of this group's -isms. There is a lot of drug-taking, especially marijuana, the plant that grows wild under my window. Hot-boxing – turning your car into a colossal bong – is popular, with a lot of time spent giggling and red-eyed.

There is an unbridgeable divide between us. It is not that I am not, on some level, racist, with a wonky set of assumptions about how and why the world works. I am in my Barbie-in-Africa stage, trying to save the world, one black child at a time. But the idea that black people might have thicker skulls and so smaller brains is so horrifyingly absurd I cannot conceive of anyone believing it. I am still foreign, this place is still foreign, but slowly I learn the long, strange and twisted histories its peoples carry within them. One night over beers and a *braai*, one of the group boasts that he belongs to the AWB, the *Afrikaner Weerstandsbeweging* (Afrikaner Resistance Movement), or, as a relative would have it: Afrikaners Without Brains. The disrespect is earned: the AWB are neo-Nazi white supremacists who terrorise and murder black South Africans.

Meanwhile, I try to acquire isiZulu, finding that my lack of language, inability to understand, makes me a representative of the colonisers of Great Britain, of the Imperial columns that march in red across the veld. Or the tourists on their coaches, visiting townships like zoos. But the night class I attend at the University of KwaZulu-Natal, taught by a white man, coupled with bashfulness, leaves me stuck behind the wall of unknowing. *Sawubona*, I can say, I see you – 'Hello!' – and *hamba kahle*, go well – 'Goodbye!' I am shamed by the pleasure even this creates and remain behind the wall of incomprehension.

I find a job teaching 'study skills' in Umlazi, a rambling township on the outskirts of Durban. Driving down the motorway, taking the turning, the weather so sultry I drink can after can of cream soda, a bright green drink that forever after tastes of 1995. Its blue sky, horizon to horizon, broad green fields of sugar cane. Durban is semitropical, verdant. Like any town, Umlazi has neighbourhoods, from the perfect matchbox homes with pretty gardens to the extended houses on bigger plots to the corrugated-iron shacks rammed up against one another.

Schools are low to the ground, built in a U-shape, and very full of children: shy, studious or as exuberant as a box of bouncy balls exploding across the classroom floor. They are as immaculate as city bankers, school uniforms pressed into perfect creases. Some smell strongly of wood smoke, from the wood for which their mothers forage and burn. With no chimney to draw the smoke, just a hole in the roof, it penetrates everything. I am something of a *naif* here and allow a cocky student named Thabo to give me what he calls a 'baby kiss'. I take this to mean a chaste kiss on the cheek, but it turns out to be on the lips. Thabo is delighted and dances with joy. I am mortified, and worried about losing my job.

The job itself is an exercise in futility. That I am entirely unqualified to teach does not seem to matter, nor the fact that I have no understanding of daily reality for these children. 'What shall I do, Miss, if I hear something outside and I am too scared to study?' asks one small girl. 'Well, why don't you go outside and reassure yourself that it is nothing?' I suggest. She objects: 'But I might get shot!' I am culturally illiterate; nothing I say to them is of any use. The only person I know to be educated is myself. I begin to grasp the ethical complexities of development work. The missionary nature of it, the removal of agency, the elevation of helper over helped. This year 'teaching' in Umlazi puts a question mark over development work that never entirely disappears.

The township roads have no signs, and my small red Mini is so unreliable that I borrow another car. Every time I set out, there is a slight girding of the loins, some challenge to it. This is not entirely an over-reaction. Thousands of people spend every day of their lives in Umlazi, but I am white, my skin a clear indicator of guilt, whichever way you cut it. And, as my uncle helpfully reminds me, there is always the example of Amy Biehl, the American Fulbright scholar murdered in the Cape Town township of Gugulethu in 1993, to keep me nervous. Young white woman, murdered by a marauding hoard of black men. See the pattern? White South Africans are trapped by the fear of a mythological danger they themselves have made all too real.

Many white South Africans have never set foot in one of these settlements; in years to come, black entrepreneurs earn a decent living showing tourists around. Poverty tourism. Later, my (white) boyfriend tells me that it was not until volunteering in Mamelodi, a township near Pretoria, that he felt his nation's shaky foundations. How black people lived, the dirt roads, refuse-strewn, running with sewage, the shacks with corrugated roofs. Having spent years watching apartheid unravel on British television, I cannot understand.

'Do you realise,' he asks, 'that there is a civil war going on in your own country?'

'What are you talking about?' I ask bewildered.

'Northern Ireland,' he says, not without satisfaction.

These are the days before the anarchy of the internet, when even in Britain the establishment, through a handful of newspaper and television proprietors and the BBC, controls the flow, the tone, of news. Not that that is an excuse.

Now I wonder about this, and about the specific occluded knowledge of the internet. How a search for the old Cape farms brings up joyous photographs of energetic cyclists spattered with mud or elegant bedrooms decorated in linen and cool greys. The slavery and atrocities of their past erased, nowhere; the persistence of ignorance; the ways knowledge can obtrude, break through. The ignorance contract, Professor Melissa Steyn calls it. A learnt turning away from the knowledge that white comfort and convenience comes at the price of black freedom. The way white children are sutured into dominance, the needle and floss of everyday subjugation. The way that ignorance persists into adulthood, so that just twenty-five years after the end of apartheid, when the dust has barely settled on centuries of white supremacy, grown adults can demand that black people should 'get over it already'.

September 1996

Casting around for my own small path in this brand-new country, I move to Johannesburg, where the jacaranda shed their violet blooms over the city streets; leave Durban behind in search of a new home, new job. My mother frets about what I am doing, so far away. Growing up, I should tell her, but instead send a long letter about everything else on blue airmail sheets, thin as onion skin under my pen.

I share a house in Bezuidenhout Valley, named for Frederik Bezuidenhout, who buys the old Doornfontein farm in 1861. Bez Valley is to the east of Johannesburg's city centre, surrounded by mine dumps from old gold diggings, a grid of single-storied Victorian homes, brick boxes topped with red-coated corrugated roofs. The front steps are painted a deep glossy oxblood and inside the ceilings are ornate pressed tin. There is no central heating, and the nights get very cold in Johannesburg's highveld winter. These houses are home to a proud community of Portuguese and Greek immigrants and old Jewish families.

I drive to work in downtown Johannesburg with its grimy pavements, buy a *mealie* from the woman who *braais* the corncobs over a small brazier at the corner of Rissik and Bree Streets. I am the office intern, struggling to get pieces in the paper. The newsroom opens on to the sub-editors' desks, where they check copy and lay out the paper on giant screens. The subs smoke inside, and cigarette fumes hang suspended above their desks. I sit in on the news conference every morning, get sent out on puff stories, search for titbits for the news-in-brief column.

Most of the team are still white, just a couple of years after the end of apartheid, with one black reporter and an Indian secretary. The atmosphere tastes of spite. The news editor, a beautiful older woman, wears a heavy face of make-up. On the brink of marriage to a third or fourth husband – office gossip is not entirely clear – she is the target of much whispered scorn.

'Why does she wear so much make-up?' I ask her deputy, a malicious skinny man in his thirties who lives with his mother and has a crush on Lady Di.

'I went on a conference with her once and saw her without any make-up,' he replies. 'It was frightening.'

The photographer has worked in the South African press for years. He has photographed everything: armoured police carriers driving into the townships, clouds of tear gas, dead bodies. He ignores the bitchiness. A young black woman joins the team. She is entirely unapproachable, head held high and aloof.

'The only reason she got that job,' a white male colleague mutters, 'is because she's sleeping with the editor.' I look at her and at the editor. I start to seek other work when the British public-school boy, just a couple of years older than me, asks me to do his typing, a task that appears nowhere in my job description. It occurs to me that neither of us should have jobs here in this country, where we are foreign, living off the fat of our privilege. Only years later do the sexual and racial dynamics of the newsroom come into focus in my head.

Soon I am lost, all at sea, no idea what to do with the future that gapes in front of me. I pitch freelance articles, walk the dogs in the park next to the house. One day another dog streaks past.

'Off, Rocky, off,' shouts its owner angrily. He is burly, shaven-headed, white. The huge Alsatian has tackled one of our dogs and is worrying at her head, leaving her with a torn eyelid.

The following month we are woken at dawn by the *boom, boom*, of bass across the park from a car parked on the grass. My friends walk across to ask the driver to turn the music down. The young man standing by the car pulls out a gun, lets it hang idly by his side. 'He knew not to point it at us,' they say when they return, 'because then we could call the police.' They are hyped up on adrenalin and fear.

Another morning we find the security gate and front door standing open, a shiny square in the dust where the stereo had sat. A sprinting teenager snatches my bag at a community centre as I (stupidly) swing it by its strap. A housemate is car-jacked at gunpoint. The razor's strop is close to the surface, keeping us off-balance.

I try to persuade young black men in bars to sign postcards asking the Nigerian government not to execute Ken Saro-Wiwa and other Ogoni activists. I tag along when the Secretary-General of Amnesty International, Pierre Sane, meets Cheryl Carolus, ANC politician, Struggle veteran, and later South African High Commissioner to the UK.

'I don't need lectures from students,' she says, looking at me with disdain. I have not yet learnt the subtle power of dress and am wearing a royal-blue T-shirt with a long black skirt and sandals, carrying a child's pink-and-black backpack.

I meet my boyfriend's school and university mates from Pretoria, white men who like to drink and talk about cars. Pretoria is the conservative core of white South Africa. They have girlfriends who are slim, and made up, and look at me askance. I meet other white South Africans: artists, writers, people who questioned the status quo, quiet activists against the apartheid state. Reluctant heroes, in another country they might have lived peaceful counter-cultural lives. In totalitarian South Africa, refusing to conform made one an enemy of the state. Now, these people are in the strange and privileged position of living in the future they craved.

A housemate, who is researching a PhD on the poor-white problem in South Africa in the 1920s, comes home one evening full of glee, brandishing the copy of a letter she has found in the archives.

'Look what this guy writes about your great-grandfather,' Lis crows. 'Look! He says: "May the hound of hell chase him over the blue rocks of buggery, over the red rocks of hell, and may his arsehole become a festering sore."' I am not certain what to say to this. ' "The day he dies we shall walk a hundred miles over broken bottles and tin tacks with our bare feet just to shit in his grave," ' she recites gleefully. There is something personal in this gloating, but I remain bewildered.

In English schools in the 1980s, we study the French Revolution, the world wars, the Crusades: our minds empty of the history learnt by South African schoolchildren. It is not our history, which we imbibe with our little bottles of milk before Margaret Thatcher snatches them away. That is D-Day and the ships setting sail for the coast of France, which, on a clear day, we can almost see. It is 1066 and all that, Henry the Eighth and his impressive number of wives.

If at home Prime Minister Jan Smuts – or the Oubaas (the Old Boss, or Old Master), as we refer to him with nonchalant smugness – looms large, it is an impersonal, ignorant looming. There are books on the shelf, collected papers, biographies, histories, but they remain unread. The letter Lis brandishes, written by an émigré Russian tailor to Prime Minister Smuts during a general strike in 1922, leaves me none the wiser. (The strike, which has never crossed my path before this day, continues as a blank space for another twenty years.)

Growing up, we don't know much about South Africa or our great-grandfather's role in its awful history, but we hear the pride in our parents' voices. Later, we try to downplay how responsible our relation might or might not be, try to distance ourselves from the Nationalists. Later still, when a friend refers to Smuts as an apartheid leader on Facebook, I am horrified, the inaccuracy meaningless to her, but a disgrace to me. Even later than that, once I have begun to parse out my own place, the responsibility of my own family, there is the flare-up around the statue of Jan Smuts in Parliament Square, which ignites the fuse that brings it all exploding into the light.

But we are not there yet, and in 1996 I am blind to the decisions my great-grandfather made about striking workers or African land, blind to how decisions he was party to are playing out across the country, finding their awful fruit in Truth and Reconciliation Commission (TRC) hearings. I drive cross-country to one of these hearings, across the flat fields of the highveld, sallow in the winter drought. Behind me are the towers and dust of Johannesburg, the newspapers blowing down the streets; the minibus taxis rammed full of people, conductors hanging off the passenger door, chanting their destination. There is a crowd outside the civic centre when I arrive, women in orange ANC T-shirts and bright wraps, babies tied to their backs in blankets. I park on wasteland nearby, look around for my friend Derrick. Suddenly the air fills with roaring, everyone turning to look as a helicopter comes to its slow rest on a neighbouring field. A portly African in a purple shirt and elegant black suit ducks out under the blades, holding his tie.

Inside the centre, the low-ceilinged room echoes with subdued coughs and snuffles. One by one, the witnesses are called. It is a laborious business, establishing names, places, dates. The elderly African on the stand begins to weep. 'I just want to know what happened,' he says.

> I, we, were living in that place and one day he went out and the next thing they found his body in that *donga*. He was wearing his blue coat. I could recognise it straight away. They had cut him; they had cut his arms and his face. I just want to know what happened. He was my only son.

The wife of the accused takes the stand. She is beautiful, petite, with delicate features and fine skin, green silk suit, coiffed blonde hair. 'No, I don't know. Sometimes he went out, and I did not know where he went,' she says. 'Often at that time, you know, it was so confused, and there was lots of fear. I did not always know where he went.'

Finally, the accused himself stands up. He is appropriately banal, with his grey face, hair and suit. He takes the oath. Nothing changes.

These TRC hearings are supposed to put South Africa's pain to rest after the end of apartheid, to offer a way forward: two thousand people, perpetrator and victim, telling their stories over seven years at hearings broadcast live across the nation. More than twenty thousand people are found to be victims of gross human rights violations between 1960 and 1994.

The Government of National Unity – the name celebrates a unity they are aiming for, not a unity they have – has as its Minister of Justice Dullah Omar, who we will meet later as his brave hands tremble when he speaks out in the face of white men armed with the uniform and guns of the previous government, who were unified in a different way. In consultation with more than fifty civil society organisations, the Government of National Unity and its Minister of Justice decide that this restorative approach is more helpful in healing and moving forward than a retributive approach like Nuremberg. Seven thousand perpetrators apply for amnesty; less than a thousand receive it.

I interview two Argentinian forensic anthropologists in their sleek hotel room in Johannesburg. They are elegant, calm, civilised. Each day, they travel by car to Rustenberg to find, exhume and examine the bodies of people killed by the apartheid regime. Argentinians, too, carry the heavy burden of the disappeared, the military dictatorship leaving its trail of blood dripping all over their nation. These Argentinians are friendly but wary, stepping meticulously around the who and the where. Nevertheless, when the story runs, I receive a telephone call from the TRC. Who is on the line is not clear, but the message is: cease and desist; I am queering their pitch, warning the perpetrators.

Truth? Reconciliation? Some people lie, some are doubly wounded by having to remember what they have been trying to forget, and a quarter of a century later it can feel as if the country has barely moved on at all into the future it so desperately wanted. Did the road to reconciliation end with the TRC? Would real reckoning have helped? After the TRC winds up, too few perpetrators are brought to justice: the criminal justice system unable, or unwilling, to cope with the burden of investigation and prosecution.

We move across the road into the old servants' quarters behind a friend's house, next to a tiny swimming pool no one ever uses. I paint the cramped walls in careful pastels, buy a futon for the corridor, which doubles up as a dining and seating area. I feel at home here, with my futon and pastel walls, my intimate ties. But I know enough to know that I am still foreign, or – here's another word – alien, belonging to another person, place or family. It is a sentiment shared by the Department of Home Affairs as I learn a year later when I pick up the phone (still then a handset attached by a curling cord to the cradle), the shiny Bakelite receiver, and the voice on the other end asks when I intend to leave.

My hold here has always been tenuous, cobbled together with uncertain work permits, and perhaps, I think, they are right: the people who slip across the Mozambican border at night, trudging silently through the bush in search of a better life, they are truly Africans. There is no question of their belonging on this continent. Whereas I, with my white skin, my loyalty to immigration authorities' ways, my tongue that speaks only English, all this marks me out as an alien.

This thought slips in before I can stop it, and then I think of all the pale-skinned people of this country who have nowhere else to call home. All the darker-skinned people at home in Europe. And then I think not of skin colour but philosophy, that I am European, a child of the benighted Enlightenment, which has led to the erasure or denial of so many other systems of thought. I am not a child of *ubuntu*, that too-often hijacked southern African sense of a human as only human through their connection to other humans. In isiZulu: *Umuntu ngumuntu ngabantu.*

Such a system of classification through philosophy slips and slides, much more difficult than skin colour, but perhaps truer to our inner selves. In any case, after this, I am always on the outside, only present on a tourist visa: visiting, temporary. More than a decade later, I emerge from a cinema in suburban Wimbledon, transported by the time machine of a film back to 1995 where again and again, I am part of an audience that cowers under raincoats and umbrellas as barefoot women in green pinafores and *doeks* (headscarves) push water off a rugby pitch with brooms and water sprays from players' boots as they skid up and down the field, 'the ball like a bar of soap' the commentator says in an uncharacteristically poetic turn of phrase as it slides upwards out of the player's hands into a future where South Africa will win the Rugby World Cup, and it will be seen as a blessing on this new Rainbow Nation.

Invictus – undefeated, unconquered – the name of this film about rugby, which is really about nation-building, or trying to piece together a whole shattered country, but which is also the name of the poem Nelson Mandela recites under his breath in his cell in Robben Island, his head bloody but unbowed. One team, one nation, despite rugby's status as the intimate friend of Afrikaner culture and the apartheid regime, just a year after one nation became a political reality and I think this is the high point of the Rainbow Nation, as Chester Williams scores the winning try and Mandela steps onto the pitch in a Springbok jersey. Two black men, carrying the torch of the white man's game onto the international pitch and winning.

Or perhaps the high point comes a year later when things get switched around, and South Africa wins again, Bafana Bafana triumphant at their first African Cup of Nations. And I am there too, at Soccer City for the quarter-finals where rain cloaks the pitch again as the crowd chant Feesh, Feesh, as Michael Fish scores, Shoes, Shoes, as John Moshoeu follows. We watch Bafana Bafana win the final on a television in a bar on Johannesburg's Rockey Street, and soon the streets are wild with honking cars and dancing. Victory in the black man's game kicked over the goal line into white territory.

Later, after the Department of Home Affairs asks me to leave, I must follow history from afar, reading the country's runes through newsprint and screen, watching from a distance as this miracle turns out, like Francis Fukuyama's thesis, to be built on sand. Hope and forgiveness undermined by the impossibly complex tangle of history, inequality, violence, poverty, corruption, toxic social dynamics and structural under-education. When I revisit Bez Valley two decades later, the houses are neglected, subdivided and rented out to refugees from other parts of Africa. The paint peels off security gates under hoops of barbed wire. 'Zuma Denies Blocking State Capture Probe' shout the *Star* newspaper billboards outside the corner shop where I used to buy a single cigarette and a can of cream soda on my way home from work.

In 2016, I share a meal with old friends in Cape Town. They are people dear to me, although distanced by time and geography. In

1996 when I live in the servants' quarters behind their house, the recent trauma in their lives is unapparent to my naive twenty-three-year-old self. Just two years previously, a few months before 1994's elections, Rachel's sister Clare Stewart is found dead on the side of a road in rural South Africa. She is shot. An active ANC member, the family believe there is a political motive behind her killing.

She leaves two children, a boy, Themba, eight, and a little girl of fifteen months – Puleng, the little girl is called, Sesotho for 'blessing of rain'. Rachel is raising Puleng while her brother John raises Themba in Zimbabwe. I babysit, take her to the supermarket. The positive attention I get as the apparent parent of a mixed-race child in this, the newly minted Rainbow Nation, is an unexpected and guilty pleasure: 'Oo, isn't she gorgeous,' a fellow white shopper coos.

'Why are they called spring onions?' Puleng asks. 'Is it because they jump up?' Driving home, she winds the window down and sticks her head out, tongue lolling like a small dog. She runs around with a jumper on her head, pretending she has long, red hair instead of her beautiful fluffy curls. I love her.

In May 1997, Rachel and her brother Pete attend the TRC hearings in Mooi River. Clare's murder has not been solved, despite pressure from Amnesty International. Two decades later, I find the records of the hearing online. The commission hears a Zulu woman tell how her daughter was stabbed to death as she ran, her baby strapped to her back. Later Rachel and Pete describe what they know of Clare's murder. They have requests: could the Truth Commission find out where the presumed murder weapon, lost by the police, has gone? Could it obtain Clare's security file from the security police? And ask her ANC recruiters about her activities? The commission makes no promises.

At the TRC hearings, the spectral queue of victims is black, mostly male. White women, English and Afrikaans-speaking, peer at African society as if through smoked glass; they are complicit in apartheid. They do not protest or try to thwart it, even if they vote against it. Some, a vanishing few and one of my aunts among them, are on the other side of the glass, their lives braided with African lives through their choices of work, husband, home. As I look at this list of names, at Clare's, which glows like a small white daisy on a field of brown, I realise the road I have been travelling has taken me to an unexpected place.

Perhaps I start this book with the misapprehension that in retelling the long-forgotten stories of women, I am writing on the side of the oppressed, striking a righteous blow. But, as I walk down into the chasm of South African history, I find that in a country where race is the fulcrum to everything, writing about white women means writing about how they are the tools that keep the box of white dominance firmly shut. And, as I open my ancestors' graves, I find the screwdrivers in their hands.

III

Margaretha Retief

1787–1884

Give a girl an education and introduce her properly into the world, and ten to one but she has the means of settling well, without further expense to anybody.

Jane Austen, *Mansfield Park*, 1814

What some call the Cape gentry

Margaretha Louisa Retief. The cold dead hand at the centre of this book. Silent, un-memorialised. She could be another kind of silence entirely – an Emily Dickinson, hiding poems under her stinkwood bed – but then there are all those children, the immaculate gentrified life. The letter condemning the abolition of slavery. I am drawn to more itinerant souls – to her niece who takes off over the horizon, to Angela van Bengale – but it is Margaretha and her ilk whose lives shape my great-grandmother's and my grandmother's and so have a role even in mine, two hundred years later. This fathomless well of plenty, lined with the bodies of slaves, these rolling green vineyards tended by chained hands, bleeding from the tough stalks, stained deep purple. The imprint of servitude.

1 July 1811
A bright chill winter's day. The white of the Moederkerk in Stellenbosch is striking against the deep blue of the sky. The oaks planted by Simon van der Stel a hundred and thirty years before cast complex shadows on the dusty carriageways. A wedding is going on. The bride wears high-waisted muslin, a lovely blue mantle down her back. Her groom sports a cutaway coat, his hair tied back in a pigtail. We are here to witness the marriage of Margaretha Retief, aged twenty-four, to Gideon Johannes Joubert, aged twenty-nine. First cousins, the church teems with their blended families, pure Huguenots all of them. No one speaks French any more – favouring the creolised Dutch of early Afrikaans – but, still, they know who they are.

Margaretha's parents are here, and so too her brother Piet, not yet covered in blood. Piet has sold Gideon his farm on the outskirts of the thriving market town, and it is here they retire for the wedding party. Kromme Rhee lies seven miles north, a Cape Dutch mansion with six large windows across the front and intricate scrolling on the gabled facade. Lit only by mutton-fat candles, which cast a coarse, yellowish sort of light, men and women eat and dance all night, swigging local wine. Slaves have prepared a feast: ham, tongue, turkey, cakes, sweetmeats and game. The bride might be fashionably dressed, but she offers no genteel chat or refined feeling, laughing and applauding her husband's rough jokes. Drunk, ladies and gentlemen alike are given to indiscriminate kissing and worse. The party goes on into the following morning, and guests hang about for days.

This is an excellent time to be a Cape wine farmer, with preferential tariffs on Cape wine exported to Britain, and the couple's first years flow as smoothly as the Klippies River on its route down the east side of their farm. Newlywed, with the bloom of expectation on them, the Jouberts work hard. Travelling extensively in the Cape, German physician and explorer Heinrich Lichtenstein publishes *Travels in Southern Africa* in English in 1812. 'They are instructed in every branch of domestic economy necessary for forming good wives,' he says of Afrikaner women, praising their kindness tempered with resolution – thanks, he suggests, to the pastoral life and maintaining authority over servants and dependants. Equal to their brothers in inheritance and what education is available, Cape Dutch women will be influential in one of the most formative events of South African history. But to get there we must first track back to before Margaretha Retief's birth in the winter of 1787.

Sixteen years after Anna Siek dies, the quietude of the eighteenth century is giving way to the turmoil of the nineteenth. Everything will change. Railways, electricity, telegraph, telephones will come. White men will explore great tracts of – to them – dark continent, mapping the earth's surface as never before. Seventy million people will leave Europe to colonise other continents, disregarding existing inhabitants. Far away, on the southern tip of Africa, the ripples will break on the shores of the Cape, becoming great waves, ready to sweep away the Dutch and all their instruments.

For now, there is local trouble: skirmishes between settler, San and Khoikhoi to the north and north-east. But the amaXhosa offer the biggest challenge. Through the eighteenth century, people across southern Africa have more and more contact with European traders, settler and Xhosa people finally meeting at the Fish River, in the Zuurveld, the sour veld, in the Eastern Cape. Xhosa women grow corn, watermelons, pumpkins, tobacco and sorghum. For men, hunting is the thing. And cattle. They and the *trekboers* have this in common, their love of cattle. *Trekboer* evolves into Boer – Dutch for farmer – each holding huge farms on the eastern frontier. For a few years, amaXhosa and Boer rub along together, but in 1779 war erupts. The amaXhosa seize twenty-one thousand cattle before being massacred by a Boer commando. What follows is a hundred years of intermittent warfare, one of the most protracted battles against Europeans by African peoples. By 1787, the situation is so poor that the farmers call it a *stormjaar* – a storm year. Farms are ablaze, cattle stolen all along the frontier.

For Margaretha Louisa Retief, 1787 is anything but a *stormjaar*: born into the middle of the Cape winter, safe in the sheltered valleys of the Western Cape. She arrives on a thriving farm near Wagenmakersvallei (now Wellington) forty-five miles from the bustling port of Cape Town, where visitors complain of terrible roads and open sewage. Descended from successful Huguenot families, Margaretha's parents are wealthy, members of what some call the Cape gentry. They marry in 1772 near Paarl, then Jacobus hears that land further north is up for sale, with mountain grazing, water and deep black soil. And so Jacobus, his pregnant wife, Deborah, and their three children make the two-and-a-half hour move to De Krakeelhoek, renaming it Welvanpas. It marks the distance the colony has travelled in a hundred and fifty years, this journey from 'twist', or 'struggle', to 'well suited'.

Born in November 1780, the baby Deborah carries will become Piet Retief, Voortrekker hero and martyr, a leader in the Great Trek of the 1830s, which sees disgruntled Boers migrating eastward to escape British domination. There is disagreement about his actual birthplace, but the family are convinced that he arrives at Welvanpas – during the apartheid era, the precise birthplace of a pillar of Afrikaner mythology is important. During the recreation in 1938 of the Great Trek, which sees grown adults dressed in the bonnets and dresses of a bygone era board ox-wagons and travel over mountain and grassland to Pretoria, the ox-wagon representing the Retief Trek visits Welvanpas. A photograph exists still of the family solemnly arrayed on the *werf*, the wagon and historic homestead behind them.

But in 1780 the Great Trek of 1835 to 1840 and all that flows from it lies in the future and these are the Retiefs at Margaretha's birth in 1787. The little girl born when the days are warm but the nights cold and the mountains peaked with snow will live for ninety-six years, so long that a photograph of her exists as a very old lady. Her eldest brother, Francois, is thirteen, and future Voortrekker hero Piet, always a reckless charmer, is seven. Margaretha shares a bed with her sisters while the boys sleep in an outside room. They have a tutor and can read and write, and Margaretha dutifully embroiders her siblings' initials and dates of birth on a sampler. Welvanpas is a political household, and the children – especially Francois and Piet – soak it up, chewing the latest Company outrage over and over until only a piece of resentful gristle remains.

By now, the late 1780s, the Dutch East India Company – the most thrusting, vibrant business the world has ever seen – is a doddering corrupted dowager. After two centuries, her warehouses are decaying around her, rats eating the last of her measly stores, her overseers drinking themselves into a rule-bound stupor. The Anglo-Dutch war does for her in the end: the Company loses 43 million guilders, and operating loans wipe out the rest. The Dutch are jostled by the violent idealists of the French Revolution, and in the winter of 1794, as the French Revolutionary Wars drag their murderous carcass from city to city, French troops enter the Dutch Republic. The Orangists beg the British to protect their foreign assets, and the British, anxious to keep French hands off the strategic Cape port, agree.

Margaretha's world is the thatched farmhouse, the fields of wheat and vines, the occasional Sunday visits to church in Paarl. Sewing quietly in the corner, she hears talk of a king beheaded in France, soldiers fighting. In the crisp winter days of June 1795, stranger news arrives – British ships have sailed into the Cape harbour, and soldiers are fighting skirmishes behind Table Mountain. In September, as they plant lettuce and cucumber, the ground covered with small bright daisies, Margaretha's parents, her older brothers, even the slaves, are abuzz with the news. The British have taken the castle, the site of the VOC fort that Krotoa watched being built a hundred and forty years earlier, without a fight.

'The grey mare'

Margaretha's childhood is an ambiguous time at the Cape – the certainties of VOC rule punctured by the British arrival, the colony remaining in suspended animation until the British claim it as part of their empire in 1806. By now, Margaretha is nineteen. The Cape is strategically essential, especially during the Napoleonic Wars, and the British balance reform with placating the burghers. But the Afrikaners are thrown into an odd frontier zone – coloniser and colonised. We can hear their newly awkward position in the attenuated voice of a Scottish socialite, Lady Anne Barnard, who marries Andrew Barnard, a handsome soldier ten years her junior, when she is forty-two. Wresting an appointment for him as colonial secretary at the Cape from her high-placed friends, the couple arrive in 1797.

I am smitten with Lady Anne when I see her drawings of slave and Khoikhoi maidens at the Vineyard Hotel in Cape Town, and read Antjie Krog's interpretation of her life in poetry. She is a romantic figure, intelligent, attentive, opening the door onto Cape life at the turn of the eighteenth century. It is absurd, of course, to project oneself onto people from another age, and I am deflated when she turns her clever, cutting pen against the 'Dutch': 'Why cannot Englishmen enjoy their superiority as Englishmen, without eagerly marking to the Dutch how much they despise them?' she asks.

Lady Anne loves to denigrate the Dutch, for their missing front teeth, for their pride in their fat wives with large bosoms. But she admires the slaves, with their 'smooth clear copper skin, the timid but ill-behaved black eye . . . some yards of fine black hair, twisted up in a knot behind and secured with a gold bodkin,' adding ironically that if she spoiled one such, or a woman 'of half-caste' presumed to sit down in the presence of a Dutch person, 'I suppose I might as well get on board my ships and go to England next day; no Dutch person would speak to me again.' When her husband dies, Lady Anne brings his mixed-race daughter by a Cape slave back to Britain to live with her, a daring act in Georgian times. What the child's mother feels about the loss of her daughter, I cannot discover.

Lady Anne is charming, observant and entirely convinced of British superiority. From the moment the British arrive, the Afrikaner hears how stupid, ugly and outdated she and all Afrikaners are, how childish her language, how dull her society: Afrikaner identity evolves under pressure from British identity. As always, people feel the hurt of whichever loyalty is under assault, and rush to its defence. Patronised by the British as crass and barbarous, Afrikaners discover an unsuspected love for their fellow burgher, and Afrikaner women intensify their scorn against women lower down the pecking order: the slave women, the 'Hottentot' women they use to suckle their children.

To the Georgian chattering classes, then, to Lady Anne, the Cape Dutch are a backward sort of folk, their social lives confined to coffee, chat and family gossip. And, indeed, to Margaretha and Gideon, the world revolves around Kromme Rhee (although they think nothing of riding for three or four hours on a Sunday to visit family). Determined to establish their superiority, the British belittle Margaretha and women like her for sitting all day 'with her coffeepot constantly boiling before her', seemingly 'fixed to her chair like a piece of furniture'.

Whatever a superior Georgian lady might think, every human plays the lead in their own story and Margaretha's story is Kromme Rhee. Quiet now in the early days of marriage, it will soon be noisy with slaves, servants, children. Small and dark, with the narrow Retief face and close-set eyes, Margaretha keeps the keys to the house on a big ring attached to her apron. She is what Lady Anne refers to as 'the grey mare' – the better horse, in charge. As a Cape Dutch woman, governed by Roman-Dutch law, she can sign contracts, buy and sell property, open a shop selling eggs and fruit, start an inn to put up travellers, without the express consent of her husband. British women at the Cape, governed by British law, have much less power. Even so, as a married woman, Margaretha is a minor.

But she runs Kromme Rhee like 'a state in miniature': to either side of the front door are the front room and the main bedroom with highly polished yellow-wood floors and Dutch tiles in the porch. A wide central corridor leads to a second living room, more bedrooms and, finally, the kitchen, the engine room of the house, painted dark blue to discourage the flies. Slaves and older daughters rise before dawn to knead down the bread dough before baking it in an oven next to the open hearth. Even yeast is made at home. Margaretha and Gideon take a wagon into Cape Town to buy coffee beans, rice and great jars of spices. Meat is salted, smoked or pickled in vinegar. Yards of sausage are made with minced venison, pork, beef and spices, Margaretha supervising as the girls insert the mixture into cleaned pig's gut using a long-nosed sausage machine.

Margaretha's table is piled high with fruit: melons, grapes, mulberries, peaches. The slaves do the cooking, but Margaretha bustles in and out of the kitchen, directing the production of *kerri*, which must be curry: a stew seasoned with red pepper and ginger, flavoured with cucumbers and tamarinds, served with rice, *atjar* and sambals. Then there might be suckling pig or game, preserved fruits, pigeon pasties. During supper, slaves wave ostrich feather fans to keep off the flies. Margaretha scratches her favourite pointer between his ears, drops a morsel of meat into his mouth. Kromme Rhee swarms with dogs, large wolf dogs and smaller cabin curs, foxy faced, mangy and flea-ridden but helpful for hunting and driving off jackals at night.

Margaretha decides when animals will be slaughtered and butchered, producing hams to be hung on chains in the chimney to smoke, fat to be rendered down in a big pot over the fire. Soft fat goes in cooking, hard fat in soap and candles. They use the whole animal: curried tripe and trotters, sheep's head, brawn and offal. Every few months, Margaretha judges it to be soap-making time. Her daughters forage for the special bushes needed for their ashes, which are boiled and left to settle, leaving a lye solution. The hard fat is put in an enormous iron soap-pot with water and a little lye. This cooks for five days, stirred continuously by an unlucky slave. Salt is added to the sticky mixture, which separates, and when the pot cools, the soap is floating, ready to be cut into blocks.

Candles are easier: cotton wicks from worn-out sheets and the same hard fat, poured into a mould. Clothes are washed by hand, mended and ironed with hot coal irons. As Margaretha and Gideon prepare for bed, a slave brings them warm, soapy water in a half barrel and carefully washes their feet to protect the sheets. The slave does not have the luxury of sheets. In the summer, the heat and the flies are vicious. *Vliëebos* branches are hung to catch the flies, and clean cups and saucers are kept in a barrel of water to prevent fly-spotting.

All these jobs take a lot of work, many hands to hold and scrub and rub and melt and stir and pick and slice and weed and bundle, and the Jouberts do use their own hands; they are not lazy, but they also use the hands of slaves. More and more slaves, which seems short-sighted. After all, the British have abolished the importation of slaves, surely the writing must be writ large on the whitewashed walls of the *opstal*, that the practice of slavery itself is under threat? But no: within five years, Margaretha and Gideon own four people, bought from other Cape slaveholders, including Scipion, a coachman who shows off with the horses. In 1820, the first woman arrives: Carolina, a housemaid, joined by Samia a year later.

Margaretha is no warm-hearted mistress, a tense crackle of scorn accompanying her as she rustles into the kitchen and asks why the cast-iron pans have not been scrubbed out. But, in the afternoons, she sits with Carolina and Samia in the cool apartment at the back of Kromme Rhee, sewing, knitting or working on delicate embroidery. These enslaved people are feared and despised, but also needed, and even perhaps loved, especially by the children. Slave wet-nursing is falling out of favour, so Margaretha feeds her infants herself, Carolina and Samia saved that humiliation at least.

So many dead children

And there are a lot of babies to feed: Margaretha has one after another, year after year. The names blur into a Biblical litany, and I can't tell where a gap in the timeline might indicate a lost baby. Afrikaner women are proud of their large families, after all; motherhood is the heart of the homestead. Margaretha is creating the workforce, the riches, of the future.

When Margaretha has her first child, Deborah, she is twenty-five, competent, practical, an adult. But pregnancy still carries the malignant dread of hours of agony, or of delivering a dead baby, or of haemorrhaging to death. By now there are controls on midwives, and a midwifery school has been set up. The first Caesarean section performed at the Cape comes in 1826, with no general anaesthetic. But for Margaretha, if the baby fails to rotate in the birth canal, she faces hours of pain followed by the horror of the doctor piercing the baby's skull with a hook and removing the dead infant piece by piece.

Once a woman has given birth safely, the placenta is examined to ensure no pieces are left in the womb where they can cause infection, the childbed fever that still haunts all women. If the baby is premature, it might be swaddled in sheepskin, or placed in a cradle before the fire. Later Margaretha imagines Deborah falling into the fire, being trampled by a horse, or in bed with diphtheria, typhoid, smallpox – although this last is mitigated by the inoculation slowly becoming available. During Margaretha's lifetime, the stethoscope is invented, and anaesthesia (ether, and then chloroform) in the 1840s. Louis Pasteur's work on germs leads to cleaner hospitals; public health improves with better sewage systems and hospitals. Cape Town gets its first public hospital in 1818.

But at the beginning of the century medicines are botanical or contain mercury and arsenic; bleeding and emetic purges are still *en vogue*. So when little Francois, her seventh child, falls ill in 1830, aged four, with his forehead burning, a cough, his eyes red, Margaretha can only soothe his face with a cooling cloth, straighten creased bedclothes. When the red rash begins to spread three days later, the rock in her stomach gets heavier: *masels*. Everyone else is kept out of the sickroom, and Francois slowly begins to recover. One afternoon, Margaretha is showing Francois the ABC book with colourful pictures when she realises he cannot make his fingers pinch the pages.

'*Ek voel slaperig, Mamma,*' he murmurs. 'I'm sleepy, Mama.' Twelve hours later the child is dead.

Margaretha brushes his curls, dresses him in his little suit, his white blouse with its frilled collar, and his coffin is buried next to the house, the first grave in the little burial ground. I can't be sure, but when she falls pregnant just a few months later after a long gap and aged forty-three, I wonder if she is trying to replace a beloved last child, holding on to those glossy eyes, that pure affection, a little longer.

When Anna Elizabeth, aged thirteen, starts looking a bit peaky a year later, Margaretha's stomach tightens again. Past the age of eight, children are supposed to be less likely to die, and Margaretha has been teaching them to read and write, the girls to knit, sew and embroider, but poor Anna Elizabeth hasn't got the message. It is winter, the vines bare twists of red in the fields, the sky full of thick, grey cloud and driving rain. Even with fires in every room, the dampness seeps in. Heavily pregnant, Margaretha sits by Anna's bedside with her cross-stitch. A quiet child, given to sucking her thumb and reading in a corner while her brothers and sisters shout and fight, Anna slips away. Margaretha brushes and plaits her long hair, dresses her in her best dress, and now there are two graves in the little burial ground, two empty spaces in the house.

We are told women are silent in the historical record, as if in life, too, they were silent. Even the titan of Afrikaner history, Hermann Giliomee, stumbles here. The main reason women are ignored, he says, is because they left no written record, no diaries or letters. 'Historians have not deliberately suppressed the role of women in the history of the Afrikaners,' he continues, 'but because of the absence of documentation they have missed a lot.' Yet for this suppression to have been deliberate, it would have to have registered in the first place – instead there is total blindness to the patriarchy, which means glancing over women and seeing an empty space, as Danelle van Zyl-Hermann and Stephanie de Boer prove when they visit the Cape Town Archives Repository and discover letters and diaries written by Afrikaner women in the nineteenth century. These women are marked by fear and anxiety for their children, wrapped up with love, sadness and longing, unable to bond.

I find myself returning again and again to a comment from an early reader of this manuscript. 'There are so many dead children in this book,' he says, and I picture them all, baby after baby, child after child, and their mothers, stupefied by loss. It is not sentimental, this catalogue of bereavement; it is something much harder: Francois and Anna Elizabeth die just too early to be memorialised in the Victorian manner, where dead children are dressed in their best clothes, posed and photographed by a daguerreotypist, sometimes with their eyelids propped open with matchsticks.

This habit seems macabre to us, with our children protected by vaccinations and antibiotics. When women's stories are left for dead in the archive, we lose the grain of daily life and its losses. How they influence everyone's lives. These deaths come as a surprise because we have become complacent, smearing the past with the evasive term 'infant mortality'. And when our stories are forgotten it changes how we understand our bodies, explains how we end up lying down on a bed to labour and birth because it is the most convenient position for the doctor, even as it makes the whole painful process even more difficult.

I think about female lives, how even now a girl's life is punctuated by getting her period, every month swabbing blood from her inner thighs, trying not to smell, inserting cotton wool up her vagina. Then trying not to get pregnant, swallowing hormone after hormone, or having them injected, or a plastic coil inserted in her cervix. Or trying to get pregnant and blankly failing; or getting pregnant and miscarrying, more blood; or aborting, safely or dangerously but with niggling doubt. Or having the child, more blood, and a lifetime of worry and care. And so it goes on.

This is lived reality for all women, how life feels, what shapes it. Biology takes us over, and we are left coping. Women's lives have always included this endless round: recorded history, not so much. Elsje Cloete bled into her clothes, but Margaretha Retief hems old bits of linen and tucks them into her girdle, carries flowers to hide the smell. Underwear only begins later this century, so sometimes she leaves a bloody pad in her wake, fallen to the floor and shaming her with its stains.

A century of wrong

Within a decade of the British arriving at the Cape, the effects of colonisation are beginning to show up on the Afrikaner's skin: it seems browner, closer to the 'Hottentots'. What other explanation can there be for these 'Hottentots' being able to complain to the courts if their (white) employer beats them? It is an insult to the natural order! they complain. Margaretha and Gideon are outraged. To the wild, poor Afrikaner out on the eastern frontier – let's call him Freek – to this Freek, arrogant, aggressive, inclined to brutally assault his Khoikhoi vassals, it is an impossibility.

Freek, or Cornelis Bezuidenhout to give his full name, is charged with maltreating his Khoikhoi servant, Booi, and when he doesn't turn up at court a posse of soldiers, including twelve Khoikhoi, ride out to collect him. Confronted far up in the eastern hills, he hides in tumbled rocks, firing his weapon repeatedly until the soldiers shoot him dead. This is not the end of the spaghetti Western. In the next frame, Hans Bezuidenhout swears to avenge his brother's death. He rides across the dry, withered grasslands, gathering resistance against the British among the ragged frontiersmen with their mixed-race Baster women. But the rebellion is crushed by colonial troops at Slachter's Nek, and Hans dies, like his brother, resisting arrest.

When five ringleaders are hanged by the British, their execution sends shockwaves through the colony, many of whom are related to them. Nearly a century later, my great-grandparents publish a pamphlet on the eve of the Boer War: *Eene eeuw van onrecht*, or *A Century of Wrong*, a text that replicates Afrikaner nationalism long after the first flush of publication. In their words: 'It was at Slachter's Nek that the first bloodstained beacon was erected which marks the boundary between Boer and Briton in South Africa, and the eyes of posterity still glance back shudderingly through the long vista of years at that tragedy of horror.'

On Kromme Rhee, Margaretha and Gideon read the Cape Town newspapers avidly, discussing the crisis endlessly. Freek and Hans Bezuidenhout are extremists, but the Afrikaners are not happy now that British rule has begun to shake down through everyday life, now that the citadel of their privilege begins to tremble. The British phase out Dutch and old VOC structures, while Margaretha, Gideon and the other burghers resist the erasure of the Dutch language and demand bilingual education.

The arrival of the British spells the end for another key Cape institution: slave labour. With the passing of the British Slave Trade Act in 1807, the external slave trade comes to an end. All Cape slaves must now be born in the colony. And when the first large wave of British settlers arrive in 1820, they are not allowed to own slaves. In 1834, all slaves in the British Empire are emancipated, although they are indentured for four to six years.

In 1825, when the emancipation is in the air, and small rebellions have become more common, the most violent slave uprising occurs. Galant, a slave on a farm in the far reaches of the colony, persuades other slaves and Khoikhoi to rebel. Together they butcher the farmer and two other whites. Tried and convicted of murder, Galant and two others are executed. Reading the news, Margaretha shudders: what if January or Scipion, or even Carolina, takes a candle and sets fire to the thatch? Grabs the vegetable paring knife and stabs her or, worse, the tender baby flesh of her little ones? (Although slave women identify so deeply with the owner's household that they are often the ones who betray slave rebellions.)

She and Gideon are bitterly opposed to abolishing slavery, but they have no political representation through which to protest. The following winter, Margaretha urges Gideon to sign a letter, along with 114 other Stellenbosch burghers, objecting to slaves being allowed to testify without a burgher's say-so. Being only a minor, she can't sign the letter herself. The authors of this letter are heart-broken, put upon. How the Slave enjoys more privileges in this colony than his Master! They can't resist, these earnest authors, invoking the ever-popular image of a (coloured) slave violating vulnerable (white) women.

Not we, not we alone, but you all will weep over the Corpses of murdered Wife and Children. The flames of devastation will not alone destroy our habitations, but will also cause your Houses to fall to ruin! Not alone our Wives and Daughters, but also yours, will in a libidinous manner be prosecuted by our Slaves with rape and defloration . . .

In the end, it rains heavily for three days at the beginning of December 1838, when all the slaves are freed, and nobody is raped or murdered. Not yet, anyway. In Stellenbosch, Margaretha and Gideon's slaves join those who fill the Rhenish Missionary Society church on the town square to overflowing. Rosie, Abraham, Aron and the other Kromme Rhee slaves are free to leave, to live a life of their choosing. But Rosie, who sleeps in the kitchen, is attached to the Retiefs, even dour Margaretha. And where can they go? With no land, and few jobs not identical to the ones they already have, Kromme Rhee is home, with all its terrible contradictions.

It is shocking how little difference abolition makes; despite all the hopes, all the fears, the British are not about to hand over any actual privileges. Lack of access to land means Afrikaner farmers can force Khoikhoi and former slaves to work for them cheaply, entrenching the correlation of race and class. Nearly two hundred years after Angela manages to escape this suffocating correlation, it is about to spread right across South Africa, engulfing previously sovereign people with its noxious miasma.

Soon we will take a journey into the veld, into the ticking mechanism of South Africa's clock, watch the slow-motion cascade of slavery's abolition and Boer resentment at British arrogance spreading over the mountains and rivers. But, first, we must say goodbye to Margaretha Retief. It might seem a bit premature; she is only fifty in the late winter of 1838, which is when she receives news of her brother Piet out there past the mountains, by letter, or by word of mouth: whichever way, it is shocking news, news which we will learn soon enough.

As for Margaretha and Gideon, well, after abolition they remain, disgruntled but wealthy, on their homestead, a little more restrained in how they treat their former slaves. They read the Bible, write letters to relatives; Margaretha pets her dogs. She follows news in the paper, in letters, of the Voortrekkers and her Retief relatives across the horizon in their chaotic Republics, scoffing to Gideon about their termite mound ovens and their wild independence. Later, when she visits her daughter Margaretha Louisa and her husband at their smart townhouse in Cape Town, she notices the English ladies glance at her in the street, the slight raising of their upper lip as they look away.

In 1851, after forty years of marriage, Gideon dies, aged sixty-nine. Margaretha is sixty-four, young enough to help with children, to carelessly mention *Onze Jan* once or twice to her friends as they sew and gossip – 'our Jan', her grandson, Jan Hendrik Hofmeyr, first editor of *De Zuid-Afrikaan*, then MP for Stellenbosch, but most importantly in control of the Afrikaner Bond, the Cape Dutch political party. She keeps on living, roosting in the house of a grandchild, nodding by the fire in her black widow's weeds and white cap, sucking on a rusk softened in milky coffee. These anonymous *oumas* with their voluminous dark dresses are scattered throughout Afrikaans literature, busybodies in the late evening of their lives, poking their noses into everyone's business. Margaretha keeps living long enough to see my great-grandmother grow into a teenager, long enough to see the first trains steam into Stellenbosch, right up until 1884 when she dies, aged ninety-six.

~

Blank facades

In the nineteenth century, the Cape is tamed, the freedom of the early years solidified into a new country. Here a young white woman does not resist domestication – she aims for it. Land on a Monopoly square marked 'Kromme Rhee' and you win the game. Land on a Monopoly square marked 'Kromme Rhee' and you spend a lifetime reinforcing the box in which your luck came. But by the end of the twentieth century women's lives look very different and in London I am not feeling rescued by domesticity but trapped by it.

Exiled from Johannesburg, I have taken a long journey north across Africa, a journey which ends violently and abruptly in a hospital bed. But that is a story for another book and by 1998 I am in London where the rain falls, shopkeepers stare at my warm greeting and there is no cream soda in the chiller cabinet. Exile, noun, meaning: the state of being barred from one's native country, typically for political or punitive reasons. Or, a person who lives away from their native country either from choice or compulsion. Except I'm not really, am I? South Africa not being my native country, I cannot be in exile, so I consider that maybe it is more an affair of the heart, with me the errant wife, unable to cut my ties with home, but dreaming of an impossible other.

At this point, still believing I will be back in South Africa by Christmas, I enrol at journalism college where, asked our ambitions, I claim Africa correspondent and watch the contrails of aircraft mark the sky. Meanwhile more concrete seems to sprout overnight and passing cars and vans ruffle the litter as derelicts swig from cans of cider. There are lots of black faces here in Lambeth, amid the jumble of tower blocks and Russian immigrants, the fast-food chicken joints in red and yellow, betting shops in green. Young men in low-hanging trousers, neat women in shiny office-wear. I feel quite at home after Johannesburg, but really everything is different, with a hard urban edge and no warm laughter.

The most useful thing I learn, the most useful skill, turns out to be shorthand. Every week a forthright elderly woman turns up and teaches us this old-school code, every day we practise from tapes, fill reporter's notebooks, squiggles and wriggles becoming more fluid until we are flying, a hundred words per minute. Forget the vowels, it's all about the consonants, l bt th cnsnnts – difficult sometimes, to remember what the vowels were, if your notes sit too long, meaning evaporating off the page like invisible ink. We learn other things too: courts, government, libel, but I can't say how much of that sticks. We don't learn anything about big data sets, how to analyse them; or how to make a jigsaw of people's lives from social media. Those things are all just over the horizon, like the imminent demise of the very industry for which we are training.

It's another patch of misspent youth that comes in technicolour, life spending itself in white nights touched with neon, where passing cars leave trails of light in their wake, night buses hissing by in the rain, heading for Clapham, or Crouch End, or Kensington. The taste of absinthe, the dregs of the early hours. I am big-hearted, but still ignorant, othering young black Britons by asking them where they are from, in my selfish quest for a connection to Africa, to South Africa; not understanding when they bristle, or hiss like a threatened cat. A friend gives me a pool cue, but it's already a symbol of something gone because here the pool halls are snooker halls, the tables are enormous, and I am where I come from, too posh, too female, to fit in.

And then it's out into the world. This is England, 1999. Conservative, although Labour's in power. A country obsessed with bands I have never heard of, the Spice Girls, Oasis: I've missed Cool Britannia and the country has moved into a nebulous end-of-history era. I join an Amnesty International group, but instead of righteous young men there are older women, painstakingly sending letters to generals who don't care. At the newspaper we share an email address, Ask Jeeves what he thinks; sit for hours in the wood-panelled magistrates' court staring blankly at the words wrapped around the royal coat of arms – *honi soit qui mal y pense*, and *dieu et mon droit*. Or does the coat of arms hang in the council chamber, where grey-haired councillors in sensible shoes repeat themselves ad nauseam?

Meanwhile, bored teenagers set cars ablaze in a belch of black smoke, residents campaign against streets smeared with dog faeces, and beneath it all is the dull noise of a society functioning, roads being resurfaced, children taught, sewers replaced. (We still haven't grasped that our entire way of life is burning through resources that will soon be gone: clean air, soil, clean water.) It's all sclerotic, rusted up.

I grasp at any South African connection. When a street is named after Donald Woods, the newspaper editor immortalised in the film *Cry Freedom*, I dial for an interview, humbled by the self-deprecating South African voice that greets me. (It is another twenty years before I find a link to Donald Woods through a Xhosa girl brought to England by my Quaker relatives in 1932. Nontando Jabavu writes a weekly column for Woods's *Daily Dispatch* in 1977, the year that Steve Biko dies.) In the evenings, I drink wine at the kitchen table as night grows outside, emailing into the past, casting a skein down the continent of Africa. But something ties me here and as I try to work towards return I only pull the knots tighter.

How much of life is intentional, how much the result of hidden habits, bubbling up to push our hand towards yes, or no? I ask this of myself now, but I didn't ask it then, when the time was coming that I might consider marriage, I won't say 'or at least a long-term future' because really it was never going to be anything other than marriage, what with the long line of ancestral couples standing behind me, sentinel messengers receding into the past – this is how you do it, they whisper; this is how you live.

But even if that part of things is predetermined, the choice of partner is still a thing, still a vital question, even this late in the game, as all the women before have found, not that we think about any of this as we recognise each other across the floor of the council chamber. He is reading – *Sweet Thames*, the book is called, after the effluent of the nineteenth century as it turns out, but I can never after see the River Thames without calling it that name, this river which rises in the Cotswold Hills and empties into the North Sea near Gravesend, this river with its ever-changing flow, owned by the diminutive, the familiarity.

We marry in 2003, everyone dissolving into giggles as he pronounces my unwieldy Afrikaans name. We are given a bottle of *Vin de Constance*, that sweet Cape wine first fermented by Elsje Cloete's great-grandson, squat and dark with a thick wax seal, and in the kitchen of our London flat I split the wax, pour myself a glass and take a small mouthful of the wine, unctuous and golden. Identity, *terroir*.

After that there are still nights where I imagine us there, but it's getting harder and harder to find a way back and soon enough, eight years after I leave South Africa, I find myself fixed by biology, by a baby in her crib. Time flows on, inexorably, but I am fixed like a stone on the riverbed, moss growing on my rounded flanks, trapped inside the house, domesticated. The current of workers, students, others on the move flows over and around me as I sit, learning how life will be.

In those early weeks, my mother hands me two slim notebooks, one she had kept for me and one her South African mother kept for her, and I too start a journal of baby's weight, sleep patterns, feeding. Later, when a friend pages through the three generations of notebooks and asks, 'But why keep them?', I am unable to answer him, ashamed of female labour expended on this apparently pointless task. It seems like nothing, mothering: something natural, innate, but it needs to be taught and learnt. When she has her first child, my grandmother Cato labours thousands of miles away from her own mother; by the time my mother has my older sister, Cato has died: neither has a maternal guide.

Cato turns to Truby King's baby-care bible, *Feeding and Care of Baby*. Mr King suggests that baby should be breastfed every four hours and only cuddled for ten minutes a day. My mother follows another expert, Dr Spock, and the path left by Cato – these notebooks represent painstakingly gleaned experience. As for me, well, Gina Ford's *The Contented Little Baby Book* is *en vogue*, but it is my mother who suggests the regular feeding intervals that save my sanity.

What passes from generation to generation? Tastes: the *Cookery Book for South Africa*, passing from my great-grandmother to my grandmother to her cook, who feeds the *bobotie* to my mother, who in turn feeds it to me. These first sensory memories, their smell and taste, are potent, but there are other ties we can barely feel, soft, subtle and strong as spider's silk. I imagine them weaving from branch to branch of the family tree. How to fold sock balls, chop onions without tears; how to feed, burp, sleep a baby; how to hold a family together through shared meals.

And other traits: how to avoid visitors, how to slide away from a husband's demands without conflict. That reading is next to godliness, but hands don't necessarily need to be washed. And that most unbreakable habit, that caring for children is the most important role you will ever play. Isie Smuts asks her daughter Cato in 1932: 'Such a child gives one much pleasure, doesn't he? How did you ever do without him?'

I see my mother in the kitchen back in 1980, purple syrup dripping from a muslin cloth suspended over a bowl. It is the beginnings of blackcurrant jam. We live in rural Hampshire, and she grows the blackcurrants herself, keeps bees, cultures yoghurt. She cuts our hair in strange shapes and makes our clothes. She is always there, always at home, in the house, just as her mother had been. (Until she escapes in the evenings to night school, studying O-level sciences, A-level, and a path reveals itself.) I see us all at once: myself, my mother, her mother, her mother's mother. The story repeats itself again and again.

Born in 1973, not 1870 or 1904, I am schooled for a career; it is how I understand my life. So it is a shock when those sweet dependents arrive, with all the attendant conflicting emotional and financial needs. During these years, I flail between joy and despair, exiled from my old life, and, even now, grey misery laps at the corners of my mind at the memory of bleak hours at the playground, pushing swings. Empty afternoons breastfeeding the baby while the toddler plays on the floor; trapped in what novelist Doris Lessing calls 'the Himalayas of tedium', excluded from the challenging, stimulating world of work.

But the truth is that work has sloughed off much of her glamour by the time baby arrives, revealed herself as a dowdy drudge, typing mechanically onto a screen wiped clean every night. And our kind, patient childminder costs so much I am almost paying to work. I cut my hours back. 'Don't you get bored, stuck at home all day?' someone asks, and I think of walking home from the playground, how my three-year-old daughter skips, inexpertly, how the skip runs down her arm into the buggy like an electric shock, while her sister, strapped in, eyeballs an approaching buggy, gazes locking as their steeds pass, latter-day jousters, how the spring light fizzes around our heads. We are outside hours, beyond clocks, unmoored from ambition, invisible from without. A little world all our own, of soft flesh, mashed carrots, nappies, singing.

At eighteen months, my elder daughter is taken into hospital with pneumonia; after a week she is transferred to another hospital, has chest drains inserted under general anaesthetic, intravenous antibiotics. At night she can't sleep without me and I push my hospital trundle up against her cot, hold her hand, lie awake. We follow her, holding the container of fluid connected into her chest by a thin plastic tube, as she trots around the ward, bashes at a Bob the Builder workbench that has lost all its sounds and most of its accessories. Nauseous, I take a pregnancy test in the hospital bathroom. My mother cancels a flight to the USA to hold my daughter as her tiny chest is X-rayed, to avoid damage to the foetus inside me.

I read so many women's words to write this book, converse with them silently, and sometimes I come up against a phrase that keeps me awake at night, so that I must walk around it, poke at it. Here is one, from a hugely intelligent book, the comment that babies are 'resolutely unmodern'. I poke at this idea, imagine small but immensely strong babies, resolute in that soft flesh, a surreal conception. Is the author writing tongue in cheek? Are babies unmodern because they are flesh and blood? Am I not fit for the modern world because I love mine? Is it because they are animals? Untamed? Because they demand attention and care, cannot be switched off? Or because they do not fit the late capitalist model where every moment is a potential moment of production, every human a potential means of production?

What this phrase says to me, why it frightens me, is that modern life is not fit for humans: it does not fit *us*; we try to fit into it. If babies are resolute about anything, it is the unconscious expression of their own humanity, how they demand that we answer with the humanity in ourselves, connect ourselves into the enriching network of others. The same author, searching for her biological clock, frets over the potential loss of time expended on the exhausting mundanities of care and I want to tell her: this is all true, all true. But children repay that labour, that time, even that dreadful sapping boredom, a thousand times over; can help connect you into life itself, into its cycles, its ebb and flow. Beyond the modern. In the long run, even if it doesn't feel like it when you are wiping down the high-chair, or a small bottom, life is enriched, varied, connected.

Umuntu ngumuntu ngabantu. I am because we are.

None of this helps when I am struggling with early motherhood. 'When are you going back to work?' my father asks, and my stomach clenches with failure. Like most misery, it doesn't last forever, it only feels like it as I wait by the swings, a riot of yellow plastic, enviously watching the woman with older children as she reads her book. Later that's me, kissing the grazed elbow brought for my inspection before the child runs off and I return to my inner world. But for a few years I feel milky as a dairy cow, and for some people – single women humming with desire in make-up and heels; the wet-lipped old man who asks me, 'What've you got in there? A litter?' – I have lost all purpose.

I am in a different world and the lines of communication have all been cut. It is a world of bodily fluids and cuddles, small warm bodies in our bed, the boundaries between humans erased. I am constantly interruptible, juggling frying pans as a small person hangs from my leg crying with angry hunger, as I pull down my trousers in the bathroom with a twenty-pound baby on my hip. No wonder people can't be bothered with me: there is no space for anything beyond biology.

There's a miscarriage in these years, spotting on my knickers in Warsaw Airport, growing to gouts of blood by the time we are circling Heathrow. My girls watch the Penguins of Madagascar happily on an iPad while I lie on a gurney behind a flimsy curtain. 'Smile and wave, boys,' says a plump anthropomorphised penguin, sleek in his feathers. 'Smile and wave,' as the sonographer slaps cold gel on a large white wand.

'No heartbeat,' she says two minutes later, as if she is bored by the whole situation. As we leave, the girls swoop down the wide blue corridors before me like seagulls.

I have a whole new society to navigate, ocean charts laid out before me: playgroups, vaccinations, huge decisions and me, unfettered by knowledge. I choose this; I choose to step out of the world of work. But it is lonely, and erasing, and I wonder now, not about whether women should choose to have children or not, but why, when we do, we still struggle to be fully functioning members of society? And, also, why my husband should bear the burden of breadwinning alone, exiled from his children's lives? From muffled sleep, I hear the front door shut as he leaves for work, only to open again as the evening bath water runs into the tub, making the plastic Dora the Explorer dance.

I think again of Doris Lessing. Later a Nobel Prize winning novelist, she grows up stifled and white in Southern Rhodesia in the 1920s. To escape, she leaves two children behind, aged eight and nine, and moves to London. She marries twice, has multiple affairs, is an active Communist. But how unhappy she always seems. In 1947 Lessing writes: 'I haven't yet met a woman who isn't bitterly rebellious, wanting children, but resenting them because of the way we are cribbed, cabined and confined.' How much has changed in the intervening decades?

We all muddle through, trying to find balance and stimulation or at least financial stability in those blank early years. The children develop, flourish; we learn, become mothers, and life grows back, even if motherhood still too often excludes women from the chance of worldly success. (Not Lessing: she writes eight books in that first decade as a single mother in London – but how restive she is in her freedom!)

By the time my third child arrives, I have become other to what I was, and he is strapped to me, even as I visit the renowned poet who supervises my master's dissertation. She eyes him doubtfully and later: 'Your baby is very good,' she says in surprise. Good, (adj.) meaning: to be desired or approved of, or, having the desired qualities, of a high standard. If the required standards are to be unobtrusive – let's face it, probably a prerequisite for an infant in a master's supervision – then he is. I am relaxed; we're in physical contact and he's only three months old.

But I am still looking for some way back into the world, some way forward out of the swamp. I have not forgotten South Africa, the impossible other, and take annual trips south, arriving in a shiny new airport, twenty-first-century anonymous and full of sleek Africans. But still there are the old difficulties, and on the plane the air hostess addresses me in Afrikaans – in this country no one could even consider the end of history.

Back home, I peruse family histories with their hand-drawn diagrams, spend weeks espaliering the Afrikaner tree, hampered by the reuse of names down the generations and serial marriages in the early years. I pilfer books from relatives, order reprints of Dutch East India Company records, click through shipping lists, genealogical webpages, deciphering texts with my rudimentary Afrikaans. No longer is the past another country. It loops the world in little packets from Iceland to New Zealand, open to anybody with an internet connection.

The books on my shelves pile up like silt and my internet history fills screen after scrolling screen. But even if Facebook can access the secret stacks where our psyches are stored, surveillance is only as good as its record keepers. In the seventeenth century these are few, and those there have quills, paper and a filing system. Which rules out women, and slaves, and people other than whites, who are seen only through the occasional scratchings of others. Nevertheless, slowly, painstakingly, I uncover women, unearth a chain of voices – mother after Afrikaans mother slotted where they belong, in their homes.

I am not the only one who struggles with domesticity: in 1911 Olive Schreiner, South African and friend of my great-grandmother, publishes *Woman and Labour*, rage burning off the page as she characterises women as 'parasitic', trapped at home by the Industrial Revolution, reliant on their bodies as sexual and maternal vessels. This book inspires my Quaker great-aunt, Alice Clark, to write a seminal feminist text, *Working Life of Women in the Seventeenth Century* in 1919. I order a copy. Women were more part of the economy when a household system of production was in place than in industrial systems, Alice writes, and I think of Anna Siek and Margaretha Retief toiling away behind the veil of history at the means of production, the wine and wheat farms.

Finally, I realise it doesn't matter if I feel one way or another about these women, because I bring different tools to the table: tin openers when they have only preserving jars; washing machines when they have mangles. I am trapped only by motherhood; these women by custom, law and the entire structure of society. Even in 1928, my grandmother is legally barred from working as a teacher after marriage. A hundred years later women's problems are the same, and different. We are no longer 'parasitic', but neither are we entirely part of the economy, carrying the double burden of work both outside, and inside, the home.

It is a troubled love triangle, this relationship between women, home and children, and central to all our lives. Still, I wonder if houses are not just where tradition lives, if they are places where change can live, where we can begin to create the lives we need: white and patriarchal, or neither of those things.

Western Cape, 2017

My husband sighs when I suggest visiting living history sites, weary of my fascination with the homes of the past, and I wonder if this response resides in his gender, women being more interested in these buildings that house our history since we were so long exiled from those other buildings, the offices, the banks, the Houses of Parliament.

I am on a journey, a pilgrimage perhaps, a journey that is geographi-
cally short but temporally almost impossible. Except we can all recognise a home, the place of a woman in that home. I am here to poke
at that relationship, at these Cape women and their refuges, their
cages, at their copper kettles and giant soap pots. I wonder, too, if I
am here to make excuses for my own domestic entrapment.

House: not only a building for human habitation but also a verb,
an active process of providing shelter or accommodation, which is
what women have done. And also: to provide space for, contain or
accommodate. 'What does it mean,' Antoinette Burton asks in
Dwelling in the Archive, 'to say that home can and should be seen not
simply as a dwelling-place for women's memory but as one of the
foundations of history – history conceived of, that is, as a narrative, a
practice, and a site of desire?'

Just north of where Somerset West sprawls along the N2 motorway
strip, Vergelegen is an easy day trip from Cape Town, if ease is what
you are looking for. The house wallows in its manicured lawns, its
agapanthus and hydrangeas, and visitors stroll in the shade of the giant
camphor trees with their swollen trunks planted by Willem Adriaan.
Looking towards the mountains, you can't see the upmarket housing
estates that border Vergelegen, encircled with walls and razor wire,
more springing from the ground from year to year like dragon's teeth.

The house is grand in the Cape Dutch way, with glossy dark wood
floors and ceilings. Cool in the heat of the day. The view astonishes,
the mountains in the blue distance. 'Imagine,' my husband says,
'choosing to put this house here when there was nothing else around.'
The hexagonal garden remains, laid to flowers, the sturdy wall still
enclosing it, but Anna Siek spent time in the kitchen, squabbling
with the *knechten*.

Lunch is an incongruous picnic at a table under the trees, all the
servers black, all the customers white, and *Amandla awethu*, I think,
the old ANC rallying cry. Power to the people, which is still not true,
especially not here, on this estate owned by Anglo American, one of
the world's largest mining companies. Vergelegen has become a theme
park, a playground designed for the global rich. There are displays in
the house, a timeline of ownership, Anna Siek, properly recognised,
although the guide on duty has no idea to whom I am referring. And,

such are the times, there are the slaves of the house, their names listed on the ceiling. Here, too, are photographs of the great and the good, hosted by Anglo American (the Clintons, Nelson Mandela, Queen Elizabeth II), giant corporations knowing on which side to butter their bread.

Cape houses were initially a maximum of three rooms in a row, walls of rubble or clay and lime mortar rendered from seashells. As settlers grew and prospered, they built grander homes with gables and wings on each end to produce an H shape. Outbuildings appeared: stables, coach-houses, wine cellars, slave quarters. And the whole homestead surrounded by a whitewashed wall: the *opstal*, this image of perfect security.

In Dorothea Fairbridge's *Historic Houses of South Africa*, published in 1922, I find a preface written by my great-grandfather. It contains some fine ironies of time and change. 'This South Africa of ours lies far from the Europe to which she is, for the greater part, only a name, and her history but a vague impression, but she has a story of which no country need be ashamed,' he writes. Wishful thinking aside, he hails Cape architecture as South Africa's one contribution to the Arts: 'Neither in Music nor in Literature nor in Painting nor in Sculpture have we anything yet to compare with the performance of older countries. The one exception is our domestic architecture, and there our production is of a unique character.' The old Cape Dutch houses are indeed great beauties, with their whitewashed facades and ornate rounded gables. The eighteenth-century houses take their inspiration from the townhouses of Amsterdam, but they have echoes of the VOC's sojourn in Indonesia. These gorgeous estates are central to the Cape's tourist trail: in the winelands around Stellenbosch and Franschhoek you can't move for fine dining, spas, luxury suites.

But this beauty unsettles; its languor disturbs. To reach Vergelegen from Cape Town, you take the N2 over the Cape Flats and past the airport, driving through townships: Langa, Gugulethu, Khayelitsha, housing set two hundred feet back from the road – alleged to be the furthest distance a stone can be thrown. Sometimes at night, obstacles are thrown onto the motorway to puncture the tyres of passing motorists who, pulling over, will be robbed or worse. (In 1710, those travelling this route run the gamut of leopards and vengeful slaves.)

More than a million people live in these shantytowns, drawn across the Fish River by the lure of work after the end of apartheid. In Khayelitsha, a quarter of households do not have electricity; each outdoor tap shared by twenty families, each toilet by ten in this place where the speed of growth and fifty per cent unemployment means gang-rule, with four murders a weekend.

Just a few miles away, Vergelegen swills with wealthy whiteness. But it is not poverty that keeps black guests away, or not only. Vergelegen, Groot Constantia, Boschendal are all part of South Africa now, but these mansions represent Europe on African soil, with all the confusion and pain that go with it. The settlers might have been building houses in the best way they knew. Still, they were also importing home to a place – to them – of wilderness and savagery, importing European art and design, symbols of European civilisation; inevitably and unthinkingly also symbols of European superiority over Africa. Of domestication.

Other realities lurk here: Cape Dutch homes were built with the unpaid coerced labour of slaves. The great medieval cathedrals of Europe were built by low-paid labourers, but those differences have been absorbed. Inequality persists, but with no easy way to check if those in poverty now descend from those in poverty five hundred years ago. In South Africa, you can be sure that someone of colour built Vergelegen, brick by brick, overseen by someone white. But it is another truth which slithers away between the neat rows of grape vines: for centuries the people, enslaved or otherwise, who grew the vines, harvested the grapes, pressed the wine, all these people were given wine throughout the working day. And these daily 'dops' drove them into alcoholism, fracturing communities in a terrible circle of dependence. Even today coloured communities in the Western Cape struggle with alcoholism, with some of the highest rates of foetal alcohol syndrome in the world.

Is this what I was expecting to find at Vergelegen? An entrapped woman, trapping black and brown in the mesh of white dominance? Isn't that what homes do – teach us who we are supposed to be, these homes that we find ourselves trapped inside, by society and by ourselves? Anna inculcates the racial order in her children, reinforcing and reinforced by society, domesticates the African landscape, because the public and the private, the outer world and the home, are in constant communication. Even if women are silent in the historical record, they are not silent in their homes, which is where children grow up, and adults live.

In search of more understanding, I continue this tour, visiting the blank facades of long-dead women, trying to scrape the whitewash from the historical record, because after Anna Siek came more and more, these women entrenched in their homes, comfortably trapped. And perhaps more so than any other is Margaretha Retief; more than any of the other women with whom I acquaint myself, she is defined by the home. First Welvanpas, where she receives her training in the arts of the *boerevrou* – the farmer's wife – and then Kromme Rhee, where she puts her training into practice.

It is an hour's drive up the R44 from Vergelegen to Welvanpas, lined with plush green vineyards. The farm is signposted from the main road, a bunch of grapes against the faded brown indicating a tourist hotspot, and blue-overalled farm women bend in the vines as we drive past, rising to smile broadly and wave. It is smaller than I expect, the *werf* where the house sits narrow against the hillside, and humbler, the buildings patched, white paint dull with age and dust. Despite the heritage signage, the coffee shop advertised on the perpetual present of the internet is closed, the small children's play area overgrown with weeds and even the vines seem patchy, although the internet claims they produce award-winning wines from the same hillsides as they've done for the past three centuries.

We park, uncertain. Wander around sheepishly on what might be private property. There is no one here any more. My mother, undaunted by her seventies, walks up towards the house, hallooing. Summoned, another old woman emerges. Or perhaps she was on her way out anyway, car keys in hand. Before I have caught up, they have discovered relatives in common, although not the ones I thought they would. Family gossip flows between them, some vestigial stream brought to life.

She is *Mevrou* Retief, last perhaps to bring her children up in this farmhouse that has seen two hundred years of Retief families grow to adulthood. 'My husband died seven years ago,' she says. 'I live by myself here now.' She has some damage to her left eye and repeatedly reaches up to replace her sunglasses where they slip off, keeps lapsing into Afrikaans. 'I speak English so rarely now – it gets rusty.' Her son still farms Welvanpas, but he does not live here. In my mind's eye, I see the bustling house of the past, the industrious kitchens, the vines heavy with grapes, the hams on hooks in the *vleiskamer*, the meat room. She reaches for her mobile phone. 'I have no landline; they stole the cables,' she says matter-of-factly. 'I don't think they will even bother replacing them. Agh, these terrible times we live in.' She seems resigned rather than worried and then, as an afterthought, 'For you too. I feel so sorry for that Mrs May; she walks so like this, so stooped.'

These homesteads do not offer a way in, only the closed door of history because between then and now there has been a great ebb and flow of female agency. Alice Clark's thesis that women have not always been as they are in the twentieth century is widely held to be true, but whether that position is better or worse is debated. Alice suggests that before the Industrial Revolution takes men off the land into factories and wage labour, women are more socially and economically active within the household economy, even if oppressed by the patriarchy. Yet she is blind to those working-class women who move into waged work thanks to the Industrial Revolution (in textile factories and potteries, down mines) and so become more independent of the home.

Alice might have pinned this sea-change to the 1600s, but more recent historians identify it as coming later and less suddenly, in the late 1700s and early 1800s, and out here, at the far reaches of Empire, in agricultural, pre-industrial Afrikaner society, perhaps it comes later still, with the discovery of diamonds, gold, coal, and the harnessing of black labour in the late 1800s, when white women's agency shrinks to a puddle of boredom inside a carpeted bungalow. But tides turn, and this way of life, too, is in decline, as white people are, challenged by the new black South African state. I turn this idea in my mind, considering that decline, its glacial pace: women still earn less than men and homes continue to represent the female realm; black South Africans' wages still come to less than twenty per cent of white wages.

We visit Kromme Rhee a few days later. It is a confusing journey with few landmarks along the nondescript roads with vineyards to either side. Away from the tourist hub of Stellenbosch, there are no other cars, except the occasional white *bakkie*. We turn left between two rows of trees, dip down into a comforting hollow and over a stream. The sunlight spangles the dust beneath the branches. Here a boom bars our way. It is strangely fortified for a provincial training college. Two uniformed and armed men emerge from the gatehouse in surprise. They were not expecting anyone. No entry to the past.

The puzzled guard tries unsuccessfully to read my British driving licence with an electronic reader. After a couple of minutes, he gives up and raises the boom. We are not sure of our destination but drive forward up the dust road. Suddenly Kromme Rhee appears across a flat expanse of lawn, unapproachable through the high fence. Restored in 1950, since 1964 the farmhouse has been used as a training centre for farmworkers. There is nobody here; we have arrived at this point in the past on a public holiday, making it a site where ghosts seem to float.

It has a beautiful aspect, this rise with the mountains in the distance and trees filling the dip below where the stream runs. The farmhouse has the traditional Cape Dutch whitewashed walls and green trimmed windows and doors. It is a long horizontal building, symmetrical, with three large sash windows to either side of the front door. The gable over that door loops in exquisite scrolls. If we could get closer, we could see the date painted on the frontage: 1759. Instead, we listen as the cicadas whirr and I wonder at how our next companion will abandon all this, this dream of the perfect *opstal*, to head off into the blue interior. How she will leave the cicadas to their whirring as she hauls her wagon over mountains, kicking over the traces of the domestic.

IV

Anna Retief

1797–1891

History is what is left in the sieve after the centuries have run through.

Hilary Mantel, Reith Lecture, 2017

In their ox-drawn kakebeenwaens

Graaff-Reinet, 1837
Four hundred miles east of Cape Town. Anna Elizabeth Retief lifts
the mammoth leather-bound Bible from the wagon seat and leads her
family back into their empty farmhouse. She reads from the Holy
Book one last time, invoking the word of God to bless everything
they are leaving behind, everything to come. The wagons roll out,
leaving the farmhouse empty except for dust.

Born into the same century, town and family as Margaretha Retief,
Anna shares her aunt's looks, the long nose and close-set eyes under a
low brow. A ranking member of the Cape gentry, secure in the
embracing vineyards of Stellenbosch, Margaretha is too comfortable
to become a Voortrekker. But in 1838, she shares the fury that sends
one of her brothers to a death so bloody that he goes down in the
annals of Boer history, and her niece Anna right across the breadth of
the African continent. Anna is the other side of the coin, the other
Afrikaner woman. One stays in the sheltered valleys of the Western
Cape for ninety-seven years, the other abandons her home in middle
age, takes her ox-wagon and crosses the frontier into the unmapped
interior.

For the Afrikaners, the Great Trek is nothing less than the origin
of their nationhood: they are brave and determined pioneers, set on
a Promised Land where they can exercise their freedom. (For the
African people living in central and eastern South Africa, the Great
Trek marks the end of independence and the start of dispossession.)
Trek heroes are all men, bearded pioneers with horses and guns,
staring into the blue distance: Gerhard Maritz, Andries Potgieter, Piet

133

Retief, Andries Pretorius. Town after town is named for them, statue after statue raised. These stubborn men set off with no clear idea of where they are going or what they might do when they get there. They are looking for personal freedom, not a better society, but their bravery, their resilience and independence, are enough for the Afrikaners.

Women are not, however, the meat in a vegetarian diet and Voortrekker women heave wagons across mountains and rivers. A British settler on the Eastern frontier observes of the trekkers 'the women seem more bent on it than the men'. Piet Retief might be the martyr, but Anna is the indomitable settler. For an Afrikaner woman, home is her kingdom; children, slaves and servants her subjects. When the Khoikhoi are made equal to the white man, when the slaves are freed, her authority shrivels horribly. Add to this negative impulse to escape a positive one: for an energetic, adventurous woman in the early nineteenth century, what a chance, what an exercising of will, a kicking against impotence.

And Anna Retief, unusually, leaves behind something that renders her visible. It comes to me by a circuitous route, Anna's story, with no original, or rather several originals, all now lost. Written for a daughter, left behind in Graaff-Reinet, or a son, isolated on an Orange Free State farm, what I am left with, or what I manage to retrieve, is a manila booklet published by the University of Natal in 1939. *Die Dagboek van Anna Steenkamp* reads the cover, *The Diary of Anna Steenkamp*.

Anna Retief chooses speech over silence. I consider how unusual she is and how, in this at least, she relates to that other Anne, Lady Anne Barnard, who leaves behind letters and diaries, claims her place in the public realm: I can find these women because they leave pieces of themselves behind. Choosing speech, they stand as representative for all the silent women, and yet they are different.

Anna Retief speaks to her daughter, her son, but she wants her life recorded, to be heard. Who listens? The *dagboek* is quoted again and again for her justification of the Great Trek: the abolition of slavery. 'It was not so much the liberation that we drove away,' she writes in her account begun in 1843, 'but the equation with whites, which is contrary to both the laws of God and the natural distinction of race and religion . . . wherefore we rather withdraw in order to preserve our doctrines in purity.' She takes herself into exile, trying to find a place to feel at home. To try to escape equality with brown people by journeying into an area populated by other brown people is not only vile but ridiculous. And how much of this is outrage at being under the thumb of the British?

Historians seize upon Anna's text, which they can see, and hold. They use it to remake the past. I seize upon it and follow another thread as it weaves the tapestry of the new nation. In tapestry, the weft threads are the colourful ones, the ones that make up the vista. The warp threads are hidden, secretly at work behind the arras. Men are weft, women warp, but here is Anna, grasping the weft. She steps outside the home, travels through the world, hijacks the male narrative.

Born in 1797, just a few miles from ten-year-old Margaretha, Anna's father is Margaretha's brother, and her mother Gideon's sister, a double niece perhaps, one of those close blood relationships in which Afrikaners specialise. But at thirteen Anna moves with her family to Graaff-Reinet, an unsettled rebellious place far out on the eastern frontier, the end of the universe, weeks from Cape Town by ox-wagon. Place of thirst, the Khoikhoi call the semi-desert – the Karoo. Dry scrubland stretches for miles out towards distant mountains, and at night the sky is crystalline with stars. At fifteen, Anna marries Johannes Hattingh, twenty-five, and they have eight children. Later, her widowed father remarries, his new wife a sister of the Voortrekker leader Gerhard Maritz. I watch the skein of resistance settling over Anna. Out here the frontier is so close that it is easy to imagine stepping over it.

The borderlands are a mess – Boer and Xhosa people have fought over land and cattle since 1779, and the British only make things worse, oscillating from missionary to military and back again. New British settlers arrive in 1820, followed by African refugees from the *Mfecane*: meaning 'crushing' or 'scattering' in isiZulu; this word refers to the widening circles of war and chaos resulting from military action under Shaka Zulu. The years 1834 to 1835 see cattle raids on Boer herds and the murder of the Xhosa king Hintsa by a Cape commando. Ten thousand amaXhosa pillage and burn hundreds of Boer homesteads, slaughter dozens of Afrikaners.

The British minister of colonies blames the Boers for starting the conflict, which proves to be the last straw. Scouts test escape routes: to the north, the dry Karoo morphs into the red desert of the Kalahari, but far to the east lie the green rolling hills around Port Natal (now Durban) and to the north-east high grasslands. The first two treks roll out in September 1835. Another leaves in early 1836, and Gerhard Maritz leaves Graaff-Reinet in September of that year, Anna's father Francois on board with his wife, Maritz's sister. No one can agree where they are going, but they all want access to the sea. By late July 1836, Hans van Rensburg's party of forty-nine have been massacred near the Limpopo River; Louis Trichardt's party reach Delagoa Bay only to succumb to fever.

Anna chafes along on her farm, desperate to head east, but prevented by her ailing husband. At forty, she is, according to the foreword to her *dagboek*, 'an exemplary and God-fearing woman, who always sought her comfort in the Bible'. She is also willing to take four wagons into the wilderness where the kitchen consists of an open fire and where food supplies are sparse and dependent on successful hunting, all with a sickly husband. Finally, the Hattinghs hitch their wagons in autumn 1837. Anna takes the driver's seat, whip in one hand. She is five months pregnant.

Anna wears her bonnet and *riempieskoene* (leather-thonged shoes), and the family carry muzzle-loading rifles that take so long to load that the women and children reload one gun while the shooter aims and fires the other. Anna keeps a loaded rifle behind the wagon seat. It is slow progress, in these ox-drawn *kakebeenwaens* – jawbone wagons, after the shape of it, like an animal's jawbone – piled high with the family's worldly goods, their chairs and chamber pots, their seeds and hoes. The wheels turn over the rough ground, lurch one way and another over rocks. They cross the Seekoei, scouting for the shallowest and slowest section of river, lashing down goods with ropes, getting everyone off the wagons and all the heaviest things unloaded. If the drift is low enough, the oxen pull the wagon across; if not, they must float it on a makeshift raft.

The little group of four wagons is slow but steady, and eventually they cross the Orange River: the final frontier between British governance and freedom. This is just the beginning. They travel across land with no roads, not even tracks, no maps and only a vague sense of where they are going. Anna's *dagboek*, her diary, reads like a Victorian adventure novel, with villains – mixed-race groups of Griqua and Baster – who steal cattle and sheep, servants who abandon the wagons. There is grass so high they almost lose the children and cattle; there are chieftains' compounds where Rolong people surround the wagons 'like two walls'. They drive across a treeless plain littered with abandoned kraals and the skeletons of clans 'demolished by Mzilikazi'. They get lost, move backwards and forwards, their cattle 'die in heaps'.

After four months, they reach the Sand River and in the back of a wagon, under deep black skies lit only with stars and the smallest sliver of a waning moon, Anna gives birth to her last child on 26 August 1837. 'Here is the word of the Lord's truth: "When the need is at its highest, the help of the Lord is near,"' she records later. But birth is a messy business involving blood, amniotic fluid, placenta, meconium and other liquids, and I think how sensible she was to have a water source nearby and daughters and a trusted former slave to help deliver their infant sister.

Three days later, the Hattinghs reach Hendrik Potgieter's trek and travel on with them, still searching for Anna's old father. The larger wagon train proves a mixed blessing, with its vast appetite for firewood and game. It sways across land controlled by rebel Zulu Chief Mzilikazi up until a few months before when Voortrekker commandos broke his power. 'Before the arrival of the Trekkers he was called the God of the Earth because he had eradicated the tribes,' Anna writes. 'We had to go through these devastated states.' They travel for days and see hardly anyone across broad sweeps of grassland, only small groups of the cowed and starving, and bodies in burnt-out kraals. Rumours of cannibalism and slaughter swirl. It is a terrible irony: precisely when the Europeans decide to move further inland, that land has been depopulated by war.

Two decades before the Great Trek, millions of Africans call the South African interior home, descendants of Bantu people who reach modern KwaZulu-Natal by AD 300, modern Limpopo by AD 500. The introduction of maize by the Portuguese in the sixteenth century leads to a population boom – maize being more prolific and quicker growing than the traditional African grains, sorghum and millet. But a ten-year drought places massive pressure on land and food, playing into the growing militarisation of a small clan down on the east coast.

These are loose-knit federations with intense inter-clan rivalry; they have the rule of law and a system of courts. The Sotho people live in towns of up to twenty thousand people, while the Xhosa people are more dispersed, living in homesteads of two to forty huts. Southern Africa's greatest military power takes root in a minor clan called the amaZulu. Under Chief Dingiswayo, then Shaka, the Zulu become a fighting machine, swallowing up surrounding clans. Shaka, who comes to power in 1817, has been much mythologised in the centuries since. He is a military tactician of genius who rules with an iron grip.

Shaka benefits from and worsens the chaos of the *Mfecane* and the impact spreads when one of his chiefs, Mzilikazi, rebels in 1823 and travels north, establishing the Ndebele kingdom in the Transvaal area, north of the Vaal River. Shaka is assassinated by his half-brother Dingaan in 1828. When Potgieter's Voortrekkers reach the highveld in 1836–7, they engage in deadly skirmishes with Mzilikazi's Ndebele people. Mzilikazi divides his people in two, half moving north and the other looping round through present-day Botwsana and Zambia before the two reunite in what becomes known as Matabeleland, in the south-west of present-day Zimbabwe.

This is how the land lies when Anna and her wagons rumble across the highveld: Mzilikazi has fled north, but Dingaan and his Zulu people still rule across KwaZulu. Five or six large Voortrekker settlements lie between the Vaal and Orange Rivers. And finally, approaching the Drakensberg to the east of the emptied veld, the Hattinghs catch up with Francois and Piet Retief.

The iklwa *has a broad blade*

It's mysterious to me how these Voortrekkers find each other out on the veld, with no map, no lines of communication. I imagine scouts setting off on horseback, looking for the wide wake of other trekkers, the wagon ruts, the ground trampled by thousands of cattle. I wonder how they find their way back to their wagons, landmark by landmark, lonely tree by stony *koppie*.

It is a year since Anna's old father left on the trek, six months since Anna set off from Graaff-Reinet. I imagine the state of them: dirty, smelly, threadbare. Travel-hardened, faces tanned and wrinkled from narrowing their eyes against the sun as they struggle over rivers and around gullies. This reunion has the rich satisfaction of old love, a new granddaughter for Francois Retief, sixty-five, to greet, and for devout Anna, an amateur preacher. Every Sunday, and every evening, Erasmus Smit holds services for these strange, pious people. He is married to Anna's step-aunt Susanna Maritz, who runs daily life on the Maritz Trek, organising cooking, washing and the slaughter of livestock.

The trekkers elect Anna's uncle Piet Retief, who set out on his own trek in February, as 'Governor of the United Laagers'. Piet approaches the trek as he does everything, opportunistically: despite publishing a manifesto in the *Graham's Town Journal*, he is not one of the principal architects of the movement. But he is charming and persuasive, and the Voortrekkers are desperate for direction. Characteristically, however, the United Laagers are soon no longer united, being unable to agree on which direction they should take.

Piet wants to settle between the Drakensberg and Port Natal (a small British trading settlement, now Durban), and his group move off eastward. They set up camp at Kerkenberg, atop the steep peaks of the mountains that stretch seven hundred miles north-east to south-west through Lesotho and South Africa. Piet hurries off on horseback with fourteen men and four wagons to explore across the mountains and negotiate with Dingaan. The Zulu king is renowned as merciless and has no reason to welcome thousands of white settlers. Missionaries warn Piet not to threaten him, not to arrive with armed men, but Piet dismisses them. They should 'be under no fear on his account for it took a Dutchman and not an Englishman to understand a K★★★★r,' he retorts.

In November, messengers from Piet ride back into the Kerkenberg camp with a letter and tropical fruits. The children suck the sweet fruit as the adults devour the letter: there is no reason, Piet writes, why the trekkers should not now descend the Drakensberg. That evening, gathered around the campfires, Anna and her family dance to old Afrikaner songs.

Getting the heavy wagons over the steep, jagged passes is another matter. Anna supervises as her sons empty these wooden mobile homes, tie great logs to the stern as brakes and swap the wheels, so the bigger ones are on the front. Two oxen are yoked in front, and teams of people hold on at the back to slow the passage down the mountain. Johannes Hattingh travels down on a litter with the other invalids. Soon nearly seventy wagons are safely over the Berg, and by the time Piet rides into camp on 27 November, one thousand wagons are spread along the Tugela River. Piet convinces Maritz and Potgieter to join him in January 1838, and the Voortrekkers scatter in family camps along a forty-mile front.

But, despite his assurances, Piet has not had agreement from Dingaan that the Voortrekkkers can settle on the Zulu people's land. He sends Dingaan a threatening letter describing the Voortrekker triumph over Mzilikazi. Disregarding opposition from Maritz and Potgieter, he sets off for Dingaan's kraal again with seventy armed men, warning the trekkers to stay together. But the cattle are lean and must have grazing, and the men must hunt buffalo or help other trekkers still in the mountains. As the men scatter, the women and children settle in to wait, washing clothes in water from the rivers and springs, mending, collecting firewood. It is high summer and the ground is green from the warmth and rain.

1 a.m., 17 February 1838
Only the rustle of small mammals in the undergrowth, the hoot of an owl, break the silence. Out in the darkness, the Zulu *impi* jog, barefoot and silent. Each warrior carries a heavy ox-hide shield on one arm, a stabbing spear in the other. Named for the sucking sound it makes when drawn from a human body, the *iklwa* has a broad blade, ten inches long. The *impi* encircle the Voortrekker camps: seven thousand fierce elite warriors. In her wagon, surrounded by children, perhaps Anna sighs in her sleep. A cairn at the foot of a nearby *koppie* marks the small grave of her last-born daughter. Born in the back of

a wagon, exposed to the cold and wet weather, the infant survived for six months, only to fall from the wagon.

It is an uneasy sleep, wrapped in blankets on the uncomfortable boards, and Anna wakes at noises breaking the profound silence. Straining her ears, she thinks she hears screams or whoops, but when she rouses herself and climbs down to whisper with the sentry, she can see no sign of anything out in the bush. She sits with her rifle across her knees, on the front seat of a wagon, eyes straining in the blackness. Rifle shots crack, she hears yells, and the sky begins to lighten, the birds to sing.

There is no communal breakfast porridge that morning, no hot coffee, just water and *biltong* in the saddle. Anna and her eldest son, Francois Hattingh, a gentle bearded fellow, check the cattle where they graze quietly in the dim morning light before riding along the river towards where the sounds came from, the other Voortrekker camps. They keep to the bushes and trees, the soft earth where their horse's hooves make less sound. Riding into the first camp, they hear groans and smell the butcher's stench of meat.

A woman rocks to and fro, her shabby dress covered in blood. At the first wagon, they lift the canvas, and 'Oh! It was almost unbearable for flesh and blood to see the dreadful scene,' Anna records. Dead and dying women and children fill the wagon, flesh torn with stab wounds, blood running down the canvas and dripping from the wagon's bed. There are fifty dead in this camp.

Speechless, Anna and Francois ride on to the next camp, and here, too, the looted and blood-stained wagons are full of the dead. 'Two hundred innocent children, ninety-five women and thirty-three men have been sent by the bloodthirsty heathens to the immense eternity.' Without a word, the pair turn their horses and trot quickly, quietly, back to their wagons, scanning the grasslands, the hills, for Zulu warriors. All that day, they pack up camp, strike tents, stow cooking pots and bedding, round up cattle. That evening they draw the wagons into a tight circle and push thorn bushes between the axels and under the shafts to keep out intruders. The following morning, they make for the large Retief camp at Doornkop.

The Natal Voortrekkers have lost half their number: men return from hunting to find their wives and children slaughtered; pregnant women and exhausted children walk for hours through the bush, straggling into Doornkop before falling to their knees and thanking God. For days after, the sound of wailing breaks the gloomy silence. The site of the massacre becomes the town of Weenen, Dutch for 'weeping'.

But what of Piet, off at the Zulu royal kraal, and the seventy men he took with him? Soon a man called Richard King trudges into the Voortrekker camp. The news is not good. Initially, Piet's meetings with Dingaan had gone well, he reports, and by the final morning Piet had in his side wallet a treaty, awarding the Boers swathes of fertile land. (That this treaty means nothing under Zulu law, where the king can only grant temporary usage of land, is lost on the Europeans.) The Voortrekkers were drinking their coffee, the coloured servants saddling their horses, when a message arrived, inviting them to the royal kraal once more.

Seduced by Dingaan's blandishments, the men left their guns at the entrance to the royal kraal, accepted milk and beer as Dingaan ordered his warriors to dance at the centre of his compound, two thousand huts encircled by miles of mimosa poles. While the Voortrekkers watched, the Zulu warriors moved into their two-horned formation. Only as the dancing men moved backwards and forwards, each wave creeping closer, did the Voortrekkers begin, too late, to worry.

At the sound of the Zulu attack whistle, Dingaan shouted, '*Bulalani abathakathi!*' – 'Kill the witches!' – and the Voortrekkers were beaten with knobkerries and dragged to a small nearby hill, Piet forced to watch his men, including his fourteen-year-old son, clubbed to death with sticks and rocks before he himself was killed. The Zulus ripped the Voortrekker leader's chest open, wrapping his heart and liver in a cloth for Dingaan, and leaving the bodies on the hill for the hyenas and vultures.

Reverend Francis Owen, an English missionary whose hut faced Dingaan's killing ground with its perpetually circling vultures, watched the murders with horror, unable to intervene. Richard King, the reverend's driver, hurried to the Voortrekker camps on the Tugela River to warn them, but he arrived too late: the Zulu *impi*s had set out for the Tugela immediately after the Retief massacre and waited only for the moon to wane before they attacked, ten days later.

ANNA RETIEF

A river running red with blood

After the Weenen massacre and the loss of Piet Retief, the Voortrekkers are in disarray. In July, the camp moves to Bushman's River, a tributary of the Tugela River. The weather waxes foul, and the camp of a thousand wagons is overcrowded. Anna's sickly husband Johannes finally dies, and 'many other family relations were also killed', Anna writes, 'perhaps because of the wet camp because it was cold, it was raining almost every day and the mud was so thick that one could not wear shoes'. All the time, the terror of the muscular *impis*, with their spears and shields, haunts them.

Two weeks later, on 10 August, the Zulus attack again, only this time there is nothing stealthy about it: 'As far as the eye could see,' Anna writes, 'their impis stretched out. It was as if the whole k****rry stormed us.' The Bushman's River camp has only four soldiers, alongside many widows. 'Now you can realize what anxiety we are having, because a woman is weak in nature,' she records. The Zulus approach with their horns outspread, armed with guns taken from trekkers. For two long days and nights Anna loads, shoots and reloads her rifle from the shelter of the laagered wagons. They lose just one Voortrekker, and one of Anna's 'faithful slave friends' before the Zulus retreat with the Voortrekkers' cattle, chanting defiantly.

The state they live in! Tents, wagons, rain, mud. Grinding fear, hunger. And Anna faces it alone; Johannes had at least been an ally even if he was constantly ill. But she knows a man in the camp in the same position, Thomas Steenkamp his name, no wife and ten children to look after. Ten plus six equals sixteen children for Anna to shepherd and feed once these two decide to marry. This is marriage not as romantic ideal, but as practical means of raising children and shelter against hardship. 'It was a lot to take care of in the hard times, but the danger in which we lived made me decide,' Anna writes. It proves a durable partnership.

The Voortrekkers move camp again, argue about retreating over the mountains. Their stubborn inability to be led makes everything worse. Gerhard Maritz dies, and with Retief murdered 'we were like sheep without a keeper,' Anna says. Into this murderous scenario, a saviour steps: Andries Pretorius is a wealthy Afrikaner farmer, and when he arrives in November, he is unanimously elected leader by these people who won't accept any leadership for very long. Within days he musters a 460-strong commando to vanquish Dingaan. Anna's new husband dresses in bandolier and slouch hat, bids her goodbye and joins them. Anna, left with sixteen children, their spouses and her grandchildren, watches Thomas canter away, the horse's hooves thudding on the damp sod.

Sure enough, on 16 December 1838, the commando wakes to find their laager surrounded by twelve thousand Zulu warriors. But clever Pretorius has positioned the laager in front of a wide hippo pool on the Ncome River. To one side lies a deep dry riverbed, and to the front there is only open ground, offering no cover. By the end of the day, three thousand Zulu warriors are dead, and no trekkers. The river runs red with blood, and this victory becomes known to the Afrikaners as the Battle of Blood River, won against such overwhelming odds that it becomes one of their founding myths. That the Boers attribute their victory to a vow made to God before the battle only adds to its allure. The sixteenth of December becomes Dingaan's Day, then the Day of the Vow and later, in post-apartheid South Africa, the Day of Reconciliation. The triumphant Voortrekkers, Anna's husband among them, head for uMgungundlovu. They find only a charred ruin: Dingaan is gone. On the nearby hillside lie the rotted corpses of Piet Retief and his men. And, in a leather pouch next to Anna's uncle's skeleton, the treaty.

'A disgrace on their husbands'

The Zulu nation fractures. The new leader, Mpande, aligns himself with the Voortrekkers, who set about founding a state, and Anna and her family arrive in Port Natal in January 1839, less than two years after leaving the Cape. But this tiny settlement of two dozen Europeans, surrounded by mangrove swamps where hippos and crocodiles wallow, is no paradise. She loses mild Francois, killed by a lightning strike, and seems numbed by pain: 'But the hand of the Lord does what he wants and death does not miss anyone,' she writes.

The new Natalia Republic has Pietermaritzburg as its capital – named for the two lost leaders, Piet Retief and Gerhard Maritz – a *Volksraad* (a People's Council) and a voter's roll confined to adult white men, despite women having been promised a voice in the new Republic. Life presses the Steenkamps onward, and they build a home, only to have it go up in a fiery mass when an inferno engulfs the camp. Anna escapes with the twelve children who live with her, but Thomas is badly burnt: stashes of gunpowder explode, fountaining in the night sky. Scores are burnt alive or maimed, along with wagons, nine fat salted cattle, soap, sugar, coffee, maize, pumpkins. The fire hits just as the camp has invested in new stores. All this in the wake of a measles epidemic.

For four painstaking years, Anna and Thomas raise cattle and farm in the lush semi-tropical hills inland, where elephants rummage through cattle kraals and trample crops. The Steenkamps' plan to continue as before, using darker-skinned people to do the hard work, falters when the Zulus, returning to their land, show no inclination to play along. Not even when Thomas raises the *sjambok* with his burnt and maimed right arm and lashes them, blood dripping from welts on the tender skin. All the Voortrekkers want cheap labour and none of them think the Africans drifting home after Dingaan's fall have any right to the land.

Anna tries to set down the Trek in ink, capturing it in her *dagboek*. Perhaps she hopes it is history now, but then the British arrive again. Can they never escape these people? The British, concerned about violence destabilising the Cape border, annex the Republic of Natalia in 1843. The women spit fire, especially when the men begin to cave, and confront the British at a meeting in Pietermaritzburg. Indomitable Susanna Smit demands to be heard: the women had been promised a voice in the colony because they fought side by side with the men, she says, and now the all-male *Volksraad* is submitting to the British, against the women's will!

The British are astonished. It is 'a disgrace on their husbands to allow [their wives] such a state of freedom,' they splutter. Four hundred women sign a petition saying they would rather 'walk barefoot across the Drakensberg' than agree to British rule, but all in vain. The *Volksraad* decides they cannot fight both the British and the Zulu peoples and the women are pushed wriggling back into their box.

Yet, in the end, Anna and the other women prevail. How could the Voortrekkers agree to settle down under British rule, a rule which enshrines in its articles: 'There shall not be in the eye of the law any distinction of colour, origin, race or creed'? They may not be barefoot, but the women repack their wagons, harness their oxen and begin the long journey back over the Drakensberg. Piet Retief's dream of Natalia sinks, and it is left to the British to destroy the Zulu empire in 1878 and after. Some Voortrekkers trek north of the Vaal River; others return closer to the Cape, between the Orange and the Vaal rivers. In 1848 the British annex this area, before handing it back to the Boers as the independent Republic of the Orange Free State in 1854. In 1852 the Boers to the north across the Vaal establish the South African Republic.

It is hard to overstate the importance of the Great Trek and the isolationist impulse. It is the trek that pushes the white frontier all the way across the southern end of Africa. It is the trek that allows the discovery of diamonds, and later gold, and the flood of white adventurers who come in their wake. I think of the frontier rabble and their murderous activities. How Anna Retief personifies colonial expansion, just as Elsje did nearly two centuries earlier, pushing the Khoikhoi out of Hout Bay, out of the Boland.

Trekking leaches into the Boer identity and as late as 1874 some head north-east in search of political independence. Thousands die. 'They dare the desert crossings in their wagons like sailors in an open boat. Indeed, seeing the trekking wagons with their dusty hoods: God – they're like tanned sails – tanned sails on a hot brown ocean,' records Carel Birkby. In this version of the story, the Boers appear as intrepid explorers, unafraid. But where a boat leaves no trace, these people leave paths all over southern Africa, an unsettling spider's web of selfishness and intolerance. Rock spiders, the British call the Afrikaners during the Anglo-Boer War, thanks to their ability to scramble over and around rocks and disappear into crannies. There is a harsh ignorance here, farmers with their skin tanned to a tough leather by the sun and their humanity warped by isolation and attack.

Anna and Thomas Steenkamp shuffle from place to place, never settling anywhere long before the British or Basotho run them off. From 1820, Basotho leader King Moshoeshoe has extended and strengthened his clan by offering food, land in the southern highveld and protection to different ethnic groups displaced by the *Mfecane*, as well as Boers. But in 1865 the conflict over land between Boer and Basotho, held in an uneasy peace for seven years, boils over again. Thomas Steenkamp, out herding his sheep on the grassland, is caught by some marauding Basotho. They stab and beat him to death.

Anna never recovers from the Trek, burning a light every night against the danger out in the dark. She loses seven of her family, survives bloody attacks, fires, epidemics and starvation, all to avoid seeing Africans as equal human beings and escape British control. In half a lifetime of searching, does this woman find somewhere to belong? She dies in 1891, aged ninety-four, on her son Christiaan's farm near Bethlehem in the Orange Free State, which has grown into a wheat-growing town with frosty winters and mild summers. In the latter part of their long lives, Anna and Margaretha are divided by more than veld and mountains. Yet no doubt aunt and niece would recognise each other still.

Anna's *dagboek* reproduces her favourite song, a Lutheran hymn, haunted by the road and the far horizon:

Wijk wêrelds-gewemel,	Away, wide world,
Ik moet naar den hemel;	I must go to heaven;
Verhindert mij niet.	Do not stop me.
Weg zonden, zwijg lusten,	Away sins, be silent lusts,
Ik wil hier niet rusten	I do not want to rest here
In's vijands gebied.	In enemy territory.

★

I type Anna Steenkamp's name into my keyboard, and webpages come swimming to the surface. A shoal of photographs. Small graveyards enclosed within rusted wire fences. A palette of dust: yellowish, greyish, under a bluish sky. The occasional cypress dark green, sentinel. Old family cemeteries on Free State farms, untended, gravestones cracked by frost. Empty of God, waiting. Or is it that the dead turn their faces away, aloof?

Anna Steenkamp's memorial stands curiously upright, a marble obelisk. In the background, prickly pears are growing, a pale bluish-green. *Opgerig deur haar afstammelinge 16 Des. 1924*, reads the lower tier. Erected by her descendants 16 Dec. 1924. Thirty years after Anna's death, someone bothers to raise a memorial to her, to stake their claim to this land. It can't be a coincidence that this is the year in which my great-grandfather is ousted as prime minister by the National Party. The year that the South African electorate begins to turn their faces towards white nationalism.

~

Legacy

Two centuries after Anna's wagons sway across the grasslands, after white nationalism flames into apartheid, we visit to find what grows in the ashes, flying into Bloemfontein airport in October 2017. As we walk across the apron from the plane steps to the terminal, I take my son's hand to stop him from walking in front of a dolly loaded with luggage, and when I look up I see the name of the airport in big black lettering above the glass doors to the terminal building: Bram Fischer International. The name of this airport has existed for only five years, and it is bewildering not only because this small but shiny building has no international flights but also because I am related to this man, a *bona fide* anti-apartheid hero in this country where I am a stranger and where shame percolates more usually than pride.

After this, we drive north for two hours through flat dustland, endless, depressing, oppressing, as it reels past in agricultural emptiness. Grass straggles through the fraying tarmac at the verge under the telephone wires that loop one to another to another. We pass the occasional sedan in silver or white, maybe a *bakkie*, or a tractor. The bump of a railway line. Tree. Dam. This is the Free State, *Vrystaat*; formerly the Orange Free State, *Oranje-Vrystaat*. Boer Republic, heart of Afrikanerdom, not a hundred miles from Anna Retief's resting place. In this tedious landscape, they could live sequestered from the meddling world with the grim purpose of a Chosen People. So they dreamt themselves. Now their airport bears, as if a burden, the name of the prodigal son, the Afrikaner who, as we shall see, refused his birthright.

Kroonstad is an unnecessary detour – but I want to see where Antjie Krog, poet of the Afrikaner conscience, grew up, where she stood shoulder to shoulder with black comrades in the ANC, where the complexities, the subtleties, of interracial solidarity came into focus. Danielle, who we are driving towards, phones. I can't work out if she is cross because we are late, or worried. Should I worry? It's a grey and beige dump, litter blowing in the wind. The Pick 'n Pay has the sweet rotting odour of dirty supermarkets. My children are oblivious to the degradation, happy with the Cadbury's Top Deck I buy to keep them quiet – milk chocolate topped with white, a reminder of childhood visits from my Aunt Sarah, flying in from Durban with a bag full of chocolate and *biltong*. My littlest grasps my hand and skips in delight at the thought of the chocolate, his short blond hair a flag in the breeze.

As we drive out of Kroonstad, there are potholes, broken windows and pavements collapsing into the street, dense with people, their clothes bright: orange, lime green, pink. Even twenty-five years ago, these pavements would have been neat, the streets fixed up and they would have been almost empty, with the occasional white person. The broken pavements, the patchy tarmac, the Africans, would have been hidden in locations on the outskirts of town. Now the streets are full of black people. Later, an elderly relative, ensconced in the bubble wrap of the Western Cape, tells me, matter of fact: 'Oh, it's a different country up there now. Everyone is black; you don't see any white people any more.'

The road out of town is rutted and passes shacks and latrines. 'My sister Sarah always says, "If you get a puncture in town, just keep driving on your rims until you're in the countryside,"' my mother reports helpfully from the seat beside me. Opportunistic car hijackings pockmark South African cities and towns like bullet holes, and we have not managed to get the sturdy 4x4 we hoped for and are instead driving a frou-frou white BMW. I steer even more carefully, just in case, feeling stupid.

That evening on the farm, my elder daughter is panicked by the mosquitoes, the heat, the dark. All three children climb into my bed; I am swamped by restless, sweaty bodies. In the middle of the night, the fat guard dog barks for half an hour. Danielle's partner Chris sleeps with a gun. During this night-time barking, he gets up, walks downstairs, through the alarmed mesh of the security gate between stairs and kitchen, and peers outside before returning to bed. A jackal attracted by our *braai* of the night before maybe. Or something else I don't want to think about.

'At least on a farm,' Danielle says, 'it is one thing or another: petty theft or brutal murder. In the city, you can be hijacked, pistol-whipped, robbed, raped.' As if that is some sort of consolation.

Chris's family have farmed this land for decades. In the field, the *mealies* are green, taller than my head; in the small copse next to the farmhouse, horses whinny and blow. Chris's passion is growing *mealies*, trading *mealie* futures. But what, I think, even when I know it is not my place to think at all, what if they are trading their two sweet children's futures for those *mealies* too? In the year before we visit, there have been 345 farm attacks in South Africa, resulting in seventy deaths. In the past eighteen years, 1,848 people have been murdered on farms. In a country where brutality is the norm, these attacks are particularly brutal. Farmers, usually white, and farmworkers, usually black, are tortured with drills and blowtorches; they have plastic bags placed over their heads. They are raped, burnt with boiling water or hot irons, dragged behind vehicles and shot.

So many people are murdered in South Africa every year that it might as well be at war: 17,805 from April 2014 to March 2015; forty-nine people killed every day in a population of 54 million. Surrounded by the deafening race rhetoric, it is hard to work out what farm murders represent – opportunistic subsistence robbery? Genocide, as some (whites) claim? Another Zimbabwe? Retribution for apartheid? The number of commercial farmers in South Africa has halved in two decades; many farms are for sale. Seventy deaths a year on thirty thousand farms, plus numerous smaller farm holdings: living on a farm in South Africa is one of the world's most life-threatening occupations. To put things into perspective, I check murder rates in the UK: 732 in 2018 in a population of 68 million.

Populist leaders sing the old revolutionary favourite: 'Shoot the Farmer, Kill the Boer'; Julius Malema tells parliament: 'People of South Africa, where you see a beautiful land, take it – it belongs to you.' Land redistribution becomes a proxy for resentment against the ongoing inequalities in South Africa. After Anna and the other Voortrekkers migrate east and north, Africans gradually lose their land and survive as sharecroppers and tenants on white farms. In 1913, my great-grandfather's government drafts the Natives' Land Act, which ensures that even this option is closed to them: black people have access to only eight per cent of South Africa's land. The South African Native National Congress are appalled, with Sol Plaatje journeying deep into the *platteland* and beyond to report the impact of this act. 'Awaking on Friday morning, June 20, 1913, the South African Native found himself, not actually a slave, but a pariah in the land of his birth,' the black leader and journalist writes in 1916. Now, thirty years after the fall of apartheid, white businesses still own around seventy per cent of farmland.

To the outrage of white farmers, who warn of famine and civil war, President Cyril Ramaphosa amends the constitution to allow land expropriation without compensation. I try to balance the expropriation by the Boers and the British with this possible expropriation, consider the internecine roots of this murderous scenario. My great-grandfather did not actually write that Natives' Land Act, but he was involved in so many of the laws that circled round to this, this violence and horror – take the 1923 Native (Urban Areas) Act, for instance, which segregates urban living space, moving black Africans into townships from where they can service white needs and forcing them to carry passes. Or the Pegging Act of 1943, which prohibits Indians from extending businesses or buying in white areas. Or this: the South Africa Act of 1909, which excludes Africans from the political process, creating a white minority state.

Farm murders are like the boil that reveals a systemic disease: millions of black South Africans struggle to hang on to an identity that makes sense to them – forced out of indigenous society, into slums and townships next to cities. And, increasingly, there are no jobs. People long to get back to the land, to earn enough to buy cattle to recreate the old ways. Chris, gentle, relaxed Chris, is a fatalist.

'Perhaps we need a revolution,' he says. 'If they rose up and took it all back, then we could start again with a clean slate.'

On the way back to the airport, we drop in at the *Vrouemonument*. I say this as if everyone knows exactly what I am talking about, but the *Vrouemonument* is obscure. The first I know of it is a trawl across the internet looking for some big fish, my search broad: 'Afrikaner women'. On my screen: the National Women's Monument. A sandstone edifice, south of Bloemfontein, finished in 1913, commemorating the Boer women and children who died in British concentration camps during the Second Anglo-Boer War.

When we arrive after a long journey between burning fields, the entrance gate is locked, the guard hut abandoned, its paint peeling. We follow the muddy tracks of other vehicles through the gap in the fence, rejoin the tarmacked access road. The horizon is a mass of grey cloud over yellow scrubby grass. Ours is the only car in the carpark. A black woman in pink overalls pushes a giant broom around with one hand, chats on her mobile phone with the other, her voice round with Sesotho. Above her rears the statue of a horse. The rider sports a slouch hat, breech-loading rifle over his shoulder. His hand reaches back towards a woman in a dress from a bygone age: long, high-necked, modest. She has a babe in arms, and her eyes are fixed on the rider, resolute but longing. The horse gallops out of the frame as they bid farewell.

My children run ahead, turn cartwheels on the engraved stones. We search the names of the dead for our own (doesn't everyone, even as the living heart beats in their chest?), find a partial match: Susanna Johanna Smuts. The obelisk reaches high into the Free State air, its curving base decorated with bronze reliefs. At the centre are the figures of two women and a child. One woman stands, eyes shaded by a large bonnet, and gazes off into the distance. The other clutches her dead child and stares blankly.

The flat reliefs speak silently across the veld to a soundtrack of gently buzzing insects. Two small sun-bonneted girls stand in front of a tent where a woman lies dying, the taller one's arm placed protectively over the shorter one's shoulders. The taller child wears no shoes. What are monuments for? *Who* are they for? A monument embodies the act of remembering, a grave without the body. If a monument stands on the veld with no one there to see it, does it still exist?

It is a particularly strange monument, the *Vrouemonument*, its roots deep in Boer men's shame at failing their families during the Second Anglo-Boer War. A failure so abject that twenty thousand Boer women and children die. That it focuses on suffering, not female resistance, is down to an Englishwoman, Emily Hobhouse, who instructs the sculptor to make his work more moving. Her appeals that the suffering of Africans should also be remembered are ignored: the act of memorialising denies a full remembering with no place for African suffering.

We enter the museum. Here in 2017, it has a heavy air of the 1970s with its wood panelling and plush upholstery. The receptionist is an Afrikaner *vrou*, all big hair and green eyeshadow. Everything is slightly shabby, the photographs curling, the documents fly-spotted. There are enormous dark paintings of battles, and dioramas with enamelled soldiers firing faintly flashing guns, the soundtrack tinny and distant in the space. Case after case of coins, postcards, pipes. In the Kruger Hall, I stop at photographs of children so emaciated they could be survivors of Auschwitz, eyes huge and blank.

'Where is he?' Cousin J. C. asks. He is looking for a bust of his namesake, the other Jan Christiaan Smuts. With his soft voice and ready laugh, Cousin J. C. is altogether more modest than the elder statesman who addresses the United Nations in 1945. But his white hair and goatee make him the image of the Oubaas as an old man, so much so that he could have served as the model for this new bust, whose unveiling was celebrated with a dinner at the museum. Never mind the bust, we find no trace of the general anywhere in the South African War Museum.

'Maybe they didn't like his politics,' my mother says, smiling. We all know it is no laughing matter: Smuts's pro-British stance later costs him an election, taking this country down its dark path to the present. Even now, some Afrikaners denounce him as a traitor.

'I can't believe all this suffering,' I say to Danielle, who has a sturdy Afrikaans surname. 'I can't believe how they suffered so much, and now it means nothing.'

'I was at a party in Johannesburg the other day,' Danielle replies, 'and this woman came in wearing a dress that had *Kill the Whites* written on it. Nobody said anything.'

I am wrong, of course; this suffering meant so much, for so long, proliferating, polluting an entire nation for ninety years and more. What comes later is widely regarded as wiping the slate clean of pity. But this monument goes some way in both creating and explaining it. Never again. One can almost hear the defiant anxiety on the highveld wind.

Outside, someone has planted flowers around the new section of the memorial, the Garden of Remembrance for the women and children who died in concentration camps and in the field, black and white. An estimated twenty thousand Africans died. 'These memorials also represent sites of reconciliation and nation building through shared suffering,' the legend reads. Later, as I flick through photographs on my screen, I see the words etched into the wall of this garden, in three languages: 'The battle against violence aimed at women and children should remain uppermost in our cultural consciousness.'

We could consider Michiel Otto at this point, and his wife Anna Siek, who cuts the legal ties between them for '*ruste, vreede en welstand*', 'rest, peace and well-being'. Or Krotoa, doubtless beaten and raped in her last years on Robben Island. We can't know what secrets lie behind the other doors. I think of the violence integral to slavery, and to colonial expansion. That the women in this story are not only violated, but support the violation of other women, and men, of different skin colours. That peoples who are traumatised by violence, their fabric ripped apart, themselves go on to become perpetrators of violence. In South Africa, despite its progressive constitution, the past plays itself out in a warped tsunami of violence against women. And a monument to the legendary courage of Boer women, long co-opted in the name of Afrikaner nationalism, is shoe-horned into a different battle.

Retracing our steps through Bram Fischer and his international airport, we retreat to the Western Cape. Here, in Hout Bay, where I am most often 'at home' in South Africa now, we experience life as wealthy white South Africans, which means fancy food from Woolworths supermarket, swimming pools, picnics at wine estates, sundowners overlooking Chapman's Peak, concerts at Kirstenbosch Botanical Gardens. I reconsider Anna Retief, the venom of her racial views. How they replicate down the centuries. How my skin crawls as white South Africans talk about 'hotnots' and their supposedly thicker skulls, and about how my own birth and lifestyle perpetuates the same divisions. Nearly two decades after I left South Africa, this is the shape of my presence here: a tourist inside a razor-wire protected compound patrolled by security guards. Or, how I think of myself: outside, separate, excluded. High on the slopes above the bay, the noise of the town rises through the clear air.

Hout Bay, named for the forests that provide timber for VOC ships in the seventeenth century, has an Elysian feel still, with its stippled sunlight and majestic trees. Three roads run into the town, all preposterously beautiful. From Noordhoek to the south, Chapman's Peak Drive hugs the cliffs overhanging the Atlantic as it batters their feet. Below are seals sleek as wet Labradors, kelp tugged to and fro by persistent waves. From Cape Town there are two routes. The first winds through the modish beach resort of Camps Bay and under the gaze of the Twelve Apostles. Cyclists litter this route, Lycra-ed legs pumping in the freshness of the morning.

But the route we take, as we try to insinuate ourselves into this town in our temporary, non-committal way, the route Elsje would have taken in 1677, is the third. The road coils around the mountain, beneath the Rhodes Memorial – yet to fall – to the stoplight where salesmen offer curios or mobile-phone chargers for the car. Then through the lush depths of Newlands, past Kirstenbosch Gardens where Smuts's path climbs the mountain, and the remnants of Van Riebeeck's bitter almond hedge still grow, the first of many fruitless attempts to draw a line between races.

Rhodes Drive winds through groves of giant Australian blue gums, alien forest planted since shipbuilders decimated the native forest in the 1600s. Then into Constantia Heights where houses cannot be seen from the road, so deep are they in their grounds, so tall are the walls surrounding them, razor wire glinting in the sun. Over Constantia Nek and down, down, the twining road into the valley.

There are paddocks with horses, the Disa River running along the valley floor. Whitewashed faux-Cape Dutch estates flank the road, and then to the left appears Imizamo Yethu: 18 hectares, home to fifteen thousand people, thirty-three per cent unemployed – many without running water or sewerage, although it does have electric light. Here the Disa River has the highest level of E. coli ever recorded in South Africa.

Above the township, the mountain turns its implacable buttresses, the speckle of corrugated iron and planks clinging ever higher, squeezed in between boulders, ticks on the undercarriage of a great beast. These shacks frequently catch fire, flames spreading fast between the densely packed homes. People die. From the plush dwellings on the hill, people like us watch helicopters scoop water from the ocean in gigantic buckets and dump it on the rising smoke.

In the late 1980s, invasions by squatters raised the ire of white property owners in Hout Bay, and in 1991 450 families were placed on forestry land on the side of the mountain overlooking the harbour to create Imizamo Yethu. Nowadays, Hout Bay is a melange of wealthy white landowners, black isiXhosa speakers and, above the port in Hangberg, coloureds. Imizamo Yethu is also home to people from across sub-Saharan Africa, from Angola to Zimbabwe. Every day, the vast inequities stare every member of the population in the face.

Nervous whites keep crime at bay with a three-thousand-strong Neighbourhood Watch, linked by radio and conviction. This is a way of life, the Neighbourhood Watch website proclaims. It feels more like war: white residents battle-ready behind their electric gates, locked in their panic rooms, the beams of their alarm systems activated. It all smells of the usual confusion of Boer independence and the desperate attempts of a minority to maintain their advantages under siege.

Just past the roundabout into Imizamo Yethu, past the fortified police station, stands an authentic Cape Dutch farmhouse. The whitewashed gabled frontage abuts the road, the windows and door painted a traditional dark green. Kronendal: site of the land awarded to Willem van der Merwe in 1677. The farmhouse itself was built after the Van der Merwes left: the back gable dated 1713 and the front 1800.

It is a long time since Elsje Cloete was here, when elephants still wandered through the trees: almost 350 years. From up on the hill, we cannot see Kronendal, but it is impossible not to read the truth, which the buildings and trees obscure up close, to read the great scars left by centuries of racial stratification.

Elsje Cloete, Anna Siek, Margaretha Retief, Anna Retief: these women are present at the source of racial bigotry across South Africa. By the 1800s, racial categories at the Cape have solidified, whatever fluidity there was has disappeared, baked hard, and now Hout Bay encapsulates those divisions. Centuries after slavery was abolished, decades after apartheid was abolished, their legacy runs through this place like the sewage in the Disa River. I think about race, its lies and continuities, how there is no way to think about South Africa without thinking about race. How we are trapped inside this system of understanding each other, which leads to me up on the hill, looking down on big houses with swimming pools like turquoise jewels, across at ranked brick boxes, vertiginous up the slopes of Hangberg, and off to the right at the tiny tin shacks, glinting in the sun.

Bristol, 2018

I revise the family tree again, searching for understanding. Throughout my childhood, there have been rumours of 'a touch of the tar brush' – I handle this phrase gingerly, turning it in the light. My sister's tightly curling hair, said to come from our great-grandmother, whose own hair, in turn, was thought to have been passed down from slave ancestors – a cheerful glancing reference to a cesspit of rape and oppression. The family tree with which I grew up was constructed by my Great-Uncle Jannie in 1960, when obscuring ancestors of colour was more important than revealing them. A kaleidoscope, tiny tessellations, fountain from its centre, my great-grandparents' union. Even with a magnifying glass, no Krotoa, no Angela van Bengale, hides along the borders of the minute tiles when I examine them now. There is a Carolina Vryman, but who knows that Vryman denotes a freed slave?

Twice I find that the accidental loss of a generation on Great-Uncle Jannie's tree means he has lopped whole branches off. My cousin Richard, Jannie's grandson, laughs when I relate this to him.

'That was no accident,' he says.

Twist the kaleidoscope, and Carolina Vryman, also Catharina Jacobs van de Caap, is not only the daughter of two slaves but a slave herself. And one of Jannie's lost branches, I discover, is the one on which Krotoa, our eleventh great-grandmother, grew.

I am not alone: with the dawn of the Rainbow Nation, thousands of white South Africans, casting around for a way to belong, lift all the gravestones in their private boneyard to find people of colour. Who can blame them in a country that shifted under their feet in less than a generation? More than four million people went from being the pillar around which the country revolved to being strangers in their own land, just as they estranged those with darker skins for centuries. But for white South Africans – or, worse, non-South Africans, like me – to deny their responsibilities by claiming Krotoa or Angela as an ancestor seems like a sick joke. Not only is it misleading to suggest that Afrikaner origins are anything other than primarily European, but to live with the privilege and skin of a white European, as a descendant of the society that took Krotoa from her people, chewed her up and spat her out, of the society which stole and enslaved Angela, trafficked her across the ocean, is much more relevant than this rummaging around in the lost property box of racial DNA.

Why start with the minority, with Krotoa? Racial appropriation, the inner censor suggests. But I think it is the allure of chronology. Krotoa comes first on the neatly drawn timeline of European settlement of South Africa, which begins with the Dutch arriving at the Cape, each year with its short segment, like a millipede and its legs. I think of the giant *shongololo* I find by the pool in Durban: a millipede, black, shiny and as long as my hand is wide. Yet, like the *shongololo* (from the isiXhosa *ukushonga*, to roll up), history isn't just chronological; it moves in fits and starts, like the circles the *shongololo* makes when frightened, creating strange connections between segments that should never touch each other. And so, after 350 years, white South Africans, and me alongside them, rediscover their Krotoa, reassess their past.

Shongololo is also a word used by Africans for trains when they first arrive in South Africa, because they look like the millipedes with their segmented carriages. But millipedes walk in a wave-like motion, each leg synchronised. And each time the *shongololo* moults, it grows another pair of legs. I imagine time moulting, each new year shifting the ones who came before. How the new arrivals on the shores of the Cape in the 1650s throw everything into disarray, demanding their place, the radical history of white shame shuffling into motion.

Is skin any more than skin deep? Does it have any meaning beyond being a proxy for belonging? My semi-obsessive rifling through the South African press shows black South Africans are frustrated that little has changed. That, influenced by populist rhetoric, they taunt white South Africans as colonialists, suggesting they return whence they came: Holland. Here is one example: veteran Afrikaans reporter Max du Preez. Du Preez's pedigree is good, excellent even. He set up the first Afrikaans newspaper to oppose apartheid, served jail time for quoting banned people in print and continues to challenge authority now, riling everyone. For whites, Du Preez represents a racist apologist for incompetent black governance; for blacks, a racist proponent of white privilege. So it goes in South Africa's noisy democracy.

Safe behind my laptop, I am struck – as if by a fist – when an angry young black man calls Du Preez a 'kangaroo', an alien species. The irony is less exquisite cut than dull throb. I struggle to construe his meaning. The language of blood, weaponised by the National Party, has had its DNA replicated in the post-apartheid nation. And it has chosen a classically Australian animal as its vehicle of rejection. Du Preez's ancestors have been in South Africa for three centuries and, like all Afrikaners, include slaves and Khoikhoi. What makes someone belong?

By now, race is uppermost in many people's minds and Bristol, where we live, is a city wrestling with its own slave-owning past. I listen to Kwame Anthony Appiah's Reith Lectures on BBC Radio 4 as I repaint the kitchen. His urbane, faintly amused voice fills the space as I apply the paint methodically to the walls: Pearl Ashes, its name deriving from a product of potash baked in a kiln to remove impurities. Appiah titles his lectures *Mistaken Identities* and talks about creed, colour, country, culture. They are constructed identities, he says, nothing immutable about them: 'Race is a palimpsest written upon by successive generations where nothing is entirely erased.' He talks of how durable the racial fixation has proven, how it is maintained to retain privilege.

Coating the kitchen walls in pale lilac grey, I wonder if having Khoisan DNA means you belong in South Africa. Or, to put it another way, if you have to have Khoisan or other 'dark' blood to belong? Is belonging to a specific geographic area related to race? The questions are thorny and convoluted and often seem to be about justice, not race. Appiah suggests that racial authenticity is coded in cultural terms, with cultural traits seen as inalienable racial possessions. A snarl of genetics and environment: society makes skin colour central to our identities, not biology. Within colour-coded talk of cultural appropriation, I recognise my hope for some Khoisan DNA threading down the generations from Krotoa as an unspoken desire for ownership, to have a claim.

These concepts slide around, slippery as an octopus, but I follow the octopus as it slips through the tiniest of gaps, sensing this is one of the keys for which I have been looking. Race as a scientific concept stems from colonisation itself, bringing people like my European ancestors, like Elsje Cloete, into prolonged contact with different groups, and a developing interest in classification in eighteenth-century science. The Atlantic slave trade needs a justification for enslaving Africans and, more appositely for our purposes, the Dutch need a justification for taking the Cape from its original inhabitants, from Krotoa, who they call a dog when she dies.

Europeans put themselves and others into groups based on physical appearance and project onto these groups 'innate' abilities and behaviours, race becoming an integral essence, shaping more than just external appearance. With the advent of DNA testing in the late twentieth century, race's biological basis is deconstructed: there are more differences within races than between them, differences between 'race' groups accounting for only one to fifteen per cent of human genetic variability.

The wrangling continues: the new ability of computers to count huge numbers in imaginative ways, and the growing amount of genetic data that can be measured, have shown that genetic clusters do exist along roughly the same lines as continentally based racial groupings. Other biologists object that the same data undercuts groups traditionally considered to be races, that the changes are minor, inconsequential. Furthermore, because human genetic variation does not jump from group to group but changes incrementally depending on geographical distance, many people are part of more than one 'racial' grouping. It is a question that obsessed apartheid race assessors: how black is black? For them, having hair that would hold a pencil in its curls was one way of proving black was black enough.

I order a DNA testing kit. It arrives in the post, a small swab and test tube that promises to reveal the secrets of the universe. Or at least of the hidden insides of my body. I unscrew the test tube, hold the plastic end of the swab and insert the other end into my mouth, rub it against the slippery skin inside my cheek. Dropping the envelope in the post box the following day, I mock myself for indulging in genetic pseudo-science. Born of the intersection between genealogy – popularised by TV shows like *Who Do You Think You Are?* – and modern technology, these DNA tests are scorned by professional geneticists. But who can resist the illusory lure of certainty?

What am I hoping for? A physical connection to Krotoa, to Angela? Proof that I belong in South Africa? If I search deep inside, do I think DNA of colour will help lessen the load of guilt and responsibility, which weighs like a giant canker? Whatever it is, it does not appear in the results, which slide into my inbox a few weeks later. My body turns out to be resolutely northern European: thirty-six per cent British (Anglo-Saxon), twenty-eight per cent Scandinavian and fourteen per cent west European with a smattering of others. So much for the mythological tar-brush. I am disconcerted to be tied so firmly to one patch of the Earth: thinking myself a global citizen when all the codes that determine my physical self derive from human beings who moved into northern Europe thousands of years ago.

These tests are based on comparisons to DNA databases from living populations, vulnerable to systematic bias because of incomplete sampling. Given the rapid cutting and pasting of DNA down the generations, and the movements of peoples, such shared DNA can be the result of chance. And the further back you go, the less likely you inherited any DNA at all from any one ancestor. An unreliable witness, then, DNA. And dangerous. Particularly in the 2020s, when a resurgence of racial fear and demonisation shimmers like exhaust fumes over a congested motorway. The essentialising nature of ancestry DNA tests is disturbing: human beings reduced to their physical bodies. Images of 'Slegs blankes', 'Whites only', signs on beaches, buses and benches, of human beings dragged behind moving trucks, barbecued while policemen enjoy a beer, all the old horrors of apartheid, scroll across my inner eye.

It has a seductive simplicity, skin colour, as a basis for belonging. Under apartheid, blacks were rejected by the white state, literally ejected, bussed to the 'homelands'. South Africa was a white country, and proud of it. And now that has been flipped on its head. I think about what it means for Afrikaners to be called colonialists. That only the original people belong. That the Cape's original people were assimilated into a new community, and the Xhosa people arrived there later than the whites, is neither here nor there – African soil is for African skin. I consider my own knee-jerk reaction that Mozambicans have more right to be in South Africa than me, where we are both foreigners in the modern nation state.

I imagine globalisation, colonisation, on rewind, speeding back to the moment where everyone was where they evolved, but it already feels like patent nonsense, not least because we all originated in Africa. Migration is as old as humans; to disentangle everything would be impossible. Even my blood, pure northern European, carries the wounds and victories of Viking invasion of eastern England in the ninth century, Dane mixing with Anglo-Saxon, who in turn mixed with Celt in an earlier migration. We are not static. It is only the slow pace of that change that made it seem so, which allowed us to evolve. There is no empirical, final test: belonging is a feeling, not a reality.

Nations are really just the people they contain, so while you might feel you belong, if other citizens reject you, you might have to work at belonging, in order not to be deported, attacked or at the very least rejected. Especially if most of those citizens have good reason to feel resentment towards you. Under the shorthand of skin colour lie the long, complicated narratives of the human psyche. But in a country where 'African' is another term for 'black', how could a white person claim to be an 'African' without eliding centuries of racism? Perhaps,

I think, white South Africans are just that, South Africans: no longer European, not yet African. Later, I receive another email. My results have been updated to reflect new data; samples have become more complex. My DNA remains European, but there are matches to another community, partial, incomplete, but there I am: colonialist, kangaroo, South African.

V

Isie Krige

1870–1954

One often catches a glimpse of them in the lives of the great, whisking away into the background, concealing, I sometimes think, a wink, a laugh, perhaps a tear.

Virginia Woolf, *A Room of One's Own*, 1929

Libertas Parva

We have travelled a long way from Bengal, from Germany, from the 'Original People' to get here, to the lives that bind it all together, and bind me to this country to which I have so little claim. I think about naming. How it is an act of hope, of faith. A reaching into the future, and a shackling to the past. Words that rattle their chains. My mother and my sister are named for my great-grandmother: acts of ownership that keep this woman alive long after her ashes are scattered across the South African veld.

Sibella Margaretha Krige who became Isie Smuts: much of her durability stems from her marriage to Jan Smuts, a child prodigy who goes on to become a politician, philosopher and author of the League of Nations. But also: a man later scorned for his hypocrisy and racism. None of us are named for our great-grandfather, but his life and achievements dominate the stories we are told, our founding myth. So bright a presence is he that I have to squint sideways to make out the features of the woman in the wings.

Isie gives her life happily in her husband's service, yet she does not submit to the role of political wife. Sneered at by high society as a 'peasant woman', she speaks three languages and reads four more. Thwarted in her ambition to become a doctor, she spends her life baking bread, churning butter, darning. All his adult life, she makes her husband's underwear. Beyond the private life, this is a woman who believes women should not be in parliament and that black people should know their place, which is somewhere else, and lower than white people. We are creeping closer to the heart of the matter, and I find myself taking it all very personally.

Stellenbosch, 1888

Dorp Street is dusty beneath the young couple's feet as they stroll under the spreading oaks past the thick whitewashed buildings, golden in the afternoon light, on their way back from a day's study. It is the middle of the Cape's dry summer, but trickling water jingles in the irrigation channels, which run from the river to the gardens and farms. Up ahead stands a large thatched homestead owned by the girl's parents.

As they walk, they talk of Shelley and German literature, and Isie laughs at her *boetie*'s comments. She matriculated ninth in the Cape last year, one of a bare handful of girls and six places behind Jan. Afrikaner women remain excluded from the public world, and her parents thought her path clear: marriage and children. Instead, she chose to enrol at Victoria College, one of the first five female students. These two are not interested in food, nor clothes, nor money; their friendship is very demure, very intellectual. Isie writes poem after poem, but tears them all up.

They say goodbye, Jan turning into the house opposite, and Isie into Libertas Parva, papered in dense patterns, the fashions of Victorian Britain having made the long journey south. This is a working farm, and vineyards stretch down to the river in neat rows. The railway line runs to the north-west, the chug and whistle of trains punctuating the days. Old slave bells ring the servants to work from their cottages after breakfast outside and the first of four daily *dops* (drinks) of wine. Slavery has been outlawed for fifty years, but coloured women wash and cook inside white people's homes while coloured men and boys harvest white people's grapes and press the fruit with their feet in giant vats.

Isie's father, Japie, is a pillar of the community, and a church elder, and that evening she frowns at her brothers as they fidget through the long, droning family prayers. Her round-faced mother, Susanna, is about to give birth to her tenth and last child, and, as the eldest daughter, it falls to Isie to look after her siblings. But clever Isie, whose parents regard too much education in a woman as a waste, can speak English, Afrikaans and High Dutch interchangeably, read and write German and French, and read ancient Greek and Latin.

Isie Krige grows up in this pious household, shaped by the Cape Dutch values of Margaretha Retief, her *oumagrootjie*, alive until four years ago, rocking quietly by the fire when the Kriges visit their grandfather on feast days. But there is another Afrikaner varietal here, grafted onto the Cape Dutch tree, and as Isie helps in the kitchen she can hear her uncles' rumbling voices, the stories of the journey inland to escape the yoke of the British, of Great-Uncle Piet Retief and his murder by the amaZulu.

Spread sparsely across the grasslands of central South Africa, most Boers are subsistence farmers, the British colonists not much better off. Only the likes of the Kriges, close to Cape Town and comfortable with their porcelain dinner service, their dining table polished to a reflective pool, are wealthy. But the discovery of the Eureka Diamond five hundred miles to the north-east in 1867 has unleashed a river of capital that threatens to swamp the Boers: within five years, the new mining centre of Kimberley has fifty thousand inhabitants.

Libertas Parva is something of a hub for the argumentative grandees of Cape society – house guests include Cecil Rhodes – and when the British annexe the South African Republic (ZAR) in 1877 talk around the dining table is of little else. Romantic Isie identifies with the besieged farmers up on the highveld, but the Boers are too frightened of the Zulus to resist, begging the British to pacify them. By mid-1879, the British have conquered the warrior nation, annexing the Transkei in 1877–9, subjugating the Bapedi and the Basotho. From now until 1994, the African population remains under the iron heel of the white man.

Once the Zulus are beaten, the Boers rediscover their courage and fight annexation. Anna Retief, still alive aged eighty-four up in the Orange Free State, must sigh at this eternal goad, the way that the Boers cannot escape the British. She and the other *boerevroue* exhort husbands and sons to fight; after all, they had not battled starvation, murderous clans, leopards, lions and snakes to fall under the British yoke again. The First Anglo-Boer War lasts only ten weeks, the traditional British red jackets and white pith helmets proving excellent targets against the scrub for Boer commandos. Unwilling to pursue an expensive foreign war, the British sign a peace treaty in March 1881.

★

I peer at photographs and try to reconstruct people around the ancient light stamped on the shiny paper. We are getting closer to the present, the detritus of the past thickening with our improved methods of remembering. So much floats in the vessel of the internet; it is an enormous soap pot, melding everything together in a mass, rampant with unrefined knowledge. In the first photograph, Isie is eleven. She rests her arms on the back of a basket chair, solemn in a knee-length shiny black dress, boots and black stockings.

In the second, a couple appear, solid folk with clear, broad faces and thick necks. These are well-to-do farmers, the parents of Jan Smuts, who grows up fifty miles to the north. In the third photograph, a pale, lean boy with large eyes: Jan, accepted by Victoria College in 1886. And in the fourth, an older Isie. Petite, elegant, with close-cropped hair and big eyes. Isie is nearly sixteen when her parents welcome Jan into their home; she and Jan are soon inseparable. They are a lovely pair, with their patina of youth.

Isie worships Jan, with his intense blond energy, and saves all his letters. The first is a love letter, for her seventeenth birthday: 'You are the only one in whose society I feel alone, by myself, as if there is no second one, as if we two are one . . . I love you as my own soul,' he writes. *Selections from the Smuts Papers* brim with Jan's letters to Isie, but nothing flows in the opposite direction. (Legend has it that Isie burns her letters when she finds the cache Jan saves from his female friends. Perhaps a letter she writes following his death in 1950 holds another key: 'I did not think that everything would have to be so public and that everybody would know all one's private affairs when someone died,' she writes.)

Victoria College is, of course, a fortress of whiteness and while Jan teaches coloured children at Sunday school I am startled – horrified – to read in Tom Macdonald's hagiography of 1946 that Isie was sorry for these children 'that they had been born because they had been born in sin, a blending of white and black blood'.

In 1891, Jan wins a scholarship to Cambridge University and sets sail. He stays away for four years. Isie is twenty-one, and free, and in her loneliness dreams of being a doctor, but the Krige family will not spend their limited funds on a girl and so she trains as a teacher. For five years, she writes in chalk on a blackboard, facing rows of wooden benches, dressed in a long skirt with cinched waist, a blouse with puffed sleeves. Less than half of white children can read and by law they are taught in English, so Afrikaans children are less educated, feeding the cycle of English domination of business and the trades. (Only a very few African and coloured children attend mission schools.) Some of the children are taller than little Isie, and she is never strict.

Later the story I hear is that Isie is so maternal that she devotes her life to her children, like my grandmother, and my mother after her. Yet, peering closely, I find women with dreams, thwarted by poverty and gender: teaching is the only path open to an educated Western woman for the next fifty years, except for a few doctors. Even in the 1990s I am pushed towards medicine by my parents, and for the three weeks I am at medical school sixty per cent of my fellows are women. For Isie's generation, a century earlier, even the choice between teaching and medicine is removed upon marriage: it is the life partner who will determine how that life will look.

'Ik doe'

Stellenbosch, 1 May 1897
Rain spatters on the mud outside. A fire roars in the grate. There is no wedding feast, no band nor dancing, and the bride is a full twenty-six years of age. The couple standing together in the *voorkamer*, the front room, of Libertas Parva are soberly dressed. It has been a long road to get here. For the past five months, Jan has been away in the Transvaal after failing to find work in the Cape on his return from Cambridge. Their old friend, Professor Marais, intones the words of the old Dutch marriage vows.

'*Ik doe*,' says the bride. I do.

'Henceforth,' announces Marais, 'you go down life's pathway together.'

The next morning the Smuts leave on a train that chugs its way from the lush vineyards of Stellenbosch up and over the Hex River Pass, through the short darkness of South Africa's first railway tunnel and out into the brightness of the Great Karoo. Jan lives a thousand miles inland and it takes a day to cross the dry scrubland, where sheep graze and eagles circle high above. Sometimes the train startles a buck, or bright red desert flowers break the khaki expanse of bush. Prince Albert Road, Beaufort West, Three Sisters, De Aar, Oranjerivier. The train stops at Kimberley, bustling with miners and speculators, before making its way across the grasslands settled by Boer farmers fifty years before. Bloemhof, Klerksdorp, Potchefstroom, Vereeniging and, finally, Johannesburg.

Isie's legs are stiff after so long seated, despite alighting at stops to buy refreshments as the steam engine idles and puffs, and Jan helps her down from the train. They engage a pony and trap for the short drive to the house on Twist Street, which runs up a *koppie* near the centre of town. Isie recognises the heavy ox carts of the Boers, their bearded drivers. Everyone else is alien to her: they have poured in, hoping for work on the rich seams of gold. There are Africans – VhaVenda, Batswana, Basotho and amaNdebele labourers who live in slums on the outskirts. There are poor whites, tenant farmers, their clothes in rags, but only six thousand of the fifty thousand whites are Afrikaners. The burgeoning city produces a quarter of the world's gold.

She sees rough men – who look ready with their fists or a *sjambok* – bars, gambling houses and dog-fights, and even drinking canteens for Africans. There are prostitutes in chiffon and satin, sashes and painted faces; men in light waistcoats and proud moustaches who speak many languages and seem in a hurry – who, she knows, could not care less about the Boers. Worse than this, the foreign companies who monopolise the gold and diamonds would rather employ Africans than more expensive Afrikaners.

The next stage in South Africa's turbulent history is on the boil, thanks to the riches hidden in her hills. In the mid-1880s, while Isie is at school, massive gold reserves are discovered in a ridge running east to west through the Transvaal and the influx of fortune-hunting *uitlanders* (outsiders) that this discovery unleashes threatens to swamp the two little Boer Republics.

By 1890 Cecil Rhodes is prime minister of the Cape. His company, De Beers, owns ninety per cent of the world's diamond production

An engraving of the Khoikhoi guarding their cattle and sheep at night. From *Caput bonae spei hodiernum* (1719) by Peter Kolbe, the German who helps Anna Siek draw up her will in 1712.

The Vergelegen estate in 1706, before Willem Adriaan van der Stel is deposed and Anna and Barend move in.

Margaretha Louisa Retief, born in Wagenmakersvallei (Wellington), 1787, dies in Stellenbosch in 1884.

Lady Anne Barnard, writer and artist, who travels to the Cape in 1797 aged forty-seven, and stays for five years, turning her acute eye and pen on society in the colony.

Lady Anne's watercolour of an enslaved woman, Teresa, nursing the child of her master Jacob van Reenen on his Ganzekra farm, 1799.

Despite looking eerily like her aunt, Margaretha, Anna Retief abandons the comforts of Cape life to join the Great Trek into the interior in 1837.

Under orders from King Dingaan, Zulu *impi* attack Voortrekker *laagers* near present-day Weenen, 17 February 1838.

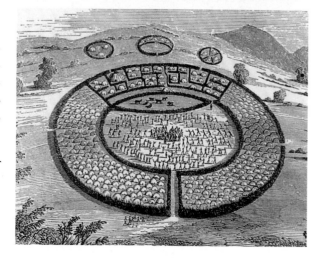

Dingaan's royal kraal where Piet Retief and his men are captured and killed. The *isigodlo*, or king's family quarters, are at the top of the large circle. Outside the circle are the military kraals of the king's regiments. To the left, out of view, is Reverend Owen's camp.

Sixteen-year-old Isie Krige, as she was when she walked home with Jan to Libertas Parva, Stellenbosch, in 1886.

A Boer woman and her starving chi in a British concentration camp durin the Second Anglo-Boer War, 1899–190

On the steps of Zorgvliet, Pretoria, 14 April 1907. Back ro Ds Botha (minister, Stellenbosch), Cato Smuts, Jan Smuts, Jaap de Villiers (advocate). Middle row: Daisie Krige, Isie Smuts, Japi Smuts. Front row: Ber Santa Smuts.

Jan Smuts and his youngest daughter Louis, named for his friend and mentor Louis Botha (South Africa's first prime minister), on top of Table Mountain, *c.* early 1940s.

Jan Smuts holds the author's mother (his granddaughter), Sibella Clark, in the doorway of Hindhayes, Street, Somerset, 1944.

Daniel (aged ten), Cato and Bancroft Clark outside the Hyde Park Hotel, October 1942, where Cato's father stays during the war. He is in London to address both Houses of Parliament.

By 1956 apartheid is in full swing and, with it, growing racist fears.

Cato and her three daughters look up at the newly unveiled statue of her father in Parliament Square, November 1956.

Elegantly turned out as always, Nontando Jabavu poses in the Strand, 1961.

Petronella Clark and Lionel Sylvester, Swaziland, 1966/7. Unlike in neighbouring South Africa, here they can associate freely.

Bancroft Clark, the author and Sarah Clark, Durban airport, 1982.

...vester, Pedder and ...rk families on the ...k steps of historic ...pe farmstead ...oot Constantia, ...pe Town, 1984.

Sibella Margaretha Pedder (née Clark) and Sibella Margaretha Pedder, junior, under a portrait of Sibella Margaretha Pasman (1693–1778), Groot Constantia, 1989.

Thousands queue in Soweto to cast their votes in the country's first elections with universal suffrage, 27 April 1994.

and he dreams of painting the map of Africa the pink of imperial Britain from the Cape to Cairo. By 1895 the area from the Limpopo River in the south to Lake Tanganyika in the north is officially named Rhodesia. But the Boers up on the highveld and the African and coloured peoples in the Cape won't get out of his way. So he forces Africans and coloureds off the Cape electoral roll and in 1894 the Glen Grey Act sets aside areas for Africans on tiny plots, which the oldest son must inherit, forcing other sons into jobs. It is the first, cruel step towards apartheid.

When the infuriating Boers continue to defy him, denying outsiders the vote and controlling freight and dynamite, Rhodes commissions Leander Starr Jameson to foment a revolt, to allow him to invade. When no revolt transpires, an impatient Jameson invades the Transvaal anyway. He is captured, and Rhodes forced to resign. The Cape seethes: the Afrikaners outraged, the English humiliated. The Boer republics stockpile weapons. Isie and Jan are Cape Afrikaners, but they feel themselves Boers and the train they catch from the Cape runs parallel to Anna Retief's long wagon ride: north-east across the mountains and away from the yoke of the British.

The house on Twist Street, when Isie arrives, feels small, the rooms poky, the walls flimsy, after the white-washed solidity of Libertas Parva. She cooks, keeps a servant for the heavier housework. Dust from the mine-dumps insinuates itself through every crack, clothes heavy with it after a walk. When it rains, the violent electrical storms of the summer months that build in black banks of cloud, the streets are mired in mud. Jan buys a piano and they sing German songs in the evening. Their home is a sanctuary for friends from the Cape as they drink coffee, talk of politics and the fear of war. The newspapers are full of the argument between Kruger's *Volksraad* in Pretoria and the big mine bosses in Johannesburg. They want cheaper rail transport, cheaper dynamite and they want the vote.

Isie soon falls pregnant. As war edges closer, Jan makes more money, they move to Doornfontein and, on 5 March 1898, Isie gives birth to twins. But Johannesburg is a dirty mining town with rudimentary medical care and Koosie and Jossie, a boy and a girl, die within a month. Two tiny bodies, two tiny coffins.

The Smutses move thirty miles north to the capital, Pretoria, a sleepy town of roses, bearded Boers and their stout wives. Grieving Isie is relieved to leave Johannesburg for the wide, tree-lined streets filled with slick pony traps and covered ox-wagons. Jan has been appointed State Attorney under President Paul Kruger: at twenty-eight, he is responsible for upholding law and order in the Transvaal. Isie persuades him to swop his usual brown suit for tail-coat, stiff white shirt and black-striped trousers, and they rehearse the oath of office. Later, Jan travels with President Kruger to meet British representatives to avert war, and spends long hours in his study or in meetings with other politicians. I find snapshots of him in the history books, where he is 'quick-thinking, impatient and often rude'. These are Jan's first steps into the power that will define not only the couple's future, but South Africa's.

In April 1899, Isie gives birth to another son, Jacobus Abraham Smuts, or just Koosie, like his dead brother. These are happy months, but outside war is creeping closer.

On 1 June, Jan writes to Isie from Bloemfontein, where he has accompanied Kruger to meet British High Commissioner Alfred Milner: 'I hope that when I return . . . I shall find you both fatter and that my big son will be a good way further on in weight and intelligence.' He adds: 'Milner is as sweet as honey, but there is something in his very intelligent eyes that tells me that he is a very dangerous man.'

Milner wants the British to act against the upstart Boers or face irrelevance in South Africa, undermining their authority globally. He is not interested in Kruger's substantial concessions and the talks collapse. With tears running into his beard, the Boer patriarch exclaims: 'It is our country you want.'

In September 1899, Jan falls ill, and Isie copies a memorandum for him on how war could be prosecuted. 'South Africa stands on the eve of a frightful blood-bath,' she writes, and the Afrikaners will emerge 'either as an exhausted remnant, hewers of wood and drawers of water for a hated race, or as victors, founders of a United South Africa'. This is not the only document she transcribes. With war becoming inevitable, Jan and Isie pen an impulsive hundred-page document enumerating the injustices Afrikaners have suffered at the hands of the British. Jan helps write it, and Isie translates the thirty thousand words of High Dutch into English, transcribing it in her close hand, her austere face bent seriously over the paper, brown curls escaping the piled hair. The stories that pepper the text come from her child-hood: motley settlers like Jacob Cloete 'contain the noblest blood of old Europe as well as its most exalted aspirations', the quest for land across the Cape Frontier was a 'pilgrimage of martyrdom', Great-Uncle Piet Retief 'the most courageous and noble-minded leader'.

'Once more in the annals of our bloodstained history has the day dawned when we are forced to grasp our weapons in order to resume the struggle for liberty and existence,' she writes. The spirals of history have brought Slachter's Nek, the Great Trek, Piet Retief round again. In their enthusiasm, Jan and his loyal wife create a text that goes on reaffirming the Afrikaners' wounded pride, their bitterness and inse-curity, finding fruit in the toxic nationalism of the National Party.

'Am I not a Boer woman?'

Pretoria, June 1900
Isie tucks a startled Koosie under her arm and runs, long skirts tangling around her legs. She hitches them up as the whirr and crash of British shells shake the buildings. The streets are crowded with fleeing wagons and cattle. A man, his face covered in a scarf, throws a brick through a shop window nearby. Jan pushes her through a doorway and gives Koosie a hasty kiss before running off, dodging the falling debris. He is focused on the government's gold and coins, £500,000 worth, and its munitions, still in Pretoria vaults. British troops, outnumbering the Boers by ten to one, nearly surround the city.

When war broke out late last year, Jan was left chafing at home, snapping at Isie and finding excuses to make frequent trips to the battlegrounds. Isie had been confident as commandos won battles against the arrogant and underprepared British and laid siege to Ladysmith, Kimberley and Mafeking. But when British reinforce-ments landed, her confidence faded. When the British took Johannesburg, President Kruger left Jan in charge of rescuing the Boer assets, and she knows that he too must leave or face capture.

The gold exits the city on one of the last trains out, shells raining down as it pulls away, and then comes Jan's turn. Isie stuffs his saddlebags with *biltong* and sugar, clean underwear and socks. There is a last-minute check for documents, a clutching embrace. Then Jan gallops off into the gloom to join the Boers in the Magaliesberg mountains to the north. Darkness draws in outside, the house suddenly quiet and empty, the temperature dropping.

Isie lights the candles, puts a match to the fire laid in the grate, Koosie toddling after her, clutching at her long skirts. 'Mamma, mamma,' he prattles. Isie lifts him onto her hip and kisses his fat cheek before putting him back down among his cotton reels. She takes the telegrams and papers from Jan's desk and rolls them into neat cylinders. Standing on a chair, she carefully pushes the papers into the hollow bamboo of the curtain rods. Clambering down, she leans back to inspect her work: there is no sign of the documents from any angle. That evening she sews the 200 gold sovereigns Jan has left her into a belt. Opening the lid of the hot-water boiler, she drops the money belt inside.

The following morning, 5 June 1900, the British march into Pretoria. They congregate on Kerkplein – Church Square – Lord Roberts and General Kitchener taking the salute on horseback from serried ranks of khaki-clad soldiers. Pith helmets and cheers rise as the Union Jack flies over the Legislative Building. British soldiers search Isie's home, rifling through her belongings. She offers the hungry young men freshly baked bread, and they never so much as glance at the curtain rods or the boiler.

After this, Pretoria is a town under occupation, and the soldiers who wander the streets wolf-whistling at the girls and bantering in their British accents are a constant reminder that the Boers are fighting for survival, but all Isie can do is wait, scouring the newspapers for any clue as to Jan's whereabouts. Food and coal run short, the water supply fluctuates and the doctors are overworked and under-trained. In mid-August, she changes Koosie's napkin one afternoon to find that he has diarrhoea. He is fifteen months old. Cleaning him up as best she can with limited water, Isie sends her servant to fetch the doctor, who examines him and leaves, only advising Isie to keep an eye on him. The next morning she struggles to wake the toddler, who now has a cough, his nose and throat full of mucus. Two days later, he has convulsions. Frantic, Isie sends for the doctor again, but there is nothing he can do. 'Oh *Boetie*,' Isie writes to Jan a year later,

> how I did yearn for one word of comfort from my husband when our last little treasure was taken from us and I knelt by his death-bed *alone*. How utterly alone I have felt ever since he left and how I long for his little pattering feet and his merry voice and clinging hands God only knows.

Isie telegrams Jan, but the telegram does not get through. She is forlorn under the corrugated-iron roof, the cold Pretoria night pressing in. Ella de Wet, wife of a fellow Boer soldier, comes to stay in the empty house, takes her to the printer to have the black-rimmed cards, with their pitiful photograph of a living Koosie, prepared. 'But I won't grieve you by talking thus,' Isie tells Jan, 'for am I not a Boer woman and can I not bear what has been laid on my shoulders as well and as bravely as the rest?'

Photographs of the Boer War show pyres of smoke rising above the veld from burning homes. From organs to porcelain serving dishes, women bury everything to prevent troops from destroying them as young British soldiers, humiliated by earlier defeats, flex their muscles. In the *Collected Papers* are glimpses of this scorched earth. In August 1901, Jan notes: 'Dams everywhere full of rotting animals; water undrinkable. Veld covered with slaughtered herds of sheep and goats, cattle and horses. The horror passes description.' Unable to defeat the wily Boer commandos across the grasslands of the highveld, the British army hits them in the soft underbelly of home and hearth.

The *Vrouemonument* erected in 1913 portrays Boer women as pitiful victims, but these women are tough, their defiance fuelled by propaganda that represents Boer women as courageous, morally upright and dedicated to political independence. I come across a photograph of a Boer woman standing in front of a tree. She wears a long black skirt and snowy-white blouse, draped in bandoliers, eyes resolute beneath a slouch hat. In one hand, she holds the reins to her horse, in the other a rifle. In the absence of their husbands, Boer women become the heads of households: they fight off British troops with revolvers; hide in forests, reed-filled rivers and up mountains in what become known as *vrouwen laagers*. It is not such a stretch – after all, Boer women like Anna Retief have been fighting off Zulu *impis* and Basotho warriors for sixty years.

In June 1900, when the British have taken every town and are laying waste to the veld, the Transvaal leaders are close to surrender. Boer soldiers, a ragtag collection of farmers and foremen, desert to protect their homes and families. Martinus Steyn, Orange Free State leader, is outraged, and not only him: Boer wives refuse to feed their returning menfolk and taunt them for their cowardice. The Transvaal is shamed into fighting 'to the bitter end', and the war enters an acrimonious third phase.

The *bittereinders* (the bitter-enders), under Louis Botha, Jan Smuts, Christiaan de Wet and Koos de la Rey, sabotage railway lines, steal supplies and harry the British troops, before blending back into the landscape. The British partition the entire area with barbed wire and blockhouses. By the time Isie writes this rare surviving letter, thousands of Boers and Africans have been rounded up into segregated concentration camps. The concentration camps are not the world's first, and they are not originally set up to make the Boers suffer and die, but that makes no difference in the end. Isie begs to be interned, but she is banished to the small village of Albert Falls in the British colony of Natal and sits out the war, surrounded by lush greenery, a mother without a child, a wife without a husband. No Anna Retief, she is quiet, clever and kind, and can only knit scarves and visit the camps.

Walking up the hill to the Pietermaritzburg camp, it looks neat enough, the conical white tents on their bare ridge of long coarse grass, and the British authorities allow Isie past the checkpoint. At first, the camp looks strangely normal, the Boer women immaculately dressed in long skirts and voluminous sleeves, holding kettles or pots over the fire, offering their children food. But as Isie murmurs to them in forbidden Afrikaans, she finds many have arrived destitute, in the clothes in which they were taken, some without underclothes. Her head begins to ache as they tell her there is not enough wood, no public ovens, no system for dispensing rations. Over the months, the children she hears laughing as they run between the tents become subdued and listless, baking under canvas in the summer, freezing and damp in the winter.

Being near a large town, water comes from the town reservoir; there are wash houses and pail latrines and Isie watches as a team of Africans, bottles of chloride of lime or carbolic in hand, empty and disinfect the pails. (Even in a concentration camp this work is done by black people, not white.) Nevertheless, forty-seven interns die in September 1901, twenty-five of them small children. Measles is the big killer, and its hangers-on, pneumonia and bronchitis. Isie listens as the doctors scold the Boer women staring blank-eyed over their dead children: they really should keep their tents, their plates and cups, clean!

Upcountry things are worse: 154,000 Boers and Africans are in camps. Emily Hobhouse, the British welfare campaigner, writes: 'I saw crowds of them along railway lines in bitterly cold weather, in pouring rain – hungry, sick, dying and dead. The rations were extremely meagre and when, as I frequently experienced, the actual quantity dispensed fell short of the amount prescribed, it simply meant famine.'

Thousands die, of typhoid, dysentery and starvation. These are the large-eyed skeletons in the South African War Museum's photographs. By October, the death rate is 344 per 1,000 and children under five rarely survive. Hobhouse returns to England, but her reports are received with hostility. In late 1901, a commission of British women under Millicent Fawcett arrives. Shocked, they recommend better rations, provision for boiling all drinking water and more nurses. These improvements cut the death rate dramatically, but it is too late: 4,177 Boer women, 22,074 Boer children and up to 20,000 Africans die in the camps. So many dead children, so many defeated mothers. No wonder Isie eats nothing but the occasional biscuit, barely sleeps.

Meanwhile, Jan writes: 'I have never been in better health or spirits in my life; military life agrees wonderfully with me.'

The war approaches its true bitter end. More and more Afrikaners desert to fight for the British. In the early winter of 1902, two British officers ride into Jan's camp bearing a white flag. As Transvaal State Attorney, he is needed at a peace conference in Pretoria. Travelling upcountry, Jan sees Boer commandos: 'starving, ragged, clad in skins or sacking, bodies covered in sores'. Despite desperate objections from those who prefer annihilation to surrender, the Boers vote for peace by fifty-four to six. The Boers recognise British sovereignty and are given £3 million to rebuild. It is a defeat, but the *bittereinders* can hold up their heads.

They are not the only people affected by this war fought over terrain where four-fifths of the population are black. Africans take part on both sides, and 115,000 are held in the concentration camps. With the Boers away fighting, Africans reoccupy land, including the entire western Transvaal, where the Kgatla people build new kraals, dig new gardens. Up to 120,000 black and coloured men fight for the British. For the Boers, it is a terrifying glimpse of black power, and it colours Smuts's racial views forever. Before the war, the British promise to consider African and coloured claims for the vote. But during the peace conference they allow State Attorney Smuts to draw up a proposal. He postpones the decision on voting rights for non-whites: the Republics will be able to decide for themselves whether whites should retain the reins of power. No prizes for guessing which way they choose to go: it is yet another turning missed on the road to apartheid.

The war is over. Isie weighs seven stone, wracked with aches the doctors cannot diagnose, but which I picture as alienation soaking into her marrow. Jan writes: 'I know you must be suffering horribly and that no calm of mind can make up for the ruin of the body. Still I hope you will be patient for a little longer yet,' and I think that it is her mind that is ruined. And I know her well enough to imagine she will keep on being patient, a veritable Penelope, waiting cheek on hand, elbow on protectively crossed legs. But never again will she give up her independence in waiting for him: she might wait, but she will do it on her own terms.

She expresses no resentment in a postcard to Olive Schreiner in June 1902, from a sanatorium in Pietermaritzburg: '. . . when I shall therefore see my darling I do not know, but I want him to visit all our people in the W. Province before returning to fetch his troublesome wife who must needs get ill <u>now</u>.'

Jan has ridden to inform his loyal troops of the surrender before touring the Cape families, along with his aide-de-camp Tottie Krige, Isie's brother.

Isie returns to the Pretoria home left in disarray by the Imperial Yeomanry two months later. 'I hope someday you will have another little one to comfort your heart,' writes Olive after a visit in September. A British Intelligence report on Jan notes: 'His wife [is] a dreamy, untidy woman with a large knowledge of Greek. Lost some children during the war and it preys on her mind. Hates the English and everything connected with them.' Isie tells Jan: 'I shall disinherit any of our daughters if they marry English men.'

This is not a happy ending

After the Boer War, Isie is marked by suffering, eyes sunken and deep lines running down to the corners of her mouth. 'The iron had entered her soul,' a friend observes. In an ironic foreshadowing of her future status as Mother of the Nation, her anguish mirrors the land and the people in it. Ten per cent of the Boer population has died, and even Milner admits the land is 'virtually a desert, almost the whole population living in refugee camps along the railway line'. While Milner sets about creating efficient administrative structures and economic recovery, Isie painstakingly rebuilds her family. Towns and cities gain better housing, sanitation and public transport while Isie falls pregnant almost immediately with Santa, born in August 1903 when she is thirty-two.

Boer resentment is so bitter that when she goes into labour Isie insists, between contractions, on having the old *Vierkleur* flag draped over her bed. Her child enters life under the flag of the Transvaal Republic, not the Union Jack. Isie has six babies in eleven years, although she folds the flag away after the first, and Jan hides in his work, buying nearly a dozen farms. These provide the couple with financial stability, but the resident Africans, dispossessed of their land and working as tenant farmers, pay the price. (Thanks to the Glen Grey Act and the war, which leave many homeless and jobless, African migrants oscillate between the reserves and shanties on the outskirts of white towns. These are not healthy places, and the authorities use an outbreak of bubonic plague to force Africans to live further from white towns.)

With Paul Kruger dead, Jan and Louis Botha set up a political party, their conciliatory attitude towards the British infuriating Isie, who refuses to join Jan on the election trail in case she embarrasses him. In the evenings, Zorgvliet, their family home, is full of comrades, smoking pipes and planning while Isie listens and scrapbooks every newspaper article on her husband. '*Plakking*', she calls it. She spends her days baking, keeping the children fed and clean, darning, ironing and sewing. Every evening she and Jan share a cup of tea and discuss politics. But marriage is an evolving creature, and just when Isie might have been expecting her happily ever after, Jan's absence turns out to be not an aberration, but the way things are. Worse than that, she will have to share him.

Pretoria, 1907
Outside, the sun burns stark on the scrubby grass, the red earth. Inside, the house is murky, with heavy floral curtains and dark-brown walls. Isie picks up the toddler, lays him onto the embroidered counterpane. Jan has long left this bedroom, unable to share his sleep with a crying baby. His bedroom lies down the hall. Isie tries to keep the squirming body still with one hand, undoing the safety pin holding his nappy together with the other. Out the window she can see Jan and Margaret walking away, down the dusty street, stepping out of the path of a passing carriage. Jan talks, Margaret leaning towards him and nodding, her waist tiny between the puffed blouse and long dark skirt, her neck elegant under sleek piled hair. Isie can see herself reflected in the window, wistful eyes and a wide mouth. The shapeless apron.

Japie wriggles determinedly, and she looks down, lifts his legs by the feet and wipes his little bottom with the triangle of linen as she takes it off. Damp flannel to clean the genitals, muslin to pat dry, and then she replaces the nappy with a clean one from the pile neatly pre-folded this morning. Japie's belly swells round and tight above the nappy. Isie pulls the woollen leggings back up over the chubby thighs and lifts him onto the floor. Yesterday Jan and Margaret did not return from their walk until lunchtime.

The nappy is rinsed in a bucket and put into the washtub with the others. She will scrub them by hand, put them to boil on the wood-burning range. She must get James to bring in more wood. Then the mangle, then the hanging out to dry on the line stretched across the yard. There is a crash from the kitchen – three-year-old Cato pulling the pots onto the floor again – and Isie is worried about Santa's streaming nose.

Time to put the soup on. The bread will be risen by lunchtime. Has Betsy finished washing the floor? Perhaps she'll take Cato into town when she goes to buy the meat for dinner. She can leave sick Santa and the baby with Betsy. The onions and carrots are kept in a wire basket in the pantry, underneath the icebox. She peels and chops at the oil-cloth-covered table, half listens for the creak and slam of the fly screen on the front door.

Twenty years ago, she and Jan walked on the hills above Stellenbosch. Now he and Margaret carry on their own conversation at mealtimes, about nature and religious mysticism, and about Cambridge. About Quakerism and John Bright. And it's in English, always in English. Does Isie mutter to herself, '*Vind jou eie man*,' (find your own man) before scolding herself for harbouring un-Christian thoughts? Later, when she writes to her mother in Stellenbosch, she sticks the stamp with the king's head on upside down.

Isie comes to terms with the relationship in the end, although she cannot resist writing to Margaret a few years later how 'very glad' she is to hear of her engagement, after all 'you really only find out what life is after you get a husband and children of your own'. She has to come to terms with it because it lasts forever: once they are all dead and gone, the list of Margaret Gillett's papers includes letters spanning four decades, drafts of the first biography of Smuts, correspondence about the publication of the Smuts letters. The rustling presence of these surviving historical documents supports Jan's reputation as an outstanding intellect and leader, with Margaret as the Keeper of the Flame – Isie's years of cutting and pasting are curiously irrelevant.

Item one: a scratchy piece of cloth – gifted to my grandfather as a toddler from his Aunt Margaret, woven at Emily's school. Jan meets Margaret on the Cape Town docks in 1905 as she disembarks with

Emily Hobhouse, who has returned to South Africa to set up weaving and spinning schools for Boer girls. The tweed itches so badly, Jan complains, it makes him feel like an ostrich. Item two: a letter from Jan to Isie from the SS *Herzog*: 'One of the most pleasant and beautiful days that I have had in my life,' he writes, after spending a day on Gran Canaria with Margaret.

The pair share a ship to England in early 1906 and discover the mutual admiration that spawns a letter a week for forty years and Jan's deeper association with England. He visits Margaret Clark's family in Somerset and attends Quaker Meeting with them, finding this quiet, rural England, with its sober non-conformist Friends (as Quakers call each other), more charming than aristocratic circles in London. This England appeals to him, the England of John Bright, Margaret Clark's grandfather, the great reforming Liberal MP, instrumental in the repeal of the Corn Laws. Not the imperialists and jingoists, the Joseph Chamberlains. But Isie does not share this interest, it is a part of his life separate to hers, Margaret's realm, and she never visits England.

What is worse for Isie, Margaret is just the first (although perhaps the most important) of many women. Historians have long pawed the letters Jan leaves behind, twenty-three thousand in all, many addressed to women other than his wife. Romantic or intellectual, platonic or physical? Late in life, he tells his foster daughter Kathleen crossly: 'The only woman with whom I have danced is my wife – and she remains the only one.' (A reminder of how buttoned-up Afrikaners are.) This does not stop him from pursuing other intimacies. He admits: 'I have a weakness for women, not in the sexual sense, but from some inner affinity and appeal.'

I am outraged on Isie's behalf, but there is no evidence that she finds any of them – beyond the first – troubling. As I work my way through the historiography, the pawing takes on a tabloid edge: Piet Beukes devotes a whole book to *The Romantic Smuts*. But that Jan should choose Emily Hobhouse, Olive Schreiner, Margaret Gillett, says something about Isie too: these women are clever and, forced to stand outside the chambers of power, have a perspective Jan values; they challenge, but do not compete. No doubt, he enjoys the element of awe. A man prepared to treat a woman as his intellectual equal.

Peering into Jan's life, historians plonk Isie on the pedestal marked 'sacrifice'. What a challenging posture to maintain for a lifetime: bent in half, offering one's self up on a platter. Here's an alternative: in that first decade after the Boer War, barefoot and pregnant in the kitchen while Jan runs around with Margaret, Isie takes stock of where she finds herself and makes a decision. No international trips, no travel to Cape Town for the parliamentary session when the children are young. Separate bedrooms. This is not a happy ending but something more tensile: a partnership that can weather passing storms of emotion.

As Jan puts together the building blocks of a country, Isie puts together the building blocks of her life. She remains in Pretoria when he travels to England in 1905 to push for self-rule, and the Republics are given self-governing status just four years after the war. In February 1907, Smuts's Het Volk party wins a landslide in the Transvaal elections and he becomes both education and colonial secretary (opposing Mohandas Gandhi over equal rights for Indian labourers). As Jan drafts the constitution for a new united South Africa eighteen months later in 1908, Isie plays with her babies on the beach in Cape Town.

How much of the blame for what happens later can therefore be placed on him provides endless material for historians. For a supplicant like me, it represents a potential nexus of shame, but for others, I find, it is a nexus of pride – instead of 'four tin-pot' countries, South Africa gathers into one mighty nation run along Westminster lines. But a federalised structure might have better suited these fractious states and in this constitution, with its need to appeal to the race-obsessed Boer republics, only the Cape keeps the non-racial franchise.

Cape politician William Schreiner, Olive Schreiner's younger brother, remarks that enshrining the division between people of different colours in the constitution is to 'build a grand building upon unsound and sinking foundations'. And even Jan's first biographer, Keith Hancock, notes his career-long habit of letting the 'Native Problem' drift, because of the difficulties of dealing with it, and all the deadly results this habit dragged in its wake. What might have happened, Hancock asks, if he had chosen to put his mind to this problem?

When in 1909 Isie moves for the last time, ten miles south of Pretoria, Jan is en route to England to push for the Union of South Africa. He sends long letters of instructions, which she ignores. Doornkloof is bare veld when Isie and Jan buy it, but they purchase a

British officers' mess for £300, transporting it by rail to the nearby village of Irene. This large and uncomfortable structure, with wood-lined corrugated-iron walls and a tin roof, is positively Spartan: baths are for Sunday nights when the boiler is lit. The house leaks when it rains, and Isie rushes around with basins. Freezing cold in the winter, she hangs thick Basotho blankets over the walls. Stiflingly hot in summer, the evenings are haunted by the loud creaks of contracting iron. Yet, strange creature, she is happy here, in this ersatz *opstal* for the twentieth century, she and Jan recalling fondly the Cape farm-steads of their youth. I find a photograph of Louis Botha and Jan Smuts in a carriage, a woman at the rear wheel, toddler in arms, clearly pregnant. Isie, I think, catching my mother in her profile and around the eyes. Her brown curls are piled up, her angular face some-what stern.

Meanwhile, Jan builds his career. In 1910 Botha's South African Party wins the first general election and Jan is given three ministries. They are opposed by the future National Party, who want independ-ence from Britain. Late into the evening, the Smutses chew over the issues as Isie sits with her mending on the *stoep* (veranda). They know how hard it has been in the post-war recession for poor whites to rebuild their homes or find jobs. With few prospects, poor whites flood into Johannesburg, but the towns and cities are suddenly full of Africans, previously hidden on farms and reserves, working in factor-ies and mines for half as much as whites, jostling for position on city pavements.

Black and white alike live in poverty on the edges of towns, and, even worse, mix, socially and sexually. In 1911, Louis Botha and Jan Smuts's government limit a range of jobs to whites only. In 1913, their Natives Land Act divides land between black and white: Africans, who make up eighty per cent of the population, are given just seven per cent (increasing to 13.5 per cent in 1936). This solidifies the process begun centuries earlier, dispossessing Africans and locking them into labour. This Act, only repealed in 1991, is part of a ribbon of legislation that unfurls into apartheid, leading to homelands, influx control, pass laws and the Group Areas Act.

On service to humanity

September 1914

Spring wheat sprouts green across the fields and Isie is heavy with her ninth and last child, born when she is nearly forty-four. Thousands of miles to the north, the horrors of the First World War are unfolding across Europe. She rereads Jan's letter in shock. Their old friend Koos de la Rey has been shot dead by mistake. Minister of Defence, Smuts is a target now that pro-German Afrikaners, outraged at the planned invasion of German South West Africa (now Namibia), have taken up arms against the government. The police have advised Jan not to sleep at home and she must have a police guard to stay at Doornkloof. Twelve thousand rebels face off against forty thousand Afrikaner loyalists but three months later the fighting is over, with three hundred men dead. Nevertheless, the schism that continues to divide this nation is clear and gaping.

Isie and Jan are parted for four years by the First World War, Jan commanding troops across Africa before leaving for London, where he joins the Imperial War Cabinet. 'We are both on active service to humanity,' he tells her. While Jan visits the royal family at Windsor Castle, she reluctantly entertains British diplomats at Doornkloof, disappearing for a shower as their cars pull up, reappearing, hair damp. While he confers with the British Commander-in-Chief in Mesopotamia (a region of Iraq), she lugs baskets of provisions to wounded soldiers at Roberts Heights military hospital, dishevelled curls blowing over her face.

Isie untangles Jan's income tax and saves money from his salary. The rains come, and the veld grows green again. Sporadic letters with news and speeches service the tie between them, travelling thousands of miles by train and boat. Isie's are long and newsy, Jan's full of instructions: how his pigs should be cared for, how two hundred oaks should be planted. But no letter can undo the miles, and for these years they live separate lives. In England, Jan spends his scarce leisure time with Margaret Gillett and her sister Alice. I uncover a small album in the family archive. Here are Jan, Margaret and Alice in the Berkshire woodland they call Paradise. Here is

Margaret's husband Arthur, cooking over the fire, narrow-faced and weak between breakdowns, here Jan, golden, stern, pouring what looks like wine into a milk jug. They lie on grassy pasture, trees behind them. Between the unsmiling dark-haired sisters with their Bloomsbury glamour, Jan is a man at the height of his powers, enigmatic, self-contained, lionised.

Alice never marries, and for many months she and Jan are dangerously close. Isie's husband is energetic, intellectual and has the bearing of a Scandinavian prince. Alice is researching *The Working Life of Women in the Seventeenth Century*, at the London School of Economics, where she has won a scholarship. This is a woman as bright and driven as Jan himself. The pair exchange passionate letters. Alice moves to London, and in July 1919, sailing home, Jan writes to her: 'What a tremendous past it has been,' the letter reads, 'with all its wild romance, all its agonies and exaltations! Is anything still left? Will they ever come again, the long long dances?' Infidelity? These days the Quaker book of discipline, *Quaker Faith and Practice*, has a section on marriage. 'Unfaithfulness is not necessarily physical,' it reads. Alice, born into Street Quaker Meeting, is surely familiar with this concept. Jan undoubtedly thinks himself so upright and moral a citizen as to be beyond reproach.

After signing the Treaty of Versailles, which he regards as disastrous, Jan's ship docks at Cape Town in August 1919. While Isie has been keeping the home fires burning, he has had another 'good war'. He is feted by the British and is now one of two principal drafters of the covenant of the new League of Nations. Tick tock. There is no time to take breath: days later Prime Minister Botha dies, and by 3 September Jan is in Cape Town, ready to shoulder responsibility for the nation. 'Yes, life is hard; for us it has been a heavy oppressive burden for twenty-one years. How much longer?' he writes to Isie.

Prime Minister Jan Smuts leads South Africa from September 1919 until 1924, living intermittently at Groote Schuur, Rhodes's state mansion. His wife, who does not like the great echoing rooms, the Persian rugs and statuettes, and who resents the Cape for failing to employ Jan two decades earlier, joins him only occasionally. She is forty-eight, her choices made, her life at Doornkloof, and, while she feels Jan's promotion is no more than he deserves, the pattern of their lives will not change now.

Descriptions of Isie tend toward the old woman with grey curls and round glasses, her black dress with its large white collar. But behind the old woman drift the ghosts of her past selves. In a soft-focus portrait from around 1920, when Isie is nearly fifty, she poses with a rose in her right hand, huge sad eyes pale with light. A studio portrait of the entire family shows her in another mood, with a slight suppressed smile, quizzical eyes over an angular nose and an untidy dark bob. After years of wearing her hair long because her husband likes it, she has cut it by holding up each curl and snipping it.

On shopping trips to Pretoria, the children notice people murmuring to each other in her wake, about her hatlessness perhaps, her lack of make-up, or her dress. In this hat-wearing age, Isie owns only one. She makes her own clothes, and her daughters', in dark practical colours. No kind of political wife, Isie can recite the Bible in Greek, but is often found reading magazines she should be packing for hospitals and old-age homes, distracted by the 'delicious' love stories inside. (Doornkloof overflows with books, in the bedrooms, the passages.) Flattery leaves her cold, and she treats earls and farmers the same. This levelling nature appears in her frugality, and she keeps a room full of used boxes and sheaves of brown paper, ironed ready for reuse. She has an embarrassing habit of asking the value of gifts before accepting them.

The house swarms with children, visitors, relations, politicians, wives, the needy. Every afternoon after school, Isie waits, barefoot on the *stoep*, to greet the children before they rush off into the veld to play with sticks, paddle in the streams. Sentences begin in Afrikaans and end in English now, time having rubbed the sharp edges off the grief of the Anglo-Boer War. There are pets – meerkats, a monkey, a crane, Sally the lioness, Jerry the kudu bull who stands menacingly over visitors, trapping them in their cars. Isie cuts two oranges in half and hangs them outside the kitchen window to watch the birds. She shares a double bed with the smallest child while, when he is home, Jan sleeps on the *stoep* on an iron bedstead. 'They prefer this tin hovel, crawling with screaming children and cluttered up with every sort of junk,' Lady Daphne Moore complains.

★

Doornkloof is stimulating and unconventional and human beings are treated with warmth and kindness. But I struggle to place the Africans – who make up eighty per cent of the population – inside this house. So many historical sources ignore Africans altogether that, as J. M. Coetzee observes in *White Writing*: 'the black man becomes a shadowy presence flitting across the stage now and then to hold a horse or serve a meal'. And so it is at Doornkloof – Isie reminds her children to make their beds, wash their underwear, before sitting down to breakfast made by James the cook as she tidies, smiling at Annie Mofakeng, the housekeeper, as she bustles into the kitchen. An old man called Jeremiah waits in the corner, beaming as she enters. 'So many of our black folk are just children,' Isie says of these people who live behind the main house, or further away, in single-roomed shacks kept scrupulously clean, lit by candles and kerosene.

Sarah Gertrude Millin visits Doornkloof in the early 1930s to research a biography of Jan, a decade after publishing *God's Stepchildren*, a novel about what it presents as the tragedy of racial mixing – and we have already heard Isie's views on 'miscegenation'. This strange, nasty word carries so much colonial distaste that it all but falls out of the language in the mid-twentieth century. It comes from a time when white racism is shameless, the natural law of things. In South African novels of this era, authors flaunt words like *flaw*, *taint* and *degeneration*. (After 1945, even the gurus of apartheid are careful not to use eugenics as a basis for their ideology.)

Millin dwells on the smell of 'k★★★★rs'. It is shorthand for the beast: the odour of African men 'taints the night air'. Their touch carries a mortal, spiritual danger: 'He nervously washed his hands after taking theirs; but even his soul, having touched the sores of their souls, seemed to him in need of cleansing. He feared the contagion of the godless.' Here lies the underbelly of whiteness, the DNA of cruelty, the – to subvert Millin's imagery – flaw, the taint, in the nation's blood. A direct line runs from this, through segregationist laws, which keep the white population safe from 'pollution', to the roasting of bodies on barbecues, to bullets ripping through children's bodies.

How does Doornkloof fit into this extreme scenario, where the children love gentle Annie, but Andries the farm manager beats the African farmworkers? Where photographs show the African inhabitants watching, expressionless, as the Smutses, on a jolly camp-ing expedition to the Rooikop farm, wander in and out of their huts? Where Jan's farmworkers can grow their own crops, by which I mean they are permitted to do so, despite this being banned by the 1913 Natives Land Act? There is a fissure between a public policy, which damages many lives, and more generous private behaviour.

But Jan does hold racist views, and there is no evidence to suggest his wife disagrees. In 1895, he claims, 'unless the white race closes its ranks in this country, its position will soon become untenable in the face of that overwhelming majority of prolific barbarism'. During the Boer War, he unwittingly echoes Gideon Joubert in 1826: 'when, to escape violation and nameless insults at the hands of their former servants, now wearing the British uniform, Boer women and girls seek refuge in the mountains'. And in 1947, when he is an old man: 'I am . . . proud of the clean European society we have built up in South Africa, and which I am determined not to see lost in the black pool of Africa.'

Jan Smuts fails, time after time, to address the problem he accepts will always be the most significant facing the nation, and indeed he actively makes it worse. Before South Africa becomes one country in 1909, rich men of all colours in the Cape can vote while in the other three colonies only white men can vote. In the Act of Union that Jan draws up none of these change. Margaret writes: 'I wish some big things had been different in your act of Union . . . I have a great belief in Afrikanders not wishing to leave women outside their own liberty, and also in their being too great to perpetuate the foolish words about European descent.' But history proves her blind to the true nature of the people she calls Afrikanders.

When Jan and Isie are in their formative years, slavery has been abolished across the British Empire, but little else has changed: black is still poorer than white, black still serves white, reinforcing the perception that a black person is less valuable, and less able, than a white person. Anyone who questions the truth of this has only to read the newspapers to rediscover how dangerous the black man is, how violent; how poverty is their natural state.

As the white world turns towards ideals of equality in the post-war era, paying lip-service to change is relatively straightforward for Europe, with its tiny black population; and for Australia, Canada, the

northern United States and for New Zealand, which have extermin-
ated most of their native populations and are quietly assimilating or
sequestering the remainder. Meanwhile, white Europeans benefit
from African labour and raw materials, through colonies and, later,
neo-colonial power. In South America with its mixed populations,
things are more subtle still.

But in South Africa and the Deep South of the United States even
incremental change is difficult. Both have sizeable populations of
both black and white, raised in a society where the white man is the
master and the black man the servant. To achieve equity here, whites
must give up their power, their privilege, who they think they are. In
both places they resist and white supremacy takes root, a virulent
controlling racism, an echo chamber where legislation reinforces
what whites already think they know: how stupid the blacks are, how
servile, how savage, how dangerous. How much they deserve to live
in their shacks on the outskirts of white cities.

Volksmoeder

Burning letters, disappearing for a shower, this woman always avoids
attention, building a private life in her ramshackle tin palace on the
veld. But the public eye follows her anyway as she puffs up Table
Mountain in the late summer of 1930 and her photograph appears in
the paper until 'all Cape Town has been talking of her feat', her
husband tells Margaret. 'The Queen of South Africa' she is called
in the 1930s, to her disgust. So when a secret must be concealed, its
concealment is more difficult, and more important.

As a child, I am aware of faint murmurings about another person.
Someone not included in the list of aunts and uncles, her name
suppressed behind tightened lips. A cuckoo in the nest, trying to steal
the family's gold. Who's in, who's out. Who gets to call themselves a
Smuts. The stakes are high. It is not attractive. And it is not until the
Pandora's Box of DNA genealogy testing opens nearly a century later
that the truth flies out.

In 1918, baby Louis is eight, and the older children are at boarding
school, but not Santa. Santa is at home, perhaps going to school

nearby, and she is a tender fifteen, with a high forehead and straight blonde hair. She is very interested in chickens, which might sound strange, but later she runs her own chicken farm, so it has utility in the end, this interest in chickens. She is credulous, loving and always willing to think others know more than she does. Doornkloof remains isolated, down its track, and Santa does not have many friends. Meanwhile, her mother is tangled up looking after the younger ones, running the household; her father absent for years fighting battles for the British.

So when Santa begins to hang around the farm manager, saturnine Andries Weyers, who is nearly ten years her senior, Isie does not necessarily notice. Teenagers live their own secret lives, hiding in plain sight, with their private thoughts, hastily concealed, furtive, trying out life for size, how they might be once they step beyond the parental boundary. There are nooks and crannies on Doornkloof, folds in the land, unoccupied farm buildings and acres of unaccounted time. Andries, who beats the farmworkers but spoils small children, is a raffish sort: later, in the 1930s, my grandmother separates him from the young Englishwoman brought along to look after her children, so smitten are they with each other.

It is hard to piece together what happens, which people have conspired to hide under veils of misdirection for a century, and because it seems disrespectful to speculate, some sort of sordid rifling through their dirty laundry. Still, I cannot stop my own mind from forming its conclusions, and I imagine Jan rigid with anger, sixteen-year-old Santa sobbing, Andries a supplicant, abasing himself. Birth out of wedlock means ruin for Santa and perhaps an end to Prime Minister Smuts's career. So Santa is sent away, maybe to Durban, to have the child in secrecy, under cover of an assumed illness, and then returns without the child, and in August 1920, when Santa is just seventeen, my grandmother writes: 'Santa is now completely used to boarding school. She seems to be healthier and can do more work.'

All of which means someone else must know the scheme of events, perhaps Mrs Whyte, who mysteriously takes up residence at the Irene Club with a small ward for a year, before they both arrive at Doornkloof in 1922 where they stay, although Mrs Whyte seems a sad character, someone who gets brought in to help with this living problem and then stays for years, an aimless being. The ward's name is Kathleen, and, despite the secrecy, rumours about her parentage eddy and flow down the years – is she Jan's illegitimate child? Or Santa's, born before she marries Andries Weyers in the mid-1920s? Not until a hundred years afterwards does one of her grandchildren take a test for a genealogy site and find his DNA related by blood to other Smuts descendants: Kathleen is the daughter of Santa and Andries Weyers.

Despite the gossip that flows over the *stoep* at Doornkloof, this secret never leaks out; not once in forty years does Santa, who grows into a sensible, conservative woman, mention that Kathleen belongs to her. Not when her siblings make snide comments about the 'poor little orphan', not when she marries Andries and has three more children, never in all the years they are married, which is until Santa dies. And Isie? She takes Kathleen on; of course she does. What else would she do? She has built her life around taking people in, what her children call 'Ouma's lame ducks', like Deneys Reitz, the teenage commando who collapses from malaria in 1906 and Isie nurses for three years. But Isie and Jan never formally adopt Kathleen, leaving her in a limbo that haunts her entire life, this child who is a gift, but also a threat; who, invited to play at Santa and Andries's house as a little girl, fantasises that they are her parents.

Isie takes on this dangerous secret, mothers this lost soul, just as her country begins to see her as a kind of *volksmoeder*, a people's mother, which sounds ominously like the *volkswagen*, the people's car, which will soon be conceived by Adolf Hitler. A car for the people who are a homogenous whole, or will be just as soon as they can strip out all the Jews and Roma, all the homosexual and otherwise less-than-ideal Aryans. And so Isie, in her eccentric complexity, will be presented as a mother of the people who would reject her if they knew what kind of mother she was, taking on this child born out of wedlock.

Even with Kathleen around, Doornkloof subsides into silence as the older children grow up and Jan travels. This emptying nest drives Isie out into the world, or could it be a sudden rush of freedom to the head? Party-political work in support of her husband, talking to the *boerevroue* in Afrikaans; and, later, speeches at women's clubs in Johannesburg, in English. What would they talk about but their children? How would she reach them but through their homes? She likens South Africa to a fractious family, appeals to the Women's South African Party to 'give the baby time to grow'. Isie, the unifying mother, taking on the country as she has taken on her illegitimate grandchild. The suckers of the ivy run fast and true round the women's hearts: deny the family and risk being cast out, lonely in the world outside; risk damaging the family that succours you. They are bound happily into the homogenous nation.

It all reeks of old dark furniture, carpet beaters, twin beds. Where are the women with their horses and guns? Have they put on their housecoats? Are they building the nation, one loaf at a time? In her *Women and Labour* of 1911, Olive Schreiner suggests that no woman of any race or class will challenge their position in society 'while the welfare and persistence of their society requires their submission'. This only ceases, she says, when 'women's acquiescence is no longer necessary or desirable'. She writes to Isie, promising her a copy of the book: 'I know you are not very much interested in the woman's question, but I'd like to send it to you just because I love you.' Who knows if Isie reads this work, accepts any of her friend's findings? Now, twenty years later, she might concede reluctantly that women should have the vote, but the idea of women in parliament fills her with horror.

Women's political rights are recognised very early in some frontier societies: Wyoming women are the first to be given the vote in 1869. Indeed, Voortrekker women expect the same even earlier before horrifying the British with their forthright demands. And now, a century later, when women in Europe and North America are throwing themselves under horses, chaining themselves to railings, Afrikaner women stay meekly at home, which is their role in the battle against the black man and the British. What pure South African irony it is that when white women are handed the vote in 1930 it is to wipe those repugnant black marks from the Cape electoral roll, by reducing African and coloured male voters to an easily dismissed ten per cent. (Black voters are removed from the Cape roll in 1936; in 1960, they are denied all representation.)

Fear of *die Swart Gevaar* – the black danger – rises, whipped up by Afrikaner nationalists in their successful election campaign of 1929.

Yet if the Afrikaners are suffering from the drought and the Great Depression, other races suffer more. Nothing will grow on the exhausted, eroded soil of the African reserves. Men travel long distances to find waged work on farms and mines. Africans and Indians resist the rise in oppressive legislation, but to no avail. In opposition, Jan suggests a system to safeguard white domination while allowing some blacks to climb the social hierarchy: a non-racial franchise based on wealth and income. So many chances to avoid the road to apartheid missed.

There are voices in the wilderness, but too few to make themselves heard. If only, when the wider world was turning away from prejudicial laws, South Africa had listened. But it stands unique among the British colonies: it is not Australia, New Zealand, the United States or Canada, where settlers all but wipe out the native population. Nor India, where whites play a limited leadership role. And it is one of only a handful of colonies with an ethnically divided white society. All this plays into the impossibly tangled web of loyalties and competition.

Whatever the differences in outlook between Nationalist leader Daniël Malan and Jan Smuts, laws introduced by all parties in these two decades provide the framework for apartheid. Slums are torn down, blacks moved to new townships outside the city, better jobs are reserved for whites, pass laws are enforced, Africans in the Cape are stripped of voting rights. Afrikaans becomes an official language in 1925, purified of its *kleurling* (coloured) roots into the language of the Boer. The fortress of Afrikanerdom rises: railways nationalised, protective tariffs and subsidies put in place, state-run iron and steel industries set up.

But men and women like Malan want more. In 1933, when Hertzog's National Party goes into coalition with Smuts, Malan, appalled, takes his Purified National Party into opposition. A letter from Isie to Margaret illustrates how close she sits to this work:

> We had a meeting last week of our SAP Head Committee . . . and then Dr Malan and 6 others left the Fusion party . . . We are glad to be rid of him, but hope he won't do too much mischief among the young students at Stellenbosch.

That mischief is not long in coming: the next few years see a secret battle for the grassroots of the National Party. Malan's hardliners take over branches, provincial committees, candidate selection commit-tees, all the dull but vital paraphernalia of politics.

In 1938 Afrikaner nationalism reaches a new peak, and even Isie is at her sewing machine, running up smocks and bonnets for the new Great Trek. Ox-wagons parade across the country, visit Piet Retief's birthplace at Welvanpas. Women converge on Pretoria to lay the foundations of the Voortrekker Monument. Under the foundation stone, they bury a copy of the Voortrekker vow at Blood River in 1838 and that unreliable historical document, the land deal made between Piet Retief and Dingaan. Standing at the Blood River site in Natal, Malan speaks; the Afrikaner has begun his second Great Trek, he says, but now: 'Your Blood River is not here. Your Blood River lies in the city.' Just as the Voortrekkers beat the Zulus at Blood River, so they must beat the Africans in the new cities, and I think of the river running red, the bodies of Zulu warriors clotting the water like tree trunks on a log drive.

'Keep the good and forget the bad,' Isie tells her friends as they knit on the *stoep* at Doornkloof, repeating the sentiment on political plat-forms across the country. But watch as a poor tenant farmer, living in a shack on another man's land, reads the scorn in Englishmen's faces or must compete with black men. What's the use of a woman safe in her farmhouse preaching to him? The Afrikaners are *laagering* their wagons. And before the circle is complete another world war will add a layer of bitterness, laying the groundwork for the National Party to sweep to power in 1948.

'Sarie Marais'

Die Volk: as sinister in South Africa as in Nazi Germany, the blood and soil of a racially unified Aryan nation. No surprise then that when Britain declares war on Germany in September 1939, many Afrikaners slither towards the Nazi camp; even Prime Minister Hertzog wants to remain neutral in what is surely a battle between good and evil. But my great-grandfather does something right, saving

South Africa from the eternal shame of supporting a regime that rips the gold teeth out of the mouths of Jews they have gassed, weaves their hair into work clothes and liners for the boots of U-boat crews. Parliament votes, Smuts wins. He becomes prime minister again, and South Africa enters the Second World War for the Allies.

To Isie, nearly seventy now, her husband is back where he belongs, but the Afrikaners are not happy; many hate Prime Minister Smuts: traitor, turncoat, appeaser are the words they use. German spies could be anywhere, and ahead of them the *Ossewabrandwag* – the 'ox-wagon sentinel': the paramilitary anti-British, anti-war group – is formed by disgruntled Afrikaners in 1938. Doornkloof is under threat again. A guardhouse, security posts and gates appear; armed police lurk in the trees; visitors are stopped and questioned. Protestors gather at the Voortrekker Monument in Pretoria. Fearing an attack on Jan's life, machine-gun posts are set up. Isie works away in the kitchen through the long, dark hours, nagging at her daughters to make more flasks of steaming, creamy coffee, send out Cambridge rusks and oranges to the policemen. The danger passes, but in late 1942 police arrest Olympic boxer Robey Leibbrandt as he prepares to assassinate Jan, for the Third Reich.

South Africans fight in the Desert War, and in the Italian Campaign, eleven thousand are killed in action. Isie's sons serve in Kenya, North Africa and Italy, her daughters in South Africa. Jan travels for months each year, consulted by Churchill, Eisenhower and others, appointed Field Marshal in the British Army in 1941. In the general election of 1943, he wins a huge victory. It is to be his last. Isie joins Jan on engagements now, they travel in a convoy of polished black cars, pennants flying, complete with motorcycle outriders as pedestrians wave and cheer. Isie moves between Cape Town and Irene, Jan's return to premiership meaning a return to Groote Schuur. The couple shun the grander rooms, choosing the cosy library as their sitting room, with its fireplace and easy chairs, its books and radio.

22 December 1944

Dial in to a radio show and you might hear the guttural g's and rolling r's of the old Afrikaans favourite 'Sarie Marais' on the lilting tongue of Gracie Fields in her radio studio in California, while two continents away Isie, with her wiry grey curls and round glasses, her shapeless black dress, tunes in through the Doornkloof wireless on a fine summer's evening. Thousands listen in movie theatres and army camps across South Africa and the deserts of North Africa as stars pay tribute to Ouma Smuts on her seventy-fourth birthday.

Noel Coward jokes about casting his top hat and tailcoat aside for the open shirts and shorts of the farmer she told him she preferred when they met. Sybil Thorndike, Bob Hope, Bing Crosby: they all send messages of goodwill in the mannered accents of 1940s Hollywood. Cheesy and unutterably dated, this concert raises £76,000 (over £2 million now) for South African troops. Appointed head of the Gifts and Comforts Fund at the beginning of the war, Isie inches reluctantly into the spotlight as her fund dispatches radio sets, socks, glory bags containing string, scissors, needle and thread, wool, safety pins to soldiers. It sends Bibles, and every Christmas a tin of toffees along with a photograph and message from Jan and Isie – 'Ouma and the Oubaas'.

Isie has left South Africa only once, to visit the Victoria Falls, but in 1941, and again the following year, she flies to Egypt. Arriving in Cairo, she visits soldiers in the desert, in rest camps, hospitals and recreation centres; white troops and coloured troops (not allowed to carry weapons, they are drivers and labourers). Received with cheers of 'Ouma', Isie chats to soldiers over tea, promising to write to wives and mothers. Later she pens each letter by hand. If Isie loves 'her boys', she finds the grandees more difficult. The ambassadors and generals and their ladies dine at 9.30 p.m., she reports with astonishment, her usual bedtime. And they sit up so late after dinner!

Short and bespectacled, Isie has grown into the Grandmother of the Nation: the Africa Star ribbon – for South African troops prepared to serve anywhere in Africa – is Ouma's Garter, the brandy ration Ouma's Stuka juice. By the next decade, Isie and Jan will be abandoned by history, with no constituency in the National Party, the global community moving towards a rhetoric of racial equality. But in these days she proves a reassuring symbol for a world in darkness.

Isie falls asleep through films now and during her husband's speeches, which she stubbornly insists on attending. In December 1942, she suffers a mild stroke, and in 1944 another, bigger stroke puts her out of action for months. Jan writes to Margaret: 'She is the real cement in this family and if she were to go the house would fall to pieces. And what would become of me in the latter days?'

'Every evening, when everyone else was in bed, she would go over to his room, and they would sit discussing things,' Larissa Smuts, a granddaughter who lives at Doornkloof in the late 1940s, tells me. Absent for so much of their married life, Isie is still the key that keeps him ticking over.

In 1945, Jan joins the San Francisco conference, which creates the United Nations Charter. His star riding high, Anthony Eden calls him 'the doyen of the Conference – quite unrivalled in intellectual attributes and unsurpassed in experience and authority'. But his hypocrisy does not go unnoticed, at home or abroad. Increasingly, the old statesman is caught: too racist for the new world order, not racist enough for white South Africa. In August, the first atomic bombs drop on Japan: the Second World War is over. In South Africa, industrialisation leads to a surge in the number of urban blacks. White anxieties about vanishing 'in the black sea', as Malan puts it, rise. Jan suggests recognising Africans in white areas, relaxing pass laws and easing labour restrictions to nudge the white electorate towards power-sharing. He includes no proposal to increase black parliamentary representation, so the Natives Representatives Council reject his ideas.

Meanwhile Doornkloof sees a post-war baby boom: five new grandchildren in just a year. Frail now, Isie proudly shows visitors the snowy nappies flapping in the breeze, the prams lined up on the driveway.

'Like a dream it has gone by'

Doornkloof, 1947

In the photograph Queen Elizabeth, a sizeable frothy hat perched on her head, strings of pearls at her neck, turns toward Isie, mouth open to make a charming remark. George VI sits on Isie's right and behind them the two princesses, smiling happily in their neat blouses, all collar and puffed sleeves, looking as if they could leap on a horse and canter off across the veld. Jan is not there: parliament sits in Cape Town, and he is still prime minister. Instead, all six Smuts children and a clutch of grandchildren gather on the front *stoep* to greet the royals. Santa and Sylma, who have brought over their best china, pour the tea – even for the royal family Isie will not 'play Mother'.

Doornkloof is not the royal family's usual habitat. It is dark and shabby and smells of coffee, *bobotie* and *melktert*, those Cape foods Isie has brought with her from the past. It is nothing like the carpeted, light-filled homes of English-speaking South Africans with their neat gardens. The values here are Afrikaner: family-centric, ascetic, plain-speaking. Through this visit, the king and queen signify their respect for the Afrikaner; in receiving them, Isie suggests that the horrors of the Anglo-Boer War have been forgotten. 'A Queen visiting a queen,' Jan says, although the contrast can hardly be greater.

The British royal family traverse South Africa for two months, racking up over ten thousand miles by train. It is an ambitious but fruitless attempt to shore up support for the faltering empire, for the king whose head still adorns stamps and coins – even if Isie no longer sticks those stamps upside down. For Jan and Isie, the empire is a safe harbour, but they are out of step with most Afrikaners.

The following year, 1948, South Africa's white electorate steps beyond the pale. And it becomes the Smutses' *annus horribilis* too as Isie's life continues to plot its course parallel to her country. In January, Mohandas Gandhi is assassinated, Jan's old adversary over Indian rights. In May, the National Party sweeps to power, unseating Jan, and begins to implement apartheid. In December, Jan Hofmeyr, Jan Smuts's heir apparent, dies unexpectedly. (Hofmeyr is Isie's second cousin, another of Margaretha Louisa Retief's great-grandchildren, but he opposes the removal of black voting rights and restrictions on Indians buying land. As long as we assign value to the people of our country on the basis of their skin colour, he says in 1946, we will force our nation to endure what Socrates termed the lie at the depths of our souls. His early death is a huge loss.)

But it is another death that diminishes Doornkloof. One October Sunday in 1948, Kitty, wife of the elder Smuts son, Japie, phones to say he is unwell. By the early hours of Monday, he is dead of cerebral meningitis, aged forty-two. Isie is so quiet and calm that her husband frets, and I think of Anna Retief and gentle Francois, struck by lightning in 1839: 'The hand of the Lord does what he wants and death does not miss anyone.' Still vigorous but increasingly ill, Jan finds being in opposition frustrating. On Dingaan's Day, 1949, he addresses the inauguration of the Voortrekker Monument. 'Let us not be fanatical about the past and, by romanticising it, get on to the wrong track,' he says.

It is too late.

On 24 May, Jan turns eighty, receiving the freedom of the city of Cape Town with three hundred thousand lining the streets to watch. On 29 May, he suffers the first of many heart attacks. For the remaining weeks of his life, he stays at Doornkloof. He is, finally, home. On the eve of their fifty-third wedding anniversary in April, he writes to Isie: 'When I look back at it all today it seems like a dream. And like a dream it has gone by – incredibly fast.' Sixty-three years earlier, in his very first letter, Jan wished: 'that our mutual love may be pure and unselfish, that in whatever relation and circumstances we may be, it may grow from more to more, and, if possible, be never dissolved.'

On 11 September, sitting down to prepare for bed, he slumps forward and never recovers consciousness. The Smuts children dress the field marshal in his uniform for his last campaign. Professor Guy Elliot drives over to Doornkloof, and Isie meets him on the *stoep*, standing under a single dim electric light. 'She feared she might break down,' he says later, 'and that was unthinkable, particularly in front of her family, for was she not now the head of the family, and whoever heard of the head of the Smuts family breaking down?' The family listen to the news of Jan's death on the radio at 9 p.m. Before she goes to bed, Isie performs her usual tasks: ironing, feeding the cats, washing up the teacups.

Later there are cables from the king of the United Kingdom – 'the force of his intellect has enriched the wisdom of the whole human race' – and a letter from Churchill – 'a warrior-statesman and philosopher who was probably more fitted to guide struggling and blundering humanity through its sufferings and perils towards a better day, than anyone who lived in any country during his epoch'. Isie does not attend the military funeral in Pretoria, does not see the coffin on the gun carriage, drawn through the streets lined with onlookers, the charger draped in black, with riding boots and spurs reversed. Her lone wreath of Cape heather rests on the flag-draped coffin. It is taken by train to Johannesburg and cremated. Isie and her children scatter the ashes at the memorial stone on the *koppie* behind the house.

At nearly eighty, Isie does not stray far. In the evenings, she answers the thousands of letters she receives (even more now that Jan is dead), she crochets and continues her *plakking*, the unchanging occupation of fifty years. The articles about Jan just keep coming, but she finishes them in the end, 150 albums. On 25 February 1954, Isie complains of a tight chest, and her daughter Louis arrives in the late afternoon with Professor Elliot. Isie dies soon after. Her body, too, travels through crowded streets before being cremated, and her ashes scattered at Doornkloof, joining Jan and Japie, and the three lost babies.

A shilling life

I find myself judging Isie by my twenty-first-century mores, condemning what I see as weakness in case it taints me. But women are whole human beings, bundles of characteristics warped by the patriarchy, shaped by time, giving rise to singular lives. I think all this while comparing Isie to Emily Hobhouse and Olive Schreiner – a circle of friendship that centres around the Boer War, the dark heart of Isie's story, despite their starkly different lives.

Emily Hobhouse is an irritating woman, cloyingly affectionate and manipulative. Lord Kitchener agrees, calling her 'that bloody woman', but the Boers adore her. She is a heroine. In 1926, when her ashes are buried at the foot of the *Vrouemonument*, my great-grandfather gives the funeral oration. 'In that dark hour when we as a race were practically doomed to extinction, she appeared as an angel, as a heaven-sent messenger,' he proclaims in his usual flowery manner. 'Strangest of all, she was an Englishwoman. Now she lies buried in the hearts of a grateful nation.'

It doesn't stop in 1926. In 2013 Afrikaner telecom billionaire Koos Bekker and his hotelier wife Karen Roos buy the Hobhouse family home in Somerset, south-west England: Hadspen House. The resulting beauty is worthy of a sugar baron. I stalk the country retreat on the internet, with its apple-tree maze, its cider press and spa. The reviews are reverent. More importantly for my purposes, they reveal a tasteful scattering of Emily Hobhouse memorabilia and even a cocktail named the 'Emily'. I wonder what the ingredients might be: it is so dissonant my head hurts.

Emily Hobhouse does not originate at Hadspen House. A poor cousin of the Somerset Hobhouses, she is born in Cornwall to a reclusive, ailing clergyman, and only his death frees her, aged thirty-five. This upbringing seems to destabilise her, leaves her gasping for affection, and belligerent in her care for the unfortunate. Connected to the British establishment through her Hobhouse relations, a Liberal MP recruits her as secretary of an anti-Boer War committee in 1900, and she sets sail for the Cape to visit concentration camps and deliver aid. At this point, fifty children are dying every day. So stubborn is Hobhouse, so shocking her descriptions, that in the face of bristling hostility she forces the British government to investigate her claims.

After the war, Hobhouse provides ruined Boer farmers with oxen and ploughs. She and Jan Smuts meet in July 1903, and so begins a long and fruitful friendship: it is Hobhouse who opens the doors of power in London for him. It is also Emily Hobhouse who introduces him to the Clark family, which makes a fundamental difference to me, enabling my grandparents to meet and marry. She is, however, what Jan, in a 1917 letter to Isie, describes as 'a little mad', a humanitarian shockingly rude to human beings, a mess of contradictions.

In another of the belittlements that litter the history books like toilet paper stuck to a shoe, historian Thomas Pakenham dismisses Emily Hobhouse as a dumpy middle-aged spinster. What he sees as her failure as a woman – her sub-standard appearance, her inability to be a wife or mother – allows her to visit the concentration camps, to campaign. As a woman in a man's world in 1900, Emily cannot compete on male terms. Being connected, intelligent, determined, resourceful is not enough. To have agency as Emily Hobhouse does, a woman must have psychological differences that make regular female life impossible. Vanity, egotism, courage, desperation, all strong enough to fracture the glass that walls women off, allowing her to step through into the action.

Is it inevitable that Hobhouse is frantically lonely, conflicted about her choices? Later she visits Zorgvliet, becoming besotted with the Smutses' baby daughter, Santa. She writes to Isie: 'the rise and fall of governments and (political) parties and the well-being of colonies and suchlike – to fill the blank caused by the absence of a home and children . . . I deem the rearing of one baby far more important than all those things piled together.'

I turn to Olive Schreiner to understand more of how these women experience life. Feminist, pacifist, socialist: Olive becomes a crucial and freethinking writer. Like Emily Hobhouse, she balances a problematic personal life with unorthodox success. Born in 1855 in what is now Lesotho, the ninth of twelve children of German and English missionaries, she is self-educated and brilliant. Like Isie, she finds herself too poor to pursue her dream of being a doctor. In 1883 she publishes *The Story of an African Farm*, a feminist tale of life on a Karoo ostrich farm, still regarded as the first great South African novel. It tells the story of a girl who, faced with rigid Boer conventions, fights to decide her own fate.

It is a close and loving friendship, Isie's and Olive's: more than a hundred letters from Olive to Isie survive, moles breaking the surface of Isie's life, bearing tales of the rich soil beneath. Here we have a tin of biscuits left in Stellenbosch for Olive; here plaintive sadness that there will be no shared holiday to Gordon's Bay this year. It is not all female solidarity; Olive is too unconventional for that. Her letters to Jan are coy, and she uses her letters to Isie to get to him. 'Tell *Neef* Jan,' she writes in 1908, '. . . he's not to go on dancing on the head of my Indians like he does; & that when I die, he must take care of all my black people for me!!! I shall leave them to him in my will.' Olive fights for racial justice, unlike Jan.

Like the heroine of *African Farm*, Olive Schreiner fights to decide her own fate. She travels between South Africa and England, tries to heal society through her writing, forms close friendships with radical figures such as sexologist Havelock Ellis and lives on her husband's isolated farm. She writes key texts and makes political connections, but struggles with health and isolation. Olive tries marriage, tries to be a mother but loses her child and has multiple miscarriages. Her marriage founders, and she moves to England, only for the First World War to break out. Eventually, she dies a lonely death in December 1920 in a Cape boarding house. Is all this inevitable too? Olive stands as far outside the patriarchal norm that Isie seems to represent, our faithful Penelope, as Emily Hobhouse does.

For centuries, the closest most women come to power is to be married to it. But there are ways other than Isie's of handling such a marriage. Late in life, Jan becomes close friends with Winston Churchill and Churchill's wife proffers a tantalising alternative. Clementine Churchill is central to Winston's political life, his partner in elections, campaigns and world conferences. She is chair of the Red Cross Aid to Russia Fund in the Second World War, and much more. Clementine puts Winston first – with his depressions and fiery temper, his rash decisions – and her own concerns second. All but one of their four children have difficult lives involving alcoholism, multiple marriages, suicide and gambling.

Perhaps it is Winston's mental health, rather than Clementine's priorities, that affects their children so badly. I cannot accept that Isie had to stay at home and look after the children or bear the blame for their misery, with all that implies for female emancipation. Children must be nurtured, but why must this mean that women stay trapped at home? I feel as if I have put on someone else's jumper, woollen, itchy, tight. The stark, dated contrast in Isie and Jan's marriage infuriates me: the triumphant masculine, the stifled feminine.

But life is not one size fits all, and its truth lies as much in the folds and seams as in the overall shape. Or, to put it another way, Isie does not play a bit part in her husband's life: she plays the lead character in her own. The complex intelligence moving behind the public persona gives the lie to the perception of her life as stifled or failed. The life she leads is her choice, as much as it can be, and it is a symptom of the era that this choice feels like no choice at all. She is born into a culture where male and female realms are distinct: public/domestic. The choices she makes for Jan are the choices of a proud Afrikaner *volksmoeder*: with his brilliant mind and charismatic spirit, she believes that he will save the Afrikaner people; must she not support him?

The family unit remains central to Afrikaner and Boer societies. To this day, Afrikaner parents are deeply tied into their children's lives. 'Demonstration of affection within a highly controlled and structured family environment has no consistent equal within other South African families,' writes Professor Jonathan Jansen, first black vice-chancellor at the University of the Free State. 'This strong love for their children therefore translates into a deep and abiding interest in all aspects of the child's life.' There are few roles for women outside this family unit in the early twentieth century, and Isie takes the path most likely to offer her fulfilment and security.

But after the separations and agony of the Anglo-Boer War, Isie insists on her own space to exist, refusing to travel with Jan, sharing a bed with the children instead. She is not just the wife of a politician; she is herself. These small shifts inside a marriage, invisible to anyone outside it, are small patterns of female resistance.

Emily Hobhouse and Olive Schreiner achieve greatness, but they struggle to live outside the status quo, suffer sadness, loneliness, poverty. Isie, trapped within the scaffold of Afrikaner society, lives a reasonably fulfilled, comfortable life. The concept of duty is no longer fashionable, with its undercurrent of coercion: we learn that freedom, for growth, for self-actualisation, is a right, almost a responsibility. Yet duty can act as a kind of trellis, training the tendrils of life into a fruitful array. Following a dutiful path can be a way of moving forward in this world of infinite choice.

I think in the end Isie *is* free, wandering into Pretoria hatless and untidy, asking princes of the realm the price of their socks. She does as she pleases and what pleases her is to stay at home as much as possible, children and animals underfoot. Why it pleases her is a complex melange of personal experience, character, history, culture, society and chance. Without pressure, great people will continue to be great men; increasing equality of power, finance and opportunity mean more great people are already great women. But we do not all want, we are not all able, to climb mountains. Clementine Churchill, perhaps, wants to name seas. Isie wants to potter around the garden.

~

'Without my past, I have no future'

I find myself at an ending, or what should be an ending. But my powerful great-grandfather leaves a long tail behind him, like a comet. It hangs in the night sky for generations after. We who come later take up the burden of this life, stagger forward under the weight of its story, repercussions ringing in our ears like a depth charge. This process starts before I am born and will continue on beyond me.

Doornkloof, 2016
The Big House, my mother calls it. The road runs parallel to the railway line, protected by a concrete fence, the straight road – just a track then – my grandmother would have walked and cycled a century ago to get to school in Irene village. It swings left over a small bridge, and the surface changes from tarmac to red earth. To the left stands the Weyers' house, where my mother's cousin Louis – the judge – lived, and then his son Philip. Later there were intruders and now the low brick structure with its large rough front lawn looks abandoned. Is this the place where as a child I saw the snake inside, which was killed, and proved to be a puff adder?

To the right stands Great-Aunt Santa's house, now an upmarket guesthouse catering for business people. Sixty-five years have passed since my mother visited as a child. The luxuriant grass, sprinkled with river water, stinks gently; the grounds where Santa ran her chicken farm now the site of faux-Cape Dutch guest suites. The management all seem to be white, the serving staff all black. My children cannonball into the freezing pool while I sip a gin and tonic and make notes. It is excruciating, the persistence of wealth and power.

The next morning, we grind up to Doornkloof over the dirt road. The circular drive looks rutted and uneven, fenced off with plastic tape and iron stakes, so we continue round to the back. In the carpark sits a crushed Portacabin, as if it has been hit by a falling tree. Not much has changed in the twenty years since I was last here. The long, enclosed veranda running the length of the frontage, the white lace ironwork framing the front gable, the red corrugated roof. We walk up the steps. Inside, it is dark as ever, although the internal walls have been painted a pale green rather than the dark forest shade Isie chose. How claustrophobic it must have been. In the front hallway, the massive dinner gong hangs from two elephant tusks.

People welcome us, all white, all delighted to have interested visitors, all embarrassingly honoured to meet us. Later we find ourselves featured in the Friends of Smuts House newsletter. For some, Jan Smuts remains a legitimate hero, a South African statesman surpassed only by Nelson Mandela on the world stage and relatively untainted by the spectre of apartheid. Long ignored, his profile has been raised by the recent publication of two books by Richard Steyn, a former newspaper editor.

The soft-spoken, soft-bodied woman at the till doesn't want to charge us, although the museum is desperately short of funds. She talks of her children moved abroad, to Ipswich, to North America, her youngest a ballerina sought by Russia. 'I don't know what will happen to me now,' she says placidly. The house guide is elderly; his skin, tanned by tobacco and sunshine, glows a deep brown around the blue eyes, glazed with cataracts. He regales us with off-colour tales of pretty women he has shown around. Remnants of another country. The house, too, has the smell and feel peculiar to heritage sites in poorer countries: deserted, musty, irrelevant. The roof is leaking, the floor collapsing. Dealers target exhibits: there is a torn section where a medal has been levered off, gaps in the display case of pens and keys.

In a cabinet: two yellowed christening gowns, trimmed with lace. Isie's own, from 1870. The money belt she stitched to hide the gold coins Jan gave her as he left for war. The black-edged mourning cards announcing the death of Koosie in August 1900. In her bedroom are family photographs: here a large photograph of Rollo, the brother who died in a shooting accident in 1912, dark-haired and handsome. Here a younger Isie, austere, surrounded by her six surviving children. And carefully arrayed on the bed: a pair of Mills & Boon romances.

The general manager, Anne, is a warm, vigorous woman whose intelligent enthusiasm cuts away the effect of her limp and white hair. She and my mother discover common ground almost immediately, although it is thousands of miles and fifty years away: Swiss Cottage in 1965, the Tube stations and swimming pools. 'I took some friends to see where I used to work a few years ago,' Anne says, 'but the building had gone. There was a big glass box there instead.'

She takes us into the curator's room. Down one side stands a row of filing cabinets piled with cardboard boxes. 'This is it,' she says. 'These are the papers.' She opens a drawer and, with tender care, takes out a file of dark shiny grey cardboard tied together with narrow green ribbon. The paper is so fragile it is flaking, the newspaper cuttings gummed in neat rows. It is one of Isie's *plakking* books. Anne takes out another, in slightly better condition. I had imagined large photo-album-type books, but these are hand-made A4 folders in various configurations. '1901,' it says in Isie's handwriting at the top. Page upon page of newspaper reports of the Boer War. Isie bound together these first drafts of history and created an Urtext with her husband at the centre.

There is no money to maintain this house, to protect the papers from damp or fire. The history it contains means nothing in the new dispensation, an irrelevance to a black culture trying to assert itself, needing to tell its own stories. It is an odd sensation. 'Without my past, I have no future,' says Anne sadly. 'Who said that? Benjamin Franklin, I think.' The greatest interest comes from the thieves, intent on stripping the house of its small assets, its medals, pens, keys. Even the library sits behind Perspex because books keep being pilfered.

I am reminded of a journey I take twenty years before through the north of Mozambique, where the road is so poor that it takes three days to cover one hundred miles. As the rice lorry lurches from pothole to pothole, we can dimly make out, through the dark glossy leaves, a railway running alongside the road. Half collapsed, over-grown with creepers, the bannisters and bars of the electric line are as chaotic as fallen dominos. Two decades previously, that hundred miles would have taken a couple of hours by rail. Entropy, decay, the European occupation being erased by the forest.

Why should Doornkloof matter to the new rulers? After centuries of having their land stolen by the white man, their families separated, dignity stripped, what possible interest could they have in deifying such people's history? I don't know why I am surprised. Perhaps we expect to find things as we left them, the pencil still on the table, the coffee still warm. To turn and find the dead alive once again, the status quo firmly in place, that first film still fresh.

In 2015, the site became subject to a land claim: a man called Jacob Gumede filing a petition for five hectares of the nineteen-hectare area, including the plot upon which the house – declared a national monument in 1966 – stands, on the grounds of historical dispossession. It is hard to know how much further the Big House can limp into the future. 'I don't know how long we can carry on with the economy like it is, and there is so much violence now, everywhere in the world,' Anne says, a woman bewildered – as so many of us are – by the seeming collapse of everything. Then, 'Let's say goodbye with a South African hug,' she says, embracing us both.

Decline and fall. Jan Smuts International Airport, the airport we fly into in the 1980s, smuggling our relationship to power inside our minds, becomes Oliver Tambo International in 2006, thus neatly symbolising the transfer of power from white to black. But statues of old white men continue to litter South African cities in a strange afterlife, the result of Mandela's philosophy of reconciliation. That deeply entrenched inequalities between the races persist leads to the removal of Rhodes's statue at the University of Cape Town in 2015, a move largely sanctioned by South Africans. But when the protest comes to the UK it is another story.

In 2016, back in Cape Town, I have lunch with once-little Puleng Lange-Stewart, her hair now dread-locked, the red jumper long forgotten. Puleng and her partner study at the University of Cape Town (UCT), and over coriander-flecked boerewors and grilled aubergine, conversation turns to the 'RhodesMustFall' demonstrations of the previous year, their reach up the Atlantic to Britain. 'Yes,' they agree, 'we really made you sit up and listen.' Despite our perch in this holiday home up on the hill, I am taken aback to be identified with colonising Britain, embarrassed that the primary emotion 'RhodesMustFall' appears to stir up at home, at least until the George Floyd protests, is outrage at the ingratitude of the Rhodes Scholar who leads the campaign.

My family's confused relationship with imperial power appears on film in footage from November 1956, which shows my mother as a teenager staring up in silent black and white at a newly unveiled statue of her grandfather in Parliament Square, alongside her mother and sisters. The British Pathé newsreel shows seated ranks of dignitaries and Clementine Churchill in place of her 'indisposed' husband. The bronze statue, designed by Jacob Epstein, has Smuts in his army uniform, leaning forward slightly, arms behind his back like some ice-skating general.

Already in 1956 Margaret Gillett is questioning the wisdom of raising a statue to Smuts when South Africa is engaged in anti-British ferment. Smuts's biographer, Keith Hancock, writes to her:

> Your reference to the Jameson Raid and the Prime Minister hit the situation exactly to my mind. It is an appalling world to put up a statue. I think Churchill is very well advised in getting out of his function in the ceremony.

Despite this rocky start, the statue stands peacefully in Parliament Square for over half a century, held in high enough regard by some that they repaint it green in 2017.

Statues are about nation-building, of course: about how a nation (re)creates its past, what it remembers to create its future. The Voortrekker Monument near Pretoria goes up not in the aftermath of the Great Trek but a century later in the 1930s, when Afrikaner nationalism is rising. Who we choose to remember, who we choose to forget. Statues are about power, about identity and belonging: national, cultural, personal. That is why they are toppled after revolutions and why battles surrounding them are so fraught. Churchill proposes the statue of Jan Smuts after his death in 1950, a promotion of empire and a reminder of South Africa's role in two world wars, just as South Africa is cutting its ties to that empire.

In 2017, wrangles over statues turn deadly when a thirty-two-year-old civil rights activist is killed at a confusion of protests over the removal of Confederate General Robert E. Lee in Charlottesville, Virginia. My god-daughter emails from Warsaw with a homework query. Can we judge historical figures with the moral values of the present, she asks, and should statues of George Washington and Thomas Jefferson in the United States be knocked down because

they were both slaveholders? Removal of the Founding Fathers —
now that would be a revolutionary act. But what is this, if not a
revolution?

At home, just as English South Africans deny any responsibility for
apartheid even as they rely on the fruits of the system, safe in their
solid houses, with their running water and electricity, as black hands
dig the coal that keeps the lights on, so do the English themselves fail
to register their own collusion with systemic racism and globalised
oppression. The impact of colonial policies remains so distant, so
invisible, it is easy to deny complicity. People take pride in their imperial past and are not prepared to entertain feelings of regret or shame.

Unlike South Africa, where every story is contested, Britain's
narrative of itself has been long-running, powerful and unified,
stretching from King Arthur and his legendary Round Table through
1066, the Civil War, the Industrial Revolution, the British Empire
and two world wars. It has been able to encompass such extremes of
empire as Smuts and Gandhi by letting one version of the past keep
running and adding to it. And by suppressing versions that threaten
the whole. The ironies of imperial history are strung like threads
between the statues in Parliament Square: Winston Churchill, Jan's
former enemy, later ally and friend; Mohandas Gandhi, his admired
adversary in the fight for Indian rights in South Africa; Nelson
Mandela, who gives his life to the struggle to reverse policies at least
partly put in place by Jan; Millicent Fawcett, who leads the Fawcett
Commission into the Boer War concentration camps.

When Millicent Fawcett's statue is unveiled in 2018 — Parliament
Square's first monument to a woman — my mother, listening to BBC
Radio 4's *Today* programme, is concerned about the statue of her
grandfather. At this point in history, she needn't have worried, the
present is still blind to the past, but this is deeply personal — change
our history and who are we? As I grow up, family mythology holds
my great-grandfather to be a 'man of his times'. Isie reveres her
husband and his abilities and achievements, her views on race tally
with his, as do those of most white South Africans born in the late
nineteenth century. But Jan's vision is always broader, and later he is
widely condemned for his hypocrisy: instrumental in 1945 in writing

the inclusive Preamble to the United Nations Charter while supporting white supremacy at home.

How some of the arguments go: my great-grandfather was no
more racist than most white South Africans and less hard-line than
the architects of apartheid. To be any kind of politician in South
Africa in the early twentieth century, it was necessary to tell the
(white) electorate what they wanted to hear. Or this: Saul Dubow
arguing that it is Smuts's 'political longevity in a rapidly changing
world' that leads to the contradictions. When he dies in 1950, the
world has shifted from the white commonwealth of the First World
War into the post-1945 world of anti-colonialism and democracy.
Public morality has evolved. How many statues would be pulled
down if moral judgements were applied evenly? I ask myself, whose
morals should we use? Lord Kitchener, responsible for the deaths of
tens of thousands in the Boer War camps; Winston Churchill, who
allowed millions of Hindus to starve in 1943; Jan Smuts, who drafted
the legislation enabling apartheid. The British Empire is yet to have
its full reckoning.

Mandela himself, in *Long Walk to Freedom*, said of Smuts: 'I cared
more that he helped the foundation of the League of Nations,
promoting freedom throughout the world, than the fact that he had
repressed freedom at home.' Mandela, of course, famously emerges
from prison with reconciliation fixed firm in his mind as the only way
forward, a conception that sometimes seems to have been welcomed
by white South Africans as a get-out-of-jail-free card. So I wonder
now how much weight to give this generosity.

In the strange summer of 2020, demands for the removal of the Smuts
statue in Parliament Square become public. We have been expecting
it for some time: Christ's College, Cambridge, Jan's *alma mater*, has
been under pressure from students to remove a portrait and a bust of
the university's former chancellor since 2015, when the University of
Cape Town statue of Rhodes is taken down and the #RhodesMustFall
campaign sails for Britain, demanding the removal of the Rhodes
statue outside Oriel College, Oxford.

In June 2020, campaigners in Bristol, the city where I live, inflamed
by the murder of George Floyd by police officers in the USA, pull

down the statue of seventeenth-century slave-trader Edward Colston and stand on his neck for eight minutes and forty-six seconds in memory of George Floyd before throwing him in the harbour. #BlackLivesMatter gains momentum, and I am watching it unfold on the television when my phone pings and my brother, or his WhatsApp avatar, reports in a few typed words: 'Smuts in Parliament Sq. just called out on C4 News.' I find it almost straight away as the algorithms kick in, on fire tonight with Black Lives desperately Mattering, www.toppletheracists.org and I click on that and zoom in on the tiny map and tap the blue pin, and up it comes: ·

London
Jan Smuts statue
Parliament Square, SW1P 3JX
Jan Smuts was the instigator of segregation and apartheid in South Africa and is commemorated by a statue in Parliament Square, just across from the statue of Nelson Mandela, who devoted his life to tearing down the racist institutions Smuts built.

There it is. Three miles from where I sit, the statue of Edward Colston lies at the bottom of Bristol Harbour: the currents of history are strong and tug at the neck of statues. I know a statue is not alive, just hollow space representing a man, and that the man himself has been dead – I calculate slowly – seventy years. But, still, I hope he is not pulled down, rope round his neck, a lynching, a retribution.

It is all very personal: guilt, shame and pride percolate. I do not hold the scales of justice, my knowledge is small and occluded, and I struggle to understand what I think. On the one hand: the creation of the League of Nations, his unflagging work towards defeating Hitler, the Preamble to the United Nations Charter, which surely continues to resonate as a force for good. Millions helped. On the other: irreparable damage caused to entire African societies. Millions of lives ruined. But this balance sheet is a red herring: a murderer would not be found not guilty just because he was a life-saving medical doctor.

As I start out on this book, I approach Margo Jefferson, author of luminous memoir *Negroland*, about upper-middle-class black life in

Chicago, and ask her how I can possibly carry it forward. She thinks for a minute. 'All you can do,' she says, 'is approach it with courage and humility.' Now I consider what this means. Courage I can manage, but humility? Humility is much more complex. Humility, noun: the feeling or attitude that you have no special importance that makes you better than others; lack of pride.

White people have a problem with humility, not necessarily through any overbearing pride, but because we are conditioned not to *see* whiteness: we assume it is the global norm, the universal way of things. Others are always found wanting when compared to whites. But it is not only that which gives me pause. I parse my emotions, anxious not to find myself at fault, but it's a hard ask when there's a statue of your great-grandfather in Parliament Square. I wonder about pride, consider its tribal basis. Pride by association. But if there is shameful pride, there is also a counter-balancing burden. Guilt, noun: a feeling of worry or unhappiness that you have done something wrong. And: the fact of having done something wrong or committed a crime.

I think about guilt and collective responsibility, about the Great Man problem – which is related to the statue problem. How a Great Man does not come from nowhere, has roots and influences and stands inside a society, a tradition. How the whole idea of a Great Man allows such a person to become unmoored from their society, so that all the pride, all the blame, rests on their shoulders alone. A crime as big as apartheid is not the act of one man: it is a collective act – and white women are part of that collective, no matter how oppressed themselves. I think about the history of such a crime, the pre-history, cause and effect, all the footsteps we have traced across the South African landscape. When one person becomes shorthand for a whole system, this allows the system to go underground. In short, pulling down one statue is not enough.

Yet it is a start, a digging away at the foundations, the opposite, I think, of the 'white-washing' it is accused of being. When these statues rest in place as if no crime was committed, as if they are a pure source of pride, surely that is 'white-washing' history: both making it white, and cleansing it of sin. This is not a matter of identity politics, which too often strip away the complex reality of what it means to wake up human every morning. After all, human beings live among the weeds, that straggling dirty place of feelings, opportunity, self-delusion, misunderstanding, self-interest, altruism. It is an examining, a careful moral reckoning, so that, in the words of the preamble to the United Nations Charter, signed by my flawed, brilliant great-grand-father: 'We the peoples of the United Nations determined to reaffirm faith in fundamental human rights, in the dignity and worth of the human person, in the equal rights of men and women'.

I consider how to lay down this pride, the icon that hangs round our necks, that holds us back, holds us suspended in the values of a time long past. How to lay down the guilt and shame. But all this is part and parcel of being human, the baggage so many of us must learn to open to the light. I turn the irony of this book, made on the axis of Jan Smuts, on the lathe of my mind, how we reshape the past to create the future. Something peers at me from the shadows. A response, a query: how to live with this legacy, this crooked line that runs from Krotoa to slave-owning Margaretha Retief and on to me through the branches of these Afrikaner trees, the roots of white supremacy that still bear fruit today. How to dig those roots up, expose them to the light so that they might wither.

But I also see that my line deviates, runs not into apartheid but up a different tree, grafted on to foreign stock (enemy stock, even, from a Boer perspective). How, as we will see, by moving six thousand miles north, by jumping continent, my grandmother shifted the crooked line. How, because our main influences lie in the horizontal ones of generation, not the vertical ones of heritage, it is England where I grow up, am educated, which does most to shape who I am. My grandmother, meanwhile, remains South African, Afrikaans; it runs through her like a streak of fat through *biltong*, and, despite her choice to leave, she would be bewildered by the disrespect shown to her father, who all the Smutses accept as a demigod. But her children are English, her children's children even more so, and time rubs the gilt from even the most burnished of gods.

VI

Cato Smuts

1904–68

There is for all of us a twilight zone of time, stretching back a generation or two before we were born, which never quite belongs to the rest of history. Our elders have talked their memories into our memories until we come to possess some sense of a continuity exceeding and traversing our own individual being.

Conor Cruise O'Brien, *Maria Cross*, 1952

Mealie-*meal porridge and blackjack leaves*

When it comes to writing about my grandmother, who is gone but not gone, who I never knew but who was always close, I am stuck. Our lives bleed into each other and I struggle to keep distance. I read the neat Afrikaans in the archive, translate hesitantly. *Liewe Mamma*, the letters begin. I visit Doornkloof, where she was raised; Hindhayes where she raised her own family. I have her passports, their stamps of inter-war Europe, Turkey, the Holy Land and, most of all, South Africa and returns to England. But I am searching for a way into this bifurcated existence, for the fork in the road between these two countries, these two possible futures.

This road begins in post-Boer War Pretoria, with a baby named Catharina – Cato, for short. Born in the early hours of a December day in 1904, weighing six pounds, she has an elder sister and a mother struggling with loss and bitterness. An early studio portrait shows two little girls posed and solemn in black bombazine and frilly white pinafores, heads shorn and feet bare. Later, matters improve: children play with sticks, fire and snakes; canoe and swim in the streams while their mother gossips on the *stoep* – these Afrikaners are more sociable than the reserved English, with multiple circles of connection that they parse out on first acquaintance and keep well maintained. It is closer to the African way – the spirit of *ubuntu*, that African philosophy of togetherness – than they would care to admit.

Cato is bundled off to Pretoria High School for Girls almost the moment she turns ten, but she seems to thrive at this English-speaking boarding school, English slang peppering her letters home with her friends always 'swotting', or 'holding thumbs'. It's an odd childhood:

week after week at an English boarding school, and then home to the old tin palace on the veld, with its pet kudu. By 1919 her father wields more power than any other man in the country but the world of parents is always a half-understood backdrop, and Cato catches only glimpses: a coffin in Pretoria's *Groote Kerk*, General de la Rey's embalmed face waxy in the candlelight; railway journeys to the Cape, camping in rented houses and visiting the beach while Pappa orchestrates the Union of South Africa.

When she arrives in Johannesburg in 1922 to study teaching, the trams rattle along newly renamed Jan Smuts Avenue. And when poor white workers, riled by mining companies' attempts to cut wages and promote cheaper black labour, explode into violent rebellion, it is her father who declares martial law. Trying to get to class at the new University of the Witwatersrand, Cato is caught in the middle of this strike with its red banners and marchers, the pitched battles between 'natives' and strikers. Later the students crowd the window of the women's residence as explosions rock the darkness.

Prime Minister Smuts orders aircraft to bomb the rebels, troops to fight on the streets. The crack and rattle of gunfire comes from beyond College Hill and the nearby Rand Show Grounds are crammed with six thousand refugees. The girls watch, nervous and excited, as aeroplanes glint in the sun and fire on rioting workers. Cannons burst into action, and Red Cross ambulances race to and fro. A week later, all is calm, but two hundred people die in this strike. It is this brutality that puts Prime Minister Smuts out of office two years later, and reveals the unsteady ground beneath South Africa's feet.

The backdrop to the strike is very different to Johannesburg's dense twenty-first-century landscape, with a beautiful Art Deco centre of new buildings bearing grand names like Astor Mansions and Clarendon Court. The centre is surrounded by tree-lined suburbs, the yellow mine dumps a commanding presence. South Africa's cities and towns are becoming white spaces: the Smuts government passes the Native (Urban Areas) Act in 1923, which defines Africans as 'temporary sojourners', only welcome in white areas to do their dirty work. This comes on the back of the 1913 Natives Land Act and earlier, when Africans living near Johannesburg's centre are moved ten miles south-west during a plague scare in 1904. Many more live in sprawling Alexandra, to the north, which by 1916 has a population of thirty thousand but no tarred roads, street lighting or sewerage.

For a young white woman like Cato, who rarely shows any interest in politics, these shifts are largely invisible. White South Africa is a melange of tennis at the club, and big game hunts, of small country stores hundreds of miles from anywhere, where Livingstone's exped-ition to the Zambezi in the 1860s is a living memory. It is a world with fewer boundaries, more danger, than the Europe from which it is derived. People are hit by trains, gored by bulls, struck by lightning in their living rooms. They drink Lysol bleach and shoot themselves.

But African and European cultures continue to buffet each other as they have for hundreds of years. Decades later, a childhood friend writes to Cato, recalling a long-ago camping trip. How they were washing in the river early one morning when:

> A group of African girls came down with calabashes on their heads to fetch water and walked in single file across the stepping stones between us and the sun which was casting long shadows from the trees and from them towards us, so that the shadows were long level bars across the golden sunlight.

Inside the minds of white people, Africans are just shadows on the grass, boxed, jailed and partitioned out of sight. But in reality they are still there, and African life remains intact in pockets across the landscape.

Zoekwater, 1925

The car is high, and square, with huge narrow wheels and running boards, and it takes Cato and her friends all afternoon to travel from Zoekwater to where the Rain Queen's compound sits, twenty miles away, up near the border with Southern Rhodesia and Mozambique. The road corrugates, little water furrows crossing every fifty yards, and as afternoon turns to evening something snaps, an axle or a spring, and the car shudders and stops, rocking, the burr of cicadas rising into the sudden silence. The friends trudge up the steep stony hill in the dusk, arriving at the kraal of the Rain Queen after dark.

Living under a rain belt in the parched heart of the Limpopo, the Rain Queens of the Balobedu are believed to have the power to control the clouds and have ruled for three hundred years. The only queen in southern Africa takes wives from villages throughout the area as a form of diplomacy, but she never marries: her official mates are chosen by the Royal Council. The Rain Queen does not appear in public and communicates with her people through her councillors, usually men.

For generations, rulers consult the Rain Queen during droughts, and even apartheid's reptilian leaders P. W. Botha and F. W. de Klerk pay their grudging respects. In 1994, Modjadji V keeps an important visitor waiting. Only after Nelson Mandela buys her a car to help her up the steep slopes to the Royal Compound does she speak to him in person. In 2001, Modjadji V leaves the throne to her granddaughter, who reigns for two years before passing on herself, leaving the Rain Queen's throne empty, waiting for her daughter to come of age.

In 1925, Rain Queen Khetoane Modjadji III, who rules for sixty-three years, is more welcoming, or perhaps less weary of disrespectful outsiders. She orders a hut and sleeping mats prepared, a supper of *mealie*-meal porridge and blackjack leaves, which, try as she might, Cato can't choke down. In the morning, a basket of oranges arrives for Cato, as the daughter of General Smuts, with an invitation to meet the Rain Queen herself. It is the start of a long association.

Cato returns to the Rain Queen's compound in 1937 with her husband and father to visit her friend Eileen, one of the 1925 party. Eileen, who has married Cato's cousin, is living among the Balobedu, studying their way of life. Later the couple publish the seminal study *The Realm of a Rain Queen*, and Eileen Krige becomes South Africa's preeminent social anthropologist. In 1937, the Smutses' visit is so fleeting that the Rain Queen wonders how anyone could leave knowing that a sheep was being slaughtered. 'In fact they thought this so strange that I have given them to understand that we're sending the Oubaas the hind-leg by post,' writes Eileen.

Snail fever

Mid-Atlantic, March 1926
The ocean stretches its gunmetal spine 5,200 nautical miles from
Cape Town to Southampton and as the propellers of the *Balmoral
Castle* push her ever northwards, the light is blinding, the sun glinting
on wavelets. I picture Elsje Cloete aboard a tall-ship in 1658, travelling in the opposite direction; Angela van Bengale sailing across the
Indian Ocean a year earlier. Cato is twenty-one, old enough to know
her own mind, even if she does not yet know that she too travels to
stay. She has left behind a suitor and a proposal on her passage from
one life to another, on this journey which is not a whim but a plan.

Passengers play quoits, read, chat in deckchairs, and all the time the
sound of the ship's orchestra, playing light classical music, floats over
the thrum of engines as shearwaters and petrels circle the vessel. Cato
has been angling to visit England since 1923 and here she is, en route
for Cambridge, shepherded by Margaret Gillett. Compressing the
two-year University of the Witwatersrand honours course into one,
she has passed with first-class marks. Short and stocky, brown hair
bobbed and finger waved, Cato makes no claims on beauty, but her
eyes laugh and she charms all the young men on the ship. There are
no Afrikaners among them – while the Union of South Africa is a
British colony, and movement between the two nations is fluid, most
Afrikaners have no interest in the hated invader.

The *Balmoral Castle* is a mail ship that carries up to 650 passengers.
Built in Glasgow, requisitioned as a troopship in the First World War,
carrying soldiers to Gallipoli in 1915, here she is, repainted in the
livery of the Union-Castle line – lavender hull, vermilion funnels
topped in black. Every Thursday at 4 p.m., a mail ship leaves
Southampton for Cape Town, just as another ship leaves Cape Town
for the northward journey. By now the passage takes only two weeks,
but Cato, who will make this voyage a dozen times, always struggles
with seasickness, its cold sweats and dizziness.

The ship docks at Southampton in late March and driving to
Oxford Cato wonders at how small the fields are, how big the

churches, how good the roads – all tarred! She feels quite at home in the Gilletts' redbrick Victorian villa, caught in a whirl of upper-middle-class Englishness and dressing for dinner. She is not at all homesick, although the distance warps time so letters from home arrive announcing crises already weeks in the past. The weather is cold and wet, the trees and flowers verdant. As she settles into her Cambridge boarding house, spring is becoming summer and unlike South Africa, where darkness falls like a shutter, the evenings are long and delicious. She cycles for miles, enjoying the meadows full of primroses, the May trees foaming white, the sweet air of their scent.

She has a place at Newnham, one of only two women's colleges. (Women are not awarded a proper Cambridge degree until 1948 and only in 1987 is the formal limit of one female student to nine males abolished.) But these are the Roaring Twenties and Cato can eat a peach melba sundae or attend the University Geographic Club and eat *pois polyhedriques, pommes geodesiques*. She can visit Scottish country houses clad in a blue pleated skirt and floral jersey, with a new crepe de chine frock for the afternoon. Or she can ride across Europe in a charabanc, draped in furs under a cloche hat. (Cato has no real interest in fashion, but the buying, selling and making of clothing, her own and others, takes up a lot of space in all her letters. By now: 'Skirts are so short that mine sit almost above my knees!')

In her first passport, issued in 1926 in Pretoria, Cato is listed as a 'British subject by birth', recalling that short window between the fall of the Transvaal Republics and the Union of South Africa. Gradually ornate stamps cover its pages, large dark eagles surrounded by gothic Germanic print: *Osterreich, Magyar Kiralyi Kovetseg Belgrad* – travel to Eastern Europe is still possible in the years before the Second World War. Yugoslavia, Hungary, Germany, Switzerland. Budapest, the wonderful bridges, the Royal Apartments, the Parliament. Vienna, Munich, Strasbourg, Paris, where she climbs the Eiffel Tower. She visits Italy and kisses the Pope's ring. In Amsterdam, she admires the familiar gables on the buildings that line the canals, and finds she can speak and understand Dutch with ease. How different all this is to the empty horizons of the Transvaal, a window into the world of upper-middle-class Britons, the cosmopolitan moneyed classes, reminiscent of the Grand Tours of the seventeenth and eighteenth centuries.

Cato is clever and hardworking as well as fun-loving, and is one of three women to obtain first-class honours in geography. Jan's friendship with Margaret keeps her secure, her 'South African daughter', Margaret calls her, and I hear old desire brimming. Bonds thrum between plain-speaking Afrikaners, born into a country where sophistication is an ill-afforded luxury, and Quakers, who aspire to a simple life of the spirit, even if their lives have been adulterated by the large fortunes amassed by Quaker industrialists. Cato's adopted aunt and uncle are wealthy and upper-class and Arthur works in the family bank, which later merges with Barclays. They are kind and helpful, if rather stifling.

Margaret catches the inconvenient cross-country line to Cambridge, and Cato holidays with them. In Rome for Easter 1927, she runs into her future sister-in-law in St Peter's and impresses her with her Italian. It is all very E. M. Forster, twenty years and a World War since the publication of *A Room with a View*. Just as Forster-ish is the impoverished death of Emily Hobhouse in a genteel nursing home in Kensington aged sixty-six, from pleurisy, heart problems and cancer. Her burial, which Cato attends, is curiously quiet and peaceful, unlike the elaborate ceremony in Bloemfontein four months later when her ashes are interred at the Vrouemonument, and Cato's father makes his flowery eulogy. There is nothing remotely Forster-ish about that.

Cato is drifting ever further from South Africa, and by now she has made the visit that will shape her entire life. In October 1926, like her father twenty years before, she visits the Clark family in Street, Somerset, and like him finds much to admire, not least a young man named Bancroft Clark. The village of Street houses the eponymous Clark shoe company, one of many successful businesses set up by Quakers in the eighteenth and nineteenth centuries when they are excluded from public life (Cadbury, Rowntree and Fry's, Barclay's and Lloyd's banks, these are all Quaker in origin). This business will prove surprisingly important in Cato's life, but she is more interested in the young people who dance to the gramophone, play croquet in the shadow of the yew hedge and sit up late, talking.

Bancroft, the eldest son, studied at King's College, Cambridge, and is close to his Aunt Alice, with whom Jan became perilously intimate during the First World War. With light-brown hair and a strong nose, Bancroft is a serious young man with no emollient charm, only a straight line of talk. All his life he can barely conceal his impatience with those who can't follow that line, but Cato takes it up and twists it around him. She is totally unlike the young Englishwomen who, to Sarah Clark's chagrin, pursue her handsome son. 'While you do your hair in that charming manner (which you know I genuinely admire) nothing can spoil your good looks, Bancroft Clark,' Cato writes, back in Cambridge.

The route from Street to Cambridge cuts cross-country: Bath to Oxford, skirting the Downs, looping on past the Chilterns and across the Fens. Endless hours with few trunk roads and limited signage. Over the next eighteen months, Bancroft undertakes this journey time after time in a car as wobbly and uncomfortable as a high-backed chair. Pistons and dynamos break, giant pigs leap from hedgerows, his avoiding swerve taking the Baby Austin onto two wheels. But nothing can spoil his pleasure at seeing Cato again and from now until her death in 1968 the chain of letters is unbroken.

Meanwhile, Cato is fascinated by the door her father's fame opens onto English high society, particularly the chance to be presented at Court. For English debutantes, this is what Jessica Mitford calls 'the specific, English upper-class version of the puberty rite', involving something like a virginal wedding dress. Afrikaner Cato is a zebra in a field of thoroughbreds at this do, with her white crepe de chine gown and georgette train, her ostrich-feather fan and imitation pearls. All this costs £30, £1,300 today, and after three hours of waiting in a black cab, she excitedly enters the Throne Room. King George V and Queen Mary sit on twin thrones under a crimson canopy, along with the Prince of Wales. The king looks tired and the prince grumpy, but at least the queen turns on the charm.

Bancroft pokes fun at Cato for all this – his friends are other non-conformists and wealthy tradesmen, the despised radicals of *A Room with a View*, and all his life he votes for 'the socialists'. Or perhaps it is less Forster and more Bloomsbury; after all in his bedroom Bancroft keeps a wardrobe daubed with cherubs and clouds: the 'Fry Cupboard', painted by Roger Fry – Quaker, Bloomsbury stalwart and lover of

Vanessa Bell. Luckily for Cato, such fluid sexual relationships are not part of Bancroft's repertoire.

The Quaker milieu exposes Cato to a new model of femininity, which is how she finds herself in Queen's Hall, London, one summer's evening in 1928, windows open, packed hot and close. Faces damp, the 2,400-strong audience fan their programmes, which list women's names in a roll-call of achievement. They are waiting to hear speeches in favour of an anti-war agreement between Germany, France and the United States. Cato reads the note from Hilda Clark, Bancroft's aunt, again, and looks up at one of the banners that hang from the walls. 'Blessed are the Peacemakers' it reads in brown letters on a cream background, embroidered by Alice Clark during the Boer War. Secretary of the Women's Peace Crusade, a socialist movement reviled by government and newspapers, Hilda has asked Cato to speak.

Standing, boyish-headed, Cato reads a message from her father and indicates the banner made 'when your people were killing mine'. She hopes a new era is dawning 'for all the races, white, black, and yellow – must find a way of living together'. In 1928, it is by no means obvious that the Afrikaners will win the peace, constructing a state in their own image, nor that their way of living together will be to live apart. Later Hilda tells Jan and Isie how proud she was of Cato, but neither of them are interested: that is a space reserved for sons. From Cato's perspective, if she never delivers a speech again it will be too soon.

In any case, now her Cambridge degree is complete, Cato must return to South Africa to pay off her debt to the education department. The separation from Bancroft is excruciating for both of them, anticipating the years apart as something like eternity. But the *Kenilworth Castle* has barely left Southampton before Cato is wracked with another kind of pain. And when the ship arrives at Madeira she has to be strapped to a stretcher and awkwardly lowered onto a small boat. The dark, handsome doctor who visits her in the hotel pronounces it an inflammation above the appendix and advises a restricted diet. We've come a long way from Fytje Cloete expiring near the Liesbeeck River, but medicine is always an occluded art and when Cato developed excruciating abdominal pain at Cambridge the doctors had been at a loss, despite their shiny new X-ray technology.

Uncle Henry Gillett, the family physician, even suggested that old female malady, hysteria.

Accurate diagnosis finally arrives at the Cape, three weeks later: Cato does not have hysteria but bilharzia, or snail fever, a disease caused by parasitic flatworms that live in snails in the rivers and lakes of the Transvaal. These blood flukes burrow through human skin into the bloodstream, migrating to soft, safe environments for their eggs: liver, bowel, kidneys, brain, where they stay quietly for years. (Even now, bilharzia kills 200,000 people per year in sub-Saharan Africa.) The worms have been in her body for so long that her bladder is irreversibly damaged. She needs injections and can't teach this term, and possibly not next.

By October, she is stuck in Johannesburg General Hospital and when she does finally get back to Doornkloof the family irritate her, time dragging in their somnolent life. Nothing has changed when she has changed so much! Cato tries to follow the map she and Bancroft drew up, but without him she wanders in a foggy no-man's-land. Yet it is not a bad plan, waiting for two years: a woman gives up so much for marriage in 1928, a man so little. Aunt Margaret and Cato's father hatch a plan for her to run Millfield, the Clark family seat, hoping to knock out of her head 'the silly idea of working or studying after marriage,' she writes indignantly. Bancroft cannot understand why this riles her so much, but I sense societal pressure massing like storm clouds over the veld.

Soon the strain of separation hurts too much, as if a living thing were being pulled apart, and their cables cross in mid-Atlantic. Aunt Margaret writes pompously: 'The ties between the two families are becoming old, and are bound up with much that is very stirring and very deep-rooted in the story of this country.' Bancroft sails for the Cape and they marry spontaneously one summer's day in Pretoria, with a car mechanic and Sylma as witnesses. Much later, I find a letter from Sylma, written in 1968. 'Do you remember how put out the Gilletts were when you got home and produced the marriage certificate?' she writes. 'They were still busy drawing up the announcement for the press, bringing in Emily Hobhouse, when you escaped for a walk without even being congratulated.'

This is it, I think, the fork in the road, the paths diverging.

Formally excluded

Yet how similar the roads look. Cato arrives in England as a wife in the interwar years, aged twenty-four and with expectations of an academic career, but while the road here is greener, with rain and sometimes even snow, the direction of travel is parallel. She is a wife, and homesteads stream behind her like contrails: Vergelegen, Welvanpas, Kromme Rhee, Libertas Parva, Doornkloof and now Hindhayes.

Chocolate-box-perfect under a high-pitched roof, in 1929 Hindhayes does not even have a proper bathroom. They wash in a tin bath in the kitchen. It is midwinter in England and the only vegetables available are roots – swede, parsnip, potatoes. Homesick, Cato asks her mother for South African recipes: bottled tomatoes, pike with onions, tomato *breedie*, apple jelly, *bobotie*. Isie sends the *Cookery Book for South Africa*. Cato herself cannot so much as boil an egg, but luckily, just as in South Africa, there are the servants for that. These women cook, clean, answer the door and telephone, undertake occasional shopping. They get one evening and two afternoons off a week and a visitor or a stroll in the evening is allowed if requested.

Early feminists draw parallels between marriage and domestic service, but what connects Cato and her working-class servants? She can dismiss these women at will, rifle through their belongings, control who they see, fire them for being unreliable, or on suspicion of stealing. How relieved she is when live-in servants are away! It is a strangely intimate relationship without the South African colour bar where the distance between white mistress and black servant gapes – in letters, African servants are seen arriving late for work or not at all. Bancroft dubs their South African servants 'thy slaves', but Cato and her sisters laugh it off.

Meanwhile, the servants or slaves leave their stories unwritten, because they are kept too busy, or can't write, or have no paper, or even if they can write, and do have paper, no one is interested in saving the paper. I think of Isie and gentle Annie in the kitchen, how that isn't even Annie's real name, how all these women live inside houses where irritation, resentment and a craving for liking, for respect, breed like a virus. And, yet, how the very last makes delicate heart-shaped sponge cakes for our birthdays and stays devotedly with Bancroft until his death thirty years after Cato.

For now, servants free Cato from the too-quiet daytime house, and despite surprising discouragement from her old Cambridge tutor, who thinks that housekeeping will soon fill her time, she starts a third degree, an MSc at the University of Bristol, thirty miles away. In the winter, she leaves home before dawn to start up the Baby Austin, but Bancroft welcomes the change: without *kopwerk*, she tells Isie, she becomes sulky. She teaches at a local school and produces talks for BBC Radio about South Africa, enlisting the help of her old friend Eileen, who sends great screeds of anthropological detail.

Inside a large yellow envelope, with 'Will you go a little slower, please' printed in big red letters, I find Cato's notes and a pamphlet for schools summarising the talks. 'When the k****r is ill,' one script reads, 'he sends for the doctor – the witch-doctor.' This witch doctor is a weird figure, 'dressed in cows' tails, feathers, many coloured paints, often horns of cattle, and bones of various animals'. I cringe, hearing a white South African capitalise on the European fetish for the exotic, and perhaps she cringes too, as I find no further evidence of this exoticisation. None of these jobs bring in much income. Instead, Bancroft gives Cato a yearly personal allowance, and there is a separate housekeeping account. But even studying and radio work come to a juddering halt once the last, vital, piece of the domestic puzzle slots into place.

Hindhayes, November 1931
Cato writes to her mother from bed, where she has wallowed for the past week, Jacob Daniel nestled in his basket next to her, with his little mop of red hair. They'll call him Daniel, she writes, 'Japie' is too difficult for English pronunciation. The birth had been arduous, the midwife and doctor helping Cato with the sickly chloroform that took away the pain, and even consciousness. Later, there had been bleeding, stemmed by the nurse compressing her womb. Feeling her nightdress sticking to her despite daily washes from the maternity nurse, she looks forward to Sunday when she can shower.

Downstairs, thuds and hammering are Bancroft unpacking the new pram – she smiles at the English aversion to ordering a pram before the baby has safely arrived and asks her mother for an Afrikaans book for children, with stories and verses: baby Daniel should speak his mother's tongue. She writes: 'They are putting Daniel's name in an old Bible and I wonder how we spell your names. Sibella Margarita or Sibylla Margaretha?', thus mangling the precise combination that will later unpick the locks of genealogy. Finishing her letter, Cato picks up Daniel's notebook and carefully records his feeding and sleeping times.

Cato does leave Daniel with a nurse to return to her research, but when she has Giles barely a year later, that is the end of it. Her Cambridge supervisor's prediction has come to pass and there is no path back to work, or at least not to paid work that doesn't centre around children. In the 1930s, women do not work after marriage, being formally excluded from teaching and clerical occupations: they are restricted to low-paid 'woman's work' – laundry, dressmaking, domestic work, factory jobs. Some marriage bars remain in place up until the 1970s. The voluntary work middle-class women turn to – Infant Welfare clinics, school governorships, family-planning clinics, in Cato's case – helps glue society together, but it is largely invisible.

Over the next forty years, Cato's life will be centred around Hindhayes as cupboards are mouse-proofed, pipes insulated, an Aga added, walls repainted and repapered. The garden will be her joy. She proves to have green fingers and – besides much-admired showy blooms at the front – out the back there are more flowers, but also fruit and vegetables: tomatoes, carrots, potatoes, rhubarb, raspberries. There is an orchard that produces apples, pears and plums and is home to geese, ducks and pigs. The rich Somerset soil, heavy rain and a regular gardener mean that even during the rationing of the war years the family will remain well fed, the children chubby and rosy-cheeked. Every year at Christmas, the Clarks give away plump geese.

But all this is in the future and Cato has not yet learnt how to manage this life, what will make it bearable, and for now she frets at home, bored and frustrated. It is a condition many new mothers would recognise, but Cato's problem is worsened by her servants: she has too little to do and her natural network of mother, sisters, cousins and old friends is six thousand miles away.

Little ice floes

And so she takes the long voyage back. Over four decades, Cato will make this journey dozens of times, with and without children, while her husband travels the globe, building the shoe business. Like Isie and Jan, they will chafe at being separated, but I consider that the separations offer all these people space to breathe, to be someone different, the canvas of their partnerships stitched together by the thread of weekly letters.

The early part of this first voyage in 1933 is horrid, Cato prostrate and sweating as the ship rolls, hairbrushes and pens clattering to the floor and rolling noisily about. Giles, in his little hammock, cries out for attention and no one has the strength to give it. But then how rich and satisfying it is to be home once more, to set foot on South African soil, hear Afrikaans, taste *biltong* and *mebos*, avocado pears, pineapples, figs!

If the tastes delight Cato's tongue, so too does her own language as the gossip flows like a river over the *stoep* at Doornkloof, Afrikaans flooding her synapses. It comes back surprisingly fast, her language, but none of Cato's children ever masters their mother tongue: little Daniel always looks quite blank when addressed in Afrikaans and she doesn't try again. I wonder what difference it makes, this translation from Afrikaans to English, which is the only way her children know her. A price attaches to émigré life, a tear in the fabric of the heart, unable to drink at the well of origin for years at a time. Cato has not yet realised how English her life will be, 'how way leads on to way'. In England, she still hankers for the old pleasures of home, writing twenty letters a month to her mother, sisters and friends, subscribing to the *Cape Times*. Her father visits England regularly, but Isie never comes.

Fifteen years later, when the war has undermined the established pattern, Bancroft urges his wife to travel back to South Africa less often. After all, one trip costs a third of their annual income. Cato ignores him, but while she can flow to and fro, navigating the smooth waters of white internationalism, for others there are rocks under the surface, or even great locked gates through which they cannot pass.

Emigrating to Australia or South Africa in the era before cheap air travel leaves England a distant memory for most. And some are cut off by more than money: even now white South Africans find international travel easier than their black counterparts.

The truth is that it is easy for Cato, not easy in the sense of specific humanness, which makes any kind of exile a wound, but easy in the systematic sense, where she has the human capital to move at ease over the surface of the earth. So she can catch a ship, or fly like a bird, and find herself at home in South Africa, or in England. But the same is not true for everyone, this fluidity of self, this plasticity: for some the self is made crystalline, by officials and observers, by other people.

I am thinking of another young South African the Gilletts take under their wing in 1932: unlike Cato, Nontando Jabavu is African, and her experiences reveal the hidden scaffolding of whiteness beneath Cato's seamless transition. Nontando's parents, who are part of the small Xhosa intellectual class fostered by Victorian mission schools, are keen for her to have a British education. (Her family, Nontando says, is in its fifth generation of Westernisation: neither purely Western nor purely Bantu, neither black European, nor white Bantu.) And so, supported by the Gilletts, she sails for England and a Quaker boarding school in York.

Like Cato, Nontando makes friends with the Clark family and visits Street. But soon enough, after school, she develops an interest in left-wing politics and activism. Cato, exposed to the same Quaker values and behaviours, develops no such interest, perhaps because she has no need of it. Later, just as Cato marries Bancroft, so Nontando marries Mick Cadbury Crosfield, another Quaker. But where they were delighted at Cato's marriage, the Gilletts are frustrated when Nontando does not return to South Africa to do good works, as they intended. Yet their very intervention makes it difficult for her to return to a country that increasingly perceives her as sub-human.

Cato's friend Eileen Krige, as befits a leading anthropologist, is acute about the ebb and flow of racism, noting Kitty Smuts's outrage at having to share the Gilletts' dining table with Nontando and an Indian visitor, being served by white girls. And her discomfort at appearing at Covent Garden in company with this 'native' girl. To a white South African like Kitty, Nontando is simply a South African 'native' and, as such, should not be served at all, let alone by white girls. To a mixed-race South African like novelist Peter Abrahams, who meets her in London, Nontando is a 'Black Briton'. Nontando herself, who becomes a successful writer and journalist, is having none of it: 'I belong to two worlds with two loyalties; South Africa where I was born and England where I was educated,' she writes.

Cato and Nontando break free from South Africa, floating like little ice floes across the world's oceans, but where Cato can melt into rural England, Nontando is restless, peripatetic. The hazy no-man's-land she inhabits between isiXhosa and English creates fractures that allow her to step back and forth through the mirror of race and identity. In 1960 she writes of 'the old and intense delights in being with my people again', mirroring Cato's own *crie de couer*. 'When I think: Hurrah, I shall soon be off to England, there comes like a quick reaction the thought: but my God, fancy having to say good-bye to all this.'

For Cato, the journey back in 1933 reveals just how much her life will occur in-between now, between England and South Africa. She sails happily, if sickly, between the two with her little boys and once home sinks into provincial life: the occasional Quaker Meeting on Sunday, factory dos, amateur dramatic productions, country Christmases.

In 1934, this Christmas is a jolly affair with a party of twenty-nine. But all is not well with the children; threadworms in November, followed by flu, lay Daniel and Giles low, and in the days after Christmas, they eat less and less. By New Year's Day, Giles burns hot and feverish. He asks for water, but brings it all back up. Even then, Cato writes a letter to her mother, wishing her Happy New Year.

By evening Giles's blond curls stick to his head with sweat; he breathes rapidly, too weak to cry, his pulse fast. Until midnight there is still hope. But when the second bout of fever takes hold, Giles's small heart cannot withstand it. By half-past three, he is dead.

The next morning Bancroft leaves Hindhayes clutching Giles's small body wrapped in a blanket. He drives the thirty miles to Bristol with Giles in the back seat. In the drear of winter, the trees are empty, the land brown and grey. Cato stays at home, Daniel still being ill, and because, it is later said, she couldn't face it. Who could? She is pregnant again, and Bancroft worries that she might miscarry. Giles's body is cremated, his ashes scattered in the borders at the Gothic cemetery of Arnos Vale. 'A few days before,' Cato writes to her mother, 'one would have said that such a thing was impossible.'

In the 1930s, twenty times more English children die than in 2019 and before the widespread use of antibiotics one in ten children under five dies. Nevertheless, children of the middle-classes, with better food, shelter and healthcare, die much less frequently than poorer children. Giles's death reverberates through the family. Bancroft trudges over the moor, Cato is more self-contained: 'What is gone is gone, and nothing can bring it back,' she writes to Isie, who lost her Koosie thirty-five years before. Later the children complain of the close watch Cato keeps over them, and I am reminded of the wistful letters of the 1800s, the women never able to love without fear again. So many dead children.

Those who emigrate find their lives changed in almost all the fundamentals: geography, climate, society. But even they cannot escape filial love, which cascades down the generations. Migrants love and are loved by those they leave behind for a lifetime. This is as true in 1935 as it is in 1658 or 2019. In 1969, Sylma writes to Bancroft:

Dear little Giles, we here have all always remembered him as a quite exceptionally beautiful baby . . . how lovely it was to see Cato again, and to see her children: England was so much further away then than it is now, and she had to brave that long ghastly seasick voyage to come and visit us.

'Ons kleinspan'

But, as Isie found, dead children cannot stop time or war, even if time has stopped for them. Some accommodation must be made and Europe is settling into darkness now, with Cato in a front-row seat. When Jan gives the Rhodes Memorial Lectures in 1929, she and Bancroft accompany him to Chequers to stay with Prime Minister Ramsay MacDonald and his beautiful dark-haired daughter Ishbel, feeling quite at home with their modest lifestyle. The Oubaas is to discuss the League of Nations with the prime minister again before he leaves for America.

Cato has a bilious attack and misses one of the lectures, so I do not know if she hears that the best way 'to civilise the African native is to give him decent white employment'. Or her father admit that the 1913 Natives Land Act had not given the Africans enough land, yet that separating black and white was still the best arrangement. It is doubtful that Cato would have disagreed, but the Quakers surrounding her certainly do.

Here's another snapshot of history: Emperor Haile Selassie, in exile from Ethiopia following the Italian invasion of 1935, giving a talk at the Crispin Hall in Street. He lodges at Fairfield House, just thirty miles away from the Clark household. The souvenir programme shows his Imperial Majesty in full regalia: high gold-embossed collar, medallion and chain round his neck. Selassie says only a few words through an interpreter and Cato cannot help but notice the sadness around his eyes.

And another: it is 1934 and Bancroft, breakfasting at the Savoy with his father-in-law, finds Uncle Arthur defending the Soviet Union against Smuts's attacks. By 1936 the Clark family are still skiing in Switzerland. Bancroft reports from Munich:

> flags hang out of many houses, red with a black and white *hachen krews*
> – there are a few men about in Nazi uniform some looking a bit swin-
> ish – but there are many in army or flying corps uniform – they salute
> in the normal military way . . . I have however yet to see a Jew! The
> silly Heil Hitler raised hand is sometimes used . . . Many men wear the
> Hitler toothbrush.

The ships, on the other hand, are full of Jews: 'You would think it a German ship if you listened to the passengers in Tourist and third – almost all German Jews,' Bancroft writes en route to the US in 1936. South Africa too sees an influx: 6,500 Jews arrive from Germany from 1933 to 1939, although the racist South African Aliens Act of 1937 slows the flow. Cato writes from Doornkloof in February:

I also saw [cousin] Hennie and Saartjie in the hospital. Hennie treated us to a storm of hate against the Jews: he thinks they are a menace to the non-Jewish doctors and they are swarming to Johannesburg from Germany, Poland and Russia now.

She is anxious about being stuck in South Africa with a war on while Bancroft and baby Jan are in England. Bancroft replies: 'Germany is planning war just as soon as she is able so far as one can see . . . And in Street everything is peaceful and quiet and spring is here.'

But even peaceful Street, marooned on the green lake of the Somerset Levels, is more closely connected to the European continent than can be seen on the surface, reflecting itself back and blinding the casual observer. And so when Cato returns home she finds herself alongside other Street women, sewing sheets, stuffing pillows with feathers and mattresses with straw, scrubbing floors, as they prepare an unoccupied Georgian mansion for refugee children. Following the bombing of Guernica and Bilbao by German and Italian warplanes in April 1937, Quakers have evacuated four thousand Basque children to Britain, with Edith Pye, Aunt Hilda's partner, travelling to Spain to help arrange the exodus. Arriving in Britain, the children are dispersed across the country. They stay for two years.

Bancroft finds his Aunt Hilda infuriating, and he gives vent to his frustration in letters to Cato. In March 1933, he writes after seeing Hilda in Paris: 'She had been in Geneva on her usual fruitless (at least so they seem to me) errands.' Hilda's work is impenetrable to him, but she and Edith, who lie in the same grave at Street Meeting House, are the lynchpin of many humanitarian causes, including helping to found Save the Children in 1919. They are at the forefront of female networking and lobbying in the inter-war years, which results in the quiet professionalisation of the maternal realms of charity and caring into today's non-governmental sector. Perhaps what Bancroft sees as 'tiresome' is the sheer bloody-mindedness necessary for women to undertake such work in the face of (male) resistance.

I am reminded of Emily Hobhouse and Olive Schreiner in how Hilda and Edith, standing outside heterosexual marriage and children, wield agency. And how infuriating they can be. These women also have a crucial impact much closer to home than Bancroft realises – they all nudge his father-in-law towards female suffrage, internationalism and the League of Nations. I think about how these women challenge Jan Smuts over South Africa's racial policies, how the Clark children are brought up on stories of their feisty great-aunts, what difference that sense of agency makes to a young Quaker girl: Cato's daughters grow up under a radically different flag to the *Vierkleur* of the old Boer Republics.

Cato herself has no inclination for leadership or organisation, but she is supportive of Hilda and Edith and takes the minutes for Edith's League of Nations Club. By the late 1930s her notes are full of the plight of refugees as they wend their painful way across Europe.

Street, 3 September 1939

Cato is running up black-out curtains on the sewing machine, the family's gas masks arrayed on the dining table. Barrage balloons float over nearby Somerton wireless station, back-garden bomb shelters have been built, plans drawn up for the mass evacuation of children. Two days ago, German troops invaded Poland, and Hitler is ignoring British and French demands for their withdrawal. Cato takes her foot off the sewing machine pedal as Neville Chamberlain's voice comes through the new wireless: 'I have to tell you now that no such undertaking has been received and consequently this country is at war with Germany,' he says solemnly.

The winter of 1939 is the coldest for forty-five years, and at night the snow's glittering whiteness means that, even with the black-out, it is not dark outside. Petrol is rationed, but Hindhayes has coal, food and clothing aplenty, and a heavily pregnant Cato feels almost ashamed when so many are suffering death and cold. In March 1940, she gives birth to a longed-for daughter, and gives her the longed-for name of Petronella. Her parents, remembering the starving skeletons of the Boer War camps, pressure her to evacuate to South Africa, echoed by Bancroft, who pictures the undernourished Viennese waifs saved by Aunt Hilda after the last war. Passage is booked for June 1940 but Cato wavers.

She knows that ships are taking a circuitous route to avoid U-boats, the black-out covering the port-holes making the cabins hot and stuffy at night. And that, in January, the Union-Castle line lost the second of fourteen ships. Sailing in convoy from England to Beira, the *Dunbar Castle* had hit a mine seven miles from Ramsgate, settling on the seabed thirty minutes later with the loss of ten lives. On the morning of the sailing, suitcases packed and goodbyes said, Cato and Bancroft change their minds, unable to face the uncertain future apart. In total, 144 passenger ships are lost during the war.

Night after night now, Cato tries to settle the children as waves of German aircraft drone overhead, aiming for the docks and factories of Bristol, or jettisoning their bombs at random. In November, an attack on Bristol lights up the sky for miles around. Bombed out, her dentist turns up in Street. Before long, Cato is making Hindhayes welcoming for two evacuees, who are bewildered by the chickens in the back garden, the deep country silence at night. These are not the sweet labelled urchins of archive footage, but two teenage girls: Cato receives 10/6 a week to support them.

In 1943, pregnant again, she reorganises the house to sleep twelve – Jannie is in the cloakroom with the coats and shoes. It is not just evacuees: Bancroft's friend Friedl Scheu, Austrian Jew and Vienna correspondent for the *Daily Herald*, sends his wife and daughter to Hindhayes. Friedl had been interned by the British for four months, back in 1940, but he writes: 'There is no scar to heal as the predominating impression of my internment was the loyal and warm-hearted way our friends have stood up for us.' Cato and Bancroft's hospitality is part of wider Quaker work around Jewish refugees. The Basque evacuation lays the groundwork for the *Kindertransport*, which rescues ten thousand children from Germany and Austria from December 1938. Street constitutes part of a web of Quaker action, which sees the Society of Friends awarded the Nobel Peace Prize in 1947.

And, despite the world war, this household is still growing, Petronella followed by another daughter in August even as Cato wonders if it is wise when the Germans could invade, or cut off food supplies. She is not alone: fearing a population decline, the British government portrays women as contributing to the war effort through pregnancy. In 1940, Lord Woolton, Minister of Food, addresses Britain's women through their radios, 'We are the army that guards the Kitchen Front,' he says. The government pours money – and milk – into children's wellbeing with free or subsidised milk, orange juice, cod liver oil and vitamin tablets, and more maternity beds.

Cato boasts of what she calls '*ons kleinspan*' (our little team), her contribution to the future of Great Britain (the Afrikaans only underlining the contradictions of nationalism), but she frets at her inactivity. Bancroft's shoe factories provide boots for soldiers, even torpedo parts, and her brothers and sisters serve in the South African forces, but what is she doing? The glamorous code-breakers, plane trackers and Land Girls are celebrated now, but like many women Cato still can't break out of the box marked 'wife and mother'. Women march to demand nursery places so they can take up war work and Clarks provides hot meals to staff and schoolchildren to free up women to work in the factory. Meanwhile, Cato volunteers for the Red Cross and the Infant Welfare Centre, weighing children, offering advice on food and medication.

Self-deprecating as always, Cato discounts the support she offers to her father, by now Field Marshal Smuts, who is deeply engaged in the imperial war effort. When she tells her mother: 'In England, he is almost regarded as a god,' she is not exaggerating. In 1940, Churchill's private secretary even puts forward a plan to appoint Jan Smuts prime minister of the UK, should anything happen to Churchill. Cato has no interest in the limelight and little interest in the world in which her father moves, but she visits him in the Hyde Park Hotel for a week at a time, despite the bombing. Her brother Jannie is the Oubaas's *aide de camp*, and Kathleen is serving in England with the South African Women's Auxiliary Air Force. Met at Paddington Station by Oupa's big official car with its South African flag, the children love rattling around his huge suite. Their joys are simple: rowing on the Serpentine, moving staircases and underground trains, double-decker buses and trams.

The Clarks never do go hungry. Bancroft writes to Isie in November 1943: 'We do well, pike fish from the river, hares or rabbits from the fields, eggs from our hens, honey from the bees, fruit and vegetables in plenty each in its own season – no frozen apples from Canada now! Mushrooms and walnuts.' They are further sustained by careful parcels from Cato's sister Santa in South Africa full of *biltong*, sweets, dried fruit, sugar and Boer tobacco – the rare and precious taste of home momentarily erasing the impassable miles.

A lost and shrinking world

8 May 1945
Victory in Europe Day. The bedroom window at Hindhayes opens to the night air, the scent of wisteria floating in. The blackout has been folded and stored, and Cato reads in bed, her lamp a small beacon, while out on Street Hill, and all the other hills around, great victory bonfires roar and crackle. Fighting will continue in the Far East for another three months, and Nathan Clark, serving in Burma, will only reach Liverpool Docks the following year, but for Street the war is over.

Cato has not been back to South Africa since 1938, so when her father, on his way home from signing the United Nations Charter in San Francisco, offers to take her, she grabs the opportunity. They fly, a first for Cato, hopscotching from airfield to airfield across Europe and Africa, and she relishes the freedom and stimulation after so long tied to home. In Stresa, they stay in the Grand Hotel, immortalised by Hemingway in *A Farewell to Arms* and lately vacated by the German SS. Cato meets two Italian women who have hidden partisans in the hotel attics. In Rome, they lodge in the house of Mussolini's education minister, who has absconded with the French Foreign Legion while his wife haunts the top floor. At Giza, she scrambles inside the Great Pyramid, stooping and crawling down long galleries to find the Pharaoh Khufu's grave rooms.

A fortnight later, Bancroft follows in a 'great flying boat', sheltering in a cool Khartoum hotel from the intense heat, describing for five-year-old Petronella how the pilot brings the plane down low over the mouth of the Zambezi, revealing vultures, flamingos and white pelicans 'whose beak is so large it can hold as much as his belly can'. The flavour of these documents is distinct: it is a lost and shrinking world. I find a circlet of coarse dark strands. In Bancroft's handwriting, the tag records: 'from elephant shot by Andries Weyers on the Mashi river in Angola between the river and the Rhodesian boundary, 1954'.

South African Airways introduces its first intercontinental flight in November 1945: thirty-four hours with stops in Nairobi, Khartoum,

Cairo, Castel Benito and Bournemouth. As the years tick by, the speed of transport increases, and while Cato travels by ship until the 1950s, jet engines and the falling cost of air travel means that by 1977 the Union-Castle line ceases to run, its mail and passengers lost to jet aeroplanes, its cargo stowed in container ships.

Back in 1945, Cato finds her mother cheerful but Doornkloof infested with rats and bees. Buzzing inside the walls, they sting Cato awake at 5 a.m. The Oubaas receives a triumphant homecoming parade through the streets of Pretoria, his wife at his side at the family's insistence. This annexation of South Africa's civic life to the Smuts family is perhaps a mistake. The country is evolving: only Afrikaans is heard in Pretoria now, and even in Johannesburg there is less English than before the war.

North-West Province, April 1947

With the war over, Cato has returned to her regular, if costly, visits home. The new baby does not accompany her. Instead, she brings Petronella and Jan, seven and twelve respectively. In all these travels, her children are largely left behind, and they are sent to boarding school at eleven. She claims to Bancroft: 'I am very sad to be away so soon again from them all, even if thee does not believe it.' Whether anyone believes it or not, it is the price she pays for nourishing her South African side.

At home in Somerset, Cato is absorbed by the daily round: buying envelopes, stamps, toothpaste and shoe polish for school trunks, taking tea with her mother-in-law or Aunt Margaret, organising party games, taking the children out for picnics, invigilating exams. She spends happy hours offering advice to young mothers at the Infant Welfare Clinic. The era of plentiful servants is fading and, although she still has help, some jobs are taken over by appliances – by 1948 Hindhayes is home to a Bendix washing machine. Visits to South Africa are a respite from this daily round, and a place to relax into the comfort of old connections.

This time, she is visiting the farm given to her and her sister, Louis, by their father. Sticky, reddish mud clots around the car's wheels as they near the homestead and Denis McIldowie, Louis's husband, goes for help. Warmed by the autumn sun, Cato rummages for pencil and paper and scribbles a letter while she waits. In the field nearby, a secretary bird struts in its black knee-breeches. Cato looks up to see if she can spy Denis's long form returning with a team of oxen to pull the car out.

Kromdraai – crooked turning, after the crooked river that runs through it – lies at the northern end of South Africa's maize triangle, and is run by a manager, worked by Batswana labourers. The mud road is tarred in 1956, cutting down the journey time from Irene, two hundred and thirty miles away. From now on, this farm makes enough profit to fund Cato's trips home, even in dry years. This is no mean feat: in 1949, the trip costs £535, £13,000 in today's money.

Meanwhile, the Tswana are reduced to a peasantry. This dispossession begins during the *Mfecane* when the land is claimed by Boer farmers, but it worsens when Jan Smuts's government drafts the Natives Land Act of 1913 – Africans are barred from owning the fields they till for the next eighty years. Some move to slums and townships near white cities, some migrate to the mines, but they do not forget the land that shaped who they are. Cato, who has a modern, capitalist claim to Kromdraai, takes the profit of their labour. (Later, some of this land passes to her children, whose claim is even narrower. This too is part of being an emigrant: to inculcate love of the motherland in one's children, to continue to stake a claim.)

Change flares across the veld now: the royal visit of 1947 no more than a desperate attempt to stamp out the flames, and when Cato returns again in 1948 her father's long sojourn as the figurehead of South African politics is over. This is not immediately obvious to his family, who conflate the post of prime minister with their father, a curious fishbowl effect that leads Cato to complain, in the wake of the ominous anointing of the National Party: 'The problems connected with the Oubaas' loss of office are very serious, the most immediate being where he is to live during the session.' Still, she writes: 'We all hope it will not be very long before he is back in the position of Prime Minister.'

Two short years later, the Oubaas is dead, his death coinciding with the birth of a separatist South Africa. In 1949 the Voortrekker Monument is inaugurated, and more than 250,000 people attend to worship at the altar of their mythic past. To the Smutses, it all seems like a big mistake and Louis writes: 'Really even to a non-thinker like me the position is fraught with danger – in so many ways running parallel with Hitler's early moves.'

After Isie dies in 1954, the grass at Doornkloof grows green and lush, but they all know something has ended.

Glimpsing the basilisk

Ageing is like running on top of a spinning ball. Once the slang you speak, the music to which you listen, the exams you pass are the gold standard. Then a new generation grows up, and yours is out of fashion, downgraded. Parents die, siblings, friends. Santa writes in 1959: 'Do you remember the happy trips we used to have in bygone days with all our dear ones still here? I often feel so home-sick for those far-off days.' What of a country left behind? What if the soft border of passports becomes the rigid border of time? You assume you can return, but the country you remember no longer exists; you assume you understand, but the society you once knew has changed.

Cato never gives up her claim on South Africa. 'I am torn between sorrow at going and joy at arriving,' she writes in 1950, but it could have been penned at any point in the decades before or after. She is equally at home – and not – in both places, emigrant and immigrant. The words stem from the root *migrare*, Latin for 'to move from one place to another'. My grandmother is, I think, much closer to the swallows that swoop and roll over the reed-lined rhynes crisscrossing the Somerset moors, before migrating south to skim the surface of the dam at Doornkloof, than those moneyed Brits who in the twenty-first century travel south each winter to enjoy the cocooned lifestyle of the white Western Cape.

What is more, Cato, although distanced from what was once home, is still welcome there, unlike Nontando, who records in her tender memoir of amaXhosa culture, *Drawn in Colour*, a 1955 visit to South Africa, where she cannot live because of her marriage to a white man. 'As soon as I stepped out of the plane with its relaxed international atmosphere, I could feel the racial atmosphere congeal and freeze round me,' she writes. 'The old South African hostility, cruelty, harshness; it was all there, somehow harsher than ever because Afrikaans was now the language.'

Law after law regulates the lives of black South Africans ever more tightly: every South African must be classified into a racial group; public premises, vehicles and services can be segregated by race; black people cannot marry white people, nor have sex with them; black people must carry a passbook that permits movement between designated areas. On a trip into town, Nontando and her stepmother are desperate to relieve themselves. But there is only one ladies' lavatory, and that is for Europeans only. 'So we had to walk to a deserted part of the town close by and squat in the short grass, overseas gloves and all!' Nontando recalls. I am reminded of the 'urinary leash' on which Victorian women were kept in Britain by a lack of public facilities. How much less welcome are African women in the white spaces of 1950s South Africa?

This is not a problem Cato ever encounters (and I doubt she feels the need to mark her respectability with a pair of gloves). For her old friend Eileen, her absence renders her incapable of understanding her motherland. 'On the Native question, Cato remained more conservative than she would have been had she continued living in South Africa and been subjected to new currents of thought here,' she writes after Cato's death. I salute Eileen's loyalty, although I am unconvinced. After all, Cato visits South Africa almost every year during the 1950s and early 60s, jet engines having cut the journey from three weeks to a day or two. And even at home in Street, juggling everything from tuberculosis inoculations for the cow to planting red cabbage and spinach, she maintains a busy correspondence.

Those letters show her old friends finding the temperature hard to bear, starting infant-welfare centres and mothers' sewing circles in the townships and, as Cato writes in 1954, counting 'native and coloured women among their real friends'. One friend helps to found Black Sash in 1955, a group of white women who initially join together to protest the removal of coloured voters from the Cape roll, and others join Black Sash marches. Later, banned from protesting in groups, the Black Sash maintains silent vigils as lone figures outside government buildings, staring implacably at government ministers. Later still they are arrested, detained, kept under surveillance and harassed.

Yet white women vote for apartheid, repeatedly. The demands of nationalism that frost-shocked the blossoming lives of Afrikaner women in the early twentieth century are going strong. I come back again and again to the frog in its gradually heating water. Who among us would know when the time had come to leap? What would Cato have done, had she stayed? Some of her family are less radical than her friends. In March 1960, police in Sharpeville open fire on Africans protesting against pass laws, killing 67 and wounding 186. Santa agrees with the police: 'If they won't listen to reason and obey orders they must learn the hard way.' Like many whites, she looks north to a rapidly decolonising colonial Africa and fears the worst.

But in 1960 a letter arrives at Hindhayes. 'We hear that a certain cousin of ours has been detained under the Emergency Regulations,' Santa writes. 'Her husband – a well-known QC – is too prominent to be detained.' Reading this letter over the coffee cups and toast crumbs, Cato knows perfectly well who she is referring to, thinking back to that little Krige cousin, Uncle Tottie's daughter. Molly was always feisty, standing up for others, even when they were at Pretoria Girls High. She did teacher training, she remembers, and later married Bram, who is lovely but perhaps more crusading than is sensible. She folds the letter, wondering how Molly is coping, and puts it back in its envelope.

Bram Fischer, whose airport we arrived at earlier, is defending Nelson Mandela, Walter Sisulu, Joe Slovo and others accused of attempting to overthrow the government at the Treason Trial. In the wake of the Sharpeville massacre, the National Party government has outlawed the ANC and declared a State of Emergency. So when the doorbell at the Fischer home rings at 2.30 a.m., one April morning, Bram struggles upright in bed, hand out for his horn-rimmed spectacles. But it is not him the security police have come for.

By the time this letter lands on the Hindhayes' doormat, Molly Fischer is in detention in Johannesburg, one of eighteen thousand activists arrested. After eight days of hunger strike, Molly, aged fifty-two, has 'lost two inches everywhere'. She leaves prison in July. The Afrikaans authorities are especially punitive to Afrikaners perceived to have betrayed their race, but there are other costs, not least to activists' children. Nelson Mandela describes how his daughter refuses to hug him, exclaiming: 'You are the father to all our people, but you have never had the time to be a father to me.' The sacrifices are extreme, but later Mandela and other comrades credit Bram with their shift from black nationalism into non-racial pluralism. 'I fought only against injustice, not my own people,' Mandela writes of Bram. He could have said the same of Molly.

The Clarks have the *Guardian* newspaper delivered every morning, and in late 1963 and early 1964 Cato follows from a distance as Bram defends Mandela and others at the Rivonia Trial. These defendants, on trial for fomenting violent revolution and sabotage, face death by hanging, but it is apartheid that is on trial in the court of world opinion. Mandela and others are saved from the gallows, but closer to home the news is darker: the day after the trial ends, Molly Fischer dies in a car accident. Bram Fischer never gets over his wife's death. Put on trial for being a communist, he goes on the run for 290 days, is recaptured and sentenced to life in prison. He dies in April 1975.

When Aunt Margaret dies in 1962, Cato is left to care for the Smuts letters, and despite her fears of 'Congo-type destruction' the precious papers are sent to South Africa. She worries that the 'increasingly Nazi' National Party government might open the papers to the public before the stated date of 1986 in an attempt to smear his reputation. Yet Jan is not so much discredited as wiped from history. In 1960, white South Africans vote, by a narrow margin, to reject the British Crown and become a republic.

For the Smuts children, South African politics are tied into loyalty to their father and pride in their heritage. They oppose South Africa becoming a republic, but cannot conceive of South Africa under multiracial rule. When Hendrik Verwoerd, 'the Architect of Apartheid', is assassinated in 1966, Sylma writes: 'No one has ever doubted his sincerity and integrity and his strength of character is something we in this corner of Africa badly need.' Perhaps Cato's conservative outlook is not surprising. She worries, but Sylma reassures her that they are untouched by the township violence reported in the press. 'It's like we used to worry about you during the war,' she observes.

There is still a little room for the old ways. After Isie dies, Louis and Cato pay her housekeeper, Annie, a stipend, and in 1967, Annie makes the long, expensive journey to Doornkloof. She wants to consult Santa about the government buying her land and is distressed to find her gone. (Santa dies suddenly of a stroke in 1966.) Her hair snow-white, thin, and walking with a stick, Annie asks after all the children and grandchildren individually. 'Thank God, Louis McD's lawyer, a bit of a k****rboetie, will gladly see her and fix it all up for next to nothing,' Sylma writes to Cato.

And some room for new ways: when Kathleen (Santa's unclaimed daughter) moves to Botswana with her husband, they make friends with President Seretse Khama and his white English wife, Ruth. The Khamas have returned to Botswana in triumph after being exiled by the British government, which had been put under pressure by the apartheid regime, appalled at a mixed marriage. For Kathleen: 'Yes, the face of the world is indeed changing, and we are so fond of the Khamas, the colour being no bar to our friendship.'

In 1963, Cato and her youngest daughter, Sarah, visit Petronella in Nigeria. Her son might predict that her hair will turn white when she sees Petronella among the black Africans, but Cato takes it in her stride, noting among Petronella's Nigerian friends, 'No servile approach to Europeans, but a kindly approach and a self-assurance that I had never seen in South Africa.' Self-assurance would be a tall order indeed in a society as determined as white South Africa to ensure that Africans remain subservient. But while Cato can observe her mother country's slide into ever greater cruelty from a distance, she cannot distance herself from the changes it wrote into her body so long ago.

That blithe spirit

In 1959, the bilharzia that saw Cato taken off a ship at Madeira more than thirty years before comes home to roost. One spring evening, preparing for bed, she stops, takes stock and says to Bancroft: 'I think I am having a stroke.' From then on, she is in and out of hospital with a stomach ulcer, high blood pressure, kidney infections, all made worse by the stroke, which affects her hands and gait.

Each visit to South Africa seems like the last now and in 1967 Cato and Bancroft visit Namaqualand. They see the desert flower: orange, yellow and purple, but later that year Cato has another stroke and never recovers. She dies a year later of heart failure, just two years after the beloved sister who she followed so closely into the world of post-Boer War Pretoria, and younger than any of our women since Elsje Cloete in 1702. A post-mortem finds her bladder badly scarred by bilharzia.

It has been a happy marriage, but the future Cato rejected in the Oubaas and Aunt Margaret's plans in 1928 is close to the one that comes to pass. Marriage, and children, reduce her future to fit the shape of Hindhayes. I think of the road not taken, of Cato's old friend Eileen who stays in South Africa and spends her life on the *kopwerk* Cato craved. Meanwhile Cato has years and years – four decades – of a full house, children to raise, a household to run. She invests love, spends her intellect piecemeal – on family-planning clinics, school boards and on historian Keith Hancock while he writes the first biography of her father.

I fiddle with the threads of Cato's tapestry and wonder, struck with sorrow at the thought of that clever young woman of 1926. Does the denial of fulfilment feel so cruel because there was a glimpse of another life? Did it matter to her, this merry soul of whom in 1973, an old friend writes: 'I still think of that blithe spirit with great joy'?

Later Sylma writes to Bancroft: 'Marriage to Cato made you different from your brothers and sisters – as it made her different from hers. Together you formed the two halves of a complete whole.' Later still, a cousin posts a photograph on social media of the Clarks gathered in the 1930s, black and white faces staring unforgiving as eagles from the past, good Quakers upright in linen. Except Cato, soft as a dove, who carries the secret scars of bilharzia picked up in the South African lake where she paddled, skirts hitched up in her *broekies* (underpants). Transplanted, she holds a fat bonneted baby, one of seven who fails to master their mother tongue, part and parcel of the slippage from one generation to the next.

~

Bitter fruit

Fifty years later, after the toxic rhetoric of the Afrikaner has subsided into acrid aftermath, I visit Hermanus in October 2018. Reading the *Cape Times* in the spring sunshine as the starlings call to each other, I have the sudden sensation of floating in an alternate universe, the sticky residue of blood on my hands and in my hair. The newspaper reports the exhumation of six members of the Pan Africanist Congress's armed wing, hanged in 1963 on the state gallows and thrown into a pit. Provided with money, pangas and knives, the six had travelled from Cape Town to the Eastern Cape, where they killed a chief.. This happens as Bram defends Mandela against the state, and just before Molly dies.

I pick carefully through the newsprint. One person's freedom fighter is – we all know this, don't we – another's terrorist. Through this trough of Old Testament killing, those in power are reframing the country's collective memory. It is another turbulent year in this loud, disruptive democracy: President Zuma's removal from office, the capture of state assets by ANC flunkies, land expropriation without compensation. With so much at stake, words ricochet around this newspaper: 'propaganda', 'traitors', 'white monopoly capital'.

Whites continue to live in houses with swimming pools, blacks in corrugated iron shacks with sewage running down the path outside. Resentment festers in anti-white propaganda. Is this the end-point: a nation fatally divided along racial lines? The cauldron of race, deprivation, privilege and power bubbles away. Identity politics look like new clothes draped over the old race mannequin.

I remember another moment of disorientation, two years before, when an acquaintance, a white Englishwoman long married to a black South African, speaks her own truth: 'My African relations laugh at the way the white people fret at the corruption and what is going on in government. I think we should stop interfering; it is their turn now.' I stay silent, imagine my silence effacing my physical presence so that she cannot hear my thoughts, which I have no right to think. I silence myself because I am foreign, and because it takes time to work through the thickets of oppression and privilege.

But later I think about shame, and self-silencing, which Professor Samantha Vice thinks should go along with a moral recognition by white people that they are an ongoing problem in South Africa: 'One would live as quietly and decently as possible, refraining from airing one's view on the political situation in the public realm, realising that it is not one's place to offer diagnoses and analyses, that blacks must be left to remake the country in their own way.' I repeat this sentence to myself, hear how it skirts the dangerous line of scapegoating a minority, denying their democratic voice, at odds with the constitution so carefully drawn up, with Mandela's vision.

But it is also unrealistic. It is not in the political arena that white hegemony persists, but in all other arenas: in the boardroom, the bathroom, around the *braai* and at the airport. Political silence will not change that. White South Africans retreat into unremorseful arrogant silence, or complain too loudly about encroachments upon their privilege. Black South Africans, infuriated by the slow pace of change, shut down and blame whites. It is not silence that is needed, but care in how speech happens, what is said, what is chosen.

'Up until four or five years ago, white people would phone into SAFM radio and complain. They would be cut off immediately. Then they stopped phoning. Now it is black people phoning in and complaining about standards, the grubbiness, the roads being potholed. People are outraged by the corruption,' Cousin J. C. says back in Hermanus when I have put the newspaper away. People are not just their skin colour – they are also citizens infuriated by the failures of government. But, he adds, 'White people's lives are getting smaller and smaller: you just build your house, go to work, play golf. It's a different country. If the newspaper, the *Cape Times*, criticises anything, it is a coconut; anything a white person says – they are a colonialist.'

How to live as a white person in this new country? I think of Jan Smuts House, the decay, the leaking roof, the papers rotting in filing cabinets. 'Sometimes I think we should just set fire to the Big House, burn it all down, finish, *en klaar*,' says J. C.'s sister. 'Rather than this sadness of seeing it gradually falling down.'

7.30 p.m., 17 July 2007

Late coming home, my cousin Richard pulls into his Johannesburg driveway in the midwinter dark. Sensing movement out of the corner of his eye, he assumes it's the neighbour. Until he sees the gun at the window and the little white Citigolf in the rear-view mirror. Driving in South Africa is a game of Russian roulette, with seventeen thousand cars hijacked every year, nearly fifty every day, and more than half in Gauteng. And now there's a live bullet in the chamber.

Two men force him into the cramped rear seat-well of the Citigolf, while another drives off into the darkness with the stolen car. There's a gun in his side and the two coloured kidnappers, teenagers, really, are on edge, hammering questions at him in Afrikaans. Does the stolen car have an immobiliser? What's his PIN? He tries to recite the Lord's Prayer, but is so rattled he can't remember it, so prays for his family instead.

He can work out roughly where they are by the turns they take, the lights flickering overhead. They pull onto the motorway out of town, headed towards Soweto. Which is not good. The teenagers' hands are shaking and they seem high, two broken boys from broken homes with only the dubious protection of a gang. Lord forgive them, he prays, and feels forgiveness move in himself. The car comes to a stop and he is pulled out, forced to kneel on the dirt road. One of the boys puts the gun to his head, cocks it. They want more information, about the car, bank details. Then one of them is on the phone, '*Ja, ons sal hom na jou toe bring.*' ('Yes, we'll bring him to you.')

More driving and then a big man looks in, says, 'Yes, go and finish the job.' The gangsters take a side road off the motorway, pull him out of the car, tie his hands together with his own leather shoelaces. And perhaps it's the effects of surreal terror, but as they are tying them he remembers 80s TV action hero MacGyver flexing his wrists as the baddies tied them together, thus leaving more space between them. So he flexes his wrists, just in case. And then he's lying face down in the veld and it's so cold.

For weeks he blanks out what they say next, these two young men, although at the time he understands them perfectly, understands what the stakes are, thanks to the years of school Afrikaans, the tongue of his forebears, after all. What the boys say to each other is: 'Let's shoot him,' and: 'No, let's leave him.' Miraculously, mercy triumphs. And as the sound of the Citigolf recedes, he is up, freeing his hands (thanks, MacGyver), running barefoot, careering into a barrier in the dark, leaping over what later turns out to be a three-foot-high cattle fence, running, running.

Days later, he revisits the scene with his parents. As the wind ruffles the sparse grass growing through wire and broken glass in this quiet spot, they meet an old African farmer. Hidden by a rise from the nearby motorway, it is the perfect place to dump a body, as the old man knows, having found several. 'God was with you that night,' he says.

How do you live with a gun held to your head? It's a question with which many South Africans of all colours live, along with the contradictory knowledge that they are the lucky ones. For Richard there is counselling, PTSD for a while and deep gratitude to his hijackers for their mercy, especially the one who refused to shoot him. He is haunted with regret that by now the two men who spared him will have been unable to resist the second or third kill order and graduated to murder. 'I've never harboured a moment's bitterness towards them,' he says. And then he adds something surprising: 'I think it's been incredibly liberating.' Liberating, (adj.): providing a release from a situation which limits freedom of thought or behaviour. Or: freeing a place or people from enemy occupation.

It's not just Richard, with his pragmatism and faith, who responds in this way. Many South Africans I meet are like this, clear-sighted, with a deep understanding of the violent discordant inequality, the desperation with which people live, the struggle just to survive. To eat, to have somewhere to belong. Having faced fear and chosen forgiveness, they have achieved a real sense of *ubuntu*: I am because we are, even as you hold a gun to my head. Not everyone reacts this way, of course, as the emigration rate shows. But, for some, it is a way to live in this torn and patched-up nation. For Richard and his wife Anne, as it turns out, it is a decision they reached years before.

April 2020

While the coronavirus continues to roam the earth, looking for somewhere to spend its seed, I reach out through the murkiness of the internet. Darkness lurks outside my study, the garden concealed by night. When the app gives its welcoming chime, and Richard and Anne appear on my laptop screen, moving in that hitched video-call way, we smile at each other, filled with some sort of joy. Distance multiplies, six thousand miles from Bristol to Cape Town, unable to take even a single step towards each other, and yet under lockdown we are in the same location.

Richard and I are a long way from the eight-year-olds making lemonade in a suburban Johannesburg garden, although our lives have kept pace with each other, through university, the peregrinations of youth, marriage, children. Just as I returned to England, and being English, so Richard and Anne returned to South Africa and being South African, which, when you are white, means complexities run very close to the surface. Especially if your great-grandfather is Prime Minister Jan Smuts.

But Richard is confident and astute, while his wife is warm and pragmatic, so when issues arose around having children, and with thousands of babies abandoned every year due to poverty and gender-based violence, Richard and Anne looked towards adoption, specifically cross-racial adoption. Which is why I am calling them in the depths of a global pandemic. In 2006, this decision made them pioneers, rather than outcasts, but it still took a while: six weeks of counselling, a marriage questionnaire, meetings with adoptive parents and adoptees. Until suddenly the waiting was over and there was Anne, holding baby Emma in a nursing home in Johannesburg. And there was Richard, stepping through the door to see his wife holding his daughter. And there they were together, two young white people driving carefully home, a ten-day-old black infant in the back seat.

When Richard was hijacked a year later, it was Anne and Emma he prayed for, crushed in the rear seat-well of the white Citigolf, thinking of how Emma had already lost one set of parents. Eighteen months after the hijacking, the family moved to Mauritius, for work and health reasons, but they always intended to return. And, indeed, after Emma came Christina in 2008, a lovely plump baby with a rosebud mouth. Second time round proved much easier: ten minutes with Emma in tow and the social worker was urging them to fill in the paperwork.

It feels revolutionary to me, this decision: imagine Emma and Tina with their dark skin and African hair brought into those lily-white households of the past. To where people of colour are where they always were: servants, or slaves. Family remains our most basic unit of belonging, how we make sense of the world, where we come from. Most often still families are formed by biology, and even if class, education, language, geography, are all more truthful indexes of fit, skin colour glows more brightly. So when parents have one skin colour and their children another there is ample scope for confusion. For Richard and Anne, their family's fabric is even more knotted, with one peach-coloured child nestled alongside the brown. Because after Tina came Sam, a birth daughter. 'The baby won't be the same colour as you,' Anne warned her daughters, and there was all sorts of biology to navigate.

And finally Michael, a son. Nearly two when he arrived, Michael had only ever left the modest children's home in Kimberley to visit the clinic. But he didn't cry when they put him in the car with his new sisters, not even when they drove for three hours, to a friend's home in the mountains. For a few weeks Michael was fast as lightning, but almost totally silent, his tiny brain ticking over at the sound of English instead of Afrikaans. These days he is a whirlwind of love and energy.

How far we have come from Anna Retief, who treks into the wilderness rather than be held equal to a brown person. 'Our children are coconuts,' announces Richard through my screen, in his cheerful way, leaving me slightly shocked and double-checking if it isn't the insult I think it is. That the term 'coconut' – brown on the outside, white on the inside – exists as an insult is tied into the philosophy of black consciousness, the need to find value in blackness, to resist assimilation into whiteness. That this insult fails to meet its mark on a white man is perhaps not surprising. It is a good description, he insists. 'My children are white Anglo-Afrikaans Christian South Africans, with brown skin,' Richard says: culture, not colour.

I think about visiting Cape Town in 2018, the children bombing into the pool, Anne and I gossiping about education, moving house, the usual parent stuff. I ask how the children are settling in at their new inclusive school after the previous (mainly white and rather posh) one.

'Do that thing the African girls do,' Anne says when Emma comes into the kitchen, 'that head wiggle.' Emma wiggles her head obligingly in an 'oh no you di'n't girl' kind of a way. I think of Krotoa, dancing between two cultures until she can dance no longer; Nontando Jabavu, dismissed by Peter Abrahams as a black Briton, by Kitty Smuts as a South African 'native'; my cousin Sarah, half-coloured and entirely English. Identities are complex, and contingent, and evolving.

Children live in a strange dreamland with no past and no future, the eternal present, like dogs or hens. In the bath, Sam feels left out because she is the only one with peach skin, but, 'Look, we're twins!' little Michael exclaims happily when he and Sam dress in matching outfits. Both things are true in a world with no contextualising time-line. In the dreamland, parents police the ignorance contract, act as shock-absorbers for environmental racism, which saturates the air like napalm. Those bigoted old fools in the extended family are hard to avoid, until they ask you to please leave your black children at home when you come visiting. Or this: when Emma is small, Richard and Anne take her to see a relative, who scoops her up in a hug, exclaiming, 'What a lovely little *k****rtjie!*' Deep in the dreamland, Emma hugs back. Great-Aunt Daphne is cut from a different cloth. Aged ninety-two, she tells a cousin sharply: 'My great-grandchild is African, and she is the apple of my eye. You can get out of my house if you are going to be racist.'

But we all lose our place in the dreamland eventually, wake into an awareness of our place in the timeline of history. Emma refuses to enter a coffee shop full of skinny blonde women in athleisure gear for reasons she cannot articulate; at a new school white hangs out with white, black with black, and she is uncertain of her place, choosing the African children until another pupil asks aggressively, 'Why can't you speak Xhosa if you have brown skin?' Micro-aggressions, macro-aggressions, experiences of being black, of being black with white parents, race and class ensnarled in a great ball of barbed wire, running down the litter-strewn track between township and suburb.

Emma thinks of studying French as a means of reaching the Europe with which she identifies. Her younger sister currently feels at home with her township friends. Just as there is no one 'whiteness' – between the Afrikaners and Anglos, the Greek and Polish and Jewish South Africans, and me, with my provisional foreignness – so there is no one 'blackness'. I reconsider the question I didn't ask Richard, how the term 'coconut' narrows the possibilities of black identity down to one.

Anne says: 'We are encouraged to talk to our black children about their ethnic background and language of origin. But then we are treating them differently, and we don't know everything about all their parents, so which language do we use? What if we know about one set of parents and not another?' Silently I add my own questions: would talking about different backgrounds entrench the notion of an essential difference between people of different skin colours? Is that inevitable in a world obsessed with antecedents?

Cross-racial adoption, legalised in 1991, hovers around the ten per cent mark. It's been remarkably easy, Richard and Anne say, but I notice they make very deliberate choices. About where they live, where the children go to school, what kind of social contexts they put themselves inside. And the older the children get the more they notice, the ignorance contract beginning to fray: why are waiting staff always black, customers white? More and more South African families find themselves crossing and re-crossing these boundaries, searching for what makes them themselves. But the racial rhetoric in South Africa grows louder, the voices on the radio shouting out their rage, their discontent.

I wonder if it is possible to be more rooted than Richard and Anne. How much devotion does a country require? Stupid of me, I think. The country requires nothing; it is a mute, unresponsive table of earth. It is the masses huddled on its surface who make the choices, ascertain the level of devotion necessary. And it is hard sometimes not to feel unwelcome, when your skin is the colour of the old oppressor. Unwelcome, the word derives from the Old English: prefix of negation + *willa* pleasure, desire, choice + *cuma* guest. Guests who are not wanted. Fighting always to stay. Anne, who grew up on a farm in KwaZulu-Natal, is a Zulu speaker. In Zulu: *azemukelekile*, they are not welcome. Not welcome on farms either. I think back to the farm on the platteland, to Danielle and Chris and the careful *mealies*, to my restless children and the dog that barked in the night-time.

This continues to be South Africa's paradox, her mosaic of human stories, these connections and fractures across the lines of colour. The euphoria of peaceful transition, those years I was privileged to share, fades. The dream of a genuinely multiracial nation, where whiteness does not cling to its way of being but opens itself to a redemptive acceptance of complicity and moves forward, struggles to become a waking reality. A new generation is born, ripping open long-established divides.

As I write this, a few years after my meal with Rachel and Puleng Stewart, the story I started so many pages ago, way back in 1996, my phone pings and I thumb on the alert to find Rachel, telling me that her sister Clare's case is being covered by a social justice publication in Johannesburg. Clare's murder remains unsolved since she was shot in rural KwaZulu-Natal in November 1993. Reopened by the Truth and Reconciliation Commission in May 1997, two investigators travelled to northern KwaZulu-Natal in December of that year. But they reported in March 1998 that serving policemen were implicated in the murder and witnesses were terrified of coming forward. Not only had the murder weapon gone missing, but so too had the associated paperwork.

The investigators recommended that Clare's case should be reopened for possible criminal prosecution, but, as with hundreds of other cases, this has never happened, for reasons that remain cloudy, but which might have something to do with ANC concerns for their own reputation. Along with thousands of others, Clare's brothers and sisters and her children, Puleng and Themba, have been left in limbo for twenty-five years, the fate of their loved ones unsolved. It is possible Clare was killed by the security police and the local Inkatha Freedom Party as a result of her ANC membership, or perhaps because she had access to sensitive information from her work on a cattle project.

Time moves on, taking perpetrators and witnesses with it, and the likelihood of prosecution recedes. But now, Rachel reports, hope is on the horizon. Some apartheid-era crimes have been reopened with the slow restoration of the National Prosecuting Authority in the post-Zuma years. In 2022, the National Prosecuting Authority announces that it aims to work through all the TRC referrals by 2027 and has appointed twenty-five prosecutors and forty investigators. Clare's killers may finally be brought to justice.

I realise there is no end to history, particularly not in this broken, joyous nation. Because, despite everything, South Africa remains an exuberant country. Nontando Jabavu observes in *Drawn in Colour* in 1960:

> despite slum conditions Southern Bantu have an indestructible gaiety, bubble with vitality, are infectiously cheerful in the most adverse circumstances. General Smuts once commented on this temperament as being one of the compensating factors dispensed to us by Nature in an age-long exposure to the harshness of our bare continent.

This compensating factor, this indestructible gaiety, persists through the wreckage and dispossession of the Native Land Act, all the Acts of General Smuts's and other parliaments, which see Nontando's Southern Bantu comprehensively trashed.

When wildfires sweep Canada and two hundred South African firefighters disembark in Edmonton to offer their help, they break into harmonised hymns of praise in the arrivals hall, sashay on the spot. This joy bubbles up everywhere, and everywhere is held in balance by darkness. In Westville Prison, incarcerated Zulus sing as they hitch up their trousers before lifting one leg with controlled precision, stomping it down, kicking high into the air and falling flat on their backs, smiling with shy pride at their war dance. South Africa continues to simmer with pain and joy, with rich and textured life. As an elderly relative says: 'At least the news is always news here.'

I think of Cato, her choice to leave the country of her birth and the difference it made to me. Of all the women who came before her, shaping the country into this warped polity. Of the farmers, the white people frightened of the myth and reality of violence. Of Chris and his revolution, of the Smuts grandchildren and their resignation, of Puleng and Rachel hoping for justice, and of Richard and Anne and their children, the Rainbow Nation reflected in all their eyes.

In our parallel tale, beyond my personal, foreign concerns, South Africa is coming to the fruit of it all, spiralling down into the end game of white supremacy. And the English grandchild of the *Volksmoeder* will reject the entire ethos of her forebears, of her iconic grandparent, embracing a different way of being, a different country, through her choices as a woman, of husband, of children and of occupation.

De Rust, Karoo, 2012

The superette is gloomy after the bright sun. It smells of yeast and maize meal, the *koeksusters* gleaming golden in the glass cabinet. The farmer's wife behind the counter smiles as she puts them in the grease-proof paper, says something in Afrikaans to my blonde daughter, who twirls in her summer dress. We step out into the high empty air off the veld, stand on the *stoep* next to the barred window, the peeling Coca-Cola sign. A man in blue overalls walks up the steps, empty bottles *toyi-toying* in his Checkers bag. A farmer drives past, tanned hairy arm resting on the open window of his *bakkie*, labourers staring blankly from the flatbed. 'Sorry, Mama,' says a woman in a headwrap, ducking past me. My teeth are already breaking through the sugared crust. It is too sweet, but I give in every time. Back in the car, I hand my mother a dewy Coke and she points the car out of this little town to where there are only yellow fields unfolding behind us like furrows from a plough.

VII

Petronella Clark

1940–

Ga se lekgoa, ke motho.
(She is not white, she is a human being.)

Sesotho saying

Pounded yam, fufu, jollof rice

Born in 1940, my aunt Petronella has a country childhood of shorts and dirty faces, milk and apples, and at thirteen she travels to the Mount, the school two hundred and fifty miles away in York where Nontando Jabavu studies two decades earlier. Founded in the eighteenth and nineteenth centuries, Quaker schools uphold the Quaker testimonies to peace, integrity, equality and simplicity. Pupils attend Meeting twice a week, and there are regular lectures: on the Mau Mau uprising in Kenya, the partition of India, the Alaskan 'Eskimos'.

In November 1953, a Miss Wateley gives a talk about South Africa. Miss Wateley is absolutely disgusted by what she saw, Petronella tells her mother. Black children living in shacks, poor working conditions in factories, high levels of TB, segregation on buses. Petronella writes: 'She mentioned Oupa several times, but she blamed old Dr Malan for most of the trouble, which is what he deserves.' She goes on: 'Mamma is right when she says that South Africa's politics are all wrong, but it is silly and lazy to just sit back and do nothing about them.'

Her South African aunts and uncles might mutter about the National Party while fearing being swamped by Africans, but Petronella is not a Smuts; she is a Clark, with all its English, Quaker implications. Still, it takes a certain kind of person to respond to what my husband later calls 'indoctrination'. My mother resorts to the Bible for entertainment during interminable school Meetings, but Petronella hears the call to arms.

When the time comes for university, she chooses McGill in Montreal: in their blended home of *bobotie* and jugged hare, with parents who no sooner step over the threshold than the next journey has been planned, none of the Clark children is afraid of disappearing over the horizon. Besides, Petronella yearns to be free of the apron strings of her much-loved mother, which snarl so tightly around her. McGill is English-speaking in Quebecois Montreal and rather staid: girls are not allowed to go out in slacks unless for skiing, skating or field trips. Petronella studies geography, and in the long summer break there are jobs – helping at a summer camp for the disabled one year, editing academic papers the next – but the work available is limited: geological firms don't want women at their field centres.

In February 1961, she represents Cameroon at a model United Nations summit that considers South Africa's expulsion (the real UN has condemned the South African government a year before). 'It is ironical,' she says, short cap of brown hair shining, 'that we are met here to discuss the expulsion of a member nation, when the preamble to our charter was written in 1945 by a citizen of that nation, General Smuts.' She smiles secretly to herself. Under Smuts's rule, South Africa had been moving from paternalism to equality within a multiracial state, she continues, until the Nationalists undid all his good work.

Sixty years later, I might question the Cameroon representative's faith in her grandfather's vision.

When Petronella first visits South Africa in 1947, the country captivates her. After the grey gloom of post-war Britain, with its rubble and rationing, it seems a paradise. There are dishes of strange fruit at every meal, avocado pears, pineapples, grapes; cold tumbling surf on wide white beaches. It takes time to notice that this paradise is marred, that all the servants are brown and even Petronella, a mere child, has authority over them, thanks to her white skin. In 1947 only a handful of black people live in rural Somerset and no more than twenty thousand in the whole United Kingdom. But in South Africa four out of every five passers-by have darker skin.

Due to sail home, seven-year-old Petronella locks herself in the bathroom, unwilling to return to 'starving England'. Later she sends her mother a story, misspelt in pencil on an air folder. 'Once upon a time,' the story begins, 'there was a black man and his wife. Once they lived in Africa but now they were slaves. One day they had a little boy but when he was three he was sold to a man who was a captin of a ship.' During a storm around the Cape of Good Hope, the little boy swims ashore 'and lived with his own poeple happily ever after wids.' Some preoccupations are set very early.

Fourteen years later, Petronella graduates into the dawn of the 1960s. In February 1960, British Prime Minister Harold Macmillan addresses the South African parliament in Cape Town after touring British colonies across Africa. 'The wind of change is blowing through this continent,' he famously proclaims. The British government will not block independence movements, and they will not continue to support apartheid (reality proves rather different to rhetoric, of course). Nations proclaim independence across Africa and Asia, there are demonstrations against nuclear proliferation, the civil rights movement continues. Over the years, the Peace Corps, set up in 1960, will send two hundred and twenty thousand idealistic young Americans overseas as teachers, engineers, health workers. The model UN, coupled with South Africa's Sharpeville massacre of 1960, fuels Petronella's interest in such work.

An early Peace Corps recruiter characterises the best volunteers as those who see more to the world, who are angry if they read about a human tragedy in a country of which they have never heard before. Mentally I set this against recent criticism fuelled by rising awareness of privilege, the perceived narcissism of 'white saviours' and the continuities of colonialism. Nested within a larger argument around the international aid industry, this criticism centres on the arrogance of young, untrained Westerners presuming to 'save' Africans, Asians and South Americans. Volunteering in what used – strangely – to be called the Third World has arguably always created more growth in volunteers than in the communities they serve (as I found in the townships of Durban in 1994). And yet. It is among the noblest of human impulses: to help others, to be angry at a human injustice, part and parcel of our evolution as social beings.

In the 1960s, such arguments trouble nobody: Peace Corps service is the acceptable face of postcolonial altruism. And in 1961 when the Canadian University Service Overseas (CUSO), sister to the new Peace Corps, is asked to provide teachers for Nigeria and Ghana, Petronella is allocated to Nigeria. In South Africa, her maternal relatives are horrified. Santa writes to Cato: 'Poor Petronella sizzling in the Nigerian heat, and with all the sizzling black faces around her! How I pity her.'

When Petronella welcomes Cato and Sarah to Nigeria in 1963, she has been teaching at a teacher training college twenty-five miles inland from Lagos for over a year. The only other expatriate is an American in late middle age, Marjorie Dean, who takes Petronella under her wing, providing her with soap, lavatory paper, supper and breakfast. (In middle age myself, I salute Marjorie Dean and what-ever courage it has taken to bring her here.) Petronella has a small, basic house with occasional running water and a cook-steward called Idim.

During training, she was shown graphic slides and swamped with talks, films and seminars. The English leaflet on 'Preservation of Personal Health in the Tropics' advises washing once a day; the American assumes everyone does anyway. Now she faces classes of thirty-five. Some of the students are older than she is, but a bigger problem is teaching in English to pupils who understand it about as well as she understands Russian.

CUSO volunteers are buoyed by their beliefs, but it is not – or not only – idealism that allows Petronella to cope. Simplicity is central to Quakerism (an early obsession with plain dress means that most people hearing the word Quaker still picture an eighteenth-century figure, clad in grey bonnet and shawl). Later her husband tells me Petronella has 'great powers of endurance' and I think how not caring whether the lavatory is a latrine in the garden or a flushing toilet inside allows her to live happily anywhere. Her future is shaped to the contours of this indifference and, of course, the means to choose.

Everywhere Petronella looks is rich life, not an apron string in sight: peppery mutton stew with piles of boiled rice; fried plantain for breakfast; nightclubs in Lagos where the music of Highlife sways across the dancefloor, with its jazz syncopation and complicated horn arrangements; grand receptions at the Canadian high commissioner's residence. Every Sunday, Christians walk to church in their fresh white *agbada*. At a christening in the Anglican church, the service is held in Yoruba, the women dressed in best Yoruba indigo wrappers and head-dresses and gold jewellery. Even the baby has a necklace, bracelets, earrings in her tiny pierced ears and rings on her tiny fingers.

There are intricacies of inter-racial, inter-cultural relationships to negotiate. Smooth-skinned with neat eyebrows over a Clark nose, hair bleached blonde by the Nigerian sun, pretty Petronella is not short of suitors. One young Yoruba man, looking for a white wife, promises to wait when she says she has no plans to marry. A Nigerian who has done his PhD at McGill quizzes her on mixed marriages. Even Bancroft worries about the lack of potential husbands. Some foreign women marry Nigerian men, but most whites conform to the stereotypes: sneering colonials, cynical businessmen, idealistic teachers. Bored European women idle away the hours in the air-conditioned lounges of upscale hotels. Expatriate friends of friends drone on about sending their children to the 'right' schools in England.

Once Marjorie Dean departs, Petronella's is the only white face in town, all eyes following her, or so it feels. Almost painfully reserved, Petronella blinks when someone talks to her, with a surprised laugh. But, even so, the words build up inside after days without talking to a fellow English speaker. The ruby-red Volkswagen Beetle she buys from a Greek VW dealer in Lagos helps her connect: with the police when her headlights are stolen, with haemorrhaging pregnant women or children with broken limbs as she drives them to hospital. The poor roads mean a constant need for repairs. When her windscreen shatters, Petronella knocks it out onto the latest copy of the *Observer* sent from England and continues at 40 mph. When the clutch cable snaps, she drives fifteen miles in first gear.

Perry, the other volunteers call her, in this new life where the Christmas turkey is stuffed with pineapple and oranges, and Christmas Day Scrabble is played in thirty-degree heat; where Peace Corps teachers might have a monkey, or a sulky parrot and a shy tortoise, and live in a wooden house on stilts. Her mother worries she will be lynched for her heritage, but her referees let the cat out of the bag and the Nigerians employ her anyway. She goes to the beach with French, Italian, Dutch men and women; sailing, she looks back on Lagos to see it is beautiful from the sea, the marina lined with tall, elegant buildings and palm trees.

Here nothing official is informal, and bureaucrats appear with a sheaf of notes and long lectures. But the Nigerians are broadminded on bodily matters, urinating openly at the side of the road, her students watching her through the window and commenting on how 'firm' she is with male guests as she offers them cups of tea. She visits the needlework mistress's home eighty miles away, where water is stored in oil drums in the courtyard, and the bush is full of orange and banana groves, plantain, cassava, yams. To phone Ikeja, fifteen miles away, she must book a trunk call and wait three hours – so much easier to go in person. She dreams of staying or returning to Canada, but, perhaps, 'I might get married which always messes things up and interferes with one's plans.'

Nigeria is wild and clean. Emptier, with a quarter of the people it has now, more orderly. In the countryside, there are compounds of cob-walled houses under pitched leaf roofs. Change approaches: harbours are dredged, new schools built with toilets not latrines, hopeful garages in a village without a road, let alone cars. But trouble approaches too: right from the start, Petronella hears from Hausa people how superior they are to Yorubas, from Yorubas how superior they are to Hausas. Western friends fret; after all the Nigerian Youth Congress has condemned the 'neocolonial spies' of the Peace Corps, but when Petronella's two years with CUSO are up she decides to study for an MSc in medical geography at the University of Ibadan. Established in 1948, the university is Nigeria's first.

Petronella sleeps in a single room full of bookshelves, eats in the canteen, which serves pounded yam, fufu, jollof rice. She takes field trips hundreds of miles north, mapping sleeping sickness distribution, the air so dry that skin cracks and powders, cold enough for a blanket at night, and a sweater in the morning. It is like the highveld, but with no colour bar. She swims laps in the pool at the luxury hotel. In South Africa, black Africans would be barred from swimming in such a pool; here, they can if they want to, although nobody does.

The long way back to Ibadan runs north of the Niger River, along the edge of a plateau, savannah rippling off into the distance below. The people here are 'pagan', women dressed in nothing but a string of beads round the waist, a bunch of leaves fore and aft. Compare this freedom – to be out in the world, driving through northern Nigeria, alone – with any of the women who have come before. No wonder she has no interest in getting married: these are joys still unavailable to most women in 1965.

This freedom runs through the hourglass as unrest roils Nigeria. In March 1965, riots break out at Lagos University. Petronella finishes her master's degree as Ibadan goes into lockdown: political meetings banned, police on campus, the main gate bolted shut. She leaves in July 1965, but for Nigeria the point of no return arrives six months later, with an attempted coup and the murder of Prime Minister Abubakar Balewa in 1966. Civil war breaks out in July 1967 and only ends in January 1970. More than a million people die in the Biafran war of independence.

Tall yellow aloes and dirt roads

Lesotho, January 1966
Flying to South Africa from London still includes a stop in steaming Brazzaville and another in Salisbury, which shows no sign that Rhodesia has declared herself unilaterally independent from Great Britain. Petronella has been accepted as a volunteer at the new University of Botswana, Lesotho and Swaziland in Roma and, landing in Johannesburg, her mother's relatives sweep her up. Is she going to teach 'k****rs' again? Isn't she pleased to be out of that 'wog-land' Nigeria now that war has erupted? She smiles politely, the thought of Nigerian friends in danger making her wince.

Roma is nothing like this: it is multiracial, multicultural, with 280 students from all over southern Africa. The university lies in the foothills of the high rugged mountains that make Lesotho the only country in the world entirely above three thousand feet. Gazing from the sandstone buildings across the valley floor, dotted with *mealie* fields and small stone huts, high talus slopes and cliffs rise in front of the mountains towering above them. As the light changes, the mountains seem to move: now small and far away, now huge, close and menacing. Great black clouds spume over the valley, lightning flickering, mountains hidden behind curtains of rain.

What is this place? Within South Africa, but not of it, a real black homeland, contradicting the monstrous propaganda along its borders: Transkei to the south and, by 1969, tiny Qwaqwa to the north-east. Lesotho's history is mythic: a brave mountain kingdom resisting the onslaught of white colonisation with courage and guile under King Moshoeshoe, who not only builds a nation out of the lost and dispossessed of the *Mfecane*, but bargains with an empire. In 1820 Moshoeshoe becomes chief of a clan in what is now northern Lesotho. He builds a stronghold on the sandstone plateau at Thaba Bosiu, offers shelter and cattle to refugees. Sensing the threat posed by the white man, he welcomes missionaries and obtains guns. By the late 1830s, Boer trekkers, like Anna Retief and her husband Thomas, move into western Basutoland and Moshoeshoe and his people wrangle with Boer and Briton.

After a defeat in 1868, Moshoeshoe appeals to Queen Victoria for British protection. Basutoland becomes a British territory and a British Protectorate in 1884. Moshoeshoe dies in 1870, ashamed at leaving only the remnants of his kingdom, but his shrewd action means the Basotho are the only Africans in South Africa in control of their own destiny. The only enclave state outside the Italian peninsula, Lesotho is surrounded by South Africa and economically integrated with it. But this tiny country remains an independent nation, culture intact, free of the poison of the white supremacy that wilts its powerful neighbour.

Even if the motley collection of nationalities in Roma import their suspicions alongside their textbooks and warm jerseys, Lesotho is an island of tolerance in the shark-infested waters of South Africa's separatist regime, and many swim for the safety of its shores. Over the years, I meet other whites – ANC activists, Quakers, liberal academics – with old ties to Roma. No wonder that whenever Petronella ventures into the Republic of South Africa, she retreats to Lesotho with relief. The republic is a country where jittery white women hold weekly 'pistol parties' on a firing range, carry teargas canisters in their handbags. Where police vans patrol white areas, shove Africans without a pass onto buses and dump them hundreds of miles away, across the border in an 'independent homeland' where they say black people belong but that are really reserves of cheap labour. Three and a half million Africans are forcibly removed to the Bantustans between 1960 and1985.

Writing to her parents in long fluent screeds that bely her spoken reserve, Petronella takes no prisoners. 'I can understand why Hitler came to power and met so little resistance. You just don't realise that a South African Reich has risen,' she writes.

If only they [the regime] would work hard to develop the country entrusted to them and exploit to the full its resources including human. What they are doing is just the opposite – the aim of the Bantu Education Act, for example, is to keep the k****rs in their right place – and what use of one's human resources is it when a child with an IQ of 150 is educated to become an unskilled worker?

Once started, she cannot stop:

And stories of families disintegrated because the parents cannot live together since one works in a White area, horrible accounts of what goes on in prisons, reports of injustices over pass-laws – these aren't myths and fairy-tales, but are facts. Here one is always aware of the Problem – it is for ever arising, in many unexpected places, a far commoner subject than the traditional Sex, Politics and Religion.

If you were here as I am here, you would realise just how enormous, and how tragic, is the bitterness engendered by Apartheid.

Suddenly this is all very personal: 'Take for example the other member of the Geography Department apart from Dr Schmitz and Mr Smits. He is Lionel Sylvester, from Capetown.' Lionel works as a demonstrator while hoping for a scholarship to study abroad because at home the best he could hope for would be a job in a shop. 'He has no future, or no worthwhile future, if he stays in South Africa – and all because his skin is a permanent olive-brown instead of a temporary golden-brown induced by sunbathing.'

Lionel Sylvester is coloured, one of those descendants of Angela van Bengale and Krotoa who fall on the other side of the colour line, children who Isie pities 'for they were born in sin'. In apartheid South

Africa, coloured identity is infused with the negative, marking you as the product of immorality and promiscuity. For a long time, coloured people dream of being white enough to access the means of power; again and again, they vote for the National Party, which does so much to damage them. In 1948, when National Party victory ensures they will be disenfranchised and oppressed. In 1994, when they worry about being overwhelmed by an influx of Xhosa people from the Transkei.

Lionel grows up on the outskirts of District Six, the vibrant mixed community in Cape Town's city bowl. But when his railway-man father falls to his death from an overhead pylon, his mother painstakingly saves her annual compensation and buys a house in nearby Salt River. It is a quiet, self-contained place, joined to the city centre by City Tramways and Golden Arrow buses, with an Indian grocer on every corner. Lionel has already left by the time Salt River escapes the Group Areas Act's clearances, which sees parts of District Six declared a white area in 1966, its homes razed to the ground, inhabitants dumped on the windswept Cape Flats to the south-east of the city.

Excelling in his exams, Lionel receives a bursary to attend an Irish Christian Brothers school. Apartheid narratives can narrow non-white lives into a mass of undifferentiated suffering, but Lionel does not recognise the racial framework within which he is caught until, approaching matric, he finds his options suddenly limited. English-speaking University of Cape Town is reserved for whites, coloured students attend the University of the Western Cape, but the teaching is in Afrikaans.

Afrikaans partially evolves as a coloured language and on the Flats. It is an expressive *Kaapse taal* – a Cape language – a creolised dialect. *Moet my nie vir 'n pop vat nie*, they might say: 'Don't take me for a doll.' Or *Slat my dood met 'n pap snoek*, literally 'Hit me to death with a soft snoek.' But Lionel is not likely to ask anyone to hit him with a fish: he speaks English, not Afrikaans, at home, this bookish teenager growing out of his uniform, a tall lad, head poised on elegant neck. Clever and touchy, Lionel speaks only school Afrikaans and, besides, he doesn't want to be taught by 'brainwashed professors'.

To bypass the byzantine waterways of apartheid, the Brothers send coloured students to Roma to study. And so, in 1962, Lionel finds himself crossing the narrow bridge over the Caledon from South Africa to Lesotho. For a boy brought up in apartheid South Africa, Roma feels like a window opening, a United Nations of people, all walks, colours and creeds. There are three men to every woman, and it is into this ratio that Petronella steps four years later. The two Dutch academics in the geography department work from home, and Lionel and Petronella are left to fall in love over the slide projector, Lionel's edgy garrulous charm a foil to quiet Petronella. Later they squabble over whether their relationship was frowned upon because they were teacher and student, never even raising what might seem a more significant obstacle: this relationship blossoms in an atmosphere where race is largely beside the point.

As soon as they step across the Caledon tenderness mutates into monstrosity, not only immoral but illegal. Not since the very early days of the VOC has sex between people with different skin colours been acceptable, let alone marriage, and under apartheid this has congealed into a greasy legal mass. The Prohibition of Mixed Marriages Act of 1949 prevents white people from marrying people of other races. The 1950 Group Areas Act prevents them from living in the same neighbourhood, not to mention the same house. Holidaying in Durban, Petronella dare not visit even an unrestricted beach – most are signposted 'whites only' – with Indian and coloured friends, the risk of being arrested for contravening the Immorality Act is too high. 'Morality' has a unique connotation under South African law: the 1957 Act forbids sexual relations between whites and non-whites.

The sexual side of white racism: African women – like Krotoa – were thought 'unrapeable', because they were seen as bestial and wanton and consequently were always at more risk of being raped. This obsession towards sex with black women persists among (some) white men. A fascination with the 'exotic', white men with their subtle brags about sex with African women: sex as a strange coupling, a badge of pride, experience. An owning. White racism dictates that while black women are wanton and promiscuous, so too are black men, and, what is more, they have their eye on white women. White men fear they will be compared and found wanting, 'their' women stolen. The perceived need to protect white women has haunted

South Africa for centuries. By the 1960s, police take the laws that prevent such sabotage so seriously it drifts into the absurd: they follow people, raid homes at night, inspect bedsheets and underwear. The children of such unions become the living embodiment of a crime. For Petronella and Lionel, a glimpse of this future arrives in 1966, when, travelling across South Africa, Petronella and two white colleagues find hotel beds while Lionel must sleep in the car.

I find myself reluctant to shrink my aunt and uncle to fit South Africa's toxic racism, which has metastasized into a cancer. After all, in the photographs, they are simply two young people. Petronella, in her tartan trousers and jerkin; skinny Lionel in his baker boy hat, chunky knit cardigan. Smiling, happy. Fortunately, I can offer a place where this simplicity remains true: within Lesotho's great 565-mile loop of rivers and mountains, where they are both outsiders, free to be human.

It is 11,700 square miles of rugged mountains and green valley floors, this freedom, crisscrossed by eroded gullies; of herd-boys and horsemen, cattle, goats and sheep; of tall yellow aloes and dirt roads; of the Roma campus with its avenues of poplars and blue gums. There is electricity and running water. In the winter, the cold and light are intense, and the heater drinks gallons of paraffin. There is not much to do here where they are free: a couple of tennis courts, a volleyball court. Petronella finds her students' clothing so Europeanised that at first she assumes their culture is too. But these young adults are Basotho, bound by Basotho customs, having to win their parents' approval to marry, finding money for *bohali* (bride-wealth, the dowry). There are tensions between modernity and tradition, and this gap allows the multicultural atmosphere at Roma to flourish, for a while.

Lesotho is still part of the British Empire, still tied into Moshoeshoe's deal that kept it safe. But by October 1966, the time has come to go it alone, and the capital Maseru, twenty miles from Roma, erupts with lights, flags, variety shows, piano concerts, all celebrating independence. The inevitable power struggles soon flare up. King Moshoeshoe II's sway is limited by the new constitution, and he and opposition parties tour the country complaining he has been robbed of his hereditary powers. Angry mobs stone a police station. Students strike and demonstrate, and the assassination of South Africa's Prime

Minister Verwoerd causes great rejoicing. Unlike her maternal relations, Petronella bemoans this murder with her usual clear-eyed
disdain for injustice, not for the loss of leadership, but because his
successor is sure to be worse, especially that 'Nazi Vorster'. She and
Lionel are not sleeping under the same roof in the Republic any
time soon.

Minute tan and a wig

At twenty-seven, Petronella is unmarried and childless, pursuing her
own interests alone in Africa. She returns to England in 1967 to study
for a one-year postgraduate qualification in Education in Tropical
Areas, and for the first time in ten years England is, temporarily,
home. Every radio seems set to Procol Harum's 'Whiter Shade of
Pale', soon challenged by the Beatles' Christmas hit 'Hello, Goodbye'.
Dirty, foggy London. It is a jolt after the clean light of Lesotho. The
UK is going through its own quiet revolution: the contraceptive pill
and the Abortion Act of 1967 offer women sexual and reproductive
freedom. The Divorce Reform Act of 1969 recognises marital break-
down as a valid reason for divorce.

Down in Brighton, Lionel is embarked on a master's degree at the
University of Sussex, his first trip beyond southern Africa, the 'short-
skirted dolly birds jiving in the student union' a surprise after his
conservative upbringing. The South African authorities didn't want
him to come: they want to keep all brown people within their borders
and are notoriously petty about it. Passports are only valid for border-
ing states and must be specially endorsed for other countries. Whites
can get such endorsements easily, but non-whites must produce
evidence of a university place or some such divine symbol, and by the
time Lionel's passport is returned he cannot travel by ship but must,
expensively, fly.

This new university has a School of African and Asian Studies,
something of a hub for African revolutionaries (future President
Thabo Mbeki takes a master's degree the previous year), but Lionel
feels out of his depth. At a party, the other students shun him until
they discover he is not white but coloured and cluster at his feet,

quizzing him about his experiences. He tries attending an anti-apartheid group, but they mistrust him. The fear of 'agents' percolates the movement: Pretoria's horizons are narrow, but its arms are surprisingly long, and South African spies really are infiltrating all sorts of organisations, especially universities.

Thabo is not the first Mbeki with whom Lionel crosses paths. Earlier, his youngest brother, Jama, studies at Roma and they lunch together, listening to the news. In 1964, the headlines are full of the Rivonia Trial: Jama's father, Govan Mbeki, is on trial alongside Nelson Mandela, their defence team including Bram Fischer (whose name, as yet, means nothing to Lionel). Jama picks at an orange as the news comes through: Govan Mbeki is sentenced to life imprisonment but spared the death penalty. Later Jama joins the Pan African Congress and disappears after fleeing Botswana for Lesotho in February 1982, in circumstances that implicate the ANC.

Lionel's trials are not yet over, even if they are personal rather than public. He must still run the gauntlet of Hindhayes. Even in Britain, mixed-race relationships are frowned upon in the 1960s. Earlier, the government urges British women not to marry Muslim, Hindu, Chinese or black men and in the 1930s, the dangers of 'race crossing' are trumpeted, Marie Stopes suggesting all 'half castes' should be sterilised. In Bancroft's Quaker eyes, Lionel's skin colour, his dark unruly hair, do not pose a problem: his Catholicism is another matter. But both Petronella's parents make the jumpy young man welcome, Cato trying to reassure him while worrying privately about how the Smutses will react. It is hard to understand now how incendiary this association is: the granddaughter of Prime Minister Smuts in a relationship with someone whose skin is not white. All too soon, Cato has her second stroke, and what she might have said to Petronella about the tangled web of history, racism, government policy and personal choice remains a void. For decades the family agonise about the newspapers getting hold of the story, but for Petronella and Lionel the fear of exposure is more than reputational. Jama Mbeki is just one of thousands who die in the deadly traps set by the absurdist theatre of the apartheid state.

But, despite the danger, they must go back. Where else could they go? They know people in Lesotho; there are opportunities for jobs and no need for difficult work permits and visas. And they are attached, to each other, to the country. Petronella is beginning to be an old hand at teaching, and education and the altruistic impulse has an honourable history in Lesotho. In 1833, Moshoeshoe invites French Protestant missionaries to visit him. To educate his people, he claims, but really it is himself he wishes to educate, on the challenge the Europeans represent. Three young Frenchmen arrive, and the mutual understanding and respect that evolves between these humans is a bright star on the dark quilt of colonial history.

Under Moshoeshoe's direction, the Frenchmen set up their mission at the foot of Makhoarane Mountain and he sends them his two senior sons. The village – now Morija – survives as a centre of learning for 150 years, and when Petronella returns to Lesotho, teaching qualification in hand, it is to the teacher-training college at Morija – she is neither French nor a missionary, but the impulse endures.

Morija, April 1969

The privy is outside, but there is running water and electricity, and apricot and peach trees surround Petronella's little mud house, blossoming beautifully pink and white in the spring. Morija is wooded with trees cultivated by generations of missionaries, and in August tiny yellow flowers cover the mimosa. Lionel finds a post at St Mary's High School in Roma. The rare buses take three hours to cover thirty miles, and the telephone system is erratic. Petronella invests in another VW Beetle, but Morija is isolated, and she struggles to get dependable news. She relies on an old shortwave radio, reconnecting a wire and inserting new batteries to listen to the BBC World Service. On the day of the first general election in 1970, Morija is peaceful: almost everyone supports the opposition Basutoland Congress Party and voters in their brightest blankets queue outside the polling station. As votes are counted, Congress, more radical than the ruling Basutoland National Party, appears to win by several seats.

Suddenly Radio Lesotho starts broadcasting nothing but music. Then the orchestral strains are broken: stand by for a special announcement by the prime minister at 3 p.m. Petronella hurries round to her friends' to listen. Leabua Jonathan's voice sounds deep and solemn as he announces a State of Emergency into the room's silence. After this, he works quickly: Radio Lesotho announces the opposition leader's arrest at 3.30 p.m.; Maseru and other trouble spots are put under curfew; King Moshoeshoe II is exiled; British subjects in Maseru are summoned to the High Commissioner, Peace Corps volunteers to the Peace Corps office. Petronella stays where she is.

Trouble splutters on for months. Driving south, a bus stopped in the road forces Petronella to a halt. A group of Jonathan's 'Young Pioneers' circle it, armed with rocks, removing some passengers before allowing it to move on. Staying in Leribe, in the north, the night silence is broken by flares, gunfire and circling Land Rovers. There are news stories, rumours: an opposition politician kidnapped and tortured for three days with a hosepipe; four elderly women, too weak to escape to the hills with their fellow villagers, hacked to death. Leabua Jonathan (like many others, a great-grandson of Moshoeshoe I) retains power for the next sixteen years, but Lesotho's struggles are always going to be complicated by those of its powerful encircling neighbour.

In May 1970, Petronella drives for seven hours alone across the *platteland* to attend an elaborate celebration of the centenary of the Oubaas's birth. A thousand chairs line up on the Doornkloof lawn while two thousand guests stand at the back, but the contents of the ceremony underline how far Jan Smuts lies from the Afrikaner Nationalists, to whom he must be just a soldier, not a (traitorous) statesman. Petronella's aunts greet her joyfully, and Sylma reports to Bancroft:

> [Petronella] is looking well and happy and seems untroubled by the political situation – but I always feel she's a little wary with me, just as Aunt Margaret was with Ouma, in discussing the native question and feels all South Africans are reactionary!

Neither Petronella nor her English great-aunt can speak their concerns to these Afrikaner women, the gulf between them too wide and treacherous to accommodate even one tentative step.

Far from being untroubled, Petronella and Lionel are most often seen making a dash for sanctuary as the republic's punitive laws tighten ever further: when she visits her mother's friends, or her sister Sarah who moves to Durban in 1971, or when Lionel visits his family in Cape Town. But Petronella *is* curiously unruffled, or so it seems from this distance: she condemns the corruption of apartheid, but does not allow it to wash through her, and I wonder how much of this is a result of rightness, and whiteness? For Lionel, an unclouded mind is impossible, Pretoria and her minions a corrosive insult on his skin.

Eight months later, Petronella and Lionel want to spend Christmas with his family in Cape Town, but this simple desire involves complicated planning. Lionel sets off first, leaving Petronella in Morija where snow lies upon the apricot and peach trees. She keeps close to her paraffin stove and thinks of the herd-boys freezing to death and of Lionel, travelling with two Canadians in a VW minivan. He plans to sleep in the minivan: there is no room at the inn for people with brown skin, whatever the season.

In Grahamstown, when the Canadians insist on asking if Lionel can stay in the hotel, he is shown to a hovel in the backyard. Better that than a sleeping bag in the back of a van on this cold, damp night, he thinks. Fed an excellent dinner in the kitchen, he returns to find the hovel transformed: clean sheets and blankets, an old-fashioned basin and jug, a potty, candles burning brightly. The next morning, he is woken with a cup of coffee. The following night in Swellendam does not go so well: the drivers' room smells of stale socks and cheap booze, and a woman is hiding under the bedclothes with the other occupant. Lionel retires to the VW and tries to fold his long, thin frame onto the back seat.

Petronella travels to Cape Town with her friend Sumitra who is an Indian from India, and subject to the same restrictions as South African Indians: she cannot stay overnight in the Orange Free State and must pay two rand for the privilege of driving through. Sumitra has sourced a travel guide for non-whites, so they set a course for a hotel in the coloured location in Beaufort West. But navigating rules designed to keep people apart is an intricate process and Petronella finds herself without a bed until the innkeeper phones around and finds her a bed in a white hotel. It is always a surprise, the kindness of non-whites towards her pale skin and blue eyes, which should mark her out as the enemy.

Once in Cape Town, Petronella is sheltered by Lionel's family, but he cannot bear it when she steps out into the garden with her head uncovered, hair and skin glowing pale as a lamp for every moth-like informant and apartheid agent in the city to see. To visit a drive-in cinema where coloured and non-coloured watch the same film, separated by a high fence, Petronella is daubed with Minute Tan and dressed in a wig. She emerges looking sunburnt, and the wig is replaced with a headscarf, the tan with make-up, but, just as this disguise is about to be tested, Petronella loses the car keys. When she does visit the drive-in, it is with Lionel's half-sister, classified white. Later Lionel's stepfather is injured in a car accident. Admitted to hospital, there is a great to-do about who can see him: he has been admitted to a white ward. This is Alice in Wonderland territory.

The drip-drip of threat makes Lionel fearful, Petronella contemptuous, but their commitment continues along its natural path, which makes me wonder about humans and the tensile strength of our bonds.

The following Christmas, 1971, Petronella drives Lionel to Bloemfontein to catch the Orange Express to Cape Town. Without a chaperone, they risk arrest for violating the Immorality and Suppression of Communism Acts and at the Maseru Bridge border post the official looks carefully at Lionel's light-brown skin, his dark hair and eyebrows, and asks if he is coloured.

'Yes', replies Lionel, and waits for the hammer to fall. Instead, they are waved through.

With Lionel safely on his train, Petronella drives to the *Vrouemonument* to see if Aunt Margaret's mementoes are on display. The photographs of concentration camps, the leg of a chair to which an ill man was tied to face a firing squad: it all seems designed to commemorate the evils of the British. Now the Boers perpetuate the same evil, she writes to her father, flushing 'unwanted Bantu' out of urban areas into 'homelands' that are no more than a 'hastily erected collection of tents and tin huts on a barren stretch of veld'.

Lesotho, January 1974

Petronella and Lionel keep out of sight, but they are about to embark on a course guaranteed to make the hydra of South Africa's repressive government sniff the air for its prey. When Lionel gets a job in Morija, it makes sense for the couple to live together. But in conservative Lesotho this means marriage, and marriage means messing with the Republic of South Africa's diktat against mixed marriages. (It is not my business to speculate if there is another, more biological, reason for marriage although this would sharpen these difficulties further, sharpen them enough to cut the incautious or those unable to protect themselves.)

Wary of phone taps, the family exchange coded telephone conversations, and Bancroft, visiting the Smuts relations in Irene, dares not tell them the real reason for his hasty departure. He arrives in time to see Petronella walk up the aisle of the Catholic church alone, light-brown hair swinging behind her. With a few words it is done, this tying of a Gordian knot, and the bride and groom depart for their honeymoon at the Maseru Holiday Inn overlooking the river, and beyond that the Boer farms. If they were to step over that border, they would find themselves unmarried again, because a mixed marriage contracted outside the republic by a male citizen is not legally recognised within the republic. Questions niggle. When Lionel renews his passport, should he reveal his marriage and risk not obtaining a passport because it is a mixed marriage? How then could he stay in Lesotho? Should he state himself unmarried because the marriage is not recognised in South Africa anyway? 'His wife considers this DISHONEST,' writes Petronella, and I wonder at the strength of a principle maintained in the face of an illegitimate and punitive regime.

Two hundred miles north, the Smutses splutter: what about the Oubaas's legacy, the United Party? In 1975, needing to stay in Johannesburg overnight, Petronella phones her aunts and cousins. She is met by excuse after excuse until her Aunt Louis realises Lionel is not with her and invites her to stay. As I read this back, I am close to tears, but Petronella wasn't hurt: 'I just thought they were stupid.' Even the Smutses come round in the end: later in 1975 'Mr Petronella Clark' is invited to the unveiling of a grand bust of Smuts at the Union Buildings. He does not attend.

'Not only illegitimate but illegal'

There are so many dead children in this long tale, but there are also living ones, and we are about to meet the next in line as he becomes a person distinct from his mother. Over the past three centuries, the hypothetical papers grasped by those living on the southern tip of Africa have been rewritten each time the *shongololo* of history sheds its legs. Krotoa: citizen of nowhere, being part not of a raucous modern polity but of a nomadic clan. But even pastoralists have issues of belonging or not, and she is of the outcast Goringhaikona, if you remember, fated to wander the shore and eat beached whales. Angela: a slave and perforce not a citizen. But who later becomes something like a citizen, married to a free burgher. Both of whom bear children who are free burghers of the Dutch Cape Colony.

Elsje Cloete: born near Köln, citizen of a city. Anna Siek: daughter and wife of a Cape burgher, Cape citizen? Margaretha Retief: daughter and wife of a Cape burgher, later a British subject. Anna Retief: also a British subject until she takes off over the horizon to become a wandering citizen of, one after another, Natalia, the South African Republic and the Orange Free State. Isie Krige: born a British subject in the Cape Colony, later reinforced by their victory in the Anglo-Boer War, squeaks South African citizenship with the passing of the South African Citizenship Act in 1949; Cato Smuts born a British subject, later a British citizen; and finally, Petronella, who, being born in Britain to two British parents, has no claim in this republic. I am dizzied at this shifting rollcall of identities down the centuries – no citadel nation state this – a bewilderment for patriots everywhere.

Her baby, Roger, is the actor for whom we are waiting, although at this point he is not so much an actor as a bundle of impulses. Surely with three-quarters of his ancestors in South Africa for at least three hundred years, with a great-grandfather who arguably created the country of South Africa, surely he has a claim? Roger's father, Lionel, is South African and a citizen: the Bantu Homelands Citizenship Act of 1970 strips blacks of their South African citizenship, replacing it with joke citizenship of the independent Bantustans, but coloured people remain citizens of South Africa. Unable to vote, segregated, but citizens nonetheless. But to inherit Lionel's South African citizenship, Roger must be registered as illegitimate, his parents' marriage not being recognised under South African law, and this they will not contemplate.

To compound the problem, Roger cannot have citizenship of Lesotho unless he is Basotho or has two Commonwealth parents, and to be British he must be born in Britain, which is why, seven months pregnant, Petronella boards a flight to England and boards it alone because Lionel's passport is not valid beyond southern Africa. And it is why we meet Roger cooing in his crib in August 1974 while outside tender nuts ripen on a walnut tree surrounded by the cows and deep green grass of Somerset. Lionel remains in Morija, six thousand miles south, doting on photographs of his son's beauty: it will be another six weeks before he meets him in person. Meanwhile, Petronella recovers from a life-saving Caesarean section (a reminder of how being born white, English and modern blunts the traps of female biology).

Three years later, another baby enters the scene, but this time Petronella does not fly to Britain: Lionel's passport has been renewed and validated, but biology gets in the way when the doctor confines Petronella to bedrest. Safer to have the baby in Bloemfontein, especially given the need for another Caesarean, but that is three hours' drive away in the Republic of South Africa. And while a babe in the womb is easy to carry across an international border, a babe in arms is less so. Besides, doctors in the republic are more likely to be prejudiced by the 'bruise' marks on an infant's bottom, revealing its non-white ancestry. So baby Sarah is born in a mission hospital in rural Lesotho. Stateless. Petronella and Lionel appeal to the UK High Commission in Maseru, and eventually Sarah receives a certificate of British naturalisation, an act of generosity unthinkable in these days when 12 million people worldwide have no recognised nationality.

The following year the family moves to Roma, where Petronella teaches at the university primary school and Lionel at the university. Lesotho is cut off, with little cultural activity and no chance of advancement, but for the children it is a childhood of bicycles and freedom, where their friends are of all different skin colours and hair textures and nobody cares. But, beyond Lesotho's borders, the

Sylvester children are entirely unwelcome and all the evil Petronella and Lionel hide from them lies in plain sight. They avoid explaining why they can't go to the beach, how the darker hues of their cousins on their father's side affect those cousins' lives in terrible ways. 'Lionel wants to shelter them from developing the kind of inferiority complex that he was brought up to develop,' Petronella writes to her father.

Trips into the republic are fraught with danger: this is a family 'not only illegitimate but illegal' under South African law, as Bancroft likes to say, another phrase that becomes as polished as a pebble in a river-bed, the sharp edges of its disbelief worn smooth by handling. In 1980, driving home from Cape Town through the dry scrub of the Karoo, the Sylvesters' car breaks down. The local mechanic having drowned in a flash flood, they head back to Cape Town, two hundred miles away. Soon enough, the engine seizes up again. They are stranded in the middle of the semi-desert, their crime visible across all their faces.

Lionel pulls the car onto the dusty roadside and as the engine ticks into silence Petronella gets the children out. It is hot, and quiet, aside from the occasional rush of vehicle and rumble of truck. The grey, dusty Karoo is studded with the jade-green succulence of the *ganna* bushes. Perhaps Lionel mutters angrily, or kicks the back tyre. As a large white Mercedes heading west indicates and slows to a stop, his hands shake.

The Mercedes's window winds down and Petronella steps forward and speaks in her English accent, smooth brown hair in a fat plait down her back, blue eyes wide with explanation, signalling for help. The two men, kind and empathetic civil engineers, tow the car to Touws River and then take the Sylvester family all the way to Cape Town. Nearing the city, Lionel asks to be dropped off in a coloured area, and even then the men say not a word about the family they have aboard. Illegitimate, illegal. This episode becomes a story, part of the Sylvesters' personal mythology, but there is another way of read-ing it, because the two men in the Mercedes are Christians, and perhaps see themselves playing out the parable of the Good Samaritan.

Resistance to apartheid is becoming more militant: in 1976, Soweto school children are shot by police while protesting at having to learn in Afrikaans. Black Consciousness helps to counter the toxic sense of inadequacy that festers under white supremacy, until in August 1977 its leader, Steve Biko, is arrested at a roadblock. Held naked in a cell with his legs in shackles, he is interrogated for twenty-two hours and violently beaten, suffering a massive brain haemorrhage. Later he is driven 740 miles handcuffed and naked in the back of a Land Rover to a prison hospital in Pretoria, where he dies alone in a cell.

This is the backdrop against which, in March 1978, Petronella and baby Sarah venture into the republic. Quakerism runs through Petronella, like lead through a pencil, and access to the Quaker Meeting at Roma reactivates this faith; her opposition to Pretoria's malevolence begins to run along the well-worn channels learnt years before at the Mount. Miss Wateley would be proud. Now, en route to a Quaker gathering, they find the road south to the remote border post little more than a bridle path, and the immigration official drunk. When they arrive at the Christian centre in a forest sanctuary, there is not quite enough food or hot water, but it is one of the few places where people of different skin tones can still mix.

As Petronella nurses baby Sarah, the atmosphere veers between speeches of despair and songs of hope. I picture the flipcharts and marker pens of Quaker conferences, the dowdy, decent Friends as they write a list of how they are helping people and then become terrified that the list will fall into the wrong hands. This reaction might seem paranoid until an uninvited Afrikaner appears, claiming to be a local church minister. Well-meaning Friends welcome him, but how, the only other Afrikaner among them asks suspiciously, can a Dutch Reformed pastor be absent from his congregation at Easter? Reluctantly, they ask the minister to leave, which is fortunate as he turns out to be a government plant. This is not an isolated incident: in 1971, thieves break into Friends House in London, the only items stolen relating to South Africa: files of exchange visits, donors, lists of local organisers.

The Quaker community in southern Africa has always been tiny, from the first Meeting in 1728 to the Nantucket whalers of the early 1800s who hold their Meetings on the peninsula, tucked as it is between the whale grounds of the South Atlantic and Indian oceans. In 1910, our old friends the Jabavus appear when John Tengo Jabavu, editor of the first isiXhosa newspaper and Nontando's grandfather, visits London to protest colour prejudice in the Act of Union, written by Jan Smuts. He attends Westminster Meeting and becomes a Quaker, just as Smuts solidifies his own relationships with Quakers, two hundred miles away in Somerset. In 1932, John Tengo's son DDT – Davidson Don Tengo Jabavu – complains that he must send his children to England for a Quaker education when the new Quaker school near Durban turns out to be co-educational but not multiracial.

Quakerism is a radical faith – Friends are expected to live their beliefs in the world – but with only a hundred adult members in a population of over 40 million they have minimal impact. Some valiant Friends campaign long and hard, at great personal cost, but as Petronella observes in an MPhil thesis, 'Quaker attitudes towards racial issues have a complex and contradictory history, full of ambiguities, in southern Africa as elsewhere.' At Yearly Meeting in 1981, she finds herself alongside stunned Friends who are black, or whites accustomed to living among blacks, in dormitory rooms while Friends from Johannesburg and Cape Town, primarily white, sleep in superior rooms. The elderly couple in charge of sleeping arrangements has assumed Friends would prefer to be segregated.

The relationship between South Africa and Lesotho is deteriorating. In December 1982, a friend near the Maseru border reports a night huddled in the back bedroom of his prefab home with his children, tracer bullets cracking as military vehicles cruise up and down. Forty-two people are killed in this raid by South African Special Forces, and more raids follow, as well as bomb attacks on reservoirs and fuel depots. We are almost back to when the army stops us at the roadblock and my father's fountain pen fails to work as it is supposed to because this is the Christmas that we unknowingly situate ourselves in the middle of a low-grade war between the ANC and Pretoria.

Following the Soweto uprising in June 1976, young South Africans enrol at Roma and build underground ANC networks. They bomb South African cities; the South African military and police retaliate with cross-border raids, abductions and assassinations. In May 1983, the border all but shuts as South Africa punishes Lesotho for an ANC car bomb. Caught in the queue is Petronella, who has driven Roger to the orthodontist in Bloemfontein and must spend the night cramped and cold in the back of the station wagon with her children, hunkered down in sleeping bags. I picture the 1980s version of my aunt: wholemeal pasta on her children's plates, home-made Clothkits dress on her straight back. Righteous. Not likely to be intimidated by an authority she regards as illegitimate. Bullying, she calls it in a complaint to the British High Commissioner after spending twenty out of twenty-six hours of travel at the border.

By 1985, the ark that has housed the Sylvester family for so long begins to leak: the university at Roma has ruled that jobs are to go to Basotho, not expatriates. South Africa's ban on inter-racial marriage lifts in April 1985, but under the Group Areas Act Petronella still cannot live in the same place as her children, let alone her husband. She is not even a South African citizen. What is worse, the resistance building inside South Africa has exploded into riots, grenade attacks, petrol bombs. A State of Emergency declared in July extends nation-wide in 1986, extreme force justified by the supposed communist threat and the collapse of law and order in townships. But it fuels more and more violent opposition.

News from Cape Town is not good. There have been ferocious outbreaks in coloured areas. Lionel's brother-in-law, head of a coloured school, reports that his school is 'on holiday', with no classes for some time. His own children who attend a 'white' school (private, so it can have up to fifteen per cent non-whites) do not wear their uniform for fear of reprisals by vigilante coloured gangs and Lionel's sisters shop carefully, wary of being caught frequenting 'white' stores.

It is not war, not exactly, not enough that the white population are aware. Towns and cities are white spaces, clean and safe, and the violence keeping them that way is hidden. Censored newspapers and broadcasts are empty of the deaths in detention, the riots, the police shootings. They don't even have television until 1976. The non-racial United Democratic Front (UDF), established in January 1983 by trade unions, church groups and other civic organisations, forms an internal bulwark of resistance, but it is fractured by suspicion and the rise of people's courts, violence and fear.

South Africa might be dangerously close to civil war, but the Sylvester family cannot swim against the tides of history. Lionel finds a job at the University of the Western Cape. The white school attended by Lionel's nephew and nieces accepts Roger and Sarah. Mrs Leonard in Immigration gives them multiple forms, and they navigate the convoluted rules. Before the final move, there is a graduation ceremony to attend: after four hours, Petronella's name is called, and she pushes through the large crowd towards King Moshoeshoe II, chancellor of the University of Lesotho. In her silver and blue Master of Education hood, she bows against a rising chorus of ululation. Watching this scene through the lens of history, I see all the female lives freed by teaching glitter in the silver of her hood.

Old friends turn up for the pot-luck supper: Ellen Mahomed and four children, the family of Ismail Mahomed, a former maths lecturer at Roma. Mahomed is on trial for his role in the UDF. He is also, secretly, in an underground unit of the ANC. The next morning, the Sylvesters find Ellen and the children waiting, resigned, at the border, as the South African soldiers open all their suitcases and check under all the wheel arches. (In 1994, Professor Mahomed becomes an ANC MP, serving three terms before retiring in 2009.)

If Petronella has any illusions left about the country to which she is moving, they are stripped away when Susan Conjwa arrives at the annual Quaker gathering straight from Pollsmoor Prison. A cheerful portly woman, Susan is born in the Transkei before moving to Cape Town where she works as a domestic servant, but also leads community activism against the pass laws and forced removals. As township factions go to war, she and another Quaker, Rommel Roberts, try to broker peace deals.

She describes to her fellow Quakers, safe in their white skins, the bleak police cell, the friends she finds, how they knit to fill the hours and provide a cover for conversations about how to respond to Special Branch, how these conversations sustain them through interrogation. I wonder at the saving grace of the ordinary, the click of needles an anchoring, the careful creation of something to keep someone, somewhere, clothed. The sweater on the needles seems to expand to fill the whole dank cell, an orange warmth, which will keep everyone safe, although of course it can't, and the clang of the cell door breaks the spell as the warder steps in. This is it. Petronella and Lionel have opened the cell door; there is no turning back now to the warm shelter of Lesotho.

'As long as the sun shines'

Cape Town, January 1986

This is where our story began, 334 years ago, and relationships between pink and brown people are still frowned upon by those in power. Cape Town can seem a Garden of Eden, but, if it is Eden, it is one mapped with pain and betrayal right from that first Eve, Krotoa, offered the apple of knowledge by Commander van Riebeeck. And now all are condemned to live apart.

Except for Lionel and Petronella, and it feels a heavy weight to put on their shoulders, my aunt with her polo necks and red trousers, my uncle with his bright brown eyes and barking laugh. It feels a heavy weight, but it is also a fairy story, is it not? That they are returning to this city that formed their peoples in its crucible, that they are returning to this city of division, together.

Fairy story or not, the washing needs to be done, and where Angela van Bengale had to do it all by hand Petronella is happy enough to sit, writing to her father from the laundrette as it spins. North Pine, where the laundrette resides, is a step up from a township: tidy whitewashed houses on green lawns, lovingly tended by coloured owners. Petronella can live here freely – in a white area, Lionel would have to apply for special permission. Despite the relaxation of some laws, apartheid's bureaucracy breeds like rabbits. Their relationship is no longer illegal, but after twelve years of marriage and two children it must be validated by a notary public, she writes. They find ''*n regte* Afrikaner' (a real Afrikaner) at the University of the Western Cape to stamp the document as Lionel bristles.

'It's like Nazi Germany,' a Jewish estate agent mourns when she can't sell Petronella a house while she remains married to Lionel. Another consults the Department of Constitutional Development and is warned against allowing her clients to transgress the Group

Areas Act. Do government administrators dream of forms stamped in triplicate, relieving them of guilt by proving that the inhumane treatment of another human is lawful? Roger and Sarah struggle to settle at school, with the corporal punishment, the compulsory and impossible Afrikaans. A nun at Sarah's school keeps paddles on her desk to punish her pupils. Each paddle has a name. Roger is sure to fail Afrikaans and repeat a year of school. His parents are frightened that he will be called up for National Service.

Since 1652, the Cape has been at the interface of cultures, and it has been the source of Petronella's translation from white into a mixed-race family through the vector of Lionel, but it is not fluid, this interface. Sarah makes friends with the coloured girls, hanging out in shopping malls while the cliquey white kids go surfing. She and Roger feel neither white nor coloured, Roger fitting in with either group and Sarah with neither. She feels conspicuous in her difference, the other children asking, 'What are you?'; her aunts in the kitchen, cooking Cape Malay food, her mother in the sitting room with the men.

This is not Lesotho. It is urban, troubled, and the family embody transgression. But everyone is so kind! The rented house in North Pine is reclaimed by its owner, and they move from place to place in the hunt for that elusive house, the one they can buy. There is no consensus on what the laws mean, practically speaking, and a fairy story has no answers.

In 1987, as the apartheid edifice teeters and Petronella prepares to complete payment on a house in (white) Rondebosch, the papers overflow with threatened clampdowns on couples breaking the Group Areas Act. Lionel wavers. But surely the government still wishes to avoid the embarrassment of a woman of Petronella's pedigree being in a mixed-race marriage? After all, just a year previously, Smuts's birthplace has been restored and opened to the public. By the low thatched cottage, dwarfed by the silos and conveyor belts of a cement quarry, Minister of National Education F. W. de Klerk had unveiled a plaque. 'It is essential that young people in particular be made aware of our history as it is reflected in our spiritual and material heritage,' he said, without irony. That no one invites Petronella is due, she assumes hopefully, to an oversight.

This low, white building surrounded by cement works is part of a network of houses these women maintain, those carapaces protecting them from Cape life: Vergelegen, Kromme Rhee. And those more distant, more recent domains: Doornkloof, Hindhayes. But Petronella is nothing like any of those women, and she has no house! Undomesticated, still. Or is it the relationship maintained beyond the bounds of acceptance, outside the white state?

Petronella and Lionel find refuge in the end – that house in Rondebosch. But in the townships, makeshift homes of waste wood, cardboard, plastic, corrugated iron are torched and bulldozed; the government shunts residents from Crossroads to Khayelitsha. Violence descends into atrocity, egged on by apartheid provocateurs. Suspected spies have petrol-doused car tyres placed round their necks and set alight. Necklacing, it is called.

It is during this period that we visit, repeatedly, take cheerful family photographs of feeding the pigeons under a statue of the Oubaas, ride on the lions at the Rhodes Memorial, and we must know that something is happening, perhaps from English television, because around now I write my impassioned teenage screed against apartheid. In the country itself, we do not see anything, not one thing, which makes us worry, because the violence is in a strange and twisted way confined to the townships.

Petronella writes to her father: 'Meanwhile the whites can sit in their safe suburbs saying, "Isn't it terrible how these blacks fight each other?"' She observes: 'Yet everyday life continues as normal . . . we go about our daily business, perhaps depressed and saddened, those of us who are aware, but not frightened.' This is not the whole truth, especially at night or outside the comforting bubble of white suburbs, when white fears of the *Swart Gevaar* are as strong as they have ever been.

Under the hum of everyday life, I hear the faint echoes of escaped slaves, their fires on Table Mountain, the fearful farmers below.

Life under a repressive regime has many faces, some anonymous, and even letters within families can be 'subversive statements', putting author and those within at risk of detention, and so Petronella passes letters to travelling friends, to be posted in foreign postboxes. For private circulation only, she entreats. These frightening anonymous faces push people towards the edge, and Cape Town's Quaker Meeting brims with anguish, one woman traumatised by the murder of a man in front of her.

Apartheid corrupts everyone, Lionel observes in his quick, scornful way: 'Everyone in South Africa is a bit weird.' Some white South Africans are sociopaths, some psychopaths, but most are just keeping up with their social group and perhaps we cannot avoid Hannah Arendt's 'banality of evil', how it festers in airy white homes and the cramped servants' quarters around the back. I think of Petronella's comment about a South African Reich, of the Jewish estate agent who can recognise Nazism when she sees it, of how Nazism infected the whole of Germany. *Vergangenheitsbewältigung*, working through the past, I hope bleakly that I would have been different, as Petronella is different.

Cape Town, September 1987

The weather is cold and overcast and Petronella pulls her padded jerkin tighter as she stands at the back of the concrete quadrangle, out of sight of the road along with the students and other teachers. In front of the crowd of excited pupils, a young man stands on a box, addressing them in Afrikaans. Boycott, youth, strike, protest: Petronella can pick out English words, even if the Afrikaans is beyond her. This former pupil is a worker at the local sausage factory, sacked along with many of the students' parents for striking over low pay and poor working conditions.

She is the only white, and virtually the only English speaker, in this entire coloured secondary school of a thousand children. In the two months since she started teaching here, students have already boycotted classes to protest government actions. Stories swirl of the school's occupation by armed soldiers two years earlier, of students attacked with teargas and rubber bullets. All this is part of a rolling national State of Emergency: thousands arrested and tortured, hundreds killed. Apartheid is cracking under the pressure of the fall of the Soviet Union, international sanctions and a stagnating economy, an undereducated black majority and the cost of manufacturing all those guns and explosives the police and army use to bolster this system.

How to live in this strange place? Every decision is a moral one: enjoying a film in a cinema forbidden to blacks, filling a supermarket trolley while a few miles away children have *mealie* pap for every meal, working as a teacher in segregated schools. Overwhelmingly white, Quaker women are marked by guilt, but they have a secret weapon. Imagine an invisibility cloak: no one notices you or dreams you might disagree with their system. Imagine what you could do with this cloak: offer your home for banned people to meet, bring in banned literature, collect bail money for black youths. Martyrdom is not on these women's minds: visibility and arrest would bring the work to an end. For decades, they avoid working in the system, visit townships without permission, shelter fugitives, attend trials, organise help for families and food for prisoners, offer postal schooling for prisoners or shelter to young South Africans fleeing into Botswana, set up growing and sewing projects.

In June 1986, when a statement by Soweto clergymen challenging church responses to the apartheid state is in circulation, Cape Town Quakers, including Petronella, invite the signatories to the Meeting House in Mowbray. As the morning draws near, they are anxious about who might come; most of the clergy are in detention, but less welcome guests abound. In the end, an unwelcome guest arrives as a large brown envelope with no return address. Inside are six copies of an ANC pamphlet: 'Dear Comrades and Compatriots', it begins. The Friends burn the unsolicited, incriminating documents in a picnic *braai*-pit on the outskirts of the city.

At a public meeting in Athlone, a coloured area, Dullah Omar, lawyer, anti-apartheid activist and later Minister of Justice in Mandela's government, is the key speaker. Arriving to set up the hall, the organising Quaker finds the road clogged with concrete blocks, which local youths help her shift. That evening, when Petronella arrives, the building is surrounded by armed police. When Omar enters, his hands tremble uncontrollably, but he delivers his speech as the police videotape from the back of the hall.

These women are shamed by the smallness of their actions. Yet what makes them invisible is precisely what makes it hard for them to take risks – the ties of domestic life, of small children or elderly parents. I think back to Molly Fischer, to the children scarred by their parents' choice to take the moral path into active resistance. How do those mothers who choose not to walk that path live with themselves? Some Quakers snap, shame leading to chronic depression or serious breakdowns following detention, repression and the killing of friends. Lionel worries about Petronella, his law-abiding Catholic upbringing at odds with her Quaker belief in the 'moral duty to break an immoral law'. If she is arrested or deported, what will happen to her illegal, illegitimate children?

On the walls of white classrooms, posters identify explosive devices: here is a limpet mine, here a hand grenade. Policemen visit schools and show seven-year-olds landmines and pipe bombs, and when those seven-year-olds grow up they get to handle their own explosives. From 1967 conscription is compulsory for all white men over seventeen not in college. This is where white people encounter apartheid's brutality: sheltered white boys sent into the bush to kill black 'insurgents', to watch their friends get killed and maimed, then dumped back into normal society, unable to talk about these covert wars in South West Africa and Angola. Later, conscripts are sent into townships, at war with the people who clean their toilets and wash their clothes, who take care of their children.

When people imagine Quakers, they conjure up pictures of gentle do-gooders in bonnets. But these people are ornery sandal-wearing warriors for peace. Peace is not weak or soft; it is hard-won, intricate. The Quakers develop slow methods of addressing conflict in areas with deeply rooted historical problems, in Israel and Rwanda. Aunt Hilda, with her 'fruitless' campaigning in inter-war Europe, the Society of Friends awarded the Nobel Peace Prize of 1947, these are part of a broader whole. And, in 1988, the Quaker Peace Centre in Cape Town opens its doors.

The Peace Centre works with the foot soldiers of the fight against apartheid, who have been necklacing their fellow men, women and children. By 1990 Petronella is working with untrained teachers in a squatter camp, then as coordinator of the Peace Education programme. The Peace Centre offers a home to the End Conscription Campaign, pivotal in the white anti-apartheid movement, banned in August 1988 and targeted with fire-bombings, assaults and break-ins. There are conflict resolution workshops, a sewing work-shop in Khayelitsha, a gardening scheme. And constant grinding fear of the security police.

Vote, the Beloved Country

South Africa is reaching its end game, or what might feel like one: fifty years after the National Party are elected in this failed attempt to create an eternal white state, their own Thousand Year Reich already having lasted longer than Hitler's paltry murderous dozen. The slow-motion collapse of apartheid rips at the country as the ANC's pledge to make the townships ungovernable enables a system of warlords and organised crime. The ANC and the IFP clash.

Pass laws are repealed in July 1986, and petty apartheid – the 'whites only' signs on shop counters, buses, park benches – is abolished in 1989. In September, thirty thousand Capetonians of every race walk from St George's Cathedral down Adderley Street. Outside City Hall, Archbishop Desmond Tutu speaks of his 'rainbow country'. In the general election that same month, voting still restricted to whites, the liberal Democratic Party wins the entire city, plus the southern and Atlantic suburbs.

Earlier that year, *die Groot Krokodil* (the Big Crocodile), P. W. Botha, has a stroke and is replaced as State President by F. W. de Klerk. In February 1990, De Klerk legalises banned political parties and announces Nelson Mandela's unconditional release. I watch on grainy television as Mandela walks slowly down the road from Victor Verster Prison, Winnie's hand upheld in his raised fist. But Lionel is in Cape Town itself, waiting on a Grand Parade awash with sixty thousand others as Mandela's official cavalcade makes its slow way from Paarl. He watches as US civil-rights activist Jesse Jackson has himself lifted onto the City Hall balcony decked with ANC flags so that he too can be part of history. The crowd is hot; a water hydrant is broken open. Round the corner, police shoot looters. Lionel retreats to his car, wary of teenagers who eye the camera round his neck. When a gaunt Mandela, clad in a grey suit, steps onto the balcony he can hardly be heard over the roar of the crowd.

A few days later, sitting at his desk at work, Lionel lifts his surprised head to catch sight of Mandela's tall unmistakable frame through the window. Mandela has been locked away, hidden from view, for twenty-seven years, his eminence growing in inverse proportion to his visibility. And now here he is, just outside the glass! Under the leadership of Rector Jakes Gerwel, the University of the Western Cape has become the intellectual home of the left wing. Now Mandela is enlisting Jakes's support as change snowballs across the nation. At an evening party, Lionel meets leaders of the struggle, the struggle whose end is so close they can almost taste it. It is a privilege.

Meanwhile, Petronella works as a peace monitor with the Network of Independent Monitors. Teams of these monitors collect witness accounts at political meetings and funerals, stop crises before they begin, investigate political murders, map armed activities and undertake long-term mediation. In August 1990, the State of Emergency lifts, and the ANC suspends its weapons. Prolonged negotiations begin and in March 1992 a whites-only referendum results in sixty-eight per cent in favour of reforms. But in June the violence the peace monitors work to avert erupts: forty-five Boipatong residents are killed by Zulu hostel dwellers and Mandela pulls the ANC out of talks. In September the army of the Ciskei homeland kills twenty-nine. Negotiations recommence.

14 April 1993

Chris Hani, general-secretary of the South African Communist Party, has been fatally shot in the chest and head by a right-wing extremist outside his home. Riots have broken out in Cape Town, Durban and Port Elizabeth. With a memorial service organised in St George's Cathedral, Petronella and her fellow peace monitors are on duty. Walking towards the centre in the peace monitors' distinctive turquoise cap and vest, Petronella is surrounded by milling restless crowds, too many to fit in the cathedral. Already cars are being vandalised, and as the service continues inside the trouble starts.

First, it's looting of market stalls, a minor fire set in a rubbish bin by a young man who sneers at the peace monitors' remonstrations. Then the wooden stalls go up, black smoke billowing towards the mountain, and a South African flag, still the orange, blue and white tricolour of the apartheid state, is set ablaze. Another Quaker peace monitor is left bloodied by a broken bottle (in Cape Town, unlike other parts of the country, there are no bulletproof vests under the peace monitors' tabards). Later, a policeman is shot and wounded and a young black man killed.

This is a nation teetering on the edge and it is only Mandela's intervention that pulls it back. 'Now is the time for all South Africans to stand together against those who, from any quarter, wish to destroy what Chris Hani gave his life for – the freedom of us all,' he tells the country. Multiracial elections are scheduled for April 1994. In November 1993, Puleng Stewart's mother Clare is ambushed in rural KwaZulu-Natal. In March 1994, Inkatha Freedom Party (IFP) supporters march through Johannesburg, protesting against the elections. The IFP is a Zulu organisation backed at earlier points by the apartheid regime. As they pass the ANC headquarters on Plein Street, security guards open fire. Nineteen people are killed, the bodies of the dead and wounded oozing thick blood onto the concrete and tarmac.

Last-minute jitters grip the white population, who panic-buy tins, batteries, rice. Mere days before voting is due to take place, the IFP decides it will take part after all, forcing parliament to adjust the new constitution and Electoral Act, and produce 25 million stickers for the already-printed ballot papers. The end is in sight.

Cape Town, 27 April 1994
Petronella drives past Gordon's Gym in Mowbray, now transformed into a polling station, before dawn. Alongside the gym, in a concrete culvert lined with orange crocosmia, runs the Liesbeek River, where so long ago Elsje Cloete dipped buckets into the water for her washing. Behind it rise the grey quartzite walls of Table Mountain. An hour before the doors are due to open, a long queue of people wait patiently in the dark. To her surprise, Petronella finds tears in her eyes.

Back in 1984, Breyten Breytenbach wrote: 'The gulf between Black and White, or between Whites and all the others, is so enormous that in fact we are strangers to one another. The only common ground we share is Apartheid. But we interpret that ground differently.' Yet here they are, black, white, coloured and Indian, queueing to decide their future, together. It is one of those moments in history where hope is so tangible it can almost be cupped in the palms of those waiting hands.

I am very aware of where we are now: in the Cape, proximate to Elsje, to Angela, Krotoa even, whose DNA saturates the coloured community into which Petronella is now married. Krotoa, who is exiled to Robben Island, so her double-sided tongue does not show to the Dutch the thin veneer which is their 'civilisation', with her Euro-African children, one of whom crosses the colour line. As my cousins might be thought to cross the colour line, although it seems to me they never even entertain its existence, ignoring it for an alternative narrative, their mother tongue English, no sort of translation. And now that colour line, in place since the late seventeenth century, is to be erased.

From this perspective, they fall like dominoes: Krotoa takes off her skins and puts on her sarong, Angela van Bengale's children merge into white society, Anna Siek fortifies the citadel of white culture, Anna Retief leaves the Cape in outrage at the abolition of slavery, Isie and the Boers are stripped naked by the British, Jan helps craft segregationist rule, Cato escapes, Petronella returns and gives birth to children who are illegal.

What joins Petronella to these forebears? There is the name, of course; she is branded as I am, even Krotoa's colour-bar-crossing daughter is a Pieternella. Shared geography. An adventurousness, a seizing of agency, which she shares with Krotoa, Angela, Anna Retief. Petronella's occupations are still those stamped 'woman': teaching, community building, faith work. The past sticks like clots of mud. What is missing? The house, too many little clutching hands. Is it domestication that is missing? Not only the house, but the power vested in it, the collusion with white male authority, which Petronella rejects whole-heartedly, just as her grandmother accepts it whole-heartedly.

Now, three centuries after Commander van Riebeeck set his foot on the Cape shore, South Africa itself is finally rejecting white male authority. Eighty years after Jan Smuts left African suffrage out of the

Act of Union, those Africans are voting to bring a different country into being. It's been touch and go whether they would ever get here. Petronella has played her part, helping to prepare observers for their posts inside polling stations and peace monitors to keep watch outside. They have all been warned not to take unnecessary risks. Driving towards the retired minister's apartment where she is to meet other monitors before they set out for polling stations, she hopes fervently that their conflict resolution skills will not be needed. Perched high above the city, they eat breakfast and watch the long queue of voters already snaking around a nearby polling station.

'Vote, the Beloved Country' reads the headline in the *Star*, and they do. All night, all that day, all the next day, 19.5 million people, eighty-seven per cent of the electorate, queue peacefully outside polling stations across the country. Neighbours offer food, *mealie*-meal porridge, takeaway chicken, orange squash in buckets. In white suburbs, madams vote alongside their maids and gardeners. Since midnight, they have had a new constitution, a Constitutional Court, a bill of human rights, a new flag and the world's loveliest national anthem. Halfway through the first day of voting, they run out of ballot papers and ultra-violet marking ink (which prevents people voting twice). The printing presses start rolling again.

Petronella and her colleagues tour polling stations, but the one alarm of the day turns out to be false – the accidental collapse of a tent as voters try to keep dry. Some of those voting as Petronella keeps vigil outside in the rain experienced the beginning of apartheid, the National Party victory of 1948. Now the tattered ID documents that were so oppressive are the very documents they show the poll clerk, opening the door to a new future. There is no electoral roll, anyone can vote where they like, if they can prove some sort of belonging. Some cannot read and write and need help in placing the X next to their chosen candidate, claiming their citizenship, underwriting the future of their nation. Some vote holding in their minds all those who could not, each vote representing legions of the voiceless and unrepresented of the past. And each of them, as they receive their ballot paper, make their X, post the paper into the ballot box, feels this ritual is somehow holy. A sacrament.

Because this election, whatever happens afterwards, is wondrous. South Africans, all of them, have chosen to stand in long lines for many hours, in the blinding sun and pouring rain. They have chosen the road not to civil war, but to democracy; they have chosen the ballot box over the gun. An oligarchy of white men has voluntarily, if reluctantly, negotiated its way out of power. The oppressed, violated population – forced off their land, labouring for white wealth, families torn apart, social fabric shredded, treated as sub-human – have agreed not to punish, but to share. To trust in the transubstantiation of the ballot paper into the body politic.

We all know the sweeping victory of the ANC at this election. Yet in a sense all these people are voting, not for political parties, but for the threshold itself. For the moment when the past becomes history, when renewal becomes possible. Of course the old problems will still be there: the poor will still be poor, there will still be greed and guns and corruption. It will take longer than a generation to undo three centuries of careful work by the likes of the Retiefs and, yes, the Smutses, who structured society, economy and culture to the benefit of the white man. A glance north across the Atlantic shows how long racial inequality can persist: fifty-five years since segregation ended, black Americans are still, on average, only a tenth as wealthy as white households.

This is a country where brown and black children received little or no education, where even if they did manage to scrape together some grades they were actively excluded from the skilled workforce. Where those children grew up to live in single-sex hostels and work down mines, or on marginal land unfit for farming, or in shanty towns miles from employment. A country where all the economic and social capital, the entire chain reaction of upward mobility, rested in the hands of white people. In such a country, where human beings are no better or worse than they ought to be, the deck is stacked against them all.

But right now, for the first time, Petronella's husband stands as her equal in South African society. At 3.15 p.m., in a coloured school in Athlone, near where he grew up, barred from white education, forced to live in coloured-only areas, Lionel votes. Later, taking off her turquoise cap and vest, his wife casts her vote at the same school.

Their marriage, forged decades before in the oasis of Roma, is recognised. Her children are no longer illegitimate, nor illegal. Tomorrow, a fellow member of Cape Town Quaker meeting will be one of the first black women to become an MP, and married to a white man at that. Here they all stand, on the threshold, ready to move forward together. To build a new nation.

Umuntu ngumuntu ngabantu.

Acknowledgements

To everyone at John Murray, a publisher with a suitably venerable history for this particular book, thank you for taking *Moederland* on, including Jocasta Hamilton, Amanda Jones, Sara Marafini, Jasmine Marsh, Katharine Morris, Caroline Westmore and especially my editor Georgina Laycock, for her joyous enthusiasm. The discovery that Nontando Jabavu's lovely memoirs of amaXhosa life were also published by John Murray, sixty years ago, was a private joy.

To Zukiswa Wanner and Samantha Stewart for subtle and informed reading.

To my agent, Veronique Baxter, for making me cut 10,000 words. And believing in my work.

To Rachel Leyshon, of Chicken House Books, for her generosity with advice and recommendations.

I am grateful to Professor Joanna Lewis for expertise and early encouragement, to Tobias Jones and Andrea Stuart for writing guidance and to Karl French, who put me straight when I thought I'd finished.

My great thanks to the Alfred Gillett Trust, and all the staff there, but particularly Dr Tim Crumplin and Julie Mather for all the latex gloves. And to the staff at Smuts House and the Cape Archives who row against the tide to safeguard their collections.

I am hugely grateful to Petronella Clark and Lionel Sylvester, and to Sarah and Roger Sylvester, for trusting me with their story. I hope I have done it justice.

Also to Sarah Clark, for allowing me access to her archive, and for most generous hospitality and Zulu braais.

And my mother, for everything.

To Richard and Anne Tait and their children, Emma, Christina, Samantha and Michael. Blessings be upon you.

Thank you to Charles Robertson for his capacious gossipy memory; J. C. and Ingrid Smuts for their humour and kindness; and Julia Smuts and Sandra Krige for early support.

To John Sargeant, for the books, the letters, and the memories, and to Fran Biggs and the memory of both their mothers, who used their invisibility cloaks.

To Rachel and Puleng Stewart, I offer my small tribute to Clare. May her spirit live on.

Thank you to Danielle Crouse, for three decades of friendship across three continents.

To my first reader, Jeanette Carter, who went above and beyond in applying her discerning eye to every chapter as it evolved, thank you; Kate Rambridge for her poet's ear and scholar's eye; and Monika Maurer, for wrestling with the start.

To Steven Shukor, for the title, proving news reporters never lose their touch.

And to Sandra Hamilton, who loved it first. Together through life.

I honour the memory of my beloved grandfather, Bancroft Clark, and my father, Roger Pedder, who would have loved to see it in print.

For my children, who are the next links in the chain, but also entirely themselves. And my husband, who makes home, home. I am because they are.

Finally, without the research of dozens of men and women, it would never have been possible to weave together the golden threads of this book. To them I humbly submit my thanks and my own modest contribution to the conversation. Any mistakes are, of course, my own.

Moederland took me ten years to write. But it took nine women a lifetime to live. This is my tribute to them, and an acknowledgement that this is their book as much as it is mine. This is the fruit of the family tree. None of us are perfect: we all try, we all fail. And the story is not yet over.

Picture Credits

Alamy Stock Photo: 1/The Print Collector, 2 above right/ART Collection, 3 centre/The Picture Art Collection, 8 below/Associated Press. Courtesy of the author: 7, 8 above. Bridgeman Images: 5 above left. Getty Images: 6 above left/Ejor and below/Popperfoto. Courtesy of the Alfred Gillett Trust Archive: 4 below, 5 centre right and below, 6 centre right. Emily Hobhouse, *The Brunt of the War and Where it Fell*, London, Methuen, 1902: 4 centre/photographer unknown. Gustav S. Preller, *Piet Retief*, 1911: 2 above left. Public domain: 3 below, 4 above left. Anna (Retief) Steenkamp, *Die Dagboek*, 1839: 3 above right. Courtesy of Stephan Welz & Co., Cape Town, South Africa: 2 below left.

Glossary

African languages

fufu – dough made from boiled and ground plantain or cassava, West Africa
ganna bushes (Khoikhoi) – lye bushes
impi (isiZulu) – body of men gathered for war
jollof rice – spicy West African rice dish
Mfecane (isiZulu) – crushing, scattering
shongololo (isiZulu) – millipede
toyi-toyi (isiNdebele) – quasi-military dance-step
Tsui-Goab (Khoikhoi) – God of Creation
umuntu ngumuntu ngabantu (isiZulu) – a person is a person because of other
  people

Afrikaans (and European languages where specified)

Afrikaner Weerstandsbeweging – Afrikaner Resistance Movement
arrack – rice spirit
baas – boss
bakkie – pick-up truck
biltong – salted, dried meat
bittereinders – bitter-enders
bobotie – curried minced lamb dish
boerevrou – farmer's wife
boetie – brother
braai – barbecue
breedie – stewed meat and vegetables
buchu – aromatic Cape shrub
dagboek – diary

die Groote Kerk – the Big Church
die Swart Gevaar – the Black Danger
die Volk – the People
dominie – minister
donga – dry gully, ditch
dorp – town
drostdy – administrative hub
en klaar – and finished
Hottentot – (archaic, now offensive) Khoikhoi
jjongen – boy
juffrou – mistress, or teacher
Kaapse taal – Cape language
k****r – ethnic slur for black Africans (offensive)
k****rs, mulattoes, mestiços and *casticos* – these phrases refer negatively to
    Africans and mixed-race peoples (offensive)
k****rboetie – a person sympathetic to non-whites
k****rtjie – diminutive form of ethnic slur as above
kakebeenwaens – lit.: jawbone wagons
kaross – sheepskin cloak
kleurling – coloured
knecht(en) – servant(s)
koeksusters – a plaited dough pastry soaked in sugar syrup
koppie (Afrikaans) – a small hill in a flat area
kopwerk – head work, using your brain
kraal – traditional African village of huts, or enclosure for cattle or sheep
laager – defensive circle of wagons
landdrost – magistrate in rural area
masels – measles
mealie – maize
mebos – dried compressed apricots
meid – girl
melktert – milk tart
mevrou – madam
mijnheer (Dutch) – sir
Moederkerk – Mother Church
Moederland – Motherland
mooi – pretty
morgen – unit of land, from 0.5–2.5 acres
'n regte – a real

onze (Dutch) – our

opgaaf (Dutch) – the annual account of assets such as livestock, land, crops, etc.

opstal – farmhouse

Ossewabrandwag – Ox-wagon sentinels, Afrikaner nationalist organisation

ouma – grandmother

oumagrootjie – great-grandmother

papsak – cheap box wine sold in foil container without the box

plakking – pasting

riempieskoene – thonged shoes

rix-dollars – unit of currency in Dutch trade networks 1600–1850

'Sarie Marais' – Afrikaans folk song

seekoei – hippopotamus

sjambok – large whip, traditionally made from hippopotamus hide

steenbrassem – seabream

stoep – verandah

stormjaar – storm year

Stuka – German aircraft in the Second World War

superette – small store or dairy

terra nullis (Latin) – land legally deemed to be unoccupied or uninhabited

trekboers – journeying farmers

vader – father

veld – uncultivated open grassland or shrubland

vlieëbos – fly bush

Volksmoeder – Mother of the Nation

Volksraad – People's Council

voorkamer – front room

Voortrekker – pioneer, Dutch-speaking people who migrated from the Cape from 1836

vrou – woman, wife

Vrouemonument – Women's Monument

werf – yard

zevenjaar – seven year

Notes

Unless otherwise stated, all letters quoted are held by
the Alfred Gillett Trust.

Chapter I: Krotoa • Angela van Bengale • Elsje Cloete

14 **'We embraced each other'**: Moodie, *The Record*, p. 5.

15 **'Look, Mr van Riebeeck'**: Ibid., p. 135.

15 **'It appears that'**: Ibid., p. 47.

17 **'so greased over'**: Ibid., p. 147.

19 **'in number like'**: Ibid., p. 144.

19 **'Eva', they report**: Ibid., p. 149.

19 **Khoikhoi puberty rituals**: Schapera, *The Early Cape Hottentots*, p. xi.

20 **hotchpotch of kingdoms**: Booyens, 'Jacob and Fijtje Cloeten "van Ut in 't Land van Ceulen"', p. 5.

20 **European immigrants**: Giliomee, *The Afrikaners*, p. 4.

22 **four thousand people**: Ibid., p. 3.

24 **nearly two hundred slaves**: Schoeman, *Early Slavery*, p. 63.

27 **'She seems so much'**: Moodie, p. 226.

31 **'the thoughtless wench'**: Ibid., p. 271.

33 **the double-bind of assimilation**: See Patrick Wolfe on assimilation's Faustian bargain: claim our settler world, but lose your indigenous soul, 'Beyond any doubt, this is a kind of death.' Wolfe, 'Settler Colonialism and the Elimination of the Native', p. 397.

35 **'In the afternoon'**: Moodie, p. 285.

37 **more likely to die**: Neal, 'Childbearing in Adolescents Aged 12–15 Years'.

37 **a decade of her life**: See Cilliers and Fourie, 'New Estimates of Settler Life Span', p. 83.

38 **'plays the beast'**: Leibbrandt, *Precis of the Archives of the Cape of Good Hope: Journal, 1662–70*, p. 277.

39 **Why did Zara die of suicide**: Schapera, p. 115.

39 **a 'beast'**: Moodie, p. 315.

40 **'This day departed'**: Leibbrandt, *Precis of the Archives of the Cape of Good Hope: Journal, 1671–74 & 1676*, p. 209.

41 **'drinking herself drunk'**: Ibid.

41 **'She, like the dogs'**: Ibid.

42 **the triple threat**: Diamond, *Guns, Germs and Steel*.

43 **the Khoikhoi suffer**: Elphick and Giliomee, *The Shaping of South African Society*, p. 21.

43 **'as the fire lights her up'**: Trail, *Extinct*, p. 19.

47 **'Cape slaves are scourged'**: Schoeman, p. 300.

49 **'rude wife'**: Fouché, *The Diary of Adam Tas (1705–1706)*, p. 43.

52 **'The women are as dangerous'**: Giliomee, *The Shaping of South African Society*, p. 25.

52 **'Kaffirs, Mulattoes, Mestiços and Castiços'**: Elphick and Giliomee, p. 542.

54 **After her death**: Holmes, *The Hottentot Venus*, p. 169.

54 **'The story of Sarah Baartman'**: ' "Hottentot Venus" Laid to Rest', BBC News.

63 **'It is not always easy'**: Krog, *Begging to Be Black*, p. 4.

Chapter II: Anna Siek

I am indebted to Schalk le Roux for his research into Anna Siek's life; see 'Van Tafelvallei na Vergelegen'.

68 **Putting the eggs**: Valentyn, *Beschryving Van Kaap Der Goede Hoope*, p. 103.

72 **'They are excellent breeders'**: Shell, 'Tender Ties', p. 6.

75 **delighted to have visitors**: Mentzel, *A Geographical and Topographical Description*, p. 120.

75 **'quite tolerable' wives**: Ibid., p. 116.

77 **This toleration of violence**: Africa Check, 'Five Facts: Femicide in South Africa'.

81 **'conduits for the accumulation'**: Cilliers, 'Cape Colony Marriage', p. 54.

88 **The ignorance contract**: Steyn, 'The Ignorance Contract', p. 8.

Chapter III: Margaretha Retief

102 **'They are instructed'**: Lichtenstein, *Travels in Southern Africa*, p. 112.

105 **'Why cannot Englishmen'**: Lenta, *Paradise, the Castle and the Vineyard*, p. 91.

105 **'smooth clear copper skin'**: Ibid., p. 113.

106 **'with her coffeepot'**: Barrow, *An Account of Travels*, p. 80.

106 **'the grey mare'**: Lenta, p. 270.

106 **As a Cape Dutch woman**: Giliomee, ' "Allowed Such a State of Freedom" ', p. 33.

107 **'a state in miniature'**: Lichtenstein, p. 28.

107 **Margaretha supervising**: I am entirely indebted for this detail to Helene Retief Lombard, who grew up at Welvanpas in the early twentieth century and recorded the daily life of generations of Retief women; Lombard, *The Chronicles of Krakeelhoek*.

110 **'Historians have not deliberately'**: Giliomee, ' "Allowed Such a State of Freedom" ', p. 30.'

112 **'It was at Schlachter's Nek'**: Reitz, *A Century of Wrong*, p. 17.

113 **'Not we, not we alone'**: Theal, *Records of the Cape Colony*, pp. 114–15.

119 **'Such a child'**: Isie Smuts, letter to Cato Clark, 1932, Alfred Gillett Trust, HH/FAM/30.

121 **'resolutely unmodern'**: Lewis, *Difficult Women*, p. 258.

122 **'I haven't yet met'**: Doris Lessing, letter to John Whitehorn, 20 October 1947, University of East Anglia Archives, DL/WHI/078. Much has been made of Lessing's performance as a parent, reflecting the very double standards she sought to escape.

125 **'What does it mean'**: Burden, *Dwelling in the Archive*, p. 4.

126 **'This South Africa'**: Fairbridge, *Historic Houses of South Africa*, p. xi.

129 **Alice Clark's thesis**: For more on this conversation, see, for example, O'Brien, *The Industrial Revolution and British Society*, pp. 31–53.

Chapter IV: Anna Retief

134 **'the women seem'**: Giliomee, *The Afrikaners*, p. 165.

134 ***The Diary of Anna Steenkamp***: More of a memoir than a diary, Anna Steenkamp's *dagboek* is written later, with the elisions of memory and alterations of hindsight, in Anna's original Dutch, and an Afrikaans

translation is produced in 1939. The quotations in the text are my own translation, thereby compounding the displacement in time and language.

134 **'It was not so much'**: Steenkamp, *Die Dagboek van Anna Steenkamp*, p. 11.

136 **'an exemplary and God-fearing woman'**: Ibid., p. 7.

137 **'Here is the word'**: Ibid., p. 13.

137 **'Before the arrival'**: Ibid., p. 15.

139 **Anna's uncle Piet Retief**: Kenney, *Piet Retief*, pp. 108–9. In my view, Kenney's book is a bit of a hatchet job, systematically demolishing the myths surrounding Retief.

139 **'be under no fear'**: Giliomee, *The Afrikaners*, p. 164.

141 **'Oh! It was almost unbearable'**: Steenkamp, p. 14.

141 **'Two hundred innocent children'**: Ibid., p. 17.

143 **'As far as the eye'**: Giliomee, *The Afrikaners*, p. 21.

143 **'It was a lot'**: Ibid.

143 **'we were like sheep'**: Ibid.

144 **'But the hand'**: Ibid., p. 23.

145 **'a disgrace on their husbands'**: Ibid., p. 169.

150 **So many people are murdered**: 'How Bad is South Africa's Murder Rate?', GroundUp.

150 **what farm murders represent**: Jonny Steinberg explores the painful, twisted topography of farm murders in his book *Midlands*.

150 **murder rates in the UK**: 'Homicides Fall for First Time in Five Years', BBC News.

151 **'People of South Africa'**: 'Malema: If You See a Beautiful Piece of Land, Take It', Daily Maverick.

159 **'Race is a palimpsest'**: Appiah, *Mistaken Identities*, 'Colour'.

Chapter V: Isie Kriege

170 **'You are the only one'**: Hancock and Van der Poel, *Selections from the Smuts Papers*, vol. I, p. 6.

170 **'I did not think'**: Isie Smuts, letter to Margaret Clark Gillett, 26 October 1950, Alfred Gillett Trust, HH/MCG/33.

170 **'that they had been born'**: MacDonald, *Ouma Smuts*, p. 21.

174 **'South Africa stands'**: Hancock and Van Der Poel, vol. I, p. 329.

175 **'contains the noblest blood'**: Reitz, p. 16.

175 **'pilgrimage of martyrdom'**: Ibid., p. 64

175 **'the most courageous'**: Ibid., p. 22.

175 **'Once more in the annals'**: Ibid., p. 14.

177 **'Dams everywhere'**: Hancock and Van Der Poel, vol. I, p. 157.

180 **colours Smuts's racial views**: As Shula Marks suggests in 'White Masculinity: Jan Smuts, Race and the South African War'.

181 **'The iron had entered'**: M. C. Gillett, letter to Keith Hancock, Alfred Gillett Trust, HH/MCG/37.

181 **'virtually a desert'**: Giliomee, *The Afrikaners*, p. 264.

184 **'The only woman'**: Mincher, *I Lived in His Shadow*, p. 151.

184 **'I have a weakness'**: Van der Poel, *Selections from the Smuts Papers*, vol. VII, p. 193.

185 **'build a grand building'**: Hancock, *Smuts*, vol. 1, p. 256.

187 **'We are both'**: Hancock and Van der Poel, vol. III, p. 557.

188 **'Unfaithfulness is not'**: Britain Yearly Meeting, *Quaker Faith & Practice*, pp. 22, 49.

189 **'They prefer this tin hovel'**: Steyn, *Jan Smuts*, p. 183.

190 **'the black man becomes'**: Coetzee, *White Writing*, p. 5.

190 **'So many of our black folk'**: MacDonald, p. 120.

190 **'taints the night air'**: Millin, *The Herr Witchdoctor*, pp. 10–11.

191 **'unless the white race'**: Hancock and Van der Poel, vol. I, p. 83.

191 **'when, to escape violation'**: Cited in Marks, 'White Masculinity', p. 17.

191 **'I am ... proud'**: Van der Poel, vol. VII, p. 126.

195 **'give the baby time'**: MacDonald, p. 59.

195 **'while the welfare'**: Schreiner, *Women and Labour*, p. 7.

195 **women in parliament**: MacDonald, p. 119.

197 **'Your Blood River'**: Prior, *The Bible and Colonialism*, pp. 93–4.

200 **'the doyen of the Conference'**: Steyn, p. 148.

201 **'A Queen visiting'**: Hancock, vol. 2, p. 495.

201 **As long as we assign**: Paton, *Jofmeyr*, p. 422.

202 **'She feared she might'**: Steyn, p. 529.

203 *A shilling life*: W. H. Auden's poem 'Who's Who' lists the feats of 'the greatest figure of his day', who nonetheless sighs for one who lives at home. This poem speaks about power and love, about where life resides. It begins with the line 'A shilling life will give you all the facts'.

203 **'In that dark hour'**: Van der Poel, vol. V, p. 207.

207 **'Demonstration of affection'**: Jansen, *Knowledge in the Blood*, p. 71.

213 **People take pride**: A YouGov poll from 2019 showed that thirty-two

per cent of Britons then thought the British Empire was something to be proud of, 'UK More Nostalgic for Empire'.

214 **'political longevity'**: Dubow, 'Smuts', p. 47.

214 **'I cared more'**: Mandela, *Long Walk to Freedom*, p. 46.

Chapter VI: Cato Smuts

224 **'In fact they thought'**: Eileen Krige, letter to Cato Clark, 1937, Alfred Gillett Trust, HH/FAM/49.

226 **'Skirts are so short'**: Cato Clark, letter to Isie Smuts, 20 August 1925, Alfred Gillett Trust, HH/FAM/29.

228 **'While you do your hair'**: Cato Clark, letter to Bancroft Clark, November 1926, Alfred Gillett Trust, HH/FsM/1/1.

228 **'the specific, English'**: Mitford, *Hons and Rebels*, p. 75.

232 **'When the k★★★★r is ill'**: Cato Clark, Script for BBC Schools Service Broadcast, 1931, Alfred Gillett Trust, HH/CC/47-52.

234 **'how way leads on to way'**: While drafting and redrafting Cato's life, I had in mind Robert Frost's poem, 'The Road Not Taken', in which this line appears. Frost, in his tricky way, suggests that 'the passing there / Had worn them really about the same'.

236 **Cato and Nontando break free**: Cato and Nontando inhabit what Amin Maalouf calls our composite identities. He writes: 'What makes me myself rather than anyone else is the very fact that I am poised between two countries, two or three languages and several cultural traditions. It is precisely this that defines my identity.' (*In the Name of Identity*, p. 1.)

236 **'the old and intense'**: Jabavu, *Drawn in Colour*, p. 57.

238 **'flags hang out'**: Bancroft Clark, letter to Cato Clark, 1936, Alfred Gillett Trust, HH/FAM/1/10.

238 **6,500 Jews arrive**: Cape Town Holocaust Centre.

239 **'I also saw [cousin] Hennie'**: Cato Clark, letter to Bancroft Clark, February 1937, Alfred Gillett Trust, HH/FAM/1/12.

239 **forefront of female networking**: For more on women and social reform see Oakley, *Women, Peace and Welfare*.

241 **Quaker work around Jewish refugees**: For more on Quaker work with refugees from fascism see Holmes, 'A Moral Business'; Spielhofer, *Stemming the Dark Tide*; and Bailey, *Love and War in the Pyrenees*.

241 **'We are the army'**: Davis, 'Wartime Women Giving Birth', p. 258.

242 **plan to appoint Jan Smuts**: Colville, *The Fringes of Power*, pp. 269–71.

246 *migrare*:   https://www.etymonline.com/word/migrant   (accessed 19 August 2023).

246 **'As soon as I stepped'**: Jabavu, p. 3.

247 **'So we had to walk'**: Ibid., p. 47.

248 **'If they won't listen'**: Santa Weyers, letter to Cato Clark, 1960, Alfred Gillett Trust, HH/FAM/34.

248 **'lost two inches'**: Ibid.

249 **'You are the father'**: Slovo, *Every Secret Thing*, eBook, p. 278.

249 **'I fought only'**: Mandela, p. 459.

251 **'I still think of'**: M. Arnot, letter to Bancroft Clark, 24 February 1973, Alfred Gillett Trust, HH/FAM/60.

253 **'One would live'**: Vice, 'How Do I Live', p. 335.

257 **the term 'coconut'**: Njabulo Ndebele, one of South Africa's greatest thinkers, says: 'In not apologising, the "coconut" asserts the notion that there are not only multiple "whitenesses", but also multiple "blacknesses". A "pure black subjectivity" really does not exist, because none of the multiple forms of blackness can be said to be definitive of "blackness".' West, 'Responding to Whiteness in Contemporary South African Life and Literature', p. 119.

261 **'despite slum conditions'**: Jabavu, p. 98.

Chapter VII: Petronella Clark

266 **'It is ironical'**: Petronella Clark, letter to Bancroft and Cato Clark, 10 February 1961, Alfred Gillett Trust, HH/FAM/5.

266 **'starving England'**: Conversation between the author, Petronella Clark and Lionel Sylvester, Middle Leigh, Street, Somerset, 26 April 2013.

270 **'I might get married'**: Petronella Clark, letter to Bancroft and Cato Clark, 23 March 1965, Alfred Gillett Trust, HH/FAM/5.

274 **'brainwashed professors'**: Conversation between the author, Petronella Clark and Lionel Sylvester.

277 **'Nazi Vorster'**: Petronella Clark, letter to Bancroft and Cato Clark, 12 September 1966, Alfred Gillett Trust, HH/FAM/5.

277 **'short-skirted dolly birds'**: Conversation between the author, Petronella Clark and Lionel Sylvester.

278 **Marie Stopes suggesting**: Hall, *Marie Stopes*, p. 182.

283 **'I just thought'**: Conversation between the author, Petronella Clark and Lionel Sylvester.

285 **Petronella and Lionel appeal**: British mothers can, since 1983, now pass their British citizenship on to their children.

288 **'Quaker attitudes'**: Clark, 'Quaker Women', p. 23.

288 **At Yearly Meeting in 1981**: Worse, Quaker-owned confectioner Rowntree had a fully owned South African subsidiary, Wilson Rowntree, which, in the 1980s, fired workers when they questioned working conditions and unequal pay, making them unemployable. It is suggested that Wilson Rowntree management even reported workers to the police, with horrendous consequences, https://www.rown-treesociety.org.uk/news/statement-on-rowntree-colonial-histories/ (accessed 14 October 2023).

294 **'Everyone in South Africa'**: Conversation between the author, Petronella Clark and Lionel Sylvester.

299 **'Now is the time'**: Mandela, 'Address to the Nation'.

299 **'The gulf between Black and White'**: Breytenbach, *The True Confessions of an Albino Terrorist*, p. 74.

Bibliography

Books

Adhikari, M. (2011), *The Anatomy of a South African Genocide: The Extermination of the Cape San Peoples*, Athens, OH: Ohio University Press

Bailey, R. (2009), *Love and War in the Pyrenees*, London: Phoenix

Bank, A. (2016), *Pioneers of the Field: South Africa's Women Anthropologists*, Cambridge: Cambridge University Press

Barrow, J. (1801), *An Account of Travels Into the Interior of Southern Africa, In Years 1797 and 1798*, London: T. Cadell and W. Davies

Bell, A. (2007), *Only for Three Months*, Norwich: Mousehold Press

Benade, T. (2004), *Kites of Good Fortune*, Claremont: David Philip

Beukes, P. (1991), *The Holistic Smuts: A Study in Personality*, Cape Town: Human & Rousseau

—— (1992), *The Romantic Smuts: Women and Love in His Life*, Cape Town: Human & Rousseau

—— (1994), *The Religious Smuts*, Cape Town: Human & Rousseau

—— (1996), *Smuts the Botanist: The Cape Flora and the Grasses of Africa*, Cape Town: Human & Rousseau

Birkby, C. (1936), *Thirstland Trekkers*, London: Faber & Faber

Bloem, T. (1999), *Krotoa-Eva: The Woman from Robben Island*, Cape Town: Kwela

Bloom, K. (2009), *Ways of Staying*, London: Portobello

Bosman, H. C. (1998), *Mafeking Road and Other Stories*, Cape Town: Human & Rousseau

Breytenbach, B. (1985), *The True Confessions of an Albino Terrorist*, London: Faber & Faber

Brink, A. (1994), *On the Contrary*, London: Minerva

—— (1995), *A Chain of Voices*, London: Vintage

—— (1997), *Imaginings of Sand*, London: Vintage

—— (2009), *A Fork in the Road: A Memoir*, London: Harvill Secker

Britain Yearly Meeting (2013), *Quaker Faith & Practice: The Book of Christian Discipline of the Yearly Meeting of the Religious Society of Friends (Quakers) in Britain*, London: Religious Society of Friends

Brits, E. (2016), *Emily Hobhouse: Beloved Traitor*, Cape Town: Tafelberg

Brody, H. (2001), *The Other Side of Eden: Hunter-Gatherers, Farmers and the Shaping of the World*, London: Faber & Faber

Burden, A. (2003), *Dwelling in the Archive: Women Writing House, Home, and History in Late Colonial India*, New York: Oxford University Press

Bush, J. (2000), *Edwardian Ladies and Imperial Power*, London: Leicester University Press

Cassidy, T. (2007), *Birth*, London: Chatto & Windus

Clark, A. (1920), *Working Life of Women in the Seventeenth Century*, New York: Harcourt, Brace & Howe

Clark, C. (2022), *Clare: The Killing of a Gentle Activist*, Cape Town: Tafelberg

Coates, T. (2015), *Between the World and Me*, Melbourne: Text Publishing

Cock, J. (1980), *Maids & Madams: A Study in the Politics of Exploitation*, Johannesburg: Ravan Press

Coetzee, J. M. (1988), *White Writing: On the Culture of Letters in South Africa*, Sandton: Radix

Colville, J. (2004), *The Fringes of Power*, London: Weidenfeld & Nicolson

Dabiri, E. (2019), *Don't Touch My Hair*, London: Allen Lane

Dangor, A. (2001), *Bitter Fruit*, Cape Town: Kwela

Datta, A. (2013), *From Bengal to the Cape: Bengali Slaves in South Africa*, [Kindle] self-published

De Klerk, F. W. (1998), *The Last Trek: A New Beginning*, London: Macmillan

De Villiers, C. C. (1894), *Oude Kaapsche Familien Parts I–III*, Cape Town: Van de Sandt, De Villiers

De Villiers, M. (1988), *White Tribe Dreaming*, London: Penguin

De Waal, E. (2011), *The Hare with Amber Eyes: A Hidden Inheritance*, London: Vintage

Diamond, J. (2005), *Guns, Germs and Steel*, London: Vintage

Dlamini, J. (2009), *Native Nostalgia*, Auckland Park: Jacana Media

Dubow, S. and A. Jeeves (2005), *South Africa's 1940s: Worlds of Possibilities*, Cape Town: Double Storey Books

Du Preez, M. (2004), *Pale Native: Memories of a Renegade Reporter*, Cape Town: Zebra Press

—— (2008), *Of Tricksters, Tyrants and Turncoats: More Unusual Stories from South Africa's Past*, Cape Town: Zebra Press

—— (2013), *A Rumour of Spring: South Africa After 20 Years of Democracy*, Cape Town: Zebra Press

Du Toit, A. and H. Giliomee (1983), *Afrikaner Political Thought: Analysis and Documents, Volume One: 1780–1850*, Berkeley, CA: University of California Press

Edemariam, A. (2018), *The Wife's Tale: A Personal History*, London: 4th Estate

Elphick, R. (1977), *Kraal and Castle: Khoikhoi and the Founding of White South Africa*, New Haven, CT: Yale University Press

—— and H. Giliomee (eds) (1988), *The Shaping of South African Society, 1652–1840*, Middletown, CT: Wesleyan University Press

Fanon, F. (2001), *The Wretched of the Earth*, London: Penguin

Fairbridge, D. (1922), *Historic Houses of South Africa*, London: Humphrey Milford

Feinstein, A. (2009), *After the Party: Corruption, the ANC and South Africa's Uncertain Future*, London: Verso

Flanders, J. (2004), *The Victorian House*, London: Harper Perennial

Fouché, L. (ed.) (1914), *The Diary of Adam Tas (1705–1706)* (trans. A. C. Paterson), London: Longmans, Green, https://archive.org/details/diary-ofadamtasootasa (accessed 14 October 2023)

Fourie, C. (ed.) (2008), *Romances to Remember: South Africans in Love*, Cape Town: Human & Rousseau

Frankel, G. (1999), *Rivonia's Children: Three Families and the Price of Freedom in South Africa*, London: Weidenfeld & Nicolson

Gasa, N. (2007), *Women in South African History*, Johannesburg: HSRC Press

Gevisser, M. (2014), *Lost and Found in Johannesburg: A Memoir*, London: Granta

Giliomee, H. (2011), *The Afrikaners: Biography of a People*, London: C. Hurst

—— and L. Schlemmer (1989), *From Apartheid to Nation-Building*, Cape Town: Oxford University Press

Gordimer, N. (1999), *Living in Hope and History*, London: Bloomsbury

—— (2000), *Selected Stories*, London: Bloomsbury

Haffajee, F. (2015), *What if There Were No Whites in South Africa?*, Johannesburg: Picador Africa

Hall, J. (2008), *That Bloody Woman: The Turbulent Life of Emily Hobhouse*, Truro: Truran

Hall, R. (1977), *Marie Stopes: A Biography*, London: André Deutsch

Hancock, K. (1962), *Smuts*, vol. 1, *The Sanguine Years 1870–1919*, Cambridge: Cambridge University Press

—— (1968), *Smuts*, vol. 2, *The Fields of Force 1919–1950*, Cambridge: Cambridge University Press

—— and J. van der Poel (1966), *Selections from the Smuts Papers*, vols I–IV, Cambridge: Cambridge University Press

Hannaford, I. (1996), *Race: The History of an Idea in the West*, Baltimore, MD: Johns Hopkins University Press

Heese, J. A. (1972), *Die Herkoms van die Afrikaner, 1657–1867*, Cape Town: A. A. Balkema

Hewison, H. H. (1989), *Hedge of Wild Almonds: South Africa, the 'Pro-Boers' & the Quaker Conscience*, London: James Currey

Holmes, R. (2008), *The Hottentot Venus*, London: Bloomsbury

Hyam, R. (2010), *Understanding the British Empire*, Cambridge: Cambridge University Press

Jabavu, N. (1960), *Drawn in Colour: African Contrasts*, London: John Murray

—— (1963), *The Ochre People: Scenes from a South African Life*, London: John Murray

Jaff, F. (1975), *Women South Africa Remembers*, Cape Town: Howard Timmins

Jansen, J. D. (2009), *Knowledge in the Blood: Confronting Race and the Apartheid Past*, Stanford, CA: Stanford University Press

Jefferson, M. (2016), *Negroland*, London: Granta

Johnson, R. W. (2015), *How Long Will South Africa Survive? The Looming Crisis*, Johannesburg: Jonathan Ball

Joseph, H. (1966), *Tomorrow's Sun: A Smuggled Journal from South Africa*, London: Hutchinson

Kenney, R. U. (1976), *Piet Retief: The Dubious Hero*, Cape Town: Human & Rousseau

Knight, B. (1953), *Anne-Marie and the Pale Pink Frock*, London: J. M. Dent & Sons

Krige, J. (1973), *Die Familie Krige: Herkoms en Genealogie*. Pretoria: self-published

Krog, A. (1999), *Country of My Skull*, London: Vintage

—— (2009), *Begging to Be Black*, Cape Town: Random House

—— (2009), *A Change of Tongue*, Cape Town: Random House

Lange, L. (2003), *White, Poor and Angry: White Working Class Families in Johannesburg*, Aldershot: Ashgate

Leibbrandt, H. C. V. (1897), *Precis of the Archives of the Cape of Good Hope January, 1651–1655: Riebeeck's Journal &c.* Cape Town: W. A. Richards, https://archive.org/details/precisofarchivesoocape (accessed 14 October 2023)

—— (1897), *Precis of the Archives of the Cape of Good Hope January 1659–May 1662: Riebeeck's Journal &c.*, Cape Town: W. A. Richards, https://archive.org/details/precisofarchivesoocape_5/page/n4/mode/1up (accessed 14 October 2023)

—— (1901), *Precis of the Archives of the Cape of Good Hope: Journal, 1662–1670*, Cape Town: W. A. Richards, https://archive.org/details/preciso-farchives14capeiala/page/n3/mode/2up (accessed 14 October 2023)

—— (1902), *Precis of the Archives of the Cape of Good Hope: Journal, 1671–74 & 1676*, Cape Town: W. A. Richards, https://archive.org/details/preciso-farchives15capeiala/page/n3/mode/2up (accessed 14 October 2023)

Leipoldt, C. L. (2001), *The Valley: A Trilogy*, Cape Town: Stormberg

Lenta, M. (ed.) (2006), *Paradise, the Castle and the Vineyard: Lady Anne Barnard's Cape Diaries*, Johannesburg: Wits University Press

Lewin, H. (1976), *Bandiet: Seven Years in a South African Prison*, London: Penguin

Lewis, H. (2021), *Difficult Women: A History of Feminism in 11 Fights*, London: Vintage

Lichtenstein, H. (1815), *Travels in Southern Africa in the Years 1803, 1804, 1805, and 1806* (trans. Anne Plumptre), London: Henry Colburn, https://archive.org/details/travelsinsouthero2lich

Lombard, H. R. (2008), *The Chronicles of Krakeelhoek: The Story of the Retiefs of Welvanpas*, self-published

Loos, J. (2004), *Echoes of Slavery: Voices From South Africa's Past*, Claremont: David Philip

Lovell, P. (1970), *Quaker Inheritance 1871–1961: A Portrait of Roger Clark of Street Based on His Own Writings and Correspondence*, London: Bannisdale Press

Maalouf, A. (2012), *In the Name of Identity: Violence and the Need to Belong* (trans. B. Bray), New York: Arcade

MacDonald, T. (1950), *Ouma Smuts: The First Lady of South Africa*, London: Hurst & Blackett

McGarvie, M. (1986), *Guide to Historic Street*, Street: Shoe Museum

Magubane, Z. (2004), *Bringing the Empire Home: Race, Class and Gender in Britain and Colonial South Africa*, Chicago, IL: University of Chicago Press

Malan, R. (1991), *My Traitor's Heart*, London: Vintage

Malherbe, V. C. (1990), *Krotoa, Called Eva: A Woman Between*, Cape Town: Centre for African Studies, University of Cape Town

Malik, K. (1996), *The Meaning of Race: Race, History and Culture in Western Society*, London: Macmillan

Mamdani, M. (1996), *Citizen and Subject: Contemporary Africa and the Legacy of Late Colonialism*, Princeton, NJ: Princeton University Press

Mandela, N. (1994), *Long Walk to Freedom: The Autobiography of Nelson Mandela*, London: Little, Brown

Marks, S. (ed.) (1987), *Not Either an Experimental Doll: The Separate Worlds of Three South African Women*, Durban: Killie Campbell Africana Library

Matthee, D. (2008), *Pieternella, Daughter of Eva*, Johannesburg: Penguin

Mentzel, O. F. (1944), *A Geographical and Topographical Description of the Cape of Good Hope* (trans. G. V. Marais and J. Hoge), Cape Town: Van Riebeeck Society, https://archive.org/details/geographicaltopo03ment (accessed 14 October 2023)

Meredith, M. (2008), *Diamonds, Gold and War: The Making of South Africa*, London: Simon & Schuster

Millin, S. G. (1924), *God's Step-Children*, London: Constable

—— (1936), *General Smuts*, vol 1 and 2, London: Faber & Faber

—— (1941), *The Herr Witchdoctor*, London: William Heinemann

Mincher, K. (1965), *I Lived in His Shadow: My Life with General Smuts*, Cape Town: Howard Timmins

Mitchell, L. J. (2008), *Belongings: Property, Family, and Identity in Colonial South Africa: An Exploration of Frontiers, 1725–c.1830*, New York: Columbia University Press, http://gutenberg-e.org/mitchell/index.html (accessed 14 October 2023)

Mitford, J. (1996), *Hons and Rebels*, London: Indigo

Moodie, D. (1838), *The Record. Or, A Series of Official Papers Relative to the Condition and Treatment of the Native Tribes of South Africa*, Cambridge: Cambridge University Press, 2011 (reprint)

Nasson, B. and A. Grundlingh (eds) (2013), *The War at Home: Women and Families in the Anglo-Boer War*, Cape Town: Tafelberg

Ngcukaitobi, T. (2018), *The Land is Ours: South Africa's First Black Lawyers and the Birth of Constitutionalism*, Cape Town: Penguin

Nuttall, S. and C. Coetzee (1998), *Negotiating the Past: The Making of Memory in South Africa*, Oxford: Oxford University Press

Oakley, A. (2018), *Women, Peace and Welfare: A Suppressed History of Social Reform, 1880–1920*, Bristol: Policy Press

O'Brien, P. (ed.) (1993), *The Industrial Revolution and British Society*, Cambridge: Cambridge University Press

Paris, E. (2002), *Long Shadows: Truth, Lies and History*, London: Bloomsbury

Paton, A. (1964), *Hofmeyr*, London: Oxford University Press

Penn, N. (1999), *Rogues, Rebels and Runaways: Eighteenth-Century Cape Characters*, Cape Town: David Philip

—— (2005), *The Forgotten Frontier: Colonist & Khoisan on the Cape's Northern Frontier in the 18th Century*, Athens, OH: Ohio University Press

Petrowskaja, K. (2018), *Maybe Esther*, London: 4th Estate

Plaatje, Sol (2015), *Native Life in South Africa*, Project Gutenberg eBook, https://www.gutenberg.org/ebooks/1452 (accessed 20 July 2023)

Prior, M. (1997), *The Bible and Colonialism: A Moral Critique*, London: A&C Black

Ransford, O. (1974), *The Great Trek*, London: Sphere

Reitz, F. W. (2007), *A Century of Wrong*, London: Echo Library

Rich, A. (2018), *Of Woman Born: Motherhood as Experience and Institution*, New York: W. W. Norton

Roberts, R. (2018), *Seeds of Peace: Stories of Silent Heroes and Heroines in South Africa*, [Kindle] Kusnacht: Digiboo

Rose, P. (2020), *Parallel Lives: Five Victorian Marriages*, London: Daunt Books

Rosenthal, R. (1998), *Mission Improbable: A Piece of the South African Story*, Claremont: David Philip

Ross, R. (1993), *Beyond the Pale: Essays on the History of Colonial South Africa*, Hanover, NH: Wesleyan University Press

Sachs, A. (2011), *The Soft Vengeance of a Freedom Fighter*, London: Souvenir Press

Samuelson, M. (2007), *Remembering the Nation, Dismembering Women?*, Durban: University of Kwazulu-Natal Press

Schama, S. (1992), *Dead Certainties: Unwarranted Speculations*, London: Vintage

Schapera, I. (ed.) (1933), *The Early Cape Hottentots*, Cape Town: Van Riebeeck Society

Schoeman, K. (2007), *Early Slavery at the Cape of Good Hope, 1652–1717*, Pretoria: Protea Book House

—— (2009), *Seven Khoi Lives: Cape Biographies of the Seventeenth Century*, Pretoria: Protea Book House

—— (2011), *Cape Lives of the Eighteenth Century*, Pretoria: Protea Book House

—— (2012), *Portrait of a Slave Society: The Cape of Good Hope, 1717–1795*, Pretoria: Protea Book House

Schreiner, O. (1911), *Women and Labour*, New York: Stokes

Shell, R. (1997), *Children of Bondage: A Social History of the Slave Society at the Cape of Good Hope, 1652–1838*, Johannesburg: Wits University Press

Sleigh, D. (2005), *Islands*, London: Vintage

Slovo, G. (2009), *Every Secret Thing*, [iBooks] London: Abacus

Smith, P. (1926), *The Beadle – A Novel of South Africa*, London: Jonathan Cape

Smuts, J. C. (1952), *Jan Christian Smuts*, London: Cassell

Spielhofer, S. (2001), *Stemming the Dark Tide: Quakers in Vienna 1919–1942*, York: William Sessions

Steenkamp, A. (1939), *Die Dagboek van Anna Steenkamp en Fragmentjies oor die Groot-Trek*, Pietermaritzburg: Die Natalse Pers

Steinberg, J. (2002), *Midlands*, Jeppestown: Jonathan Ball

—— (2009), *Three Letter Plague: A Young Man's Journey Through a Great Epidemic*, London: Vintage

Steyn, R. (2015), *Jan Smuts: Unafraid of Greatness*, Johannesburg: Jonathan Ball

—— (2017), *Churchill & Smuts: The Friendship*, Johannesburg: Jonathan Ball

Swaisland, C. (1993), *Servants and Gentlewomen to the Golden Land: The Emigration of Single Women from Britain to Southern Africa, 1820–1939*, Providence: Berg

Thane, P. (2004), 'The Careers of Female Graduates of Cambridge University, 1920s–1970s', in D. Mitch, J. Brown and M. van Leeuwen (eds), *Origins of the Modern Career*, Aldershot: Ashgate

Theal, G. M. (1891), *History of South Africa, 1795–1834*, vol. 3, London: Swan Sonnenschein

—— (1897), *History of South Africa Under the Administration of the Dutch East India Company, 1652–1795*, London: Swan Sonnenschein

—— (1905), *Records of the Cape Colony Vol. XXVII*, London: Clowes

Thomas, E. M. (2006), *The Old Way: A Story of the First People*, New York: Farrar, Straus & Giroux

Trail, T. (n.d.), *Extinct: South Africa Khoisan Languages*, Cape Town: Museum van de Caab

Valentyn, F. (1971), *Beschryving van Kaap Der Goede Hoope*, Cape Town: Van Riebeck Society

Van der Merwe, P. J. (1995), *The Migrant Farmer in the History of the Cape Colony, 1657–1842*, Athens, OH: Ohio University Press

Van der Poel, J. (1973), *Selections from the Smuts Papers*, vols V–VII, Cambridge: Cambridge University Press

Van Heerden, E. (1993), *Ancestral Voices*, London: Allison & Busby

Van Onselen, C. (1997), *The Seed is Mine: The Life of Kas Maine, A South African Sharecropper 1894–1985*, New York: Hill and Wang

Vaughan, I. (1979), *The Diary of Iris Vaughan*, Cape Town: Howard Timmins

Viney, G. (2018), *The Last Hurrah: South Africa and the Royal Tour of 1947*, Johannesburg: Jonathan Ball

Wainaina, B. (2012), *One Day I Will Write About This Place*, London: Granta

Walker, C. (ed.) (1990), *Women and Gender in Southern Africa to 1945*, Claremont: David Philip

Walton, J. (1952), *Homesteads & Villages of South Africa*, Pretoria: J. L. Van Schaik

Ware, V. (1992), *Beyond the Pale: White Women, Racism, and History*, London: Verso

Wilkins, W. H. (ed.) (1910), *South Africa a Century Ago: Letters Written from the Cape of Good Hope (1797–1801) by the Lady Anne Barnard*, London: Smith, Elder

Woodward, W., P. Hayes and G. Minkley (2002), *Deep hiStories: Gender and Colonialism in Southern Africa*, Amsterdam: Rodopi

Worden, N. (ed.) (2012), *Cape Town Between East and West: Social Identities in a Dutch Colonial Town*, Auckland Park: Jacana Media

Worden, N and G. Groenewald (eds) (2005), *Trials of Slavery: Selected Documents Concerning Slaves from the Criminal Records of the Council of Justice at the Cape of Good Hope, 1705–1794*, Cape Town: Van Riebeeck Society

Articles

Abrahams, Y. (1996), 'Was Eva Raped? An Exercise in Speculative History', *Kronos*, 23, pp. 3–21

—— (2003), 'Colonialism, Dysfunction and Disjuncture: Sarah Bartmann's Resistance (Remix)', *Agenda*, 17(58), pp. 12–26

Afolabi, A. and A. Adeyemi (2013), 'Grand-Multiparity: Is it Still an Obstetric Risk?', *Open Journal of Obstetrics and Gynecology*, 3, pp. 411–15

Bradford, H. (1996), 'Women, Gender and Colonialism: Rethinking the History of the British Cape Colony and Its Frontier Zones, c.1806–70', *Journal of African History*, 37(3), pp. 351–70

Brink, Y. (1997), 'Figuring the Cultural Landscape: Land, Identity and Material Culture at the Cape in the Eighteenth Century', *South African Archaeological Bulletin*, 52(166), pp. 105–12

Bystrom, K. (2009), 'The DNA of the Democratic South Africa: Ancestral Maps, Family Trees, Genealogical Fictions', *Journal of Southern African Studies*, 35(1), pp. 223–35

Chetty, S. (2015), 'Mothering the "Nation": The Public Life of Isie "Ouma" Smuts, 1899–1945', *African Historical Review*, 47(2), pp. 37–57

Cilliers, J. (2013), 'Cape Colony Marriage in Perspective', MComm Thesis, University of Stellenbosch

—— and J. Fourie (2012), 'New Estimates of Settler Life Span and Other Demographic Trends in South Africa, 1652–1948', *Economic History of Developing Regions*, 27(2), pp. 61–86

Clark, P. (2003), 'Quaker Women in South Africa During the Apartheid Era', MPhil Thesis, University of Birmingham

Coetzee, C. (1995), 'Individual and Collective Notions of the "Promised Land": The "Private" Writings of the Boer Emigrants', *South African Historical Journal*, 32(1), pp. 48–65

Crenshaw, K. (1989), 'Demarginalizing the Intersection of Race and Sex: A Black Feminist Critique of Antidiscrimination Doctrine, Feminist Theory and Antiracist Politics', *University of Chicago Legal Forum*, 1, pp. 139–67

Davis, A. (2014), 'Wartime Women Giving Birth: Narratives of Pregnancy and Childbirth, Britain 1939–1960', *Studies in History and Philosophy of Biological and Biomedical Sciences*, 47, pp. 257–66

De Boer, S. (2016), 'The Invisible Women at the Cape of Good Hope: A Study of the Daily Lives of Cape Dutch Women at the Cape of Good Hope Between 1775 and 1825', MA Thesis, Leiden University, https://openaccess.leidenuniv.nl/bitstream/handle/1887/44481/Thesis%20-%20Stephanie%20de%20Boer%20%28s0949868%29.pdf?sequence=1 (accessed 5 December 2017)

De Kock, L. (2006), 'Blanc de Blanc: Whiteness Studies – A South African Connection?', *Journal of Literary Studies*, 22(1–2), pp. 175–89

Distiller, N. and M. Samuelson (2005), '"Denying the Coloured Mother": Gender and Race in South Africa', *L'Homme*, 16(2), pp. 28–46

Dooling, W. (1999), 'The Decline of the Cape Gentry, 1838–c.1900', *Journal of African History*, 40(2), pp. 215–42

—— (2005), 'The Making of a Colonial Elite: Property, Family and Landed Stability in the Cape Colony, c.1750–1834', *Journal of Southern African Studies*, 31(1), pp. 147–62

Dubow, S. (2008), 'Smuts, the United Nations and the Rhetoric of Race and Rights', *Journal of Contemporary History*, 43(1), pp. 45–74

Giliomee, H. (2010), '"Allowed Such a State of Freedom": Women and Gender Relations in the Afrikaner Community Before Enfranchisement in 1930', *New Contree*, 59, pp. 29–60

Greeff, J. M. (2007), 'Deconstructing Jaco: Genetic Heritage of an Afrikaner', *Annals of Human Genetics*, 71(5), pp. 674–88

Groenewald, G. (2012), 'A Class Apart: Symbolic Capital, Consumption and Identity Among the Alcohol Entrepreneurs of Cape Town, 1680–1795', *South African Journal of Cultural History*, 26(1), pp. 14–32

Guelke, L. (1988), 'The Anatomy of a Colonial Settler Population: Cape Colony 1657–1750', *International Journal of African Historical Studies*, 21(3), pp. 453–73

Haasbroek, H. (2012), '"An Absolute Pillar of Strength for Her Husband and the Struggle": Molly Fischer (1908–1964) – Wife, Mother and Struggle Activist', *New Contree*, 65, pp. 87–110

Hall, M. (1994), 'The Secret Lives of Houses: Women and Gables in the Eighteenth-Century Cape', *Social Dynamics*, 20(1), pp. 1–48

Holmes, R. (2013), 'A Moral Business: British Quaker Work With Refugees From Fascism, 1933–39', PhD Thesis, University of Sussex, http://sro.sussex.ac.uk/id/eprint/54158/ (accessed 3 May 2021)

Iannaccaro, G. (2015), 'Whose Trauma? Discursive Practices in Saartjie Baartman's Literary Afterlives', *Prospero*, XX, pp. 37–63

Koorts, L. (2008), 'Behind Every Man: D. F. Malan and the Women in His Life, 1874–1959', *South African Historical Journal*, 60(3), pp. 397–421

Le Roux, S. W. (2013), 'Van Tafelvallei na Vergelegen: Die lewe en wêreld van Anna Margaretha Siek (1695–c.1771)', *South African Journal of Cultural History*, 27(2), pp. 82–116

McKenzie, K. (1996), 'Wollstonecraft's Models? Female Honour and Sexuality in Middle-Class Settler Cape Town, 1800–1854', *Kronos*, 23, pp. 57–74

Malan, A. (1990), 'The Archaeology of Probate Inventories', *Social Dynamics*, 16(1), pp. 1–10

—— (1999), 'Chattels or Colonists? "Freeblack" Women and their Households', *Kronos*, 25, pp. 50–71

—— (2007), 'Building Lives at the Cape in the Early VOC Period', *Kronos*, 33, pp. 45–71

Malherbe, V. (2006), 'Illegitimacy and Family Formation in Colonial Cape Town, to c.1850', *Journal of Social History*, 39(4), pp. 1153–76

Marks, S. (2000), 'White Masculinity: Jan Smuts, Race and the South African War', *Raleigh Lecture on History*, https://www.thebritishacademy.ac.uk/documents/436/10-marks.pdf (accessed 24 October 2023)

Meskell, L. and L. Weiss (2006), 'Coetzee on South Africa's Past: Remembering in the Time of Forgetting', *American Anthropologist*, 108(1), pp. 88–99

Mitchell, L. (2007), '"This Is the Mark of the Widow": Domesticity and Frontier Conquest in Colonial South Africa', *Frontiers: A Journal of Women Studies*, 28(1/2), pp. 47–76

Neal, S., et al. (2012), 'Childbearing in Adolescents Aged 12–15 Years in

Low Resource Countries: A Neglected Issue', *Acta Obstetricia et Gynecologica Scandinavica*, 91(9), pp. 1114–18

Newton-King, S. (1994), 'In Search of Notability: The Antecedents of David van der Merwe of the Koue Bokkeveld', *Societies of Southern Africa, Collected Seminar Papers*, 20 (London: Institute of Commonwealth Studies), p. 26

Quintana-Murci, L., et al. (2010), 'Strong Maternal Khoisan Contribution to the South African Coloured Population: A Case of Gender-Biased Admixture', *American Journal of Human Genetics*, 86(4), pp. 611–20

Read, S. (2008), ' "Thy Righteousness is but a Menstrual Clout": Sanitary Practices and Prejudice in Early Modern England', *Early Modern Women*, 3, pp. 1–25

Ross, R. (1983), 'The Rise of the Cape Gentry', *Journal of Southern African Studies*, 9(2), pp. 193–217

Scott, C. (2012), 'Whiteness and the Narration of Self: An Exploration of Whiteness in Post-Apartheid Literary Narratives by South African Journalists', Phd Thesis, University of Western Cape

Scully, P. (1989), 'Criminality and Conflict in Rural Stellenbosch, South Africa, 1870–1900', *Journal of African History*, 30(2), pp. 289–300

—— (2005), 'Malintzin, Pocahontas, and Krotoa: Indigenous Women and Myth Models of the Atlantic World', *Journal of Colonialism and Colonial History*, 6(3), pp. 1–28

Shell, R. (1992), 'Tender Ties: Women and the Slave Household, 1652–1834', *Collected Seminar Papers, Institute of Commonwealth Studies*, 42, pp. 1–33

Shiao, J. L., T. Bode, A. Beyer and D. Selvig (2012), 'The Genomic Challenge to the Social Construction of Race', *Sociological Theory*, 30(2), pp. 67–88

Smuts, C. (2009), 'A Psychobiographical Study of Isie Smuts', MA Thesis, Nelson Mandela Metropolitan University, http://vital.seals.ac.za:8080/vital/access/manager/PdfViewer/vital:9913/SOURCEPDF?view PdfInternal=1 (accessed 3 May 2021)

Society of Friends (1938), 'Racial Problems in South Africa; Report by a Deputation From the Society of Friends (in Great Britain and America) to South Africa', London: Society of Friends

Steyn, M. (2012), 'The Ignorance Contract: Recollections of Apartheid Childhoods and the Construction of Epistemologies of Ignorance', *Identities*, 19(1), pp. 8–25

Stoler, A. (2001), 'Tense and Tender Ties: The Politics of Comparison in North American History and (Post)Colonial Studies', *Journal of American History*, 88(3), pp. 829–65

Swart, S. (1998), 'A Boer, His Gun and His Wife Are Three Things Always Together', *Journal of Southern African Studies*, 24(4), pp. 737–51

Van der Spuy, P. (1992), 'Slave Women and the Family in Nineteenth Century Cape Town', *South African Historical Journal*, 27, pp. 50–74

—— and L. Clowes (2007), 'Accidental Feminists? Recent Histories of South African Women', *Kronos*, 33, pp. 211–35

Van Zyl-Hermann, D. (2011), '"Gij kent genoegt mijn gevoelig hart": Emotional Life at the Occupied Cape of Good Hope, 1798–1803', *Itinerario*, 35(2), pp. 63–80

Vice, S. (2010), 'How Do I Live in This Strange Place?', *Journal of Social Philosophy*, 41(3), pp. 323–42

Walker, C. (1995), 'Conceptualising Motherhood in Twentieth Century South Africa', *Journal of Southern African Studies*, 21(3), pp. 417–37

Wells, J. (1998), 'Eva's Men: Gender and Power in the Establishment of the Cape of Good Hope, 1652–74', *Journal of African History*, 39(3), pp. 417–37, http://www.jstor.org/stable/183361 (accessed 3 May 2021)

West, M. (2010), 'Responding to Whiteness in Contemporary South African Life and Literature: An Interview with Njabulo S. Ndebele', *Whiteness Studies: A South African Perspective*, 37(1), pp. 115–24

Wolfe, P. (2002), 'Race and Racialisation: Some Thoughts', *Postcolonial Studies*, 5(1), pp. 51–62

—— (2006), 'Settler Colonialism and the Elimination of the Native', *Journal of Genocide Research*, 8(4), pp. 387–409, DOI: 10.1080/14623520601056240

Worden, N. (2009), 'The Changing Politics of Slave Heritage in the Western Cape, South Africa', *Journal of African History*, 50(1), pp. 23–40

Xaba, M. (2008), 'Jabavu's Journey', MA Thesis, University of Witwatersrand, http://wiredspace.wits.ac.za/handle/10539/5289 (accessed 3 May 2021)

Yves, J., K. Vermeulen and S. Vellinga (2006), 'A Systematic Review of Grand Multiparity', *Current Women's Health Reviews*, 2(1), pp. 25–32

Websites

Africa Check (3 September 2019), 'Five Facts: Femicide in South Africa', https://africacheck.org/fact-checks/reports/five-facts-femicide-south-africa (accessed 3 November 2019)

Appiah, K. A., *Mistaken Identities*, 'Colour', The Reith Lectures 2016, BBC Radio 4, https://www.bbc.co.uk/programmes/b080t63w (accessed 17 August 2023)

BBC News (9 August 2002), ' "Hottentot Venus" Laid to Rest', http://news. bbc.co.uk/1/hi/world/africa/2183271.stm (accessed 16 October 2017)

—— (8 January 2020), 'Homicides Fall for First Time in Five Years Across UK Despite London Rise', https://www.bbc.com/news/uk-50925024 (accessed 24 October 2023)

Booyens, H. (2012), 'Jacob and Fijtje Cloeten "van Ut in 't Land van Ceulen"', https://cliffwoodfogge.files.wordpress.com/2016/02/cloe-te2ndedition.pdf (accessed 7 July 2018)

Cape Town Holocaust Centre, archived at https://web.archive.org/ web/20071113021505/http://www.ctholocaust.co.za/view.asp?pg= refuge_sa_2 (accessed 14 October 2023)

Chung, F. (2017), ' "Bury Them Alive!": White South Africans Fear for Their Future as Horrific Farm Attacks Escalate', news.com.au, https:// www.news.com.au/finance/economy/world-economy/bury-them-alive-white-south-africans-fear-for-their-future-as-horrific-farm-attacks-escalate/news-story/3a63389a1b0066b6b0b77522c06d6476 (accessed 4 May 2021)

Coates, T. (2014), 'The Case for Reparations', The Atlantic, https://www. theatlantic.com/magazine/archive/2014/06/the-case-for-repara-tions/361631/ (accessed 5 May 2021)

e-family.co.za, http://www.e-family.co.za (accessed 4 May 2021)

Fourie, J. (2014), 'The Truth About Domestic Workers in South Africa', https://www.johanfourie.com/2014/08/01/the-truth-about-domestic-workers-in-south-africa/ (accessed 5 May 2021)

Genealogical Society of South Africa, https://www.eggsa.org/index.php/ en/ (accessed 4 May 2021)

Geni.com, https://www.geni.com/family-tree/html/start (accessed 4 May 2021)

Giliomee, H. (2003), 'The Rise and Fall of Afrikaner Women', Litnet-Seminar Room, https://www.oulitnet.co.za/seminarroom/afwomen.asp (accessed 3 May 2021)

greeff.info, http://www.greeff.info/tng01/jansmuts.php (accessed 4 May 2021)

GroundUp (2 June 2023), 'How Bad is South Africa's Murder Rate?', https://www.groundup.org.za/article/how-bad-murder-in-south-africa/(accessed 24 October 2023)

Herbst, E. (2017), 'A Brutal Tale of Unbalanced, Selective, Racism-Inciting Media Coverage', BizNews, https://www.biznews.com/undictated /2017/03/20/media-coverage-herbst (accessed 4 May 2021)

Hobhouse, E., Archive at Bodleian Archives & Manuscripts, https://archives.bodleian.ox.ac.uk/repositories/2/resources/2830#d2e1124 (accessed 5 May 2021)

Inventories of the Orphan Chamber at the Cape of Good Hope, http://www.tanap.net/content/archives/introduction.cfm (accessed 4 May 2021)

'Malema: If You See a Beautiful Piece of Land, Take It', *Daily Maverick*, 1 March 2017, https://www.dailymaverick.co.za/article/2017-03-01-malema-if-you-see-a-beautiful-piece-of-land-take-it/ (accessed 9 November 2019)

Mandela, N. (1993), 'Address to the Nation', Blackpast, https://www.blackpast.org/global-african-history/1993-nelson-mandela-address-nation/ (accessed 24 October 2023)

Masilela, N. (2004), 'Noni Jabavu', http://pzacad.pitzer.edu/NAM/sophia/writers/jabavu/jabavuS.htm (accessed 5 May 2021)

Masola, A. (2017), 'Reading Noni Jabavu in 2017', *Mail & Guardian*, https://mg.co.za/article/2017-08-10-00-reading-noni-jabavu-in-2017/ (accessed 3 May 2021)

Morkel, A. (2009), 'The Formidable Pasman Ladies: Sophia and her Daughters', http://family.morkel.net/wp-content/uploads/2009/02/the-formidable-pasman-ladies.pdf (accessed 4 May 2021)

Olive Schreiner Letters Online (2012), https://www.oliveschreiner.org/vre?page=295 (accessed 3 May 2021)

Snabel, C., 'History of Amsterdam and its People in the 16th and 17th century', http://ringlingdocents.org/amsterdam.htm (accessed 4 May 2021)

South African History Online (2021), https://www.sahistory.org.za (accessed 3 May 2021)

Stamouers.com (1999), https://www.stamouers.com (accessed 3 May 2021)

Truth and Reconciliation Commission website, https://www.justice.gov.za/trc/ (accessed 4 May 2021)

'UK More Nostalgic for Empire than Other Ex-colonial Powers', *Guardian*, 11 March 2020, https://www.theguardian.com/world/2020/mar/11/uk-more-nostalgic-for-empire-than-other-ex-colonial-powers? (accessed 14 October 2023)

Upham, M., 'Zara', http://www.e-family.co.za/ffy/RemarkableWriting/UL09Zara.pdf (accessed 3 May 2021)

——, 'Cape Mothers', http://www.e-family.co.za/ffy/RemarkableWriting/UL14CapeMothers.pdf (accessed 3 May 2021)

——, 'Moeder Jagt', http://www.e-family.co.za/ffy/RemarkableWriting/UL15MoederJagt.pdf (accessed 3 May 2021)

——, 'Krotoa: In a Kind of Custody', http://www.e-family.co.za/ffy/RemarkableWriting/UL021Krotoa.pdf (accessed 3 May 2021)

Archives

Alfred Gillett Trust, Street, Somerset, HH/CC Papers of Cato Clark 1904–1968 (private collection)
——, HH/FAM Bancroft and Cato Clark's family papers (private collection)
——, HH/MCG Papers of Margaret Clark Gillett, 1774–1983
——, HH/SMUTS Material relating to Jan Christian and Isie K. Smuts
Cape Town Archives Repository, National Archives of South Africa, Cape Town, South Africa

Index

INDEX

Villiers, Susanna de 81
VOC *see* Dutch East India Company
volunteering 267–9
Voortrekkers 103–4, 133–4, 136–7,
    138–48
  Monument 197, 198, 212, 245
Vos, Jan 31–2
voting rights 180, 191, 195, 247
  1994 election 299–301
Vrouemonument 152–4, 177, 203
Vryman, Carolina 157, 158

Wagenaar, Zacharias 28, 29, 31, 35
Washington, George 212–13
Weenen massacre 141–2
Welvanpas 103–4, 128–9, 197
Western Cape 79, 154–6
Weyers, Andries 193, 194
white nationalism 148, 195–7
white South Africans 55, 90, 155,
    159, 163
  black ancestors 158
  ethnic slurs 52, 232
  fears of 87
  republicanism 249
  silence of 252–3
  Smuts policies 186, 213–14
  see also Afrikaners
white supremacy 50, 51, 86, 192
'white-washing' 216–17
Williams, Chester 95
wine growing 51, 55, 73–4, 78–9
women:
  activism 295–6
  apartheid laws 247–8
  Britain 277
  childbirth 109

domestic workers 84
Dutch 22
  employment 124, 129
  erasure of 110–11
  family units 207
  Great Trek 134, 145–6
  national monument 152–4, 203
  Peace Crusade 229
  racial experiences 79–80
  rights 77
  Second Anglo-Boer War 177–9
  Second World War 241–2
  sexual stereotypes 275–6
  slaves 27–8, 30, 47
  voting rights 195
  wet nursing 72–3
  see also motherhood
Women's South African Party 195
Woods, Donald 117
Woolton, Lord 241

Xhosa people 76, 82, 138
  Boer skirmishes 103, 135–6

Yoruba people 270

Zambia 138
Zara 39–40
Zimbabwe 63, 96, 138, 150; *see also*
    Rhodesia
Zuid-Afrikaan, De (newspaper) 115
Zulus 60, 138, 139–42, 143–4
  British rule 146, 169
  land rights 145
  Mfecane refugees 135
  war dance 261
Zuma, Jacob 95, 252